The Transformation of Austrian Socialism

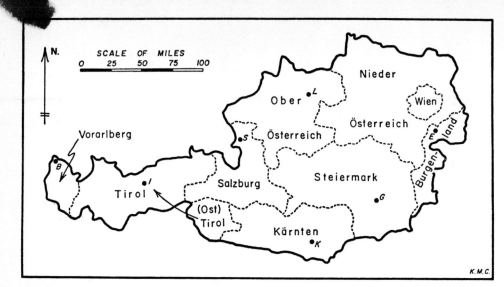

Map of Austria

B = BREGENZ   I = INNSBRUCK   S = SALZBURG   L = LINZ
K = KLAGENFURT   G = GRAZ   E = EISENSTADT

drawn by Keith M. Clayton

The Transformation
of Austrian Socialism

KURT L. SHELL *Assistant Professor of
Political Science · Harpur College of the State University of New York*

State University of New York | *1962*

to my father

Preface

The stimulus to the present study came to me through a chance remark of the late Professor Franz L. Neumann of Columbia University. In a lecture he referred to the "Americanization of European parties." It had been fashionable to assume that the American party system, characterized by lack of ideologies, programmatic overlaps, and "concurrent majorities" was moving toward the European model of clearly aligned class and program parties, of which the social-democratic mass parties were outstanding examples. New evidence began to accumulate that the historic drift may be in the opposite direction, toward the softening of the once rigid European party structures. My investigation represented an attempt to examine this phenomenon in the form of a case study directed at what before World War II had been the very epitome of a disciplined mass party.

Most of the field research on which the present study is based was undertaken during the years 1952 and 1953. I have had no opportunity for extensive trips to Austria since then, though I have attempted to keep abreast of developments and trust that they are reflected in the pages of my study. The years from 1945 to 1953 saw the forging of the postwar pattern in the heat of conflict engendered by old rivalries, political and economic chaos, foreign occupation, and "cold war." Nothing has happened since to disrupt seriously the process of transformation and consolidation which is the theme of the present book.

The editor of *World Politics* has kindly given permission to include in the final chapter material which originally appeared in an article by the present author in the January, 1957, issue of that periodical.

I owe thanks to the late Professor Franz L. Neumann, whose untimely death in 1954 deprived me of a keen and challenging critic; to Professor Sigmund Neumann of Wesleyan University and Professor Herbert A. Deane of Columbia University, who carefully read the original manuscript; and to numerous members and functionaries of the Austrian Socialist Party who facilitated my research and were usually ready to answer my questions. My gratitude also goes to Miss Emily Schossberger, whose skillful editorial advice has saved me from many stylistic lapses. Needless to say, all errors of fact or interpretation are entirely my own.

Finally, I wish to express my gratitude to the members of the Publications Committee of the Graduate Council of the State University of New York, who have considered the present study deserving of their support and have thereby made its publication possible through the University's Research Foundation.

K. L. S.

Binghamton, N. Y.
1961

Contents

The Transformation of Austrian Socialism

Introduction

Today the democratic socialist parties of Western and Central Europe are in a state of crisis. This crisis is, in some instances only, reflected by the inability of these parties to move closer toward conquest of political power and achievement of their socialist goals. For in some countries (e.g., England, Austria, Sweden, etc.) they either have in the recent past governed and may do so again or occupy today the seat of government at least as partners in a ruling coalition. The nature of their crisis is more profound. It shows itself in a loss of direction, in an increasing inability to define clearly the meaning of "socialist" goals, thus in a loss of distinction and specific mission. What we are observing is a transformation by which the traditional labels and some of the traditional terminology and mystique are retained while a transmutation of content—of ideology and policies—is taking place. Observers of the French political scene never fail to point out that the French Radical Socialist Party is neither radical nor socialist— a much abused witticism. I am suggesting that a similar observation is becoming appropriate with regard to the socialist parties this side of the "iron curtain."

The Austrian Socialist Party, the subject of this study, exhibits most clearly the transformation indicated. In the Twenties it was full of the sound and fury of Marxist class-war slogans, courting ideas of violence and "dictatorship of the proletariat," and conceived for itself the function of a bridge between Soviet communism and Western European "laborism" and "reformism." When it fell victim to persecution and suppression by the Austrian Fascist regime, the subterranean cadres making up the "il-

3

legal" party swung further to the Left, adopting the name "Revolutionary Socialists," and to methods of political struggle derived from Lenin. And yet, though the Austrian Socialist Party of today proudly proclaims its identity with its historical predecessors, no visible trace of the former radicalism in thought or temper remains. No other socialist party has traveled a longer road faster from Left to Right.

The Austrian Socialist Party is a subject worthy of study also because it is the closest approximation to the ideal type of the modern "mass party." Since 1918 it has been the strongest or second strongest electoral party in Austria. Membership is direct, individual, and requires monthly payment of dues. Yet the Party has been able to organize within its ranks more than 10 per cent of the entire Austrian population and over one-third of those who support it with their votes. The desire to gain members rather than merely votes, the urge to educate the members in socialist principles, the provisions for leisure-time activities, all these have made the Party the very prototype of what Duverger calls an "Order." [1] Its root was clearly ideological—the linkage of Marxist creed with strong class consciousness and a militant approach to political problems. And in spite of the change in ideology and policies, the structure of this mass party has remained essentially unchanged to this day. The assumption which explains my focus of attention is that—contrary to Duverger's assertion [2]—it is a party's *objectives*, its W*eltanschauung*, which represent its most characteristic features and are most influential in molding its structure and mode of action; and that these objectives are related to the political and economic setting in which a party finds itself. I assume that parties are purposeful organizations, though the purposes may and do differ for different strata, groups, and individuals within them; and that, by and large, organizational structure is adapted to these purposes, though the weight of established organizational patterns and habitual behavior introduces rigidities which render difficult any adjustment to changes of environment.

The relation between political organizations and the historical setting is particularly pronounced in socialist parties. By identifying themselves with specific needs and specific doctrines, they make themselves exceptionally vulnerable to this disabling rigidity or to self-elimination by success. Though my study centers on an examination of the Austrian Socialist Party as a separate entity, the reader should not forget that many of its

---

[1] Maurice Duverger, *Political Parties*, pp. 124 ff.

[2] *Op. cit.*, p. xv.

facets can be appreciated only within the context of external events, domestic and foreign. The Soviet occupation, the position of Austria as a pawn in the "cold war," the fate of socialist parties elsewhere, and the position of rival political forces within Austria are reflected in the changing attitudes of the Socialist Party; they have been taken into account as far as seemed necessary for an explanation of Socialist thought and action. The Austrian Socialist Party, perhaps due to the firsthand contact it had with Soviet communism in the form of Russian occupation, and with the external imposition of nonviolent political practices in 1945, was able to adjust itself to the postwar environment without splitting apart through doctrinal divisions. The existence of the rival Communist Party as well as the commitment to democracy excluded a radical alternative. In its absence the choice was merely that between abdication and adaptation. A few isolated individuals chose to withdraw in preference to an activity which seemed senseless to them. But the weight of organizational tradition and the need of party workers to be, above all, active in some capacity, assured the continuation of the organization in spite of the change in objectives enforced by the changed environment. The elaborate structure of the mass party, originally a rational tool serving radical socialist objectives, has, however, lost its function in a party restricted to the conservation of a welfare state and a mixed economy. The massive size of the structure may be misleading. The ties which hold the structure together have changed. To use Duverger's convenient terminology, the Party has moved toward an organizational structure in part "Community" [3] and in part "Association" —a pattern of interaction based on habit and individual advantage but lacking the spirit of selfless dedication characteristic of the "Order" party. Comparative evidence suggests that this transformation need by no means lead to speedy dissolution once the crisis of a sudden change has been weathered. By losing its restrictive doctrine and ceasing to be the object of fierce and possessive dedication by its members, it has become a more flexible, more adaptable, and hence a more durable political structure, assuming that no major physical or doctrinal challenge will arise to test the somewhat attenuated bonds of loyalty of its members and supporters. Concretely, the present program and the present leadership of the Party reflect the conviction that a mixed economy with a minimum of fiscal planning can

---

[3] In the very special sense used by Duverger and derived from Durkheim and Toennis: a group acting automatically, on the basis of common conditioning or similarity of experience.

assure full employment and the maintenance of the extensive welfare services established. As I shall show, no provisions for alternatives have either been made or been seriously considered. The consequences of a major economic crisis, should one occur, would be to alter entirely the picture I have drawn of the Party in the present historical period.

However detached an observer may attempt to be, it is impossible for him not to allow at times his own values and emotions to invade his judgments of significant contemporary issues. I do not pretend to be indifferent toward the process of transformation which is the subject of my study. Yet my own reaction to it is highly ambiguous. The Austrian Socialist Party of the past—an "Order" with strong commitment to radical Marxism, at least on the verbal level—was, in my view, an impediment to the establishment of a working democracy in Austria. Today the Socialist Party, as this study will show, is thoroughly integrated into the democratic state and adjusted to the process of democratic politics. Furthermore, because the past dichotomy between radical theory and frequently moderate action has disappeared, there is today less need for pseudo-radical doubletalk. As one who upholds the values of democracy, I welcome this as an indication of growing maturity and assurance of peaceful change. And yet I am aware of a feeling of loss: I regret the end to high striving and noble sacrifice, and the replacement of visionaries—though they were on occasion fanatical— by moderate and realistic men. With regard to this process I share the feelings expressed by Schumpeter:

All non-Marxist socialist groups are more or less like other groups and parties; only Marxists of pure persuasion consistently walked in the light of a doctrine that to them contained all answers to all questions. As will be seen, I do not admire this attitude unconditionally. It may well be called narrow and even naive. But the doctrinaires of all types, whatever their practical disabilities, have certain esthetic qualities that raise them high above the common run of political practitioners. . . . They command sources of strength which mere practitioners will never be able to understand.[4]

---

[4] Joseph A. Schumpeter, *Capitalism, Socialism and Democracy*, p. 305.

I

Austrian Socialism—Past and Present

Viewed formally, the Austrian Socialist Party, which since the end of World War II has played a leading role in the Austrian political life, is a new organization. No legal party organization under that name existed for almost a dozen years prior to 1945. Yet postwar Social Democracy in Austria cannot be understood unless one recognizes its history of over half a century, and realizes that the postwar founding of the Socialist Party merely marked the latest phase in the development of the Austrian Labor Movement, whose continuity was not decisively interrupted by the suspension of its public and lawful existence between 1934 and 1945.

The organization of the Austrian Socialist Party in April, 1945, was carried out by men who had all been members—in more or less prominent positions—of the Social Democratic Party [1] in 1934 or of the Revolutionary Socialists, the name adopted by the underground organization which had proclaimed itself the revolutionary successor of the legal party dissolved by a decree of the Dollfuss regime. Picking up the threads in 1945, the new Party insisted on the unbroken continuity of tradition linking it with the old Social Democracy as well as with the period of illegality. [2] The "glorious past" was at once incorporated into the "new" party's mythological heritage and the Party forthwith identified itself without reservation with that past. Although, since 1945, the Party has differed greatly, both in temper and policies, from the Revolutionary Socialists as well as the Social Democ-

---

[1] Its full name was Social Democratic Labor Party of German-Austria (*Sozialdemokratische Arbeiterpartei Deutsch-Oesterreichs; SDAPDOe*).

[2] See the first postwar copy of the *Arbeiter Zeitung*, August 5, 1945. The postwar organizational pattern was based on the prewar model. The Party succeeded in its fight for legal recognition as the old Social Democratic Party.

racy of the First Austrian Republic it does not view this change as repudiation of its past but rather as the result of natural development. Though party spokesmen will occasionally admit past errors,[3] no episode, no decision, no action, and no leading figure connected with party history has been publicly disavowed.[4] This insistence on the unity and continuity of development has led officials to minimize past conflicts and to gloss over discrepancies. As pictured by them the transition appears smooth, the evolution of the present phase out of the past inevitable and harmonious to a degree not borne out by historical evidence.[5]

In attempting to understand the Austrian Socialist Party of the present, one must therefore not overlook the historical dimension of its existence. One of the major questions that will occupy our attention will be to what extent and for what reasons the past is—or has ceased to be—an operative force in the postwar Party. First of all, however, it is necessary to provide a brief general outline of the Party's historical development in order to establish the framework for an understanding of its present policies and structure.[6]

Early History: 1889–1918

The Growth of the Mass Party

The official birth date of Austrian Social Democracy as a party is January 1, 1889. Its birthplace: Hainfeld, an obscure village not far from Vienna.

---

[3] See Jacques Hannak, *Im Sturm eines Jahrhunderts*, an "authorized" history of the Party. The breakup of the 1920 coalition, the Party's attitude toward Soviet Russia, and the handling of the riots of July 15, 1927, are treated critically by the author.

[4] The one exception is Joseph Buttinger, chairman of the Revolutionary Socialists from 1935 to 1938, who broke with the Party's social democratic tradition. The Party has made an effort to obliterate his memory by omitting any reference to him in discussion of the illegal period. Hannak merely devotes a brief and contemptuous paragraph to Buttinger's leadership. (*Op. cit.*, p. 408.)

[5] See, e.g., editorials in the *Arbeiter Zeitung*: O.P., "Die Partei," September 30, 1945; Felix Hubalek, "Die Brücke," August 5, 1945. Hannak minimizes the long-continued conflict between the Renner and Bauer wings of the Party as well as the extremely bitter controversies marking the illegal period.

[6] The following account is based on Hannak, *op. cit.*; Charles A. Gulick, *Austria from Habsburg to Hitler*; and Joseph Buttinger, *Am Beispiel Oesterreichs*. An English-language edition of Buttinger's book has been published under the title *In the Twilight of Socialism*. For the sake of convenience, all page references will be to the English-language edition.

The Party Conference of Hainfeld, at which the first program was agreed on by the overwhelming majority of the delegates present,[7] represented the climax of the prolonged efforts to bring unity into the splintered ranks of the embryonic Austrian Labor Movement. After a full year of negotiations, the two main groups, the "radicals" and the "moderates," had agreed on a preliminary set of "fundamental articles" which served as the basis for the Hainfeld "unity program." The main issue dividing the two groups was the use of democratic as against violent action in the struggle for political power. At a time when equal suffrage for propertyless laborers still appeared a distant and hardly attainable goal, and when legal organization and political agitation were impeded by censorship and restrictive decrees, the anarchist-inspired "direct force" argument held considerable appeal. In composing the differences, Victor Adler, the moving spirit behind the unity efforts, did not settle or solve the issue. The formulation adopted at Hainfeld did not rule out either the course of democracy or that of violence. They were to be looked at as means—merely a tactical question—the choice of which was to depend on the exigencies of the political struggle.

Unity laid the groundwork for an intensive and successful effort at expanding and strengthening political organization. Though "direct action" as a road to power had not been rejected as an alternative, the political mobilization of the greatest possible number of working people became the primary immediate objective. Mass organization fitted in with the ideas of "moderates" and "radicals" alike. For, whether the ultimate goal of this mobilization was conceived as achievement of universal equal suffrage and its peaceful use, or as the overthrow of the existing social order by means of "direct action" (such as a general strike), organized mass participation seemed an obvious prerequisite for success in either case. Blanqui's notion of conquest of power by a small group of determined conspirators apparently had few followers in Austria. The problem of choosing between the organizational principles of "mass" and "cadre" thus did not present itself until much later.

The Party as a State Within the State

In the campaign to "render and maintain the proletariat fighting fit both physically and mentally," [8] the basic pattern of the urban mass party quickly emerged. The organization, divided along lines of politico-territorial

---

[7] Only 3 votes were cast against it. (Hannak, *op. cit.*, p. 60.)
[8] Quoted by Hannak (*loc. cit.*) from the Hainburg program.

districts, began to cover every street, every block, every house, particularly in working-class areas. Unpaid party volunteer workers—the celebrated *Vertrauensmänner*—regularly distributed party publications and within a short time began to collect compulsory dues,[9] thus instituting a rigid concept of "membership." At the same time—and equally significant—a Central Education Office (*Bildungszentrale*) was set up by the Party, through which general *Kultur* and particularly socialist doctrine were to be passed on to the working class. The politically active segment of that class, highly conscious of its inferior position in the Austro-Hungarian monarchy, set about building for itself a proletarian "state within the state," frequently inspired and led by men drawn from the middle class. The Movement was not conceived merely as a political means to a political end. Rather, it provided a home, literally as well as metaphorically, for a considerable part of the Austrian working class. It comprised clubs and associations whose scope and interests ranged from stamp collecting to militant atheism. Each one of these organizations insisted on drawing a clear class line between itself and the rest of society. Singing, hiking, playing chess, all these were carried on in associations proudly affixing the term "worker" to their title and maintaining affiliation with the Social Democratic Party. Through the Children's Friends (*Kinderfreunde*) and the Free School (*Freie Schule*) an attempt was made to ensure that the public school system should not alienate the growing working-class child from his proletarian background or indoctrinate him with antisocialist ideology.[10] Through a determined drive against the use of alcohol, the working man was to be rescued from this particular "opiate of the people." Through the organization of cultural activities—book clubs, libraries, theaters, concerts—he was to develop a sense for the "higher things" in life; all this on the assumption that sober, well-read, and "cultured"—thus rational—working men would become conscious of the political position of their class and join the struggle for a socialist society. The atmosphere permeating the Movement was one of highmindedness mingled with socialist puritanism. Every activity was scrutinized for its effect on the class struggle; pleasure for pleasure's sake was

---

[9] For some time these dues were collected by the district organization exclusively. The Party as a whole did not adopt the practice until 1909. (*Ibid.*, p. 81.)

[10] For a detailed account of these two organizations, see Gulick (*op. cit.*, chap. 17). After World War I the Red Falcons, influenced by the *Wandervögel* and Boy Scout movements, were organized for youths in their early teens. (*Ibid.*, pp. 604–10.)

frowned upon.[11] Membership, and particularly active participation in the Party, implied acceptance of a socialist attitude in daily life (*Haltung*) in which the virtues which were assumed to be the inevitable product of the future socialist society were to be present characteristics of Socialists fighting for the realization of that society.

In the course of the two decades following Hainfeld the Party achieved its first major political objective, universal and equal male suffrage, and established itself as an important parliamentary force. An electoral reform law passed in 1896 had given all male citizens above twenty-four years of age, regardless of property qualifications, the right to elect one-sixth of the membership of the Lower House of the Austrian Parliament. In 1905, however, fired by the example of parliamentary reform in Czarist Russia, the Socialists renewed with increased fervor their struggle for *equal* male suffrage. Victor Adler, for once abandoning his characteristic caution, demanded and obtained the approval of the Party Conference for a general strike call in Vienna to force passage of a law meeting Socialist aspirations. Under the pressure of "the street" and of repeated threats of further mass action whenever a hitch in the bill's legislative progress seemed to develop, the law establishing a democratic chamber was enacted.

By 1910 an extensive network of publications controlled by the Social Democratic Party had come into existence, consisting of two daily newspapers, a dozen papers appearing several times a week, and publications devoted to humor, antialcoholism, sports, and youth activities.[12] In 1908 there appeared the first issue of *Der Kampf*, the Party's monthly, devoted to discussion of questions of socialist theory and practice; for thirty years this periodical remained the depository of the most distinguished thought produced by European Socialists.

Left and Right in World War I

The two decades of successful socialist organizing efforts, the greatly increased political weight of the Movement, and the resultant entry of a powerful block of Socialist Party representatives into parliament re-created the dilemma which the compromise of Hainfeld had tended to obscure— the question of the socialist attitude toward the existing state. Though the

---

[11] Thus, when the *Naturfreunde* (Friends of Nature) was organized as a workers' mountaineering group, Party leaders expressed dislike of working men "breaking their necks like the silly sports fans of the bourgeoisie." (Hannak, *op. cit.*, p. 157.)

[12] *Ibid.*

Austrian Party had indignantly repelled "Revisionism," the cleavage between an uncompromisingly revolutionary theory and Revisionist practice became apparent. The presence of Socialists in Parliament—a presence not utilized for obstruction—implied a changed attitude toward the state, a willingness to accept rather than to destroy its basic structure, a willingness even to help maintain it if it gave at least minimum satisfaction to working-class demands.

Within Austrian Social Democracy, this fundamentally positive attitude toward the existing state found an early expression in the writings of one of its outstanding theoreticians, Karl Renner. In a series of books published during the first decade of this century, Renner put forth the idea of an "Austrian mission," which was to combine the splintered nationalities of the Danube basin into a supranational federation,[13] thus to reform rather than to destroy the Empire as it then existed. The outbreak of the war in 1914 revealed the extent to which Renner's "proximity to the state" had become characteristic of Austrian Social Democracy as a whole, in spite of the Party's theoretical anti-Revisionism. Because of an historical accident— fortunate from the Socialist point of view—namely, the assumption of emergency powers by Austria's Prime Minister and the subsequent suspension of Parliament in March, 1914, the Socialist Party was spared the choice of having publicly to go on record in support of, or in opposition to, the war effort. However, it was dominated, no less than its German counterpart, by the spirit of "social patriotism" and did nothing to oppose the prevalent prowar sentiment. Though an invitation to enter a cabinet of national unity was neither extended nor sought, the Party, under the leadership of Victor Adler and Karl Renner, initially co-operated fully in the war effort. While this course of action was at first apparently overwhelmingly approved by the bulk of the Party—Friedrich Adler, Victor Adler's son, alone maintained an unyielding position of opposition to the war from the beginning—rank-and-file sentiment soon began to shift.

By 1916 a Left faction, opposed to the leadership's prowar policies and hostile to their foremost exponent, Karl Renner, had acquired considerable backing. At that time the Left as yet failed to carry the Party with it in its demand that the Party go on record with a call for immediate peace without annexations. Unlike the German left-wingers, the Austrian Left did

---

[13] Under the pseudonym "Synopticus," *Staat und Nation* (Verlag Josef Dietl, Vienna, 1899); under the pseudonym "Rudolf Springer," *Der Kampf der österreichischen Nationen um den Staat,* Band I. *Das nationale Problem als Verfassungs-und Verwaltungsfrage* (Deuticke Verlag, Leipzig, 1902).

not push its differences with the Party leadership to the point of division; nor did the leadership resort to repressive disciplinary measures in order to silence the violent criticism. By mid-1917 the specific Left demand for the unequivocal endorsement of peace without annexation had, in fact, become the official Party position. The impact of the Russian October Revolution and the progressive radicalization of the Austrian working class, reflected in mass strikes and a naval mutiny in early 1918, combined to increase the strength of the Left in the Party.

At the end of the war the faction which had been an oppositional minority became, under its brilliant leader, Otto Bauer, the dominant force in Austrian Socialism. Victor Adler had died on the eve of the Armistice. Though Karl Renner and the moderate-reformist wing of the Party continued to be active in prominent positions, the Party's decisions and its temper reflected from then on the more radical views of the Bauer Left. The fact that this shift in the center of political gravity could take place without a split was of the greatest significance for the future of Austrian Social Democracy. By giving expression to "revolutionary" as well as "reformist" viewpoints, it retained within its ranks socialists of widely divergent beliefs and effectively forestalled the rise of a potent Communist Party in Austria. The dilemma between radical theory and frequently moderate practice, between simultaneous acceptance of direct action and ballot-box democracy perpetrated in the First Republic, gave the Party its most significant feature, the unresolved tension which was the basis of the phenomenon known as "Austro-Marxism." At the heart of this Austro-Marxism lay conflict and compromise, tenuously maintained in a precarious balance which only optimists could consider a lasting synthesis.

Social Democracy in the First Republic: 1918–1934

Coalition and Achievements

At the end of World War I the Socialist Party suddenly found itself committed to accept responsibility for the precarious new Austrian state which had come into existence. "Proximity to the state" which, during the war, had been criticized by the Left as an unsocialist aberration of the Renner wing, now was endorsed by this same former Left. True, the new state was a democratic republic in which the working class had become a powerful—temporarily the most powerful—political factor. Nevertheless, having rejected violent revolution as a means of establishing single-party rule as "impractical," [14] Socialists now had to exercise governmental power jointly with "class-opponents" in a state which had not ceased to be basically "capitalist." In October, 1918, Karl Renner was given the task of working out a provisional constitution, and the Social Democrats entered a coalition government which prepared the transition from monarchical empire to the small republic. Did these facts make the new state "their" state? Otto Bauer, and the former Left with him, answered the question affirmatively. Yet, viewing themselves as revolutionary socialists, they could not commit themselves wholeheartedly to a state and society which were palpably nonsocialist. Bauer tried to resolve this ambiguity by an equivocation: The democratic state was valuable but only because it provided the most favorable battleground for the socialist struggle. Thus acceptance and hostility were simultaneously embraced. This political and ideological tightrope act could not be perpetuated indefinitely. But for more than a dozen years it preserved the unity of the Austrian Labor Movement and provided it with the opportunity to establish a record of social reform in the city of Vienna which was viewed with admiration by sympathetic observers the world over.

For two years after the end of World War I the Socialist Party, as the stronger partner in a coalition government, worked successfully for the passage of extensive welfare and labor legislation while vigorously defending the new state against *putsch* attempts from the radical fringe. In contrast to the German Socialists, the Austrian Party succeeded in acting ruthlessly against Communist attempts to overthrow the Republic without, however, at the same time building up the power of its conservative opponents.[15] Tactics of "incorporation" succeeded in containing and controlling potential revolutionists through institutions such as Works Councils and the military formations of the People's Guard.[16]

The political atmosphere in which these social reforms were carried through was highly favorable to the Socialist Party. The wave of radicalism which had swept large parts of Europe in the wake of the war and which, in

---

[14] It was always on grounds of the nonfeasibility of a successful proletarian revolution that Otto Bauer defended the Party's course in 1918. (Cf., e.g., Otto Bauer, *The Austrian Revolution*, abridged version, pp. 90–91.)

[15] On three occasions a Communist-led battalion attempted a coup but was beaten down by the People's Guard (*Volkswehr*) which the Socialists had organized; on the last occasion (June 15, 1919), with more than a hundred casualties, twenty of them were killed. (Hannak, *op. cit.*, p. 273.)

[16] Cf. Gulick, *op. cit.*, chap. 4.

Hungary and Bavaria, had brought radical regimes to power, rendered the Austrian middle class fearful and pliant. Leadership of the Christian-Social Party, the Socialists' conservative coalition partner, was during that period in the hands of the Party's socially progressive wing. While the forces of the conservative peasantry and the radical urban working class held each other in balance, both deadlock and civil war were avoided; due to its superior *élan*, derived from the favorable historical setting, the working class felt itself in possession of predominant power and of the political initiative.[17] It used this power, however, merely for the achievement of limited social objectives to which the coalition partner could be persuaded to give assent.

For some time the rapid progress toward practical objectives long cherished by the Party prevented any conflict between Right and Left. If there were doubts about the usefulness of the state machinery for the achievement of socialist goals, they were overborne in the minds of "Leftists" like Otto Bauer by the surge of activity and the necessity of defending what they viewed as considerable achievements against the threats of material chaos and radical illusions. Bauer and Renner were, for the time being, not divided by their differing concepts as to the nature of socialism and its relation to the state. But while Renner viewed active participation in the government of the Republic primarily as an expression of his attachment to the welfare state he saw emerging, Bauer could bear it only as long as the working class retained its predominance and while acceptance of responsibility resulted in immediate and tangible gains. When in 1920 the class balance appeared to shift in favor of the bourgeoisie [18] and the pace of social progress slackened, the Socialist Party withdrew from the government on Bauer's insistence and against Renner's counsel.

The Party in Opposition

During the remaining lifespan of the First Republic the Socialist Party assumed a posture of opposition in national politics. In the city of Vienna, where it had gained an overpowering political position,[19] the Party initiated a program of radical municipal reform which included extensive public housing and provision for education and welfare services financed, in part, by a

---

[17] Bauer, *op. cit.*, pp. 96–97.
[18] *Ibid.*, pp. 262–79.
[19] In the municipal elections of 1923 the Party had obtained 78 seats out of a total of 120, only two short of a two-thirds majority. (Hannak, *op. cit.*, p. 311.)

system of ruthlessly progressive "luxury" taxes.[20] This arrangement served the Movement too well to be exchanged for one less serviceable, since it permitted the expression of feelings of hostility toward the existing order generated by the ideology of class struggle and at the same time the generously constructive urge inherently and historically part of socialist thought. It admirably embodied Otto Bauer's conception of a synthesis between "head" and "heart," between practical reformist action and revolutionary fervor.

Outwardly, at least, the Movement, comprising the Party proper as well as its affiliated organizations with their multiform activities, flourished and grew during the twenties. By 1929 Party membership had reached a peak of over 700,000 dues-paying members, more than 10 per cent of the entire population, and about half of the number of votes the Party polled at that time. In Vienna the Party had succeeded in enrolling nearly 25 per cent of the entire population in its ranks.[21] At the elections held in 1930 Social Democracy, for the first time since 1919, had again become the strongest party in parliament, winning 72 of 165 seats. The moderates, overshadowed at the top level by the ascendance of Otto Bauer's Left, found ample opportunity to exercise their gifts in the Party's practical political and organizational work, in the activities of the affiliated Trade Unions and the large network of cooperatives. The militants, on the other hand, whether concerned with Marxist theory or revolutionary action, were given wide scope in that period. In the educational activities carried on by the Party and Marxist study circles radical formulations prevailed. And in the Republican Defense Guard (*Republikanischer Schutzbund*), a semimilitary party formation organized in 1923, a channel was provided for the energies of the less theoretically minded militants. A certain prudence of action was matched by an extravagance of language which gave the Party a far more radical appearance than in reality corresponded to the prevalent sentiments of its leadership. Though not itself a force controlling the Party's course of action, the extreme left wing could nevertheless maintain steady pressure on the "Left of (socialist) Center" leadership of Otto Bauer to prevent any open deviation—verbally, at least—from the commitment to the principles of the class struggle.

---

[20] For a more detailed discussion of the Vienna tax system, see Gulick, *op. cit.*, chap. 13.

[21] Some 418,000 members in a population of approximately 1.8 million.

Impending Civil War

By its uncompromising tone of class hostility and by its endorsement—however qualified—of the violent struggle for power as an important and probably inevitable aspect of the political process, Austrian Social Democracy contributed to the increasing political tension which caused tempers to grow short, bloody incidents to multiply and eventual civil war more and more widely to be accepted as a possible solution. At the Linz Party Conference in 1926 the likelihood of the necessary resort to violence—in defense of socialist successes democratically secured—was formally included in the Social Democratic program. The formulation was viewed as insufficiently vigorous by the radical wing and as unnecessarily provocative by the moderates. In fact, the resolve was accompanied neither by the physical nor intellectual mobilization required to prepare the Party for civil war. Torn between a policy of outright conciliation—a course openly urged by Karl Renner at the 1927 Conference, designed to secure more safely the democratic basis of the state—and that of direct and, if necessary, violent action to break the opponent's power while the political balance still seemed to favor the working class, the responsible leaders could not decide on either course and thus continued to confuse their own followers as well as their opponents.

The precariousness of this position was demonstrated by the events of July 15, 1927, one of the milestones on the First Republic's road to destruction. On the morning of this day the *Arbeiter Zeitung,* the Party's official voice, had protested in an editorial of great violence against the acquittal (by a jury) of some men accused of having fired at and killed participants in a Socialist street demonstration.[22] This editorial, intended as a substitute for action rather than a call for it,[23] contributed to incite rank-and-file emotion to a pitch which went beyond the leadership's expectation and control. Caught off guard by apparently spontaneous mass action taking the form of demonstrations converging from the outlying industrial districts on the center of Vienna, the leaders were reduced to pleading with the demonstrators—who had become engaged in a violent clash with the

---

[22] The ambiguity of Socialists attacking the verdict of a jury—an institution which they had always defended against conservative criticisms—was not lost on their opponents. It acted as a further factor restraining the leadership in its means of expressing protest.

[23] Gulick, *op. cit.,* pp. 734 ff.

police and had set fire to the Palace of Justice—to permit the restoration of peace and order. In the confused fighting which marked that and the following day, 85 demonstrators were killed and over a thousand people injured.[24] The Party leaders firmly refused to turn the melee into a civil war, pointing out to their excited followers the alleged hopelessness of such a struggle. On the other hand, Otto Bauer was apparently only too eager to interpret as permanent refusal[25] the initial rebuff of tentative Socialist conciliation moves at the hand of Monsignor Seipel, the Christian Social chancellor.[26]

In parliament the evenly balanced forces of Right and Left faced each other with growing hostility in a situation of near-deadlock due to the absence of a stable majority. Within the conservative camp the "Heimwehr," Fascist successor organization to the post-1918 irregular forces defending Austrian frontier districts, was gaining in influence. Economic crisis, manifesting itself in growing unemployment and climaxed in May, 1931, by the breakdown of the Credit Anstalt, Austria's largest bank, created seemingly insuperable problems for the weak governments of the Right. In the wake of the Credit Anstalt collapse, Seipel invited the Socialist Party to join him in a coalition government whose task it would be to put through a clearly defined emergency program. The Socialist Party viewed this offer as a trick by the chancellor to shift the burden of responsibility for unpopular economic measures, and therefore rejected it unanimously.[27] The government, supported by the Christian Socials, the Heimwehr, and the Landbund (a small peasant party), with its majority in parliament reduced to one seat, teetered ever more precariously on the edge of momentary defeat.

In the meantime a new and dangerous element began to intrude upon the Austrian political scene: the National Socialist Movement, which put both major parties on the defensive by its rapidly growing appeal. Though the National Socialists had failed to elect a single representative at the parliamentary elections of 1930 they secured 15 seats (out of 100) in the Vienna City Council in the municipal elections of April, 1932, a sinister portent of the success they were likely to score if general elections were to

---

[24] *Ibid.*, p. 746.
[25] Hannak, *op. cit.*, p. 349.
[26] Monsignor Seipel, a Roman Catholic prelate, was leader of the Christian Social Party, repeatedly chancellor, a man of great ability, and the Socialists' most powerful adversary during the entire decade.
[27] Hannak, *op. cit.*, p. 373.

be held.[28] Even in the face of this new threat, the Socialists and their traditional opponents did not subdue their hostility sufficiently to create a united front against it. Instead, each decided to fight a two-front war against the new and the old enemy simultaneously. Parliamentary democracy was widely discredited and under sharp attack by the *Heimwehr* group in the government camp. Engelbert Dollfuss, who had succeeded Monsignor Seipel in the leadership of the conservative coalition, considered it likely to bring about the destruction of his forces. After frequently circumventing parliamentary rule by the use of the obsolete "war economy emergency powers" stemming from World War I, he utilized a technical deadlock in parliamentary procedure to prevent parliament from resuming its meetings. Faced with a situation, already anticipated in the Linz program, in which democratic institutions were being eliminated by their opponents, the Socialist leadership debated at length and in anguish the question of resorting to the violent means at its disposal—general strike backed by mobilization of the Defense Guard—in order to enforce restoration of democratic procedures.[29] The decision to accept Dollfuss' action without an all-out struggle made it clear that the Socialist leaders "most at home in city councils, diets, and parliament" [30] had never seriously considered implementation of the Linz formula. They were unprepared even to take the initiative in the use of violence when driven back on their last defenses unless their adversary did so first.[31] Furthermore, it was doubtful whether such a struggle, once started, could have been restricted to the announced goal, the restoration of parliamentary democracy. For the Party was under increasingly heavy pressure from its militant wing, the very group which would have had to bear the main burden of violent action, to aban-

---

[28] In the municipal election the Socialist ranks held firm; the losses were suffered exclusively by the traditional Right.

[29] The Trade Union representatives and some moderates favored action while both Bauer and Renner counseled caution. The ostensible reason for submission was the desire to avoid bloodshed. (Gulick, *op. cit.*, pp. 1035–36.) It may, however, be suspected that the restoration of parliamentary democracy in its somewhat discredited and unstable condition did not appear to the majority of the leadership to be worth an uncertain struggle.

[30] Gulick, *ibid.*, p. 1036.

[31] Cf., e.g., Otto Bauer's speech of that time—frequently cited—in which he stated that "we could assume responsibility to the mothers of this country [for the victims of a civil war] only after we had previously done everything which would make a peaceful solution possible on the basis of democracy." (Gulick, *ibid.*, p. 1034.)

don democracy and to launch a direct attempt at establishing a Socialist dictatorship.[32]

Roughly a year separated the elimination of parliament from the suppression of the Socialist Party. Dollfuss' technique was to attack the Movement by piecemeal rather than all-out methods. Neither precensorship of its press, prohibition of mass meetings and demonstrations, nor, finally, the dissolution of the Republican Defense Guard were considered by the leadership as so vitally threatening the existence of the Party as to warrant violent resistance.[33] Dollfuss made these measures appear inherent to his struggle against the rising menace of Nazism which disturbed public peace by the violence of its agitation and frequent resort to terroristic weapons. Given the historical situation—so obviously unfavorable to the fortunes of democratic movements—as well as Dollfuss' skillful manipulation, civil war appeared to be a venture the cost of which would in all likelihood not be balanced by any equivalent socialist gain.

February, 1934: Days of Defeat

When fighting between the Socialist Party and the government forces did start, it was not as the result of any deliberate Socialist plan, defensive or offensive, but rather as an instinctive reaction, a violent revulsion by the raw nerve ends of the Party against further attacks on its organization. Officially the Party had given notice that it would consider these particular further infringements a *casus belli*: dissolution of either the Party or the Trade Unions; occupation of the Vienna city hall; establishment, by decree, of a Fascist constitution.[34] Its Right wing under Karl Renner and Oscar Helmer, backed by the Lower Austrian party organization, continued to seek conciliation with the government—a policy with which Otto Bauer at the time apparently was in sympathy.[35] By that time, however, Dollfuss had firmly decided to seek a tie with Mussolini, the price of which was final elimination of parliamentary democracy in Austria.[36] Therefore he

---

[32] Cf., e.g., Otto Bauer, "Um die Demokratie," *Der Kampf*, XXVI (July, 1933), 269–76, in which Bauer criticized those in the Party who held democracy in low esteem.

[33] The Party itself with its affiliated organizations, the Free Trade Unions, the Vienna City Council, and even the Upper House of Parliament (*Bundesrat*), continued in existence during this period.

[34] Gulick, *op. cit.*, p. 1211.

[35] *Ibid.*, p. 1212.

[36] *Ibid.*, pp. 1276–77; cf. also Paul R. Sweet, *Mussolini and Dollfuss*, published as appendix to Julius Braunthal, *The Tragedy of Austria*.

allowed the *Heimwehr* leaders to push ahead with their plans for the destruction of the Socialist Party as the major step toward the establishment of a corporate state (*Ständestaat*).

The government did not formally encroach on any of the "sensitive" areas declared inviolable by the Socialist leadership. Thus, when a leader of the Republican Defense Guard at Linz decided to resist by force any further attempts by *Heimwehr* contingents to invade and ransack their offices and meeting places under the guise of a search for arms, Otto Bauer immediately advised caution and delay. He preferred to wait for the general government attack on the "sensitive areas," which he considered inevitable.[37] His cautious advice was disregarded by the Linz militants. And when reports of the outbreak of fighting reached Vienna on the morning of February 12, 1934, the hastily assembled Committee of the Party Executive decided to proclaim a general strike while Renner and Helmer even now attempted to prevent further violence by carrying on negotiations with the democratic wing of the Dollfuss government.[38] The general strike slogan failed to bring about universal work stoppage. Hastily armed detachments of the Guard were attacked by police and army units in various districts of Vienna and several provincial towns. On the same day the government declared a state of martial law and decreed the dissolution of the Social Democratic Party. In three days of fighting the government forces had beaten down all resistance; courts-martial had sentenced twenty-one Socialists to be hanged, nine of whom were actually executed.[39] And a number of prominent Party leaders, among them Otto Bauer and Julius Deutsch, chief of the Defense Guard, had fled to Czechoslovakia to escape the vengeance of the Dollfuss regime.

The Period of Illegality: 1934–1945 [40]

Organization of the "Revolutionary Socialists"

The Party organization's first reaction to the defeat suffered was one of stunned inactivity, the next, feverish discussions—consisting primarily of recriminatory post-mortems—carried on by innumerable cells, all of them

---

[37] Buttinger, *op. cit.*, p. 6.

[38] Gulick, *op. cit.*, pp. 1281–82; Buttinger, *op. cit.*, p. 12.

[39] Gulick, *op. cit.*, p. 1302.

[40] The following account is based on Otto Bauer, *Die illegale Partei*; Gulick, *op. cit.*, ch. 30; Buttinger, *op. cit.*; also on many talks with former members of the underground movement.

Left-wing, the disorganized splinters of the mighty organization. Yet this phase did not last long. To the members of the Defense Guard, to the core of Party employees, and to the army of *Vertrauensmänner* the Party had been the most significant part of their existence; activity in it and for it had been a habit and a necessity. Nourished for decades by the belief in the invincibility of the Movement and the certainty of its ultimate triumph—beliefs which justified the sacrifices and devotion demanded—these dedicated Socialists could not interpret the defeat as anything but a temporary setback.[41] That they should accept the defeat, lapse into permanent political inactivity, or allow themselves to be integrated into the emerging Fascist regime appeared simply inconceivable. For these members of the Socialist "cadre," continued political activity of some sort was a foregone conclusion.

It did not take long before the question of succession to the defunct Social Democracy was settled. Already in February, 1934, a group of younger functionaries had formed an underground organization under the name "Revolutionary Socialists" (R.S.). Before many months had passed, rival splinter groups, such as the "Febrists," the "Spark" group, the "Red Front," all of which initially competed for leadership, had been amalgamated into the R.S. In spite of the determined rejection by the R.S. of the old Party's democratic commitment—a rejection symbolized by the change of name—this organization was dominated by the idea of the "continuity of the Movement." [42] As an organization in which all former Social Democrats wishing to remain politically active and willing to run the risks of such activity were welcome as members, it suffered all through its short history from a fundamental contradiction, which somehow perpetuated the ambivalence inherent in the very nature of Austro-Marxism: on one hand, it was determined to be considered a new, revolutionary force, independent of the old—and in the eyes of some, discredited—leaders who now led the lives of political émigrés in Brünn; on the other, it desired to be accepted as the *legitimate* successor of the legal Party.[43] The result of this conflict, which took place between fractions and individuals but also within the

---

[41] Cf. Buttinger, *op. cit.*, pp. 64 ff.; particularly the political portrait of "Frau Maier," the prototype of the "humble Party worker."

[42] Cf. Buttinger, *op. cit.*, pp. 34–57.

[43] In illustration of this point, we might cite the concluding sentence—unintentionally humorous—of a letter written by one of the members of the Central Committee of the R.S. to Otto Bauer: "And so we should like to ask you to agree to our using the title: 'Central Committee of the Revolutionary Socialists.'" (Quoted by Buttinger, *op. cit.*, p. 57.)

individuals themselves, was a wavering between rejection and glorification of the past; between a view of revolutionary methods as desirable *per se* and their reluctant acceptance as tactics forced upon the Movement.[44]

Otto Bauer, who had established a Foreign Bureau of Austrian Socialism in Brünn, Czechoslovakia, was sensitive to the widespread criticism directed at the old leadership and also aware of the difficulty of controlling an illegal organization from abroad. He therefore at once disclaimed any pretensions to the retention of decision-making powers.[45] Nevertheless, the R.S. had to avoid an open break with him not only because the Foreign Bureau dispensed funds needed for the continuation of illegal activity, but also because Otto Bauer still commanded a great deal of loyalty within the Party and continued to be identified by the outside world as the spokesman for Austrian socialism.

Though harassed by frequent arrests and the limitations which police surveillance imposed on the R.S., it quickly established an operating underground network and succeeded in maintaining it. Underground activity passed through a series of phases. In the first, marked by the fervent hope for the speedy overthrow of the Dollfuss regime simultaneously harassed by the illegal Nazi movement, the R.S. engaged in mass distribution of propaganda and in frequent public demonstrations of its "will to live." [46] The prevailing mood was one of bitterness and radicalism, born of a feeling of betrayal at the hands of incompetent and insufficiently militant leaders. The government's victory over the Nazi *putschists* in July, 1934, ending hopes for its quick demise, as well as the losses which the underground movement suffered in carrying out frequently foolhardy actions, created the necessity for developing a longer-term strategy and more concern for the physical safety of the illegal workers. The distribution of the *Arbeiter Zeitung*, now printed in Brünn and smuggled across the border, continued; efforts at strengthening the underground organization were increased; thus, under the influence of the group loyal to Bauer, the distinction between the new party and the old was less heavily stressed,[47] much to the chagrin

---

[44] The conflict is clearly revealed by the treatment given the period by Buttinger and Hannak in their respective accounts.

[45] Cf. *Arbeiter Zeitung* (Brünn edition), February 2, 1934; also, Otto Bauer, *Die illegale Partei*, pp. 63–64.

[46] Gulick, *op. cit.*, pp. 1575–76. Their essence lay in the conspicuousness of these actions designed to give confidence to friends and convey the feeling of contempt for the power of the enemy.

[47] Buttinger, *op. cit.*, pp. 165 ff.

of the determined radicals. The undercurrent of bitterness at the émigré leadership was strong enough, however, to force a reversal of this trend. At a conference held at Brünn on December 31, 1934, the radical wing forced through demands for changes in the composition of the leadership organization and for a decrease in the publicity emanating from the Foreign Bureau. It also succeeded in having the name of the organization, which, under pressure from Bauer had shortly before been changed to "United Socialist Party of Austria," restored to "Revolutionary Socialists." [48]

"New Men" Versus "Old Social Democrats"

The victory of the most extreme wing of the movement marked the beginning of the third phase, which was given additional impetus by the arrest of almost the entire top leadership by the Austrian police. This made room for the emergence of new men who identified themselves much less with the nonrevolutionary past. The new course was characterized by two tactical changes: the replacement of mass action by more truly conspiratorial activity; [49] and the decision to enter and penetrate, wherever feasible, the institutions set up by the government, particularly the official "United Labor Organization" (Einheitsgewerkschaft) rather than to attempt their destruction by boycott. The conspiratorial activities of the illegal Party clearly were not aimed at bringing about the downfall of the regime by their own efforts. Hitherto the faith in the historical inevitability of the Party's triumph had predominated even under conditions of illegality. The "New Men" who took on the Party's leadership in 1935 rejected this comfortable belief as an illusion inherited from the old Social Democracy. Viewing themselves as "realists" and criticized by their opponents as "pessimists," they pilloried the complacency of those who, though self-professed "Leftists," remained in intellectual bondage to past tradition. Honesty, the New Men's most highly valued virtue, compelled them to insist on ruthlessly dispelling smug, and what seemed to them fallacious, assumptions. In the place of "historical forces" they put "pure will to socialism" as a guarantor of eventual triumph.[50] Otto Bauer, who failed to appreciate this purely visceral optimism, saw in the abandonment of faith in the historical process' assurance of socialist victory the beginning of the Move-

---

[48] Ibid., p. 217.
[49] Buttinger (Richter) and Karl Czernetz, another prominent member of the R.S., had been strongly influenced by the Leninist views propagated by ex-members of the "Spark" group.
[50] Cf. Buttinger, op. cit., pp. 385–92.

ment's disintegration. In his view, work without rationally grounded faith lacked guidance and, equally important, lacked appeal to the masses.[51] Rigid slogans and emotionally charged rhetoric, so the New Men felt, obscured, misled, and falsified facts. To Social Democrats, on the other hand, these were unavoidable and essentially accurate, though necessarily simplified, intellectual props in the struggle carried on with the support of the masses.

While the New Men had taken over some of the leading positions in the underground movement and were surrounded by a small group of devoted followers, the illegal party still included a large number of members who were untouched by their leaders' theoretical doubts and unorthodox socialist views. In spite of the ruthlessly revolutionary pronouncements of the R.S., a return to the *status quo ante* 1934, to a situation in which they could pursue traditional Social Democratic objectives in traditional ways, seemed to them a highly desirable goal. Thus when Dr. Kurt Schuschnigg,[52] in an attempt to strengthen his regime against increasingly heavy pressure by Hitler, began to explore the possibility of restoring a free labor movement, his overtures met with enthusiastic acceptance by many "Revolutionary" Socialists.[53] They saw in this prospect of a belated "red-black" coalition for the defense of Austria against Hitler the first fruit of their long underground struggle.

Early in 1938 the border line between illegality and legal existence disappeared for a few brief weeks. In meetings and conferences the underground Revolutionary Socialists of yesterday formulated modest demands [54] as conditions for their co-operation in the government's efforts to maintain Austrian independence. Otto Bauer urged from Brünn a simultaneous struggle for national independence and internal freedom of action.[55] On the urging of Renner, the Right-wing members of the 1934 Party

---

[51] *Ibid.*, pp. 421–23.

[52] Schuschnigg had succeeded Dollfuss in 1934 as the head of the Austrian government, after Dollfuss' assassination by Nazi *putschists.*

[53] Buttinger, *op. cit.*, pp. 439 ff.

[54] These, as finally presented to Schuschnigg, included: (*a*) the right to adhere to socialism and to be politically active to the same degree as the National Socialists; (*b*) free elections in the Trade Union Federation; (*c*) permission to publish a daily paper; (*d*) guarantee of a "social" policy by the regime. The cadre of New Men refused to participate in the formulation of these demands. (Buttinger, *op. cit.*, pp. 494–95.)

[55] In an article published by the *Arbeiter Zeitung* (Brünn edition) on March 1, 1938. (*Ibid.*, p. 476.)

Executive, who had been meeting regularly since the dissolution of the party,[56] also prepared to re-enter the political scene.[57] The Central Committee of the R.S., on the other hand, dominated by the New Men, considered the conquest of Austria by Hitler's forces inevitable and busied itself with the preparation of the organization's dissolution and the emigration of its leading functionaries.

Destruction and Dispersal

The Socialist organization had not ceased to exist when it was outlawed in February, 1934. Its final destruction was the result of Hitler's occupation and of the work of the Gestapo, so much more ruthless and effective than that of the Austrian police. Those leading functionaries who had failed to make their way out of the country were arrested, though not all of them right away. In its last directive the Central Committee of the R.S. had ordered a period of "strict inactivity" for the entire organization as a precautionary measure.[58] Attempts—contrary to the directive—to keep illegal cadre organizations in operation did not achieve significant successes. The remnants were wiped out when the Gestapo, in a wave of mass arrests at the beginning of World War II, imprisoned almost the entire cadre of underground activists.[59] The Right-wing leaders who had not carried on illegal work retired to a state of complete political inactivity. Renner withdrew to his country home; Helmer took up the innocuous position of an insurance agent; and Renner's aide, Dr. Adolf Schärf, carried on a modest law practice. The Gestapo, by and large, showed little interest in this moderate (largely non-Jewish) group of former Social Democrat functionaries.

Abroad, the greatly enlarged group of émigré leaders attempted to preserve the continuity of the Austrian Socialist Movement in some form. As long as an urgent common task had imposed a degree of discipline and unity, the serious differences between the New Men and the "old Social Democrats" (as well as those Revolutionary Socialists who had not genuinely rejected the past) had not been allowed to disrupt the organization. By the force of events, the proponents of the "new course" had now been thrown into one boat with their antagonists. In their struggle for control of the "Auslandsvertretung"—formed in Paris—the New Men, however,

---

[56] Adolf Schärf, *April 1945 in Wien*, p. 7.

[57] Buttinger, *op. cit.*, pp. 460 ff.

[58] *Ibid.*, p. 485.

[59] The task of the Gestapo was simple: it used the files on illegal Socialist activity compiled by the Austrian police. Cf. Buttinger, *op. cit.*, p. 487.

were handicapped by being cut off from what had been the source of their strength vis-à-vis the Brünn group in the past: the power and support of the illegal cadre organization which they controlled. In the summer of 1938, shortly after Otto Bauer's sudden death, a compromise between the two factions was achieved which, by giving the New Men the leading role in the Foreign Bureau,[60] temporarily veiled the fundamental weakness of their position, a weakness which was in part self-imposed. For, as genuinely revolutionary Socialists who had risen to positions of leadership in revolt against opportunism and democratic compromise, they held that unless their activity was clearly furthering revolutionary socialist goals, total inactivity was the course to be preferred. Thus, by the spring of 1939, Josef Podlipnig, Secretary of the Foreign Bureau, the most determined adherent of these principles, favored the dissolution of the Bureau in view of the inevitability of war which, in his view, would render truly socialist activity impossible.[61] In April, 1940, he resigned from the Paris Foreign Bureau, accusing those who did not share his attitude toward the war of being the "intellectual heads of social democratic opportunism." [62] A few months later, at a meeting in New York, Fritz Adler—to the satisfaction of the New Men—suspended the Bureau's activities.[63] When some of the Bureau's members wished to reactivate it subsequent to the Soviet Union's involvement in the war, its chairman Joseph Buttinger (undercover name: Gustav Richter) and his followers resigned, whereupon Fritz Adler declared it to be dissolved.[64]

In London a precarious attempt to preserve the organizational continuity of Austrian socialism was maintained by the London Bureau of Austrian Socialists, set up by Oscar Pollak, who had been the editor-in-chief of the *Arbeiter Zeitung* in 1934. The close links established with members of the British Labor Party, as well as the group's belief in subordination of socialist goals to the overriding necessity of victory over Hitler, made it heir to the Social Democratic tradition rather than to the principles of the

---

[60] The publication of the monthly *Der sozialistische Kampf* was left in the hands of Fritz Adler and Julius Deutsch, representatives of the old Social Democratic Party, together with Oscar Pollak, one of the "nominal" R.S. members. (Buttinger, *op. cit.*, pp. 499–502.)

[61] *Ibid.*, p. 510.

[62] *Ibid.*, p. 527.

[63] Most of the Bureau's members had been able to make their way to New York before the fall of France.

[64] Buttinger, *op. cit.*, p. 531.

Revolutionary Socialists. No contact between the London Bureau and the former members of the Socialist organization remaining in Austria existed. The physical and intellectual isolation of the London Bureau from the forces which, in April, 1945, were active in the revival of the Party, rendered it of slight direct importance in shaping the Party's postwar development. More significant in the long run was the prolonged exposure to the moderate political climate of Great Britain of such prewar Leftists as Oscar Pollak and Karl Czernetz, who returned to influential posts in the Austrian Socialist Party after the liberation of the country.

Social Democracy Revived: 1945 and After

Reorganization of the Party Machinery

By the spring of 1945 Austrian Socialism had been in a state of suspended animation for seven years. Top leaders had retired into political obscurity, fled abroad, or been sent to concentration camps. Many less prominent functionaries shared their leaders' fate or were conscripted into the German Army. Beyond small-scale attempts to "keep in touch," scattered co-operation with Yugoslav partisans, and some contacts with the so-called "Biedermann" resistance organization,[65] no trace of organized political activity on the part of Austrian Socialists during the period of Nazi occupation can be discovered. Nevertheless, within a few days of the entry of Russian troops into Vienna, the Party organization was re-established—*on the pre-1934 pattern*. Old-time local Party functionaries, emerging from a decade of enforced political inactivity, simply drifted back to their former meeting places as soon as freedom of political action seemed assured, greeting each other joyfully with the old Party salute *"Freundschaft"*; and, in a matter-of-fact spirit, picked up organizationally where they had left off in February, 1934.[66] Some of the more prominent former Social Democratic leaders had established loose contact with each other as soon as the grip of Nazi power on the city slackened. Once Vienna was liberated they were ap-

---

[65] Biedermann, a major in the German Army, had planned a mutiny of the Vienna garrison at the approach of the liberating forces. The plan was betrayed and Major Biedermann was executed. (Schärf, *op. cit.*, p. 71.) Cf. also Richard Hiscocks, *The Rebirth of Austria*, pp. 15–20, for a more detailed description of resistance activities.

[66] This description is based on talks with local Socialist functionaries who were in Vienna in April, 1945.

proached by the Resistance Group 05, for a few days the only organized political force, to nominate a mayor and to co-operate in the setting up of a City Council.[67] To create a conspicuous focus for the reviving Social Democratic Party organization, this group established its headquarters in the City Hall—the traditional symbol of Red Vienna—and arranged to meet there daily. They were joined on April 14 by a number of "young" Socialists who acted as spokesmen for the ex-R.S. element. The re-establishment of the Party under the name "*Sozialistische Partei Oesterreichs (Sozialdemokraten und Revolutionäre Sozialisten)*" and of a provisional Party Executive on the basis of parity between the two "factions" was agreed on.[68] By April 19, 1945, the Party Secretariat had begun to function, and on April 21 the first all-Vienna conference of Party district leaders was held.[69]

The Russian occupation authorities, sole masters of the city at that time, did nothing to discourage this revival of Socialist Party activity.[70] Similarly, no obstacle was put into its path by the British authorities in their zone of occupation.[71] In the zones held by French and United States forces, however, political party activities remained illegal [72] until, by decision of the Allied Council on September 11, 1945, permission was granted to solely three parties—Socialists, Communists, and the People's Party [73]—to carry on political activities in all parts of the country. The three-party system thus established by Allied fiat displeased the Socialists because it institutionalized the split in working-class ranks while it artificially created a united "bourgeois" front.

The Provisional Government

From the first, representatives of the Socialist Party did not hesitate to accept governmental office wherever the opportunity arose. In the provinces of Styria and Carinthia, Socialists were recognized as Governors

---

[67] Schärf, *op. cit.*, p. 66.

[68] *Ibid.*, pp. 69 ff. *Sozialistische Partei Oesterreichs* is referred to hereafter as SPOe; cf. Chap. II, footnote 4.

[69] *Ibid.*, p. 88.

[70] After some minor hitches, the Party was duly registered with the Russian occupation authorities. (*Ibid.*, pp. 90–91.)

[71] Schärf, *Zwischen Demokratie und Volksdemokratie*, p. 60.

[72] Although occupation authorities apparently did nothing to enforce the ban.

[73] The Austrian People's Party (*Oesterreichische Volkspartei; OeVP*) is virtually the successor of the pre-1934 Christian Social Party.

(*Landeshauptmänner*) by the Russian and British authorities.[74] In Vienna, to the surprise and temporary discomfiture of the Western occupation powers, a provisional national government headed by Karl Renner had been formed on April 23 with the active sponsorship of the Russian authorities.[75] This provisional government, like all subsequent Austrian governments to date, was based on a party coalition. In it the Socialists held the Chancellorship (Renner), one of the three positions in the so-called "Political Council" (Schärf), and the Secretariats for Social Administration and Food; also positions as under-secretaries in the Secretariats for Interior Affairs, Education, Justice, Agriculture, Trade, and Reconstruction.[76] The government was based on the principle of complete parity of representation between the three parties. Each secretary was assisted and watched over by two under-secretaries not of his own party.[77]

The effective authority of this government was for several months restricted to the Russian zone of occupation. A Russian motion at the Potsdam Conference to extend its authority to the entire country was rejected by the Western powers.[78] As a reply to a plea by Dr. Renner, the Allied Council voted unanimously, on October 20, to recognize the government, and demanded the speedy holding of free elections.[79] Over the heated protests of the Communist Party, the government decided to readopt the Austrian constitution, once elections had been held, as it had existed prior to March 5, 1933,[80] thus avoiding any drawn-out struggle over the formulation of a new basic law.[81] Until that time the provisional government was to combine legislative, executive, and constitution-making powers, temporarily turning Austria into a unitary, centralized state.

---

[74] Schärf, *Zwischen Demokratie* . . . , p. 61. Cf. also Keesing's *Archiv der Gegenwart*, *Jahrgang* 1945, pp. 230D, 147J, and 517D.

[75] For the most detailed description of the steps leading to the formation of the Provisional Government, see Karl Renner, *Denkschrift über die Geschichte der Unabhängigkeitserklärung Oesterreichs und die Einsetzung der provisorischen Regierung der Republik.*

[76] See *Neues Oesterreich*, April 28, 1945. In September a Secretariat for Property Security (*Vermögenssicherung*) was added, in which the Socialists held an under-secretariat. (Schärf, *Zwischen Demokratie* . . . , p. 24.)

[77] Except in the case of the Secretariats for Justice and Finance; in these, nonpartisan "experts" had at their side three party representatives as under-secretaries.

[78] Schärf, *Zwischen Demokratie* . . . , p. 21.

[79] *Ibid.*, pp. 22–24.

[80] The date on which Parliament had been suspended.

[81] Schärf, *Zwischen Demokratie* . . . , p. 24.

Elections and Coalition

In the first free postwar elections, held in November, 1945, the Austrian People's Party polled 50 per cent of the total vote, the Socialists 45 per cent, and the Communists 5 per cent. All registered ex-Nazis had been barred from voting by party agreement. Even if this distribution of political strength had not rendered single-party government impossible, the then prevailing atmosphere of "unity of all democratic, anti-Fascist forces" ruled out any alternative to a continuation of government by coalition. In consequence of the weakness the Communists had exhibited at the polls,[82] their influence in the newly formed government was drastically reduced.[83] Renner became the first President of the Second Austrian Republic; the People's Party, as the strongest single party, nominated the Chancellor, Dr. Leopold Figl; and the chairman of the Socialist Party, Schärf, obtained the position of Vice-Chancellor. In the distribution of ministerial posts, the Socialists insisted on—and received—the Ministry of Interior. In addition, they were given control of the Ministry for Social Administration, Food, and of the newly established Transport Ministry. Their only foothold in the departments dealing with economic policy was an under-secretariat in the Ministry for Property Restitution and Economic Planning. The top positions in the economic departments—Finance, Trade, and Agriculture— as well as in the Ministries of Justice, Education, and the Foreign Secretariat, were held by non-Socialists.[84] This distribution was not disturbed for the duration of the government's existence—except for the replacement, by a Socialist, of the single Communist member of the government, who resigned in November, 1947.

The results of the second general elections, held in October, 1949, were greatly affected by the lifting of the voting ban for former National Social-

---

[82] A failure measured by Communist expectations and pretensions as reflected in their role in the Provisional Government. It is important to remember, however, that before 1934 the Communist Party existed in name only; it had not been able to win a single parliamentary seat or gain the support of even 1 per cent of the population.

[83] They obtained a single Ministry, that of Electrical Power and Electrification. They lost their valuable hold on the Ministries of Interior and Education as well as the many under-secretariats.

[84] The Ministries of Justice and Finance continued to be occupied by men without official party affiliations though each was known to lean toward one or the other of the two major parties. This "leaning" subsequently became the basis for party claims to occupy the respective Ministries outright.

ists as well as the emergence of a fourth major party, the League of Independents (*Verband der Unabhängigen*), which was welcomed by many Socialists. Contrary to Socialist hopes, the new party of the Right drew its support by no means exclusively from the ranks of those who had voted or were likely to vote for the People's Party. The Independents polled 12 per cent of the total vote, while both major parties' strengths were reduced by 6 per cent—the People's Party to 44 per cent and the Socialists to 38 per cent; the Communists remained at 5 per cent. Though disappointed by the result, the Socialist leaders succeeded in exploiting the even greater setback which the People's Party had experienced (by losing its absolute majority in Parliament) for a redistribution of cabinet posts on more favorable terms. Karl Waldbrunner, one of the SPOe's Central Secretaries, was appointed to head a newly organized Ministry for Nationalized Industries and Transportation, thus providing the Party with significant influence over an important sector of the economy.

In 1951, following the death of Karl Renner, an election for the Presidency of the Republic became necessary. After a bitterly fought campaign the Socialist candidate, the venerable General Körner, won in the runoff with the unsolicited support of the Communist Party and a sizable proportion of those who had previously voted for the League of Independents. In a period of business decline and incipient unemployment, the inability of the coalition partners to agree on the budget for 1953 led to a temporary breakup of the coalition and the premature call for elections in February, 1953. From these the Socialists emerged as the strongest party (measured by the number of votes cast), obtaining 42 per cent of the vote and 72 seats, while both the People's Party and—more surprisingly—the League of Independents lost electoral strength in comparison with the 1949 vote.[85] This time, however, the tactical situation of 1949 was reversed: the Socialists were unable to exploit their success. For the growing Socialist strength, coupled with the increasing acceptance of the Independents as a "respectable" political force, raised the serious thought among leaders of the People's Party of creating a middle-class bloc with the Independents which, in any coalition with the Socialists, would command a safe majority over them. Adamant refusal of the Socialist Party to entertain the possibility of

---

[85] Comparison with the first round of the 1951 Presidential election gives a somewhat different picture, considerably more encouraging to the People's Party. (See Appendix 1.)

a coalition on this basis [86] caused the People's Party to drop the proposal. But the threat succeeded in preventing the Socialists from deriving any important gains in terms of cabinet posts from their success.[87]

The coalition was not even shaken by the long-delayed withdrawal of the Four-Power occupation troops in 1955. Parliamentary elections, fought largely on the issue of the nationalized oil industry now returned to Austrian control, resulted in a sharp setback for the SPOe.[88] The decline of the Independents (now the *Freie Partei Oesterreichs, FPOe*) benefited mainly the People's Party, particularly in Vienna. But the OeVP success was not sufficiently large to permit it to govern alone; nor were the Socialists inclined to exchange their partnership for the role of opposition party. When, in 1957, SPOe Chairman Dr. Schärf, following the death of President Körner, in 1951, won out over his opponent—nominated in an obvious attempt to attract the Independent vote [89]—the Socialists interpreted the result as a decisive endorsement of a continued two-party coalition government and of the principle of "balance." [90] They made this the theme of their campaign in the parliamentary election of 1959 and succeeded in recouping the losses suffered in 1956. The SPOe emerged, as in 1953, as numerically the strongest party, though "electoral arithmetic" resulted in its obtaining one parliamentary seat less than its opponent.[91] The FPOe succeeded in stabilizing the "third camp" (at least temporarily) and even made some gains over its 1956 low point.[92] The Communists lost approximately one-quarter of their previous vote and failed to obtain any parlia-

---

[86] The U.S. authorities were widely reported to have exercised pressure on the People's Party leadership to continue the coalition in the form that had proved so stable in the past.

[87] It had been widely expected that the Socialists would, on the basis of their "victory" at the polls, claim either the Ministry of Finance or Education, both important centers of controversy between the coalition partners. The only gains for the SPOe were the establishment of two new under-secretariats (for Foreign Affairs and Trade), both held by Socialists.

[88] *Die Nationalratswahlen vom 13. Mai 1956*, Vienna, 1956.

[89] The candidate was Dr. Denk, a well-known surgeon with no political experience and no strong party ties.

[90] See the speech by Dr. Pittermann at the 1957 Party Conference (*Parteitagsprotokoll der SPOe* [hereafter cited as *PTP*], pp. 83–95).

[91] The SPOe obtained 1,953,935 votes (45 per cent of the valid votes cast) against the OeVP's 1,928,043 (44 per cent). (*Die Nationalratswahlen vom 10. Mai 1959*, Vienna, 1959.)

[92] *Ibid.* Its vote rose from 283,749 in 1956 to 336,110 in 1959.

mentary representation.[93] The 1959 election was followed by a "government crisis" of unprecedented length. For nine weeks the negotiators of the SPOe and OeVP wrestled over the distribution of power in the new government. The ultimate result indicated no significant shift in the balance of power. The position of the OeVP Minister of Finance—center of the strongest Socialist attacks—remained essentially unaltered, while the SPOe gained a somewhat nominal success in obtaining for its representative Dr. Bruno Kreisky the newly established post of Foreign Minister.[94] In the present situation of "balance of power" it is not surprising that each party contests with extreme perseverance each inch of ground before surrendering the smallest political advantage.

The Demise of "Integral Socialism"

Under the impact of coalition, economic recovery (largely with American aid), and oppressive Russian occupation policies, the balance between "Social Democrats" and "Revolutionary Socialists," nominally established in April, 1945, was not maintained. Leaving aside the question whether the bulk of the ex-Revolutionary Socialists were truly revolutionary or merely heirs of the old Austro-Marxist Left, the total liquidation of their influence on the policies of the postwar Party has marked the end of the tension between radical and moderate streams which, held together in the Social Democratic Party before 1934, was that Party's most significant feature. The expulsion in 1948 of Erwin Scharf, the foremost spokesman for the R.S. viewpoint and representative of the Left on the Central Secretariat,[95] was the most dramatic incident marking the consolidation of the leadership of the moderate (Renner) wing of the Party. With it the last remnant of Bauer's attempt to make of the Austrian Party a link between Soviet Communism and Western Democratic Socialism and a composite of radical and practical thought and action disappeared. Subsequent chapters will trace this process of transformation in greater detail. First, however, we turn to an analysis of the Party's postwar structure, with particular attention to those changes which distinguish it from the Social Democracy of the First Republic.

---

[93] *Ibid.* The Communist vote declined from 192,438 (1956) to 142,578.
[94] For day-to-day reports, see, e.g., the *Arbeiter Zeitung* between May 13 and July 12, 1959.
[95] At the time of his expulsion, however, he no longer held this position.

II

Problems of Organization

The Rejection of the R.S. Organizational Concepts

Following the defeat of the old Social Democracy in February, 1934, the Revolutionary Socialists rejected the Party's commitment to the democratic way, as well as the organizational pattern which had been adapted to the purpose of attracting a mass membership of faithful voters. Symbolically, this rejection took the form of the new name; organizationally, it expressed itself in reliance on "revolutionary cadres under whose leadership a centralized, strictly disciplined party, highly trained in the principles of Marxism, would be formed to bring about the socialist revolution." [1] At the war's end the Social Democratic tradition and the more recent Revolutionary Socialist experience had to be reconciled if the Party was to be revived as an effective political force. Yet the logic of organization which required adaptation of organizational means to political ends determined that, unless the Revolutionary Socialist group could control the course of the postwar Party's policies, its efforts to introduce organizational changes based on the experience of revolutionary struggle were bound to fail. As could be expected, a lasting synthesis between incompatible principles, the grafting of revolutionary organizational features on a democratic voter-oriented party proved not feasible.

The Party's Name

The adoption (in 1934) of the name "Revolutionary Socialists" by the underground organization symbolized the victory of the New Men over the

---

[1] Otto Bauer, *Die illegale Partei*, p. 39.

35

Social Democratic leadership, who were deeply resentful of the open repudiation of their lifework.[2] It indicated a clear break with the democratic principles of the past.

The lack of controversy which in 1945 characterized the choice of a new name for the party—in such striking contrast to the fierce factional battles of 1934—is an indication of the attenuation which the revolutionary spirit had experienced in the intervening years. The name agreed on, after brief and peaceful debate,[3] recognized the existence of an as yet unreconciled division between the Social Democratic and Revolutionary Socialist traditions. As the two groups operated in a political vacuum in which their respective strengths were completely unknown, they agreed to postpone a showdown on their differences. This decision was reflected in the clumsy name they adopted: "Socialist Party of Austria (Social Democrats and Revolutionary Socialists)."

Within a short time, however, it had become clear that the Revolutionary Socialists' claim for a position of equality was not based on the support of any strong sentiment within Party ranks. In a country occupied by alien powers and preoccupied with the most pressing problems of physical survival, revolutionary spirit was apparently at a low ebb. Thus the moderate wing of the Party leadership soon felt bold enough to rid itself of the symbolic commitments—however qualified—to revolutionary principles and of the implication of division contained in the Party's name as adopted in April, 1945. Without publicity and without encountering resistance or protest, the parenthetical part—("Social Democrats and Revolutionary Socialists")—was dropped, and from September, 1945, onward the Party became known simply as the Socialist Party of Austria.[4]

Cadre Organization Versus Mass Organization

As previously indicated, the replacement of the Social Democratic pattern of mass organization by cadres of revolutionary activists was the fundamental organizational change adopted by the Revolutionary Socialists. This change represented, on one hand, a necessary adaption to the conspiratorial techniques forced upon the Movement. But it also reflected the assump-

---

[2] See *Arbeiter Zeitung* (Brünn edition), May 27, 1934.

[3] Adolf Schärf, *April 1945 in Wien*, pp. 69–70.

[4] *Sozialistische Partei Oesterreichs* (hereafter referred to as the "Socialist Party," or the SPOe). In the *Arbeiter Zeitung* of September 30, 1945, Oscar Pollak wrote: "The official name of our Party included until recently the subtitle, 'Social Democrats and Revolutionary Socialists.'"

tion, shared by the Revolutionary Socialists with Lenin, that a tightly knit core of revolutionary activists would be required even after the conquest of power to defend the "dictatorship of the proletariat" against its enemies.[5] By its very nature Revolutionary Socialism could not develop a theory of cadre organization in a democratic state. For the R.S. leadership refused to concern itself with parliamentary democracy and a multiparty system as a future possibility, in spite of retrospective assertions to the contrary by ex-R.S. leaders.[6] Nevertheless, spokesmen for the ex-R.S. element demanded in 1945 that the cadre principle be embodied in the new Party's Organizational Statute.[7] Prior to 1934, a formal distinction between active and nonactive party members did not exist. To be recognized as a Party member it was sufficient to pledge adherence to the principles of the Party's program and join a local Party organization.[8] The new Statute, on the other hand, opened with a clause differentiating between two classes of members: Members and party workers.[9] To be classed as party workers, members had to meet certain qualifications: proof of irreproachable character and anti-Fascist convictions; steady participation in centrally organized training courses; active participation in party work. Their qualifications and thus their status as party workers were to be reviewed annually.[10]

The objective of this provision of the Statute was the establishment of an elite within the Party on which absolute reliance could be placed in any crisis. Thus the alleged organizational weaknesses of the old Social Democratic Party, exhibited in February, 1934, were to be avoided.[11] Yet the sponsors of this provision never clearly resolved wherein the activities of these party workers would differ from the tasks carried on in the past by the

---

[5] See the "Prinzipienerklärung der Wiener Sozialistischen Organisation" in *Arbeiter Zeitung* (Brünn edition) of September 22, 1934.

[6] Karl Czernetz (his name does not appear as author) explains in *Wir werben für die SPOe* (*Redeanleitung*, SBZ, September, 1948) that resort to a small conspiratorial elite was exclusively the response to Fascist suppression; that it was understood that "once democracy is regained the masses must not be left to other parties or organizations" (pp. 3–4).

[7] See, e.g., Czernetz, "Die politischen Offiziere des Proletariats," *Arbeiter Zeitung*, December 25, 1945; also the statement by Josef Gassner (*PTP*, 1945, p. 56): "I believe that the clause establishing special 'activist' status is primarily backed by the comrades coming from the illegal movement."

[8] Paragraph 1, *Organizational Statute 1919*, *PTP*, 1919, p. 112.

[9] *PTP*, 1945, p. 62.

[10] *Ibid.*

[11] Czernetz, "Die politischen Offiziere . . . ," *loc. cit.*

group of unpaid party functionaries, the *Vertrauensmänner*. Given the commitment to the revival of a democratic, electoral mass party—a commitment hardly contested and seemingly unavoidable under the circumstances [12]—the creation of an "officer corps," of a core of "all-round disciplined functionaries," [13] seemed to lack clear purpose. Otto Probst, himself a former active member of the R.S.,[14] pointed to the inconsistency of applying a revolutionary cadre concept in a democratic party. In his view, historical memories rather than concern for the organizational needs of the present and future activated the advocates of the cadre concept.[15]

Probst's criticism was prescient. The special category of "party workers" proved useless under the conditions of postwar Party activity. Not even the foremost advocate of its adoption in 1945 protested when in 1950 it was quietly eliminated from the Organizational Statute.[16] One difference between the present statute and the one in force before 1934 concerning membership qualifications remains—in theory: The Party's functionaries (*Vertrauensmänner*) are still expected to meet the qualifications of good character, anti-Fascist convictions, schooling, etc. It should be added that these specifications are either superfluous—functionaries are, by definition, active on behalf of the Party, adherence to the Party program is incompatible with Fascist views [17]—or are not enforced. Centrally directed training courses with compulsory attendance, considered the essence of the cadre concept, were discontinued in 1950 due to lagging interest and declining attendance; phenomena which were due, according to the admission of Karl Czernetz, chief of the Party's Education Center, to the failure of the courses to add meaningfully to the functionaries' political equipment. The periodic review of the functionaries' activities, demanded in the Organizational Statute, is nowhere undertaken. The requirement that functionaries submit to annual re-election by the membership also fails to

---

[12] Oscar Helmer, himself a prominent survivor of the old Social Democratic Party, considered the outcome of the debate—mass party versus elite party—a foregone conclusion: "The decision fell in favor of the mass party. It could obviously not be otherwise." ("Der Parteitag 1946," *Die Zukunft*, I [October, 1946], 6–8.)

[13] Czernetz, "Die politischen Offiziere . . . ," *loc. cit.*

[14] And subsequently one of the Central Secretaries of the SPOe.

[15] *PTP*, 1945, pp. 50–51.

[16] *PTP*, 1950, p. 204.

[17] According to several reliable accounts, the Party has shown great leniency in accepting former members of the Nazi Party as members and even functionaries (though not in prominent positions).

serve the purpose of reviewing their record because of the purely nominal nature of the election process.

The more significant alternative which the Socialist Party, committed to parliamentary democracy, had to face was whether to return to the attempt to organize within its ranks a mass of dues-paying members or whether to become an electoral party merely appealing periodically to the masses of voters for their support. Questions as to the ultimate usefulness of the perpetual quest for more Party members were bound to arise. The Party, organized as a "state within the state," had originally been the response to the pariah position of the proletariat in the country's predemocratic past. Once parliamentary democracy has been realized, this concept of the party is subject to democratic as well as revolutionary criticism. The revolutionary rejects it because it is not a fit instrument for the conquest of political power. The democrat may criticize it as an instrument unnecessary for the attainment of power, an instrument which has lost its original function and thus hampers rather than helps the party by misdirecting the activities of its most energetic members into cumbersome and dull party routine.[18]

There is no evidence that the Socialist Party ever seriously considered a basic organizational reform aiming at the abandonment of the mass-membership pattern inherited from the past.

One cannot escape the conclusion that the vast apparatus, resting heavily on tradition, has become its own justification. Its pattern of activities has been thoroughly routinized within grooves deepened by habitual practices. It provides its cadre of approximately 50,000 functionaries with a type of club life which to many of them has become a dear habit. The extensive replenishment of the Party's ranks with new members may weaken this subconscious foundation of the organization. But as these members enter the ranks of the cadre through a process of co-optation, the price of admission is conformity with the established pattern. By the time the last survivors of the pre-1934 period will have ceased to be active in the Party, the postwar crop of functionaries will in all likelihood be thoroughly accustomed to the traditional ways.

The one valid reason for the continuation of the traditional pattern is

[18] I am here suggesting—contrary to Duverger (*Political Parties, passim*)—that not only may there be an historical trend toward more highly disciplined mass parties, but that, in smoothly functioning democracies, a contrary trend—*away from mass parties* to "parliamentary" (or "caucus") parties—may exist as politics becomes increasingly specialized and divorced from simple class issues.

the Party's need for the stable financial support provided by the monthly dues of its members. By this means the Party is able to sustain its organization and propaganda work while remaining free of dependence on outside sources of income.[19]

The Problem of Socialist Shop Organization

The conflict over the principles of direct action and democratic methods was reflected organizationally in yet another question: Whether to use the members' homes, i.e., local territorial districts, as the centers of Party organization or whether it was preferable to build up Party cells in the industrial plants. At the end of World War I, in an atmosphere marked by radicalism, the Socialist leadership came under heavy pressure to abandon or modify its past reliance on local neighborhood organizations. Leftist splinter groups, as well as the newly formed Communist Party, were following the Russian example in attempts to form workers' councils in the factories as centers of political power. Workers' Councils claimed functions during this period which in a stable democracy were restricted to elected legislatures and the administrative agencies responsible to them. Yet the Socialist Party, as a political party, refused to abandon or even modify its traditional organizational pattern. In the leaders' view, territorial organization was absolutely required to fulfill what they continued to consider the Party's main function, the appeal to, and the successful organization of, the electorate.[20]

Except for one new element, the situation at the end of World War II seemed to favor a return to the exclusively geographical pattern of Party organization. The absence of revolutionary workers' councils and the universal profession of democratic sentiments appeared to eliminate the need for Socialist plant organizations. The new element, however, was the establishment of a Communist Party which based its entire structure on cells organized in industrial enterprises [21] and did not share, as events soon

---

[19] At election time, however, the Party is nevertheless forced to institute special drives for contributions to cover campaign expenses. It should also be pointed out that without the necessity of maintaining a mass-party apparatus the amount of money required by the Party would be smaller.

[20] Cf. the statement by Robert Danneberg to the 1919 Party Conference (*PTP*, 1919, p. 181).

[21] Paragraph 8 of the Statute of the *Kommunistische Partei Oesterreichs* (KPOe), adopted in 1946, provided for plant organizations as the "basis of the Party organization." (*Das neue Statut der KPOe*, angenommen auf dem 13. Parteitag der KPOe 1946.)

proved, the prevalent Socialist reluctance toward the use of extraparliamentary methods.[22] At the same time, by the establishment of an officially nonpartisan Austrian Trade Union Federation (*Oesterreichischer Gewerkschaftsbund, OeGB*), the Socialist Party had been deprived of its former reliable trade union ally. With the Socialist Party's acceptance of a share of governmental power it became more important—and more difficult—to discourage actions on the part of industrial workers hostile or embarrassing to those who claimed to speak for them. Through its shop organizations the Communist Party was in a position to exploit frictions and grievances which were bound to arise under circumstances in which it proved easy to identify the Socialist leadership with the policies resented by the workers. Some organizational effort to counter the Communist influence at the location where it was most effective—in the shops themselves—seemed thus required.

Attempts to extend the Party's influence in the plants were begun almost as soon as the Party itself had been re-established. Each Party district organization was requested to appoint "shop functionaries" (*Betriebsreferenten*) who had the task of spreading the Party viewpoint by means of education and propaganda. On one hand, they were expected to overcome the danger of "trade-union mentality";[23] on the other, they were to meet the Communists on their own ground and defeat them by use of their own means.[24] After three years of preparation by district and land organizations, the Party leadership felt ready to give the shop organizations official standing. The Organizational Statute was amended to provide for the establishment of an elaborate hierarchical structure of shop organizations, capped by an "inner executive committee." Linkage to the Party was to be assured

---

[22] The term "extraparliamentary methods" refers to political actions not connected with the electoral process, such as street demonstrations, strikes, and even use of violence.

[23] See *Redeanleitung*, "Die Verwaltung der Organisation" (SBZ, 1946), as to the tasks of the *Betriebsreferent*: "In agreement with the socialist Trade Unions and shop stewards, but beyond their scope of activity, he [the plant liaison officer] must render the power of the proletariat, concentrated in the plants, serviceable to our idea."

[24] In a statement by Otto Skritek (head of the Central Party Plant Liaison Office), the tasks of the Socialist plant organizations are described as organizing the opposition to the KP by careful preparation for the meeting, maintenance of order, presentation of a unified line in the discussion. (*SPOe-Betriebsvertrauensmann*, V [August, 1949], 219.)

by the provision that the chairman of this committee be approved by the Party Directorate.[25]

The Party's urgent need for effective plant organizations became clearly evident particularly on occasions such as the Communist call for a general strike in October, 1950. At that time Communists succeeded in mobilizing large numbers of workers for violent actions against the government and the Trade Union leadership. Yet the elaborate structure of Socialist shop organizations remained, by and large, on paper. The Party published centrally two papers for the use of Socialist plant organizations: the *Betriebs-Vertrauensmann* and *Welt der Arbeit*. In addition, it provided a number of evening courses and some week-long "plant agitation schools." [26] These efforts admittedly did not succeed in creating the closely knit Socialist cadres in the factories with which the Party hoped to balance the weight of the Communist cells.[27] By 1952 the central Party *Betriebsreferat* (Plant Liaison Office) had ceased to function and the publication of the *Welt der Arbeit* had been transferred to the Socialist fraction of the trade unions. The abandonment of the Party's efforts to build its own plant organizations as an assertion of the supremacy of the political over the trade union branch of the Movement was officially acknowledged by the repeal of the 1948 clause in the Organizational Statute providing for their establishment and the transfer of all their functions to the Socialist fraction of the trade unions.[28]

This step may be interpreted in part as aimed merely at rectifying an organizational muddle created by the simultaneous growth of Socialist plant organizations subject to Party leadership and Socialist trade union fractions under the authority of the Socialist functionaries of the Trade Union Federation, organizations whose boundaries were ill-defined and whose functions overlapped. Furthermore, the Party apparently is not sufficiently flexible to follow simultaneously two divergent organizational principles. The decision may also signify the tacit admission that the distinction between "socialist thought" and "trade union mentality" has ceased to be meaningful because of the profound changes of attitude within Party and trade unions alike. The stabilization of the Austrian economy in

---

[25] Paragraph 11 of the *Organizational Statute*, 1948; also SPOe-*Vertrauensmann*, III (December, 1948), 393–94.

[26] *Bericht der Parteivertretung an den Parteitag 1948* (hereafter referred to as *Report of PE*), PTP, 1948, p. 59.

[27] Statements by Otto Probst, *PTP*, 1950, p. 41, and *PTP*, 1951, p. 32.

[28] *Arbeiter Zeitung*, November 7, 1953, p. 2, and November 8, 1953, p. 4.

recent years, which has weakened the effectiveness of Communist agitation, has removed the strongest stimulus impelling the Party toward plant organizations. And the Party has been able to return to tasks in the realm of parliamentary politics, for which it obviously feels itself better equipped.

"Proletarian Core" and "Marginal Strata"

A Party of the Proletariat?

The Austrian Socialist Party, like all those political movements which link their fate to the rising power of the industrial proletariat, has been faced with the problem of whether to seek the support of groups and classes outside the working class; and if this question should be answered in the affirmative, what the relationship of these "marginal strata" to the proletarian "core" should be.[29]

Examination of the divisions within the Austrian Socialist Party does not lend support to the assumption, frequently voiced, that the issue is closely related to Left-Right divisions. Predominance of genuine working-class elements—as expressed in trade union influence on the political party—is widely believed to be the cause of reformist tendencies. Non-working-class members of socialist parties, frequently tagged "intellectuals" or "agitators," are widely assumed to lean to radical views. Within the ranks of labor, on the other hand, suspicion may be entertained toward "class alien elements" as likely opportunists or bourgeois sentimentalists who cannot be expected to share or represent the true, revolutionary interests of the working class.[30] Though the Socialist Party in Austria was "filled with the deepest suspicion of anyone coming from the ranks of nonmanual workers" [31] before World War I, its leadership even then was recruited to a considerable part from

---

[29] It is in terms of "core" and "marginal strata" (*Kern und Randschichten*) that the issue is discussed in the SPOe.

[30] See, e.g., the following criticism by an anonymously published Left-wing broadsheet (*Der Sozialist*, No. 10/11, November-December, 1949): "Socialism is not a matter of well-meaning people; not merely an 'ethical' demand which can be endorsed by all those who are of good will. . . . Those men from other classes who joined the workers could maintain themselves in the labor movement only if they subordinated themselves unconditionally to the interests of the workers. . . . In our Party at present a stratum exercises leadership which in part has already lost contact with the workers and in part has never possessed it."

[31] Schärf, *Der geistige Arbeiter in der Zweiten Republik*, p. 11.

these "marginal strata." Nor did ideological divisions among the leadership at any time follow class (or, for that matter, "racial") lines.[32] The present situation in which, once again, members of the middle class [33] are strongly represented in the Party leadership does not therefore differ markedly from the past. The cause for the process of *embourgeoisement* of the Party—subject of Left-wing criticism—must be sought elsewhere than in the class composition of its leaders.

The fact of middle-class leadership of working-class movements by itself has not determined their goals and methods. The Austrian Socialist Party, however, had to face rather early in its history the prospect that, while committed to the democratic road in the firm belief in the "inevitability of the proletarian triumph," the goal apparently was blocked by the Party's failure to achieve a decisive parliamentary majority solely with the support of the industrial working class.[34] Thus the Party was forced to cast the net more widely, to appeal to strata outside the ranks of industrial labor proper without giving up the claim of being a class party of the proletariat. On what terms could the Party become "national" without surrendering its role as the foremost defender of the interests of the urban working class? The call (contained in an *Arbeiter Zeitung* editorial published early in 1946), asking the Party to abandon its self-imposed confinement and to seek a broader base outside the working class,[35] represented less a radical break with past policy than a restatement of a demand which had been discussed with monotonous regularity and considerable thoroughness at the Party Conferences of the First Republic.[36]

---

[32] Victor Adler, Otto Bauer, Max Adler, Karl Renner—all of the middle class, three of them Jews—took up widely divergent ideological positions in the Social Democratic Party of the First Republic. The New Men of the Revolutionary Socialists came predominantly from the working class but co-operated closely in the R.S. with young middle-class Jews.

[33] The broad class categories are not a very helpful tool in classifying the Party's leadership. Many present leaders who, through their occupation and way of life, have become identified with the middle class (Schärf, Waldbrunner, formerly Renner) actually come from working-class homes.

[34] Of the approximately 40 per cent of the total vote that the Socialist Party has consistently polled since 1918, a considerable share has undoubtedly come from the "marginal strata." The vote for Chambers of Labor supports this view.

[35] W. H., "Heraus aus der Festung," *Arbeiter Zeitung*, April 21, 1946.

[36] Cf., e.g., the prolonged debate at the Party Conference of 1923 (in particular the speeches by Renner, Bauer, and Austerlitz). Since 1945 the question has nowhere been discussed with equal thoroughness.

Otto Bauer had engaged in some manipulation of traditional Marxist concepts in his attempt to reconcile the two conflicting imperatives—attainment of a parliamentary majority and preservation of the Party's identification with the proletariat. At one time Bauer redefined the concept of the working class to include small peasants, small businessmen and tradesmen, skilled craftsmen, and intellectuals—traditionally referred to as "petty bourgeoisie"—as comprising the "totality of those who live by the sale of their labor power." [37] On another occasion Bauer returned to a narrower definition of what constituted the "working class," but pleaded for the necessity of a political alliance between the proletariat and the "petty bourgeoisie" as the condition of the proletariat's achievement of a parliamentary majority:

Democracy permits the class struggle to be decided by the ballot, by the vote of the majority of the voters, the majority of the people. . . . Here we stand, proletariat and bourgeoisie, struggling for the majority. . . . They [the bourgeoisie] struggle for the middle strata who belong neither to the bourgeoisie nor the proletariat. . . . The task of Social Democracy becomes increasingly not only to unite the entire working class within itself but to attract the exploited strata of the petty bourgeoisie, the small peasantry and the intelligentsia, to gain for the working class the allies it needs to win a majority.[38]

Bauer's viewpoint was accepted by the Party in the First as well as in the Second Republic. To a party which considered winning a parliamentary majority as its overriding aim, the argument was irrefutable. But because it raised serious questions about the theoretical and practical link between the working class and socialism, it led to much discussion, soul-searching, and criticism concerning the effects of an alliance with nonproletarian strata. The conflict between practical necessity and the theoretical and practical dangers to the cause of socialism is clearly reflected in Bauer's apprehensive statement:

The attraction of petty bourgeois masses who are working, working hard, and greatly exploited, yet who are people of a position in life quite different from that of wage workers is not without danger. Can't it happen that the essence of our party, that which distinguishes it, that on which alone our historic mission is based, its character as a workers' party, may suffer? [39]

---

[37] *PTP*, 1923, p. 199.
[38] *PTP*, 1926, p. 259. The statement paraphrases the formulation contained in the Party Program adopted at Linz (*PTP*, 1926, pp. 172–73).
[39] *Ibid.*, p. 260.

Yet he believed that the danger he had indicated could be overcome by defining the historical task of the working class as gathering *under its leadership* ever wider strata of the population.[40] This meant to Bauer that the industrial proletariat would not only act as *primus inter pares* within the alliance but that where its interests proved incompatible with the interests of other strata, the Party would unequivocally decide in favor of the proletarian interest.[41]

The uneasy question which Bauer had asked in 1926 was being put again twenty years later when the discussion was revived:

Does this [the appeal to the people as a whole] mean betrayal of the interests of the workers? Is it a watering down? Do we cease to be class-conscious socialists? [42]

Yet the answer which the author gives to this rhetorical question indicates, by its implicit denial of the possibility of conflict between working class and the rest of the population, the change of attitude on the part of the leadership after 1945:

As long as we are conscious that the policy of which we are the carriers must represent the interests of the workers—of all the working people—we are on the right path.[43]

As the previous discussion has shown, this does not represent a fundamental change of attitude, for the principle of expanding the Party beyond its original "core" had been long accepted. Since 1945, however, the leadership has been intent on achieving this goal without attempting to square this policy with traditional socialist ideology and has put increased stress on the "national" rather than on the "working-class" character of the Movement. The elimination of *Arbeiter* from the name of the Party was an early indication of the change. The 1958 Program makes the transformation official. For it explicitly declares the SPOe to be "the party of all those who work for a living," whether they are dependent wage workers, salaried employees, intellectuals, members of the professions, and even independent producers in country and town—all those whose livelihood is not derived from exploitation through the power of capital.[44] And with this pronounce-

---

[40] *Ibid.*
[41] *Ibid.*, p. 261.
[42] Marianne Pollak, "Heraus aus der Festung," *Arbeiter Zeitung*, April 28, 1946.
[43] *Ibid.*
[44] The version of the 1958 Program here cited is that published in the *Arbeiter Zeitung* of May 15, 1958 (pp. 9–12).

ment the long-drawn ideological distinction between "core" and "marginal" strata has been consigned to oblivion.[45]

Ancillary Organizations

In order to attract members of "class alien" strata such as the peasantry and the professional and managerial middle class to the Party, organizations have been set up to serve as halfway houses for sympathizers willing to co-operate.[46] Because of the traditional identification of the Socialist Party with the cause of the urban working class the integration of these outsiders as full Party members was hardly feasible. On the other hand, the Party has been unwilling merely to appeal to these groups for voting support. It has been intent on tying them closer to the Party by "organizing" them. Its argument on the ideological level has pointed to the alleged "objective" identity of interests between the urban working class and the groups appealed to. The more effective incentive to membership in the ancillary organizations set up has, however, been the promise to further the members' interest through the Party's influence on legislation and administration.

At present such ancillary organizations exist for small peasants, artisans and small businessmen, and members of the professions and the intelligentsia. In the case of peasants, artisans, and small businessmen the Party's drive to organize them in loosely affiliated units has had very limited success. The *Arbeitsbauernbund* (Federation of Working Peasants) appears to have largely disintegrated. From a peak of 25,370 members in 1950 it has declined to a reported membership of 5,150 in 1956, and now lacks any organization in several of the agriculturally important *Länder*.[47] Membership in the *Freie Wirtschaftsverband* (Free Economic League), an organization intended to appeal to small independent businessmen—artisans and shopkeepers—has returned to a figure slightly above that of the year 1929.[48]

---

[45] Fritz Klenner, one of the members of the drafting committee, declares: "Our party is not merely the gathering point of all class-conscious workers, but has become the interest representative of the broad masses of the working population." "Das Programm der Vollendung," *Die Zukunft*, XIII (June, 1958), 145.
[46] Kra, "Die Partei, ihre Einrichtungen und Nebenorganisationen," *SPOe-Vertrauensmann*, II (May, 1947), 141–44. *Wirtschaftliche Zweckorganisationen* is the bureaucratic term by which they are officially designated in the SPOe.
[47] *Report of PE, PTP*, 1950, p. 137; and *PTP*, 1956, p. 204.
[48] In 1955 the FWV reported 24,738 members (*ibid.*, 1956, p. 196). This compares with 21,445 in 1929, as reported in the *Jahrbuch der österreichischen Arbeiterbewegung* (hereafter cited as *Jahrbuch*), SDAPDOe, Vienna, 1929.

In both cases the Party's failure to progress significantly stems from similar causes: organizational friction due to suspicion and lack of understanding of members and particularly functionaries of the regular Party organizations toward these "alien" groups;[49] the lack of appeal inherent in a program stressing rigid controls, attacks on excessive middle-men margins, and the protection of the consumer interest; and, finally, the inability of the Socialist Party to compete on equal terms with the People's Party (whose access to private and public economic power centers is far superior) in the attempt to dispense material favors to the economic groups in question.

The Socialist Party has been considerably more successful in attracting the support of professional men (*Akademiker*). Membership of the *Bund Sozialistischer Akademiker* (Federation of Socialist Professional Men, BSA)[50] rose from 2,340 in 1947 to 9,864 in December, 1955.[51] This growth is all the more remarkable because of the almost complete elimination of the Jewish element which, before 1934, had undoubtedly constituted a considerable part of the support the Party received in professional and intellectual circles. To a large extent this growth may be due to the greatly increased opportunities for careers in the public service which the Socialist Party has been able to offer to qualified members under the prevailing system of "Proporz"—the proportional distribution of public positions according to party strength. The BSA functions as the main funnel through which the SPOe fills many of these positions.

---

[49] For illustration, see the statement by Egon Bodinger (Secretary of the Federation) at the Party Conference of 1946, that "many times we have to overcome resistance in the Party itself. . . . We are underestimated. We find too little interest for our activities, from the Party Secretariat down to the local Party functionaries." (*PTP*, 1946, p. 79.) Similar complaints were voiced in 1947 (*PTP*, 1947, p. 111) and in 1950 (*PTP*, 1950, p. 95), when Bodinger criticized the official Party press for causing disgust among the peasantry and defended the latter group against the widespread charge that they "by comparison live much better than the working class." For statements in a similar vein referring to the Free Economic League, see *PTP*, 1946, p. 135; *PTP*, 1947, p. 144; and *PTP*, 1948, p. 28.

[50] Its name was subsequently changed to *Bund Sozialistischer Akademiker, Intellektueller und Künstler* (*Report of PE, PTP*, 1947, pp. 67–68).

[51] *Report of PE, PTP*, 1951, pp. 147–50; and *PTP*, 1956, p. 183. Membership of the Vienna branch of the BSA has generally made up 50 per cent of the total.

The Mass Party—Occupational Stratification

In view of the lack of success which has marked the "economic auxiliary organizations," it is not surprising that the occupational or "class" composition of the Party membership at large has not undergone any extensive changes either since the end of the war or as compared with the Party's social stratification in the First Republic. The almost total absence of relevant data makes comparison between the present and the pre-1934 situations hazardous. Only for Vienna do we possess figures which allow us to

TABLE 1

SOCIAL STRATIFICATION OF THE MEMBERSHIP OF THE SOCIALIST PARTY
ORGANIZATION, VIENNA, 1929 AND 1954

Occupation	Number of Members		Percentage of Total	
	1929	*1954*	*1929*	*1954*
Workers				
in private firms	197,156 ⎫	107,031	47.49 ⎫	36.87
in public firms	15,501 ⎭		3.73 ⎭	
Employees				
in private firms	49,170	33,608	11.84	11.52
in public firms	35,558	41,973	8.57	14.42
Free professions	7,319	5,886	1.52	2.02
Independent artisans and				
businessmen	17,875	8,524	4.31	2.92
Pensioners	9,272	30,218	2.23	10.36
Housewives	66,693	58,640	16.06	20.15
Various (domestics, etc.)	10,917	———	2.63	———
Unknown, or no occupation	6,709	5,068	1.62	1.74
TOTAL	416,170	290,948	100.00	100.00

SOURCES: *Jahrbuch*, 1930, p. 113; and *Report of PE, PTP*, 1955, p. 125.[52]

draw some conclusions (see above, Table 1). Although the two sets of figures are not strictly comparable, these changes are apparent: a considerable drop in the percentage of manual workers among Party members and a sizable increase in the percentage of salaried employees (*Angestellte*) in public enterprises, as well as a striking increase in the number of "pen-

---

[52] The occupational categories are not identical. Thus, an exact comparison is impossible. No similar set of occupational data exists for any of the provincial organizations prior to 1934.

sioners" whose share has quadrupled. As the "pensioners" are former manual workers or salaried employees, the rise in their numbers does not affect the "class" stratification of the Party, though it is an indication of the overaging noticeable among its members. The significant shift is thus the increase in the proportion of salaried employees as over wage earners, both comprised within the definition of the "proletariat." [53] The failure of the Party to attract new members among the small business class is apparent. The trends indicated by comparison of the Vienna figures emerge

TABLE 2

SOCIAL STRATIFICATION OF THE MEMBERSHIP OF THE SOCIALIST PARTY
ORGANIZATION FOR ALL OF AUSTRIA IN 1929, 1947, AND 1954

Occupation	Number of Members			Percentage of Total		
	1929	1947	1954	1929	1947	1954
Industrial workers						
in private firms	332,430 ⎱ 221,137		264,619	47.5 ⎱ 38.8		39.71
in public firms	27,110 ⎰			3.7 ⎰		
Agricultural workers	—	17,863	16,183	—	3.1	2.43
Employees						
in private firms	82,880	45,160	58,554	11.8	7.9	8.79
in public firms	59,000	67,977	90,289	8.6	11.9	13.55
Free professions	10,640	10,853	10,148	1.5	1.9	1.52
Independent artisans						
and businessmen	30,170	25,035	18,658	4.3	4.4	2.80
Peasants	—	13,366	6,669	—	2.5	1.00
Pensioners	15,610	42,395	76,236	2.2	7.4	11.44
Housewives	112,410	114,618	114,961	16.1	20.0	17.25
Various	18,410	—	—	2.6	—	—
Unknown (or no						
occupation)	11,340	12,364	10,056	1.6	2.1	1.51
TOTAL	700,000	570,768	666,373	100.0	100.0	100.0

SOURCES: Report of PE, PTP, 1952, p. 75;[54] ibid., 1955, p. 116.

[53] Though "white-collar" employees are also, according to Marxist class analysis, part of the proletariat, the distinction between them and manual workers is one of the most significant features of modern industrialized society. The impact which their increase has had on the SPOe obviously needs further study. Any offhand assertion linking this increase to the lessening of Party militancy as a causal factor would, however, be highly suspect.
[54] The extrapolation of the 1929 figures is based on an assumed total membership of 700,000. The actual membership in 1929 was 718,056.

even more clearly if the occupational breakdown for the entire Austrian organization is examined with reference to the years 1947 and 1954 (cf. Table 2, facing). To permit at least some rough comparison with the pre-1934 period, a breakdown for 1929 has been added based on an adjusted extrapolation of the Vienna figures for that year.

In the four-year span under examination, the percentage of manual workers in the Party remained unchanged, while that of salaried employees increased by 1.5 per cent. In a period in which the Party as a whole increased its membership by approximately 10 per cent, the number of salaried employees grew by almost 20 per cent and the number of "pensioners" by almost 50 per cent. On the other hand, the Party was strikingly unsuccessful in expanding—or even maintaining—its organizational position among the independent small businessmen and peasants. The failure of the Party to draw into its organizations groups outside its traditional recruiting ground is made evident by a glance at the vastly different rate of Party membership among different groups (cf. Table 3, below). If salaried white-

TABLE 3

PERCENTAGE OF SOCIALIST PARTY MEMBERS IN SOME
MAJOR OCCUPATIONAL GROUPS IN 1951 [55]

Occupation	*Total Number*	*Party Members*	*Percentage*
Employees in public enterprises	147,203	80,981	55
Industrial workers	1,192,229	241,717	20
Independent artisans, business- men, professional men	276,398	31,583	11
Employees in private enterprise	515,155	52,126	10
Agricultural workers	217,067	16,718	8
Peasants	311,526	7,875	2.5

collar employees are included in the definition of proletarian "core" stratum along with factory workers, then the Austrian Socialist Party has remained an overwhelmingly "proletarian" party. Though its greatest organizational success in recent years has been the enlistment of employees in public enterprises (most of which are administered by Socialist-dominated municipalities or the Ministry of Nationalized Industries), the numerical superior-

---

[55] The calculation is based on the occupational breakdown of the Austrian population presented in *Statistisches Handbuch für die Republik Oesterreich*, 1952, p. 18.

ity of the industrial working class is not yet challenged by this development. Once again we must conclude that in the search for the cause of the Party's *"embourgeoisement,"* the class composition of the Party's membership fails to supply us with an explanation.

Miscellaneous Organizational Changes

In the First Republic frequent reference was made by Austrian Socialists to the three equal organizational pillars of the Labor Movement—the Socialist Party, the Free (Socialist) Trade Unions, and the Socialist Consumer Co-operative Movement. In 1945, however, the official organizational link between Party on one hand and Trade Unions and the Co-operative Movement on the other was not re-established. Relation between Party and the Co-operative Movement is not based on any formal provisions. The Party Statute makes no reference to Co-operative delegates to the Party Conference nor has the Co-operative Movement been officially divided into fractions along political lines in the same manner as has the Trade Union Federation. Personnel-union in the form of simultaneous holding of important positions in the Party and the Co-operative organization provides, however, a close informal link.

One of the most significant differences between the present Party organization and that in the First Republic is the absence, since 1945, of the quasi-military Republican Defense Guard. The most obvious among the reasons for the failure to revive this organization was the presence of Allied occupation troops. This, as well as the apparently total absence of revolutionary fervor at the war's end, prevented the re-establishment of armed formations by any one of the parties and forestalled the competitive political armament race which was such a marked feature of the First Republic. In addition, the old Defense Guard had after 1934 become a Communist front organization and been discredited in Socialist—and even Revolutionary Socialist—eyes.[56]

The Socialist Youth Organization (Sozialistische Jugend; SJ)

Problems of Reorganization

Immediately after the war the establishment of nonparty "unity" organizations was widely accepted as the proper political response to the

---

[56] Buttinger, *In the Twilight of Socialism*, pp. 239–40.

downfall of the Nazi regime. The revived trade unions, the Co-operative Movement, and many smaller organizations (Nazi victims, tenants, etc.) embodied the principle of nonpartisanship. The attempt to set up a unified, nonparty youth organization was launched in 1945 under the sponsorship of Ernst Fischer, then Communist Minister of Education. The Socialist Party, however, decided to reject the claim to a monopoly position of the *Freie Oesterreichische Jugend* (FOeJ), apprehensive that it would develop into a Communist front organization.[57] It was still convinced that specific political education to counteract the antisocialist influence of school and state had to begin early.[58]

The widespread political apathy, particularly pronounced among the young, characteristic of the Austrian population since the end of World War II is frequently noted, particularly in the Socialist press. Many of the Socialist functionaries who themselves were products of a period of politically supercharged emotions, recalling their own enthusiastic activism, stand uncomprehending before the phenomenon of an apparently apolitical youth.[59] In part their complaints about "today's youth" are seemingly the result of their own tendency to view the past in roseate light and to transfer their own excitement to their entire generation. Yet it is a fact that in its attempt to attract new members the SJ has met with considerably less success than before 1934. In Vienna, formerly its strongest organizational center, membership is only about one-third of what it was in the twenties. In the rest of Austria the Vienna "malaise" is much less prevalent. Nevertheless, the SJ's total membership in 1953 was only 25,180, compared to 34,632 in 1923. The SJ has not shared in the gradual expansion of membership which the Party proper experienced in the postwar period. Rather the reverse is true: between 1947 and 1950 it lost 6,000 members, more than 20 per cent of its 1947 total.[60]

---

[57] Paul Blau, "SJ and FOeJ," *SPOe-Vertrauensmann*, II (December, 1947), 348.

[58] Peter Strasser, "Eine Lebensfrage der Partei," *ibid.*, II (April, 1947), 106.

[59] See, e.g., "Um unsere Jugend," *Arbeiter Zeitung*, October 2, 1945; Fritz Kurz, "Das Recht auf Faulheit," *Arbeiter Zeitung*, October 9, 1945.

[60] Membership in the Vienna organization in 1929 was 12,756 (*Report of PE, PTP*, 1929, p. 399); in 1946 only 4,050 (*Report of PE, PTP*, 1946, p. 47). Membership figures for the entire organization are taken from *Report of PE, PTP*, 1923, p. 86; *PTP*, 1947, p. 61; *PTP*, 1950, p. 118; and *PTP*, 1954, p. 111.

The Ambiguity of Function

The Socialist Youth organization has set itself a dual task: that of representing the interests of the young, particularly, though not explicitly, of the working class [61] and educating the young in cultural and political matters, particularly in the nature of "scientific socialism" and the Socialist Movement.[62] Because the SJ—unlike the Party at large—lacks an electoral function, the question of cadre versus mass organization is not decided by its basic function. It was up to the leadership to determine whether to make of the SJ a tightly knit community of dedicated activists or a movement bringing the largest possible number of young people into contact with socialist ideas. The traditional ethos of the Socialist Youth organization is a mixture of militant class-consciousness and romantic-puritan rejection— shared with all typical European youth movements—of the "unnatural foibles and hypocrisies" of urban civilized living (frequently identified as "bourgeois").[63] Because membership in organizations of this kind involves at least weekly meetings, hikes, etc., the merely passive membership characteristic of the mass party is ruled out. The requirement of regular, active participation prevents youth movements from becoming true voluntary mass organizations and inherently limits their appeal to an interested minority. Some functionaries would prefer to limit membership further by insistence on purism and vigorous ideological training. They see in the Socialist Youth the guardian of socialist principles and as its main task the

---

[61] The following breakdown of the occupational structure of the SJ (*Report to the SJ Conference*, 1952) shows clearly the predominantly "proletarian" nature of that organization:

Occupation	Percentage of Total Membership
Apprentices	23.2
Skilled workers	30.2
Unskilled workers	23.3
Agricultural workers	2.4
Employees	10.4
Unemployed	4.1
Pupils (*Schüler*)	5.1
Students (university)	1.3

[62] Paragraph 2, *Satzungen der SJOe* (mimeographed copy).
[63] See the discussion of this point by Strasser, "Grenzprobleme der SJ," *SJ-Funktionär*, No. 11/12 (1948), p. 195. Opposition to smoking, drinking, and social dancing is characteristic of this attitude and has given rise to frequent debate. (Cf. *ibid.*, p. 192, *Report* on debate over this issue at *Verbandstag*, 1948.)

training of an "avant-garde . . . which in the future shall take over functions in the Party and fill it with revolutionary spirit and *élan*." [64]

The "realists," who oppose them, view their organization primarily as an auxiliary to the Party, with the specialized function of "spreading socialism" among the young. They argue that without a "mass" base—which may have to be gained by concessions making membership "fun"—the youth movement would be too insignificant a body to count for anything either outside or inside the Party.[65] The efforts of the "purists" failed, above all, because their concept of a young revolutionary avant-garde was based on a fallacy: the number of youngsters willing to dedicate themselves to the socialist cause at the cost of effort and hardship turned out to be too small to form an effective cadre. The attempt to educate a sizable number in advanced socialist theory, to turn "emotional Socialists" into "fighters for socialism, well-trained Marxists," [66] had to be abandoned.[67] Though not all traces of the earlier "puritanism" have disappeared—smoking and drinking are still outlawed at SJ meetings [68]—it is by stressing the comradeship of group activities rather than the ideological content that the Socialist Youth organization has been able to attract and hold the mass of its members.

SJ and Party: Confrontation of Generations

The formal relation between Socialist Youth and the Party is determined by the Organizational Statute.[69] The SJ enjoys autonomy in formulating its bylaws, organizing its groups, and electing its executive committee (the *Verbandsvorstand*, VBVS). The organization has the right to send delegates to the annual Party Conference.[70] Membership in the SJ does not

[64] Franz Weclay in his contribution to the discussion "Kader oder Massenorganisation," *SJ-Funktionär*, No. 2/3 (1948), pp. 48–49.

[65] See the contribution of Lina Scholz to the above discussion, *ibid.*, No. 4 (1948), p. 83.

[66] Josef Hindels, "Schulungsarbeit bei der SJ," *SPOe-Vertrauensmann*, II (July, 1947), 214.

[67] The SJ-Academy, originally intended as an advanced course in socialist theory, had to be reduced to an introductory level and compressed into one semester. Even then it attracted only 14 regular participants in 1951–52. (*Report of the SJ Executive to the SJ Conference*, 1952—my own notes; statement of Erich Pogats in interview.)

[68] *SJ-Funktionär*, No. 11/12 (1948), p. 192; *Report on SJ Conference*.

[69] *Organizational Statute of the SPOe*, 1945, par. 11.

[70] *Ibid.*, par. 22, clause 6.

carry with it membership in the SPOe, nor are Party members under the age of 21 required to join the Socialist Youth.[71]

Relations between Socialist Youth and the Party have been marked by coolness and occasional hostility.[72] The fierce antitraditionalism of the youth organization which finds expression in a considerably more radical ideology as well as a certain contempt for the routinized party activities of the "oldsters" have done little to endear SJ functionaries to the large body of Party Vertrauensmänner and leaders. Each side tends to view the other with patronizing eyes, and to give it gratuitous and not always tactful advice.[73] In a period in which the Party's leadership has followed a policy of moderation, the efforts of SJ functionaries to act as a "ginger group," as the center of a real Left faction in the Party,[74] have put additional strain on the relationship between the two organizations. The apparent susceptibility of the SJ's left wing to Communist infiltration [75] has given the Party Directorate the opportunity to subject its members to loyalty investigations [76] and thereby to keep the youth organization generally on the defensive. However, more recent efforts to improve relations apparently seem to have succeeded in eliminating some of the mutual misunderstandings.[77] The

---

[71] A suggestion that membership in the SJ should be made compulsory for Party members under twenty-one was rejected by Strasser. (PTP, 1945, p. 55.)

[72] Confirmation of this general impression is found in the statement by Strasser that the "climate had been bad . . . that it was necessary to educate the party. . . ." (SJ Conference 1952; my own notes.)

[73] See, e.g., the sharp criticism of the SJ by Marianne Pollak ("Ist unsere Jugend demokratisch?" Arbeiter Zeitung, September 21, 1946) for its lack of discipline embarrassing to the Party. The existence of this mutual criticism is also noted by Czernetz, in "Jugend und Partei," SPOe-Vertrauensmann, II (January, 1947), 8–10. That this is merely the revival of a situation existing also in the First Republic is indicated by Anton Tesarek, "25 Jahre Rote Falken," Die Zukunft, V (June, 1950), 156–58.

[74] Koppe, SJ-Funktionär, No. 4 (1948), pp. 82–83.

[75] One such instance was reported to me by the secretary of one of the Party's district organizations. Others are reported by Der Neue Vorwärts, October 7, 1951.

[76] See Trotzdem, III/22, 1950; also Der Neue Vorwärts, November 11, 1951.

[77] Statement by Erich Pogats in interview. In 1951 a prominent place was given to the problems of youth at the Party Conference and 1952 was officially proclaimed "the year of youth," during which Party lecturers throughout the country were required to feature this angle. (Cf. PTP, 1951; also Redeanleitung, "Die Jugend bringt die Entscheidung," SBZ, 1952.)

greater readiness shown by Party functionaries to understand the young and not to dismiss them offhand as "wise guys" or "radicals" may, however, be primarily due to the departure of some of the leading Leftists [78] from the SJ and the subsequent consolidation of the hold exercised by the moderate wing over the organization.

The value of the SJ in the eyes of the Party functionaries is lowered by the failure of many members of the youth organization to become permanently attached to the Party. Even if the transition from Socialist Youth to Socialist Party were smooth and automatic, the SJ would not be large enough to serve as the main pool on which the Party could draw for the replenishment of its membership.[79] In fact, however, the transition from the SJ to the regular Party organization is by no means smooth or automatic. As a member of the SJ, the youngster—whether attracted primarily by the radical ideology or the romantic atmosphere of comradeship—is an active participant surrounded by members of his own age who speak his own language. Upon joining a regular Party section he finds, however, that the active functions are exercised by old or middle-aged Party workers who have a tendency to stick to their honorific positions and who expect the youngsters to start at the bottom of the Party ladder. The result is that in thousands of cases the new member, fresh from the SJ, initially eager to participate actively in the work of his Party section, becomes discouraged and apathetic and remains, at best, a dues-paying member.[80] But even if he is permitted to fill some local Party function, the routine activity which the Party functionaries have become increasingly burdened with (or addicted to) contrasts sharply with the exciting life he led in the SJ. Only where a number of SJ members simultaneously have moved into a Party section and thereby succeeded in overcoming the feeling of strangeness and isolation has this transition been a smooth process.[81] In 1948 the leadership of the SJ attempted to find an organizational remedy for this situation by planning the establishment of "transitional groups" (*Übergangsgruppen*

---

[78] E.g., Hindels, Blau. In 1950 Karl Waldbrunner, then Central Secretary of the SPOe, had already praised the increasingly responsible attitude of the SJ leaders. (*PTP*, 1950, p. 174.)

[79] Every year an estimated 15 per cent of the total membership—approximately 3,500—leave the SJ because they reach the age limit. In 1951, for example, the SPOe lost 7,629 members through death. (*PTP*, 1951, p. 10.)

[80] Strasser, "Ueberalterung der Partei?" *Die Zukunft*, III (May, 1948), 137 ff.

[81] Lina Scholz, in interview.

nach oben) within the Youth Movement. There those too old for membership in the regular SJ groups—twenty-one is the age ceiling for members
except in the case of top functionaries—were expected to remain politically
active in an appropriate atmosphere.[82] But because no clear notion existed
as to the nature of this political activity, apart from the perennial insistence
on "intensive schooling in socialist theory," this attempt to save from their
organizational limbo those too old for SJ teen-age romanticism and too
young for local Party routine proved unsuccessful.[83]

The Revival of Trade Union Organization

The Establishment of a Nonparty Trade Union Federation

Before 1934 the Austrian Trade Union Movement was divided, both
politically and organizationally. By far the largest organization was the
group known as the "Free Trade Unions," which were affiliated to the
Social Democratic Party. In 1931, 78.6 per cent of all organized workers
belonged to one of the Free Trade Unions. The remainder was split up
among Christian (14.6 per cent) and "German Nationalist" (6.8 per cent)
unions.[84] About two-thirds of all those listed as employed or looking for
employment (excepting the field of agriculture) were organized in one or
another of these unions,[85] which enjoyed considerable autonomy. Though
a supreme administrative body existed—until 1928 the *Gewerkschaftskom-
mission*, afterwards the Executive of the newly formed Federation of Free
Trade Unions—and, after the 1928 reorganization even achieved a limited

---

[82] Cf. Strasser, "Grenzprobleme der SJ," II, *SJ-Funktionär*, No. 11/12 (1948),
p. 194.

[83] According to a statement by Erich Pogats (in interview), a few such groups
were set up in an attempt to implement the 1948 decision but soon withered
away because of indifference. No new groups were organized to succeed them and
none exist today.

[84] *Wirtschaftstatistisches Jahrbuch*, 1931/1932, VIII, 164. The distribution
varied somewhat during the preceding decade. In 1921 it was 89.9 per cent, 6.5
per cent, and 3.6 per cent, respectively; in 1928, 83.5 per cent, 10.9 per cent, and
5.6 per cent, respectively. The decline in the strength of the Free Trade Union
was accompanied by a decrease in the over-all membership of organized workers
from 1,198,677 in 1921 to 917,502 in 1928 and to 740,752 in 1931.

[85] *Ibid.*, p. 141. In 1930, 816,702 workers were listed as members of trade unions
(p. 164); the number of employed and employables is given as 1,220,153.

degree of independent authority,[86] the organization was characterized by decentralization and competition among a multitude of unions.

Politically the Free Trade Unions were considered the "extended arm" of the Social Democratic Party or, in the words of Victor Adler, "the Siamese twin" of the Party with which it was united. The co-operation was so close that it was difficult to distinguish between policies of the Party and those of the Free Trade Unions,[87] except occasionally when specific divergencies arose.

After the interlude of almost a dozen years during which at first the *Einheitsgewerkschaft* (Unity Union) of the Dollfuss regime and subsequently the German Labor Front replaced the trade unions of the First Republic as the official organizations of Austrian labor, the men who revived the Movement in 1945 used the break in continuity to shape an organization which went as far as possible toward realization of the long-cherished aim of centralization along industrial lines. Even more far-reaching, however, was the decision to establish a unified Federation of Austrian Trade Unions (*Oesterreichischer Gewerkschaftsbund, OeGB*), which was expressly divorced from affiliation with any one of the political parties and aimed at inclusion of all workers who could be persuaded to become members.

The decision to establish a unified, nonparty Trade Union Federation was a reflection of the specific conditions and atmosphere prevailing in 1945. It was taken first by some leading members of the old Free (Socialist) Unions and then—when presented with a blueprint—accepted by the spokesmen for the Christian and Communist Trade Unionists.[88]

Unification appeared to provide each of the three groups with some potential advantages. The Communist and Christian groups, in the past far weaker than the organizations affiliated with the Socialist Party, could hope to gain effectiveness and means of spreading their influence by attaching

---

[86] The trade union authorities in the *Länder* were subordinated to it; affiliated unions had to contribute according to their membership. (*Ibid.*, pp. 285–86.) Karl Renner is reported as having referred to it as a mere "statistical central commission" (Johann Böhm, *Tätigkeitsbericht 1945–1947 und Stenographisches Protokoll des 1. Kongresses des OeGB*, p. I/231; hereafter cited as *OeGB, 1st Congress, Protocol*).

[87] Charles Gulick, *Austria from Habsburg to Hitler*, p. 257.

[88] The post-1945 period is marked by the (temporary) disappearance of the "German Nationalist" trade unions and the emergence of a sizable Communist fraction.

themselves to a large organization; the Christian unionists had always on principle favored a nonpolitical movement [89] and were ready to welcome the opportunity to "neutralize" the new organization and thus deprive the Socialist Party of its powerful executive organ in the industrial sphere. On the face of it, the Socialists had least to gain politically from such a change —and, indeed, there was some opposition to it within Socialist ranks. But the hope for domination of an organization greatly increased in size and power apparently outweighed the disadvantages which unification obviously would bring to the Party in its political struggles.[90]

Organizational Structure of the Trade Union Federation

In contrast to that in effect before 1934, the new structure was unified, centralized, and, by and large, divided along industrial group lines, thus realizing the aim embodied in resolution after resolution passed by trade union congresses in the twenties.[91] Sixteen separate unions were organized to form the Federation.[92] Their delegates to the Federal Congress elect a Presidium (consisting of a president, two vice-presidents, and a general secretary) which, together with 35 representatives of the individual unions —selected by them according to their respective bylaws—forms the Federal Executive (*Bundesvorstand*). In each of the *Länder* a subordinate Executive is elected by the *Land*'s trade union organizations, and a *Land* Secretary is appointed and held responsible by the Federation.[93]

The centralization of the Federation rests, in part, on the power of the Executive to appoint these secretaries who are pledged to see that the Executive's orders are promptly carried out on the lower level. Even more effective, however, is the financial arrangement by which membership dues are collected and divided. For at present all the dues collected are turned

---

[89] Gulick, *op. cit.*, p. 269.

[90] As previously pointed out, the negotiations leading to trade union unification predated party negotiations and were carried on exclusively by trade unionists. In the absence of liaison or consultation—impossible because of the preceding period of repression and the chaotic conditions prevailing—party leaders were actually faced with a *fait accompli*.

[91] Cf. Gulick, *op. cit.*, chap. 11, particularly the section entitled "Industrial Unions," pp. 272 ff.

[92] The 1893 Resolution had called for division into 17 separate unions, but Böhm explained that 16 were now found to be sufficient. (*OeGB, 1st Congress, Protocol*, p. I/227.)

[93] Klenner, *Die österreichischen Gewerkschaften—Vergangenheit und Gegenwartsprobleme*, II, p. 1620.

over to the Federation which returns 15 per cent of the total to the individual unions for their own purposes. It is thus the Executive which disposes of the bulk of the Federation's wealth and without whose assurance of support no individual union can undertake any step involving larger expenditures.[94] Since one of the main objectives of this central administration of funds is the equalization of the individual union's strength, particularly where a union's capacity to support a possible drawn-out strike is concerned, the central leadership obviously wields great influence even over the day-to-day activities and tactics of the unions. Strikes carried on without the Federal Executive's approval and support hardly ever achieve success.[95]

Membership in the unions is voluntary. In spite of occasional rumblings in the trade union press,[96] no determined drive to establish closed or union shops in Austria has been undertaken or is likely to be undertaken. The union shop is at present outlawed by the so-called "Anti-Terror" law of 1930,[97] and the Christian fraction within the Federation opposes any lifting of this legal ban.

For two years after its organization in 1945, the membership of the Federation climbed rapidly and reached a level where roughly two-thirds of all employed persons were included on its rolls. While this ratio has not changed since 1947, the distribution of organized members within the branches of the economy has altered somewhat. Most significantly, the share of the total trade union membership constituted by the Union of Agricultural and Forest Workers increased between 1947 and 1951 from 3.5 to 5.2 per cent. During the same period the number of workers employed in agriculture dropped by approximately 16 per cent. In other words, the percentage of organized workers (relative to total labor force) in the nonagrarian sector of the economy dropped from 74 to 70 per cent, while in the agrarian sector it rose from 16 to 31 per cent.[98] The degree of organization also differs, of course, considerably among the various trades, rang-

---

[94] The considerable resentment by lower-echelon trade union officials at this centralization has been exploited by Communist propaganda. (See, e.g., *OeGB, 1st Congress, Protocol,* pp. IV/255–56.)

[95] See Dr. Suse Kroll, "Streikstatistik 1951," *Gewerkschaftliche Nachrichten,* VII (February, 1952), 11–15; *Tätigkeitsbericht des OeGB,* 1958, p.I/19.

[96] See, e.g., Karl Franta, "Geschlossene Betriebe," *Gewerkschaftliche Rundschau,* VII (September, 1952), 2–4; also Klenner, *op. cit.,* p. 1704.

[97] Gulick, *op. cit.,* pp. 888 ff.

[98] *Jahrbuch der Arbeiterkammer Wien,* 1948, p. 366; *ibid.,* 1951, p. 412. For an over-all picture of membership changes in the *Länder,* see *Tätigkeitsbericht des OeGB,* 1958, pp. I/111 ff.

ing from 82 per cent in the metal and mining industry to 48 per cent in the hotel and restaurant trade.[99]

The Trade Union Federation and the Socialist Party

The establishment of the nonparty Trade Union Federation introduced an element of ambiguity into the relationship between it and the political parties, particularly the SPOe. For it was neither expected nor intended that trade union activities should be limited to "pure trade union matters," i.e., the struggle for higher wages, shorter hours, and welfare benefits— themselves, of course, highly "political" questions in postwar Austria. On the contrary, the trade union leadership saw its role more than ever as political, one which would include participation in the shaping of major economic policies. As these policies were, or soon became, the source of important differences between the political parties, the fiction of a Trade Union Federation occupying a position of neutrality toward the parties could not be long maintained.[100]

In 1945, the personnel organization of the Federation was the subject of prolonged interparty discussions before the right "proportion" satisfactory to the three partners could be arrived at. While the Communist claim for equality with the Socialists was not accepted, the result of the arrangement, made without accurate knowledge of the support which each Party commanded among the Federation's members, tended to favor the weaker partners. The usual arrangement was that the presidency of each union went to a member of the SPOe and a vice-presidency each to a Communist (until 1950) and a Catholic trade unionist. Similarly, the executive bodies of each union were composed according to *Proporz* on the basis of agreements reached.[101] From the very beginning the Trade Union Federation

---

[99] Exact figures on all trades are not available as the statistical data are not in all cases broken down along the same classificatory lines as those on trade-union organization. Nor have I been able to obtain comparable figures for the years after 1951.

[100] Spokesmen for the unions have distinguished carefully between "nonparty" and "nonpolitical." In a country where party influence is so pervasive the distinction is spurious.

[101] As an example of how the *Proporz* gave advantages to the smaller fractions in the absence of elections we might cite the composition of the Vienna Chamber of Labor. On the basis of three-party agreement, it was, until 1949, composed of 74 Socialists, 40 Communists, and 30 representatives of the People's Party. In its Executive there were 7 Socialists, 4 Communists, and 2 members of the OeVP. (Schärf, *Zwischen Demokratie und Volksdemokratie*, p. 96.)

was not so much a nonparty as a triparty organization. The fact that the presidents of all 16 trade union organizations are Socialists indicates that a close tie in terms of personnel has existed all along between Party and Federation. Moreover, some of the top Trade Unionists have held simultaneously leading positions in the SPOe or the Socialist parliamentary fraction. A certain number of seats on the Party Directorate are tacitly reserved for trade union representatives.[102] Furthermore, the top positions in all functional departments of the Federation are occupied by SPOe members. The extensive network of publications and the large educational organization are headed and largely staffed by Socialists.[103] But the official myth of nonpartisanship prevents them from using the trade union machinery which they command unequivocally for the benefit of their party.[104]

The Socialist Fraction

The formation of well-organized, properly directed Socialist fractions was begun rather slowly and met with little success for a considerable time. The establishment of a Socialist fraction within the Federal Executive [105] was followed by a double approach: the grouping together of the Socialist functionaries within each trade union, a measure which made liaison with Party organizations based on neighborhood units difficult; [106] and the establishment—at first through some *Land* organizations and subsequently on the federal level—of *Betriebsreferate* within the SPOe, which had the task of supervising and directing the Socialist Party members in each plant in their districts.[107] Neither of these attempts made much progress for several years, a fact which is attested by the recurrent expressions of de-

---

[102] At present, 8 out of 50 members of the Directorate are prominent trade union leaders. The Socialist fraction of the Trade Union Federation has the right to send 50 delegates to the annual Party Conference. This, of course, does not give the trade union wing the degree of domination which the British unions enjoy by means of the bloc vote.

[103] The official in charge of the courses for work councilors stated in an interview that "95 per cent of our teachers are comrades."

[104] Protests by the non-Socialist minority fractions against "partisan abuse" are, of course, frequent.

[105] This top-level fractionalization took place within a few weeks after the establishment of the Federation. (*Ibid.*, p. 94.)

[106] Bruno Pittermann, "Gedanken zum Gewerkschaftskongress," *Die Zukunft*, III (May, 1948), 135–37.

[107] For more detailed discussion of the institution of *Betriebsreferate*, see above, pp. 41–43.

termination to begin in earnest organizational work in the plants.[108] In 1952 the Party and the leadership of the OeGB's Socialist fraction concluded an agreement to turn the entire political activity over to the unions and to liquidate the institution of *Betriebsreferate*.[109] Until 1952 fractions in the plants consisted almost exclusively of the Work Councilors elected on the Socialist list and Party functionaries, while the mass of rank-and-file Party members working in the same plant neither knew each other nor were effectively exposed to Party influence.[110] Under the new arrangement a tighter organization of all Party members at their place of work is attempted. Special membership cards are issued and a small amount is collected as dues in order to establish contact between functionaries and members.[111]

Even the best-organized Socialist fractions will, however, be unable to fulfill for the Party the role which Socialist trade unions could assume openly. The financial resources of the Federation cannot be used to support the Party. While the fractional work which benefits the Party is frequently covered by general union funds, this cannot make up for the loss of direct trade union contributions to the Party's treasury.[112] Though, as previously noted, the personnnel in charge of the unions' educational activities is composed almost exclusively of Socialists, the demands of "unity" prevent the use of these activities for clearly Socialist Party purposes.

Party–Trade Union Alignment

The trade union press must veil its efforts to take sides too obviously in the political struggles of the day. It generally formulates its arguments

---

[108] See, e.g., Pittermann in May, 1948 ("Gedanken zum Gewerkschaftskongress," *loc. cit.*) and Karl Maisel in January, 1951 (*Der sozialistische Gewerkschafter*, I, p. 1).

[109] See above, p. 42.

[110] Ratzinger, "Sozialistische Fraktionsarbeit," *Der sozialistische Gewerkschafter*, II (March, 1952), 9–10. The author gives as an example a plant in which 1,731 workers out of a total work force of 3,434 were members of the SPOe and the Socialist list received 86 per cent of the vote in work council elections. Yet only 258 workers read Socialist Party newspapers, and the sale of the Socialist plant publication, *Welt der Arbeit*, was limited to a few copies.

[111] Fritz Konir, "Sozialistische Gewerkschaftsarbeit in Oesterreich," *Arbeit und Freiheit* (January, 1953), pp. 9–12.

[112] The difference in financial strength is very great indeed. In 1951 the OeGB's revenue amounted to 173 million Austrian schillings, while that of the Socialist Party was roughly 5.5 million. (*PTP*, 1951, p. 34.)

along lines which are largely identical with those propounded by the SPOe and furthers the Party's case propagandistically short of outright endorsement. Yet while much space is devoted to sociopolitical questions such as the need for planning, full employment, codetermination—all simultaneously expounded by official Socialist propaganda—only infrequently do articles in the trade union publications concern themselves with Socialism in its theoretical or historical aspects.[113]

The official nonparty character of the Federation has most seriously inhibited formation of a common front on purely political issues.[114] In the case of such issues as that of state support for Catholic schools, the return of property to Prince Starhemberg, or the rights and wrongs of February, 1934, the Federation either remains mute or adopts a neutral tone.[115] But on questions of an economic or politico-economic nature alignment between Federation and Socialist Party has been near perfect.[116] That the agreement of the Catholic fraction to objectives clearly opposed by the leadership of the People's Party could be obtained may be explained by these reasons: Catholic trade unionists, in contrast to the Party leadership, may themselves have been in sympathy with these objectives [117] and welcomed the strengthening of their own position within the OeVP brought about by the Federation's support. In cases where they were opposed to the goals endorsed, they may have felt that avoidance of conflict was preferable to outright struggle, particularly as the Federation's pronouncements were not backed by concrete action or plans of action.

---

[113] For examples of avowedly socialist articles, see Dr. Ernst Meyer, "Was ist Dialektik?" (OeGB *Bildungsfunktionär*, No. 38, March-April, 1953) or Julius Deutsch, "Victor Adler" (*ibid.*, No. 34, March-April, 1952).

[114] Admittedly, the border line between "purely political" and other issues is hard to draw, particularly in the economic realm. But issues such as the ones discussed below fall clearly into the political, not the economic realm.

[115] In memory of the events of February, 1934, *Solidarität* as a rule merely publishes a picture giving expression to the sorrow felt for all the victims of these events.

[116] According to unofficial statements made to me, differences did arise on certain specific issues. Thus, for example, the Socialist Party desired to end consumer rationing—widely unpopular—while the Trade Union Federation favored its retention for the period of scarcity (source: Fritz Klenner).

[117] The *Oesterreichische Arbeiter-und Angestelltenbund* (OeAAB) is the smallest and least influential of the three *Bünde* which comprise the People's Party's organization and is by no means always in agreement with its leadership, composed of agrarian and business representatives.

Indeed, it seems that the almost automatic alignment between the Socialist Party and the Trade Union Federation has done little to further the achievement of those goals to which the People's Party's leadership was determinedly opposed.[118] As Pittermann predicted,[119] the People's Party's majority in parliament and its power positions in the economy allowed it to dismiss the Federation's general policy pronouncements. In the absence of determination on the part of the union leadership to resort to "extra-parliamentary measures" as a means of supporting their demands, the Trade Union Federation appeared as little more than an appendix or megaphone of the SPOe. Agreement between Federation and Party—or at least absence of outright opposition by the Federation—is undoubtedly a prerequisite for any political action by the Party. But it would be erroneous to create an impression of two sharply differentiated bodies proceeding on parallel roads.[120] As pointed out previously, by means of "interlocking leadership" a partial merger of union and party organizations at the top level exists. Socialist trade unionists do not react any more uniformly on political questions than do representatives of other groups within the Party. Their ranks, too, contain advocates of a "hard" line, radicals as well as moderates.[121]

In post-1945 Austria the Trade Union Movement, closely linked to a party which has had a major share in the making of political decisions, has approached the economic sphere not as a pressure group attempting to extract maximum benefits for its members, but as a participant in the shaping of its decisions. The unions have continued to protect the material interests of wage workers and salaried employees, but they have done so with a novel concern for the welfare of groups not included within their organizations and for the economic situation as a whole. They largely have

---

[118] See, e.g., Johann Böhm's complaint ("Gewerkschaftsbund und Wahlen," *Arbeiter Zeitung*, September 27, 1949) that some of the most important points of the OeGB's 1945 program had not been accepted.

[119] "Einheitliche Gewerkschaftsarbeit," *Die Zukunft*, I (June, 1946), 15–16.

[120] Hindels, a trade union employee since his departure from the SJ, assured me that Socialist Trade Unionists thought primarily as Socialists. I have also been informed that votes in the SPOe Executive, on which the trade unions are represented, never divide along Party versus trade union lines.

[121] Franz Olah, recently elected head of the OeGB, and Friedrich Hillegeist, president of the Union of Employees in Private Industry, are advocates of a "hard" line. They, as well as Karl Maisel, Karl Mantler, and Anton Proksch, were leading functionaries of the R.S. and underground trade union movement.

accepted the maxim that only by an increase in the cake of national wealth could significantly larger slices be obtained for their members.[122]

The consequences of this position for all aspects of the traditional trade union policy have been far-reaching. In the wage sector struggles for higher wages have been frowned on. The wage-price level was to be frozen even if this allowed some producers to pay lower wages than they could afford to pay without having to raise prices.[123] This has involved *de facto* elimination of open industrial struggles by the unions for their objectives. Their place has been taken by negotiations at the top of the hierarchy. Results are presented as accomplished facts mysteriously arrived at, which the members are then persuaded to accept. While some union leaders dislike the apathy and resentment which such procedure creates among the rank and file and desire a return to the more exciting days of the past,[124] others—and they predominate at the top level of the Federation—consider the change in function irreversible and the hope for return to the "irresponsible" methods of the past vain. They see the wage area as part of the total economic system and consider it absurd to advocate planning in general while insisting on complete freedom of wage formation. Furthermore, by admission of its own leaders, the increased size of the organization imposes greater caution; the more imposing the structure, the greater the need to avoid risks to its existence.[125] In this new framework traditional trade union slogans have been emptied of meaning and trade union work has entered a new

---

[122] E.g., Hillegeist, "Der Einfluss der Gewerkschaft auf die Wirtschaft," *Arbeit und Wirtschaft*, II (April, 1949), 3–5. The statement is all the more remarkable because Hillegeist is considered a leader of the "radical" trade union wing within the SPOe.

[123] Mantler publicly opposed the wage-price agreements because they made the "marginal" producers, least capable of paying increased wages, the touchstone of wage-price relations. ("Zur künftigen Lohnpolitik," *Arbeit und Wirtschaft*, II [July, 1949], 1–3.) Mantler's argument was contradicted by Klenner on behalf of the official trade union leadership. ("Zum Problem der gelenkten Lohnpolitik," *ibid.*, III [August, 1949], 2–4.)

[124] Mantler, *loc. cit.*

[125] Klenner, *loc. cit.* A similar thought was expressed by Johann Böhm: "The danger is that today the OeGB is so strong that it could successfully push through demands which might go so far that they would threaten our entire economy." (*OeGB, 1st Congress, Protocol,* p. IV/223.) Paradoxically, increase in size, by diminishing the spirit of daring, has created no corresponding increase in the organization's strength. Its self-confessed unwillingness to take large risks cannot but weaken the Federation's position in negotiations.

phase. If involvement on the part of the members is an inevitable consequence of such a change in function, the leaders are willing to accept this
as a price which has to be paid for the trade unions' new role.[126]

Labor Peace

One of the results of the attitude of "reasonableness" and "responsibility" on the part of the dominant group within the Trade Union Federation
is the prevalence of labor peace in the postwar period.[127] The reluctance
of Socialist union functionaries to use the strike weapon has been increased
by the Communist agitation *for* its use. It has been the policy of the Communist fraction to exploit food shortages, inflation, and the unpopularity
of the wage-price agreements to foster protest strikes.[128] Even Left-wing
Socialists who, in principle, continue to adhere to the use of strikes as a
means of achieving material results favorable to the working class and of
increasing its fighting spirit and class consciousness, have been forced by
this Communist policy to shift their position. For they have had to face the
complex task of instructing workers about the subtle differences between
truly "progressive" extraparliamentary actions and those which serve "antiprogressive" purposes.[129]

The Communist Challenge

This change from militancy to conciliation—apparently accepted by the
majority of Socialist trade union officials—has provided the Communist

---

[126] Klenner, in interview.

[127] *Tätigkeitsbericht des OeGB*, 1958, I/19. For figures up to 1951, see the statement by Anton Proksch at the 2d Congress of the OeGB (*Protocol*, p. 40), and
Dr. Kroll, "Streikstatistik 1951" (*ibid.*). The number of workers undertaking
strike action (on the basis of these sources) in the years 1948–1958 was as follows:

1948	–	5,120	1953	–	12,695
1949	–	25,000	1954	–	21,140
1950	–	20,000	1955	–	26,011
1951	–	31,555	1956	–	43,249
1952	–	31,942	1957	–	19,555
		1958	–	28,745	

[128] See *Arbeiter Zeitung* for April 25, 1947; May 6, 1947; July 13, 1947; and OS,
"Nach dem 15. September," *SPOe-Vertrauensmann*, III (October, 1948), 321.
Klenner, *Putschversuch oder nicht?* (Pressereferat des Oesterreichischen Gewerkschaftsbundes, n.d.) gives a Socialist account of the Communist-led general
strike movement of October, 1950.

[129] Hindels, "Die Waffe des Streiks," *Trotzdem*, II (December, 1949).

Party with ample opportunity for agitation and has rendered its attacks much more dangerous than the Party's numbers alone would have indicated. In periods of acute discontent caused by food shortages, rising prices, and ostentatious luxury spending on the part of a few, the Communists were eager to fill the gap left by union functionaries turned apologists for the existing system.[130] They had only to retain the traditional arguments, using concepts and slogans familiar and dear to the workers from past struggles. Aware of the potential attractiveness of its position to disgruntled rank-and-file members, the Communist fraction has made itself the advocate of "trade union democracy," claiming to represent the true interests of the workers against the organizational bureaucracy.[131] It objects to bargaining behind closed doors, favoring discussion in open work council meetings, asks for plebiscites on important issues,[132] attacks the measures aiming at central control by the Federation Executive over the lower-echelon officials, and speaks up for freedom of opinion which allegedly has been suppressed by the Socialist-controlled Executive. The main weapon of the Socialist leadership against Communist attempts to organize strikes and disturbances has been the expulsion of Communist union functionaries from their positions and unions for violation of orders in defiance of union discipline. Thus, when in the wake of the Communist coup in Czechoslovakia the Communist fraction began to organize "action committees" on the Czech model, the Executive prohibited their establishment and expelled offending functionaries.[133] And the Communist general strike movement of October, 1950, was the occasion for their almost complete elimina-

---

[130] The following incident, told to me by one of the participants, illustrates the "governmental" attitude that trade union leaders have assumed: The headmaster of a *Gymnasium* (high school)—an active member of the BSA and the SPOe—approached the leaders of his trade union with demands on behalf of teachers who desired an increase of their "nonvalorized" salaries. The union functionary at once launched into a lengthy explanation of the reasons why the teachers' demands were unreasonable and impossible of fulfillment. Thereupon the teachers' representative angrily exclaimed: "It is your duty to fight for our interests. Leave to the Finance Minister the job of denying our request!"

[131] At the First Congress of the OeGB a Communist speaker exclaimed: "Their voice [of the union leaders] is not the voice of the working masses. Their voice is in this instance only the voice of the trade union functionaries and Party functionaries." (*Protocol*, p. IV/147.)

[132] *Ibid.*, pp. IV/69–70.

[133] Kunst, *ibid.*, p. IV/64; Böhm, *ibid.*, pp. IV/262–63.

tion from the Praesidia and Secretariats of the individual unions as well as the Federation.[134]

Work Council Elections

In spite of the fact that locally elected work councilors have frequently created difficulties for Socialist trade union leaders by advocating policies divergent from those officially adopted,[135] the Socialist leadership has considered it imperative to "politicize" work council elections, while both the Communist and Christian fractions consistently have favored "unity" or "name" elections. As the figures show, in a considerable number of cases the party affiliation of candidates has remained unknown. The results of work council elections can, therefore, hardly be used as reliable guides to the actual strength of the Socialist Party and Socialist trade union fraction in the plants and among industrial workers.

The over-all figures reveal a rather stable picture: the Socialist lists have received consistently about 60 per cent of the votes cast. The second-largest group (about 30 per cent) is that of the work councilors without official party backing. According to the national breakdown, the Communist ("unity") lists have received about 6.5 per cent and the Catholic lists 3.8 per cent of the votes.[136] The trend, except among agricultural workers, shows a slight decline in Socialist strength and a corresponding rise in the number of "no party" councilors elected.[137] Needless to say, there are

---

[134] Communist representation on the Executives of the unions is based on interfractional agreement and in most cases Communists remained members. Their expulsion from the Praesidia and Secretariats represented technically merely the disciplining of disloyal functionaries, not the breach of the interfractional "unity." (See *Gewerkschaftliche Rundschau*, V [November, 1950], 20–22.)

[135] They have been charged both with "left" and "right" deviations, with excessive resort to radical methods of struggle, and with too exclusive concern with the welfare of their own enterprises ("plant egoism"). Thus, the 1958 Program of the SPOe categorically demands: "Plant egoism must be subordinated to the solidarity of all wage and salary workers." (*Arbeiter Zeitung*, May 15, 1958, p. 11.)

[136] No comprehensive or detailed presentation of work council election results is available. *Solidarität* has published tables of the nationwide results; these are reproduced in Appendix 2.

[137] There has been considerable bickering about the political meaning of the "nonparty" lists. Socialists have generally argued that these are primarily "name lists" and can be assumed to divide roughly along the same lines as the votes cast for political lists, i.e., that about 60 per cent of them "lean" toward the Socialist Party. (See *Arbeiter Zeitung*, April 7, 1948.) This claim is almost certainly spuri-

significant differences between the positions in different plants and localities. Particularly in enterprises which had been under Soviet administration and in the large new enterprises located in Western Austria and heavily manned by *Volksdeutsche* and de-classed ex-Nazis, Socialists have had to fight strenuously, and not always successfully, to maintain a dominant position.[138]

Chambers of Labor

Functions

A major Socialist success following World War I was the establishment of Chambers of Labor.[139] One of the first acts of the Provisional Govern-

---

ous, as is shown by the results of the elections to the Chambers of Labor in which "nonparty" lists were absent and the Socialists in 1949 received 64.4 per cent of the votes cast.

[138] Thus, in the *Raxwerke* (Soviet zone) the strength of the various lists changed as follows:

	SPOe	KPOe	No Party	OeVP	VdU
1947	5	2	1	–	–
1949	4	5	–	–	–
1951	1	6	2	–	–

The following figures from the *Arbeitsgemeinschaft Kaprun*, one of the large public power developments in Western Austria, illustrate the precariousness of the Socialist position:

	SPOe	KPOe	No Party	OeVP	VdU
1949	12	4	–	–	–
1950	8	2	–	–	4
1951	5	5	–	–	6
1952	8	3	–	–	4

Subsequently the challenge to the SPOe in some of the largest centers of "insurgency" seems to have slackened considerably. Thus, at the *Steyerwerke* the Socialist list increased from 4,419 votes to 5,474, while the Communist votes dropped from 2,081 to 311 (*Arbeiter Zeitung*, October 16, 1953). At the VOEST (Linz) the SPOe increased the number of its Work Councilors from 13 to 24, while the Communist representation fell from 9 to 3 and that of the Independents from 8 to 3 (*ibid.*, November 26, 1953).

[139] *Arbeiterkammergesetz* of February 26, 1920, *StGBl*, No. 100 (1920). For their development at the end of World War I, see Leopold Stupperger, "Die Entwicklung der Arbeiterkammern in Oesterreich" (unpublished dissertation, University of Vienna, 1949); also Gulick, *op. cit.*, pp. 222–26.

ment in 1946 was to revive the unique institutions [140] whose function it is to represent officially the interests of all dependent recipients of wages and salaries.[141] Membership in the Chambers is compulsory; dues are deducted from wages and turned over to the Chambers. Their organization is decentralized: a separate Chamber exists in each *Land*, linked to each other only through the Labor Chamber Conference (*Arbeiterkammertag*), which consists of the Presidents of the *Land* Chambers and twenty delegates. This Conference meets regularly and discusses matters of common concern, but lacks directive and executive powers.[142] Decentralization, which causes overlapping of work and lack of co-ordination, is also a source of weakness vis-à-vis their opposite numbers on the employer side, i.e., the Chambers of Business. For the law re-establishing the Business Chambers provided for a Federal Chamber with extensive powers of direction over the subordinate functional and regional organizations,[143] in spite of Socialist efforts to achieve decentralization.

Technically the workers themselves are not "members" of the Chambers of Labor.[144] They merely vote for representatives (whose numbers, depending on the size of the *Land*, vary from 48 to 144) who make up the Chamber in each *Land* and who, in turn, elect an Executive consisting of one president, two vice-presidents, and from 6 to 12 members.[145]

Among the Chambers' functions, the most important are the rendering of expert opinions in all cases where legislative drafts touch on interests with whose protection the Chambers are charged; participation in the administration of economic agencies in instances provided for by law; and that of providing representatives for public authorities whenever such representation is required. In order to carry out these functions, the

---

[140] *Gesetz vom 20. Juli 1945 über die Wiedererrichtung der Kammern für Arbeiter und Angestellte (Arbeiterkammergesetz).*

[141] Directors or leading employees who have considerable influence on management, as well as some specified categories (family dependents of agricultural workers, pharmaceutical employees, etc.), are excluded from membership.

[142] The Vienna Chamber of Labor often appears to speak for all Chambers but its authority is purely informal and due to its location and size.

[143] *Handelskammergesetz, BGBl* of October 10, 1946, No. 182; also, *Stenographisches Protokoll, Sitzungen des Nationalrates der Republik Oesterreich,* July 24, 1946, pp. 612–22.

[144] In the Chambers of Business, on the other hand, each contributing firm is a member.

[145] The First Secretary is always co-opted as a member of the Executive without a vote.

Chambers have established bureaus staffed by experts who co-operate with elected committees in the formulation of policy decisions.[146]

The functions of the Chambers of Labor are intended to complement those of the trade unions. Unlike the latter, the Chambers are public-law institutions which have the right to demand information from public authorities and whose opinions must be formally brought to the attention of the Legislature and the Cabinet. Conceived at a time when trade unions were primarily thought of as fighting instruments, the Chambers of Labor, concentrating on research and education, were viewed as the potential brain of the Trade Union Movement.[147] The change in the functions of the trade unions, which themselves have become quasi-official institutions and which now carry out tasks largely identical with those of the Chambers, has led to overlapping of work and to institutional and personal rivalries. Thus the trade unions organize their own research staffs, in part to supplement the work done by the Chambers with more specific research, in part, however, also as a means to render themselves independent of the Chambers, whose viewpoint does not necessarily coincide with their own.

Elections

As the members of the Chambers of Labor are elected in a nationwide election on the basis of party lists, they are closely linked to the SPOe, which in the three elections held since 1945 obtained about two-thirds of the total votes cast.[148] The considerable support which the Independent list had enjoyed, particularly in the industrial centers of Southern and Western Austria, was greatly reduced after 1949. In Styria and Upper

---

[146] See Andreas Thaler on the organization of the Chambers of Labor in *Arbeiter Zeitung* of October 18, 1949. Separate bureaus are established for social policy, labor law, social insurance, economics and statistics, communications, and education.

[147] Karl Renner, "Arbeiterkammern," *Arbeiter Zeitung*, August 26, 1945; Johann Böhm, "Arbeiterkammern und Gewerkschaften," *ibid.*, October 22, 1949.

[148] The following figures and tables are based on "Die Arbeiterkammerwahlen," *Arbeit und Wirtschaft*, III (December, 1949), 19–22; *ibid.*, XIII (December, 1959), 344–45; and *Trade Union News Bulletin from Austria* (September-November, 1954), p. 5. (For further details, see Appendix 2.) For the distribution of seats in the individual Chambers, see, in addition, *SPOe-Vertrauensmann*, IV (October-December, 1949), 297. In 1949 the national distribution of seats was: SPOe—504; OeVP—120; KPOe—56; VdU—117; in 1954: SPOe—569; OeVP—139; KPOe—58; VdU—43; in 1959: SPOe—563; OeVP—161; Unity (KPOe)—40; FPOe (VdU)—46.

Austria the Independent list by 1954 lost more than two-thirds of its former strength; in Carinthia it was cut in half; and in Salzburg and Vorarlberg, diminished by a third of its former vote. Looking at the over-all figures, the SPOe appears to have succeeded in maintaining and even increasing its share of votes during the decade 1949–1959 in about equal measure as the OeVP. In several *Länder*, particularly Upper Austria and Vorarlberg, the two parties, however, show striking disparity (Table 4). The figures,

TABLE 4

PERCENTAGE OF VOTE RECEIVED BY PARTY LISTS IN THE ELECTIONS
TO THE CHAMBERS OF LABOR, 1949, 1954, AND 1959

	SPOe			OeVP			KPOe			VdU *		
	1949	1954	1959	1949	1954	1959	1949	1954	1959	1949	1954	1959
Wien	68.2	68.8	70.3	15.0	15.5	16.2	11.2	12.5	7.9	5.1	3.2	5.6
Nieder Oesterreich	71.3	70.3	72.2	14.8	13.3	18.4	13.9	15.6	7.5	—	0.9	1.9
Burgenland	77.2	76.8	73.4	18.2	16.8	23.3	4.6	5.5	1.4	—	0.9	1.9
Steiermark	65.2	72.4	70.7	9.5	13.8	16.1	10.5	8.5	7.9	14.8	4.1	5.3
Kärnten	63.0	71.6	69.2	10.7	12.9	14.1	6.4	5.6	6.0	19.9	9.9	10.7
Ober Oesterreich	53.5	69.8	68.0	11.9	16.1	18.8	5.8	5.8	5.1	28.8	7.8	8.1
Salzburg	54.2	62.0	61.6	12.8	18.6	21.1	5.6	3.6	2.9	27.4	15.9	14.4
Tirol	54.2	55.9	52.9	25.3	26.7	33.0	3.3	3.7	3.6	17.2	13.6	10.5
Vorarlberg	45.3	48.8	44.2	29.6	34.0	40.0	4.1	3.6	2.7	21.0	13.5	13.1
TOTAL	64.4	68.6	68.4	14.2	16.0	18.6	9.7	9.9	6.6	11.7	5.3	6.4

SOURCES: "Die Arbeiterkammer Wahlen," *Arbeit und Wirtschaft*, III (December, 1949), pp. 19–22, and *ibid.*, XIII (December, 1959), pp. 344–45.
* The Independent list was split in 1954 and 1959 between the "Independent" and "Non-Party" lists. The percentages here given represent combined totals of the two lists.

when broken down for manual workers and salaried employees, indicate that, with the exception of Carinthia, the OeVP gained more from Independent losses among salaried employees than the SPOe and that in some *Länder* (Vienna, Burgenland, Lower Austria, Tirol, and Vorarlberg) the Socialist position among them is today somewhat weaker than in 1949 (Table 5).

The trend seems to be toward stabilization of the Independent position after the disastrous setback suffered in 1954 and some headway for the OeVP, particularly among the ranks of manual workers. In the 1959 election the OeVP increased its vote by approximately 15,000 compared to the SPOe's 4,000. (Once again there are considerable variations between *Länder*.) In spite of the *relative* weakening of the SPOe position among

TABLE 5

Vote Changes for the SPOe and OeVP, 1949–1959, Among Manual Workers and Salaried Employees; in Percentages of Total Vote Cast

Land	SPOe		OeVP	
	Manual Workers	Salaried Workers	Manual Workers	Salaried Workers
Wien	+6.8	−1.7	−1.4	+2.9
Burgenland	−3.0	−6.1	+4.6	+5.3
Kärnten	+8.1	+8.2	+2.5	+5.4
Nieder Oesterreich	+3.4	−1.3	+3.2	+3.9
Ober Oesterreich	+20.5	+7.6	+7.9	+10.8
Salzburg	+4.7	+5.4	+5.8	+11.8
Steiermark	+7.7	+2.1	+5.0	+11.7
Tirol	+0.7	−0.3	+6.4	+7.0
Vorarlberg	+2.8	−1.2	+9.2	+8.2
Total	+7.4	−0.1	+3.3	+6.1

Compilation based on "Die Arbeiterkammer Wahlen," *Arbeit und Wirtschaft*, III (December, 1949), pp. 19–22, and *ibid.*, XIII (December, 1959), pp. 344–45.

salaried employees, the Socialist list did actually better there than with regard to manual workers, gaining in 1959 approximately 9,000 votes compared to the OeVP's 14,000. (For more detailed tables depicting election results see Appendix 2, Tables 1 and 2.)

Parliamentary Democracy or Chamber State?

The Chambers derive their great political significance in part from their public-law position through which they are entrusted with the official representation of the three major socioeconomic sectors, business, labor, and agriculture. They thus are publicly recognized pressure groups, institutionalized extraparliamentary rivals to the Legislature and the political parties, empowered to submit opinions on pending legislation and to draft legislation themselves. But the real reason for the prominent part they have played in the political life of postwar Austria—so prominent that some critics have referred to Austria as a "Chamber State" [149]—is to be found

---

[149] Pittermann, "Parlamentarische Demokratie oder Kammerstaat?" *Die Zukunft*, V (December, 1950), 314–17. Harry F. Johnstone (in *The Restraint of Competition in the Austrian Economy*, Economic Division of the U.S. High Commissioner for Austria, Vienna, 1951) describes the Austrian political system as a "government by Chambers" (p. 19).

elsewhere than in the mere fact of public-law anchorage. This is made evident by the fact that the Trade Union Federation, which lacks a similar official position, has played a role roughly identical with that of the Chambers. The main cause of the development is the existence of coalition between the two large parties and the close integration of the Chambers with these parties. As every major issue has had to be settled by agreement evolving from protracted negotiations between representatives of the major power blocs in society, the Chambers, aware through their research activities of the intricate facts relating to each problem, inevitably have moved into the forefront of the negotiations. Furthermore, the overlapping of leadership between Chambers and parties makes impossible a clear distinction between Chamber State and party government.[150]

---

[150] This does not mean, of course, that occasional differences do not arise or that a legislative draft emanating from an SPOe-controlled Ministry is automatically accepted by the Chamber of Labor or the OeGB.

III

Party Structure: Hierarchy, Participation, and "Inner Democracy"

Party Structure

The Party Leadership

In spite of its federal territorial organization, decision-making power in the Austrian Socialist Party is largely centralized in the small leadership institutions knowns as *Parteivertretung* (Party Directorate, PVT) and in the even smaller group comprising the *Parteivorstand* (Party Executive Committee, PVS),[1] the latter consisting of half the Party Directorate's members.[2] These bodies are annually elected by the *Parteitag* (Party Conference), composed of the delegates from all party district organizations as well as of those other organizations which were granted the right of sending delegations.[3] It is the Executive Committee which carries on the Party's business, administers its funds, controls the Party press, and appoints and controls the employees of the Party as well as of the enterprises subject to it.[4] The entire Directorate, consisting now of fifty members, must be convened only in questions of great political or financial importance, but at least once every quarter (or at the demand of five of its members).[5] Because

---

[1] The term *Parteivertretung* (PVT) will be translated as Party Directorate; *Parteivorstand* (PVS) as Party Executive, Executive Committee, or simply as Executive.
[2] *Organizational Statute* (hereafter cited as O.S.), 1945, par. 53, amended in 1957 (PTP, 1957, pp. 29, 162–63).
[3] Listed in O.S., 1945, par. 22.
[4] *Ibid.*, par. 35. The Central Party Secretaries, the Editor-in-chief of the central Party newspaper (the *Arbeiter Zeitung*), and the Secretaries of the *Land* and District organizations are appointed by the Party Directorate (*ibid.*, par. 40).
[5] *Ibid.*, par. 38.

the members of the so-called *Partei Kontrolle* (Party Control), who make up the other half of the Directorate, have the right to participate in all meetings of the Executive Committee,[6] the dividing line between Executive Committee and Directorate is in fact fluid and of little significance. Because of the size of the body, much of its work is carried on in committees.

The new version of the Organizational Statute—adopted after considerable debate at the 1945 Conference—allowed *Länder* representatives to fill half of the seats in the Executive Committee and all but two of those in the Control;[7] this constitutes a recognition of the shift in relationship between the Vienna and the provincial organizations.

If we examine the composition of the Party Directorate since 1945 and the characteristics of some of its leading figures, certain important changes from the prewar period become apparent.

Though most of the members of the Directorate were in some capacity active in the Party before 1934, a majority of them did not then occupy leading positions. Of the forty members of the Directorate elected in 1945, only seven had also been its members in 1932. And by 1951 the number of the pre-1934 holdovers had been reduced to four. Of the four men who by general agreement formed the inner core of the Party leadership in the postwar decade, only one was a member of the Directorate before 1934. In spite of the traditional Party myth that personalized leadership is unknown in the Socialist Movement,[8] these four men were until recently the most powerful leaders in the Party: Adolf Schärf, Party Chairman and Vice-Chancellor from 1945 to 1957; Oscar Helmer, Vice-Chairman and Minister of Interior from 1945 until his retirement in 1959; Karl Waldbrunner, Central Secretary of the Party from 1946 to 1956, Minister of Nationalized Industries from 1949 to 1956; and Bruno Pittermann, member of the Party Directorate (formerly since 1950, previously co-opted), Secretary of the Parliamentary Party, and Party Chairman since 1957.

Helmer, who before 1934 belonged to the Renner faction in the Party Directorate, was throughout the twenties in opposition to the dominant Bauer group. Dr. Schärf, like Helmer closely allied to Renner, was secretary to the Parliamentary Party before 1934, influential, knowledgeable, and

---

[6] They vote on all matters not formally subject to the Executive's control. (*Ibid.*, par. 37.)

[7] O.S., 1945, par. 33.

[8] A phenomenon characteristic of Socialist parties. Cf. Robert Michels, *Political Parties, passim*; Duverger, *Political Parties*, pp. 177 ff.

astute, yet without any prominent position in the organizational life of the old Social Democracy. Waldbrunner and Pittermann had both been active in Socialist student groups but achieved political prominence only after 1945. The four leaders have in common certain political characteristics: though their political roots are in the pre-1934 Social Democracy, they do not identify themselves with the specific political tactic or ideology of the Social Democracy of the First Republic. They share a dislike for Socialist theory and thus have little sympathy for the intellectual achievements of Austro-Marxism. With the exception of Pittermann, they show a marked lack of oratorical ability. In contrast to the leaders of the First Republic— Bauer foremost among them—who were impassioned "demagogues," arousing, appealing, persuading, always intent on harmonizing practice with Socialist theory, these new leaders are ill at ease in mass meetings. Although they lack the passionate commitment of their predecessors, they are skillful organizers, capable administrators, and adept at the game of political strategy. They possess qualities which meet the requirements of Austrian politics of the post-1945 type and which are an assurance that the Socialist Party, as long as they remain at the helm, will not deviate from the moderate course it has pursued since 1945.

As a consequence of Hitler's temporary triumph, the Jewish element, which until 1934 usually made up half of the membership of the Executive Committee,[9] has almost completely disappeared from the Party's top echelon. Since 1946 only two Jews have become members of the Party Directorate.[10] The disappearance of Jews from prominent Party positions has gone hand in hand with the elimination of the Socialist "intellectuals" (in the narrower sense of the word, persons primarily interested in matters of the intellect, such as writers, editors, university professors). Compared to sixteen Socialist members of Parliament in 1919 who were listed as writers and editors, the Socialist parliamentary representation since 1945 has contained only one.[11] The middle-class leaders who still are prominent at the

---

[9] Among them the personalities who dominated the Party in the twenties: Otto Bauer, Robert Danneberg, Julius Deutsch, Friedrich Adler, *et al.* According to Joseph Buttinger (*In the Twilight of Socialism*, p. 85), a tacit agreement existed that the Jews on the Executive Committee should always number, at most, one less than a majority.

[10] Among other important Party positions only one, that of editor-in-chief of the *Arbeiter Zeitung*, is occupied by a Jew.

[11] *Handbuch des österreichischen National und Bundesrates* (Bilderzeitung, G.m.b.H., Vienna, 1946 and 1950).

top of the Party are predominantly practical men: high school teachers, like Drs. Koref and Pittermann; lawyers, like Dr. Schärf; or engineers, like Karl Waldbrunner. The tension between theoreticians and "activists," which was one of the characteristics of the old Social Democracy, has thus disappeared through the elimination of the species "Socialist intellectual." [12]

Former members of the Revolutionary Socialists made up almost exactly half of the Party Directorate after 1945.[13] In 1945 both Central Secretaries came from the R.S. Since 1947, when Erwin Scharf was deprived of his post, one of the two Central Secretaries has been a former R.S. functionary. Former R.S. membership has, however, not proved a significant mark of distinction in the postwar period. In many cases, men who between 1934 and 1938 were distinguished by their youthful, revolutionary radicalism have become the most reliable and antiradical organization men.

The Party Bureaucracy

Narrowly defined, the Party bureaucracy consists of those members who are employed by, and receive their compensation from, the Party. The total number of full-time Party employees has not been revealed since 1945, but there is no reason to assume that the figure differs significantly from the pre-1934 total. Then an official report listed their number as 1,406, of whom a large percentage were employed in Party-owned newspapers and printing shops.[14] The core of the Party bureaucracy is formed by the Central Party Secretariat, located in Vienna, and the smaller *Länder* Secretariats, as well as the full-time District Secretaries with their usually small staffs. In order to tighten the Party organization by increased centralization, District Secretaries have since 1945 been appointed and paid by the Party Directorate and are therefore ultimately responsible to it.[15]

---

[12] If it were necessary to substantiate this point statistically, the list of books and articles published by Bauer, Renner, *et al.*, in the First Republic compared to the almost total absence of such publications by the leading Socialists of the Second Republic would provide convincing evidence.

[13] This statement is based on a list of prominent R.S. functionaries, compiled on the basis of Buttinger's work as well as on a statement appearing in the *Arbeiter Zeitung* (May 21, 1948), signed by a large number of them.

[14] *Jahrbuch*, 1929, p. 106.

[15] *O.S.*, 1945, par. 40. Also, Franz Popp, *PTP*, 1945, p. 42: "The appointment takes place on the proposal or after hearing the opinion of the organization for which the secretaries are appointed."

Property which the Social Democratic Party had owned before its dissolution in 1934, consisting primarily of buildings and some movie houses, was largely restored to the SPOe as the legal successor of the SDAPDOe.[16] The SPOe's most important postwar acquisition has been the purchase of the majority share in a large paper and printing enterprise, the "Steyrermühl," which was integrated into the newly organized holding company "Konzentration," which the Party had set up to unify and co-ordinate all its publishing and printing activities.[17]

If "Party bureaucracy" is defined in a less technical sense, it may be said to include all those who occupy positions in public or private enterprises as Party delegates or on the strength of their role as Party functionaries. Party functionaries who have been provided with positions in the nationalized Chambers of Labor do not receive their remuneration directly from the Party. Yet, because of the fact that they owe their positions to the Party and, in many cases, depend on it for continuation or promotion in the job, they have been closely integrated into the Party machine. Their number, though not a matter of record, increased greatly under postwar conditions when the principle of *"Proporz"* was made an essential part of the politics of the coalition.

The "Cadre" of Party Functionaries

A total of about 50,000 active Party workers, receiving no compensation for their labors, make up the organizational machine. At the head of this body of *Vertrauensmänner* stands the Party Directorate.

In each *Land* organization a Directorate—organized on the same pattern as the Central Party Directorate—forms the top of the organizational pyramid. Central and *Land* Directorates are linked by membership of at least one *Land* delegate in the Central body. Approximately 300 Party officials, many of them chairmen of District organizations, make up the membership of this top layer.

The *Land* organizations are divided into Districts, each with an elected chairman and a District Directorate, a total of about 1,500 functionaries in all of Austria. The District Directorates draw a large proportion of their members from the leadership of the smallest Party units, the Sections, of

---

[16] *Bundesgesetz vom 6. February 1947 über die Rückgabe des Vermögens aufgelöster oder verbotener Organisationen (Rückgabegesetz). BGBl* of March 27, 1947.
[17] See *Report of PE, PTP*, 1947, pp. 40–41.

which there are approximately 3,000. The overwhelming number of *Vertrauensmänner*—45,000 out of 50,000—thus fill positions in the Sections.

All of these functions are honorary, i.e., unpaid, but at the higher levels Party activity is frequently coupled with a paid public or Party position. Thus in 1951, of the 24 Vienna District leaders eight were members of parliament (one a minister), 13, members of the Vienna City Council; another was Central Secretary of the SPOe.[18] The fact that in 1951 the SPOe was called upon to fill 17,221 public positions—over 1,000 of them full-time political jobs such as mayoralty, membership in central and provincial legislatures and governments [19]—amply supports the conclusion that at the level of District chairman and above, Party functions are almost invariably linked to perquisites, political or otherwise, provided by the Party.

In terms of access to positions of political prominence and proximity to the centers of decision-making, a rough line divides the party at the level of District chairmanships. Above this line it seems proper to speak of the Party "leadership"—a group which includes the members of the Central and *Land* Directorates as well as the District chairmen themselves. The members of the District Directorates, many of them Section chairmen, form a middle stratum which acts as a two-way transmission belt between the bulk of the party workers and the top leadership, to which they have access through the person of the District chairman.

District organizations, comprising several thousand members and hundreds of functionaries, are too large to function as anything but headquarters units stimulating, servicing, and supervising the organizational life of the Sections. Yet by their possession of office space (frequently an entire building, the District *Parteihaus*) with a full-time secretary in charge, required by the Statute to maintain the organization's files, the District headquarters have become the organizational centers of the entire Party.[20]

It is below the level of District Directorates that the mass of the "unknown pioneers of the Labor Movement" carry on the Party's routine work. They are, in practice, not so much "officers of the proletariat"—the glamorous role initially assigned to them—as its "hewers of wood and drawers of water." Their activity consists above all in "looking after" the mass of Party members: their tasks are the monthly collection of dues, distribution of

---

[18] *Oesterreichischer Amtskalender 1951*, XIX, Vienna, 1951.

[19] Cf. *Report of PE, PTP*, 1951, pp. 178–79.

[20] The Central Secretariat of the Party has no over-all membership file nor does it compile its own statistics. For all organizational data it relies on the reports forwarded by lower-echelon organizations.

Party literature, and, ideally, maintaining the Party's ideological and propagandistic influence over the membership. Another aspect of the functionaries' organizational life is regular attendance at the frequent meetings scheduled by the Sections, often conducted in the back room of a saloon, at which section business is conducted or reports and lectures are given by a Party speaker.

Length of Party Membership

The three broad strata composing the Party structure—party peak, Section functionaries, and members at large—differ significantly, as could be expected, in respective length of Party membership. The hiatus of 1934–1945, which disrupted the natural process of replenishing the ranks of the organization, has transformed a normal phenomenon—the advancement into leading positions on the basis of seniority—into a confrontation of generations. Thus, to use the Vienna organizations as an example, all those who were District chairman in 1953 had been Party members before 1934; most of them had also been active during the period of illegality. Section chairmen who, in 1946, perforce came without exception from the ranks of the old Party, are being only slowly replaced by postwar recruits, at least in Vienna, where the Party was in a position to draw on a solid stock of old functionaries.[21] Though exact figures for the provincial organizations are not available, the replacement process appears there much further advanced. Thus, where—as in some provincial Sections—70 per cent of all functionaries are postwar members of the Party,[22] it can be assumed that a considerable number of Section leaders are also part of this group.

In terms of membership below the level of Section leader, the Party has largely become a "new" organization. By 1951 only about half of all *low-level functionaries* came from the ranks of the pre-1934 membership.[23]

---

[21] In Vienna's Rudolfsheim District organization (which I had an opportunity to study more intensively), pre-1934 members still filled 75 per cent of the District's Section chairmanships in 1951.

[22] See *SPOe-Vertrauensmann*, VIII (May, 1953), 152, on length of membership in the Kärnten Land Organization.

[23] *Ibid.*; my own analysis of the Rudolfsheim District, considered by Joseph Kratky of the Central Secretariat as fairly typical, produced a similar result. Average figures are, however, misleading. Sections (in the Kärnten breakdown) range from 61.4 per cent of pre-1934 functionaries to 28.5 per cent. The difference between the figures for the organizations Klagenfurt-City and Klagenfurt-*Land* appear to suggest that city organizations, where the SPOe can be assumed to have been fairly strong in the past, show a higher percentage of old functionaries.

And the percentage of *members* who had joined the Party since 1945 ranged from about 60 per cent in the Vienna organization to almost 80 per cent in one of the *Länder*.[24] Though on the basis of normal turnover figures such a wholesale change over a prolonged period should have been expected,[25] the statistical documentation of the contrast between a leadership completely rooted in Party tradition and a membership largely alien to it was received with surprise by the leaders.[26] It provides, indeed, an important clue to the changed atmosphere which pervades the postwar Socialist Party.

The Age Structure of Party Membership

The fact that a large percentage of the Party membership has been newly recruited, coupled with the realization that these new members have not been drawn from previously untapped groups of the population, would lead one to assume that the Party had experienced a great process of rejuvenation. Yet the available statistical data contradict this assumption.

Before 1934, the Socialist Party could be called a "young" organization, for it contained within its ranks a much higher percentage of youthful persons than did the Austrian population as a whole. Thus in 1930, 28.15 per cent of the members of the Vienna organization were between twenty and thirty years of age, and fully 56 per cent were between twenty and forty,[27] compared to 18 and 37 per cent, respectively, in the Vienna population.[28] After 1945, the proportionate relationships greatly changed. In 1947 the percentage of Vienna Party members under forty was only 31.26 per cent; for Austria as a whole, 37.87 per cent.[29] Or, put differently, of 100 Viennese between the ages of eighteen and twenty-nine, 27 were members of the

---

[24] *Ibid.*, and *Report of PE, PTP*, 1952, p. 39.

[25] According to the *Report of the PE, PTP*, 1952, p. 37, "roughly 5.9 per cent of the total membership leave every year." In the Rudolfsheim District the comparable pre-1934 figures were 7 per cent in 1926, 6.1 per cent in 1928, and 5.8 per cent in 1929.

[26] "This gives the explanation for much that has been inexplicable to us. We have believed . . . that the great majority of our members partook of the Party tradition. . . ." *Report of PE, PTP*, 1952, p. 37.

[27] *Jahrbuch* 1932, p. 112. Pre-1934 statistics on the Party's age structure for all of Austria do not exist.

[28] *Statistisches Jahrbuch der Stadt Wien*, 1930–1935, Neue Folge, III, pp. 9–10.

[29] *Report of PE, PTP*, 1952, p. 40.

Socialist Party in 1929 and only 13 in 1946.[30] Between 1947 and 1954 the age structure of the Party did not alter appreciably. As a glance at Table 1 will show, only 36.6 per cent of the Party membership of 1954 were under forty (compared to 39.9 per cent in the population as a whole), and 39.4 per cent were over fifty.[31]

TABLE 1

AGE BREAKDOWN OF PARTY MEMBERSHIP AND THE AUSTRIAN POPULATION, 1954, IN PERCENTAGES

Age Group	Percentage of Total Population	Percentage of Total Party Membership
under 30	27.02	18.14
30–40	15.64	18.49
40–50	20.18	23.93
50–60	16.90	21.48
over 60	20.26	17.96
	100.00	100.00

SOURCE: *Report of PE, PTP,* 1955, p. 77.

The average age of Party functionaries does not differ significantly from that of the membership at large: 72 per cent of the functionaries are between the ages of thirty and sixty, compared to 67 per cent of the entire Party membership.[32] The small difference is explained by the fact that young members do not easily become functionaries; and that the infirmities of old age frequently prevent the kind of active participation expected of the functionary.

The impression that the Socialist Party has become predominantly a Party of graying or balding heads [33] is thus corroborated by the statistical evidence: compared to 44 per cent of the Vienna membership over forty before 1934, fully 67 per cent were over forty in 1954. Between 1947 and 1954, the percentage of members over forty has *increased* in the Party as a

---

[30] Peter Strasser, "Überalterung der Partei?" *Die Zukunft,* III (May, 1948), 137–40.
[31] *Report of PE, PTP,* 1955, p. 77.
[32] *Ibid.,* p. 104.
[33] Strasser, *loc. cit.,* confirmed my own impression, gained by attendance at numerous Party meetings.

whole from 62.13 to 66.79 per cent.[34] The present age structure, taken in conjunction with the data on length of membership and on the occupational distribution of the membership, seems to lead to the following puzzling conclusions: that the Party, in restoring its membership almost to the pre-1934 level, has not simply drawn most of the old members back into its ranks; has not recruited the young; nor has succeeded in pulling large, hitherto class-alien groups into its organizational field. Two-thirds of the present membership are postwar recruits, and two-thirds of this present membership are over forty years of age. This seems to indicate that the Party today is to a considerable extent composed of men and women who, out of indifference or hostility, refused to join the Party before 1934. Attracted to the postwar Party by the changed situation in which it operates, these new members in turn contribute to the further detachment of the Party from its traditional ideological roots.

Development and Distribution of Party Membership

The Social Democratic Party of the First Republic reached its membership peak in 1929. In that year the SDAPDOe had 708,839 dues-paying members, more than 10 per cent of the entire Austrian population, and 418,055 of these, 58 per cent of the total, were concentrated in the Party organization of "Red" Vienna, whose population made up only approximately 28 per cent of the country's population. By 1955, after a period which included an eleven-year gap in the Party's legal existence, membership had again reached 691,150, i.e., 96.2 per cent of its highest enrollment before 1934. A drastic shift had, however, taken place in the geographical distribution of the membership pattern.

While the Vienna population had dropped only from 1,874,130 (27.7 per cent of the total Austrian population) [35] to 1,766,102 (or 25.5 per cent) in 1951,[36] the Vienna organization had been reduced from 418,055 in 1929 to 294,005 in 1955, or from 58 to 42.7 per cent of the total Party membership. It should be recognized that the city of Vienna in this twenty-year period underwent demographic upheavals which are not reflected in the mere population figures. Their exact nature and their impact on the political profile of the city must, in the absence of precise and detailed statistics,

---

[34] *Report of PE, PTP*, 1955, p. 113.

[35] *Statistisches Taschenbuch der Stadt Wien für das Jahr 1948*, p. 5. The population figure is for the census year 1934.

[36] *Ergebnisse der Volkszählung vom 1. Juni 1951 nach Gemeinden*, p. 3. (Hereafter cited as *Volkszählung 1951*.)

be left to surmise. Probably first in importance is the almost total elimination of Vienna's sizable Jewish community: from 176,034 in 1934[37] it was reduced to 9,049 in 1951.[38] Approximately 200,000 inhabitants of Vienna migrated to Western Austria during and after the war and almost 100,000 *Volksdeutsche* migrated to Vienna.[39] The latter, by tradition and occupational background hardly susceptible to Socialist appeals, did not replace the losses which the Socialist organization suffered through the disappearance of the Jews.[40] Furthermore, the westward migration, which took the form of moving industrial enterprises into areas deemed safer from the ravages of war or the Russian occupation, apparently diminished the size of the Vienna industrial working class.[41]

No attempt will be made to subject to detailed analysis the data assembled in Tables 2 and 3. Only a District-by-District examination, based on extensive study of demographic and economic changes as well as of the local Party organizations, could provide foundation for well-grounded conclusions.[42] The necessary material for such an examination is not available. Speculation without factual basis hardly seems useful.[43] We shall therefore have to be content with pointing out some of the more salient general features of Party developments. Table 2 gives a picture of the westward shift of the Austrian population to which the shift in Party membership is, by

---

[37] *Statistisches Handbuch für den Bundesstaat Oesterreich*, XV (1935), 8.

[38] *Volkszählung 1951*, p. 3.

[39] The population of Vienna reached 1,929,976 in 1939. By 1948 it had declined to 1,751,433. "Naturalizations" (*Einbürgerungen*) were reported as 89,000 between 1945 and 1956. (*Wiener Zeitung*, September 22, 1956, p. 2.)

[40] Though no conclusive data exist to corroborate my view, it is my impression that a large proportion of Viennese Jewry supported the Social Democratic Party. How many Jews went beyond mere voting support and actually joined the SDAPDOe cannot be ascertained.

[41] The Vienna Districts X, XI, XII, XX, and XXI, all preponderantly working-class, lost roughly 95,000 during the period 1939–1948, while Districts I, VI, VII, VIII, IX, XVIII, and XIX, heavily middle-class, showed a gain of about 20,000. (*Statistisches Taschenbuch 1948*, p. 6.)

[42] Development in individual District organizations does not exhibit a uniform picture. Thus, of three neighboring organizations in Kärnten, one, Feldkirchen, declined in membership from 1,837 in 1946 to 1,665 in 1951; another increased from 6,108 to 6,928 in the same period; and a third, Völkermarkt, grew from 1,229 to 1,882. Without a careful analysis of factors accounting for the differential developments in different Districts, any generalization would be specious.

[43] For examples of such speculative sketches, see, e.g., "Das Parteileben Kärntens," *Berichte und Informationen*, I/21 (September 20, 1946), 1–3.

TABLE 2

CHANGES IN THE POPULATION OF THE *Länder* BETWEEN 1934 AND 1951
AND CHANGES IN THE SOCIALIST MEMBERSHIP BETWEEN 1929 AND 1949,
EXPRESSED IN PERCENTAGES OF THE BASE YEAR

Land	Population in 1951 Percentage of 1934 Population	Party Membership 1949 Percentage of 1929 Figure
Burgenland	92	161.5
Kärnten	117	156.5
Nieder Oesterreich	83	96.1
Ober Oesterreich	122	115.9
Salzburg	131	131.7
Steiermark	108	122.8
Tirol	122	116.2
Vorarlberg	125	94.4
Wien	94	66.4

and large, proportionate. The deviations exhibited by Burgenland and Vorarlberg, both small frontier provinces with historical and cultural traditions peculiar to themselves, hardly affect the general picture, which is one of remarkable stability of the proportion of the population which is "organizable" by the Socialist Party and beyond which it encounters great resistance. As shown by Table 3, this barrier to expansion of membership was reached by the Party fairly rapidly after the end of the war. With the exception of the Vienna organization, which has continued to recover steadily from the severe losses it suffered—in 1947 it had only slightly more than half of its 1929 members—the picture is one of a general leveling off of the organizational expansion marking the years 1946–1948. The over-all increase in membership between 1948 and 1956 is almost entirely accounted for by the remarkable growth in the Party organizations of Styria and Upper Austria—in both instances probably due to the winning over of former Independents. The second factor is the gradual recovery of the Vienna organization which, however, remains far below its pre-1934 strength. In 1955 Party membership reached a plateau beyond which it has so far failed to move.[44]

---

[44] See the remarks of Central Party Secretary Otto Probst at the 1957 Conference (PTP, 1957, pp. 27–8). In 1956 the Party lost 3,178 members and in the first eight months of 1957 it had lost 2,065 members.

TABLE 3

PARTY MEMBERSHIP FIGURES FOR 1929, 1932, 1946, 1948,
AND 1956 BY *Land* ORGANIZATIONS

Land	1929	1932	1946 July	1948	1956
Burgenland	12,870	9,772	13,813	18,789	22,547
Kärnten	21,553	18,596	28,648	36,267	36,421
Nieder Oesterreich	124,323	102,479	105,393	130,299	124,107
Ober Oesterreich	51,089	40,607	39,291	57,035	51,574
Salzburg	13,906	10,838	15,258	19,048	20,658
Steiermark	63,673	55,572	69,971	84,239	105,603
Tirol	9,429	7,915	7,662	12,530	11,592
Vorarlberg	3,185	2,216	2,936	4,690	3,881
Wien	418,055	400,484	184,850	253,335	291,569
TOTAL	718,083	648,479	467,822	616,232	667,952

Figures compiled from *Jahrbuch* 1929 and 1932, *Reports of the PE, PTP*, 1946–1957.

The size of the core of the Party, the cadre of *Vertrauensmänner* has developed along lines roughly similar to the general membership. As Table 4 shows, it took very little time to reassemble the stock of Party functionaries. By 1947, however, further efforts to increase the proportion of functionaries to members proved largely unsuccessful. But while the ratio hardly changed

TABLE 4

NUMBER OF *Vertrauensmänner*, 1946–1955

Year	Number of Functionaries
1946	43,113
1947	49,845
1948	48,658
1949	49,542
1950	49,809
1951	49,656
1952	51,682
1953	53,560
1954	55,502
1955	57,588

SOURCE: *Reports of PE, PTP*, 1946–1956.

at all in the provincial organizations during this period, it deteriorated in Vienna from 1:14 in 1947 to 1:17 in 1955.

"Socialist Education"

The Socialist Party has always claimed to be "not a party like the others" but a *Gesinnungsgenossenschaft*, a spiritual community. This claim was based on the assumption that its members were not merely passive sympathizers but activists "filled with socialist class consciousness, acquainted with socialist knowledge, trained for the class struggle in trade unions and politics." [45] The continued adherence to the organizational pattern of the mass party has been justified by reference to this concept of the Party as a spiritual community and the insistence that the Party's main task vis-à-vis its members consisted in their "systematic education to Socialism."

To achieve this objective the Party organized the Central Education Office (*Bildungszentrale*, SBZ) and requires all District organizations and Sections to appoint, wherever possible, special committees to provide the members with systematic socialist education.[46] Compared to the First Republic, the Party faces a considerably harder task, for the Trade Union Federation, as an officially nonpartisan body, now must restrict its extensive educational activities to the narrower field of labor and union problems.

The scheme by which the Central Education Office hoped to implement the ambitious goal of "systematic socialist education" for the masses was—on paper—thorough and comprehensive.[47] The lesson of the R.S. period, with its insistence on differentiation between "cadre" and "mass," was accepted in the educational blueprint.[48] The "masses" of the Party members were to be influenced toward socialism primarily by appeals to their emotions. The functionaries—the "officer corps"—were to be inculcated with thorough scientific socialist thinking, a training which was to rid them once

---

[45] Karl Czernetz, "Die Schulungsarbeit—eine politische Notwendigkeit," *SPOe-Vertrauensmann*, I (September, 1946), 22–24.

[46] O.S. 1945, par. 21. See also "Regulativ der *SBZ*," *SPOe-Vertrauensmann*, III (March, 1948), 80, as well as "Die Partei . . . ," *SPOe-Vertrauensmann*, II (May, 1947), 141–44, for the place of the SBZ in the organizational structure of the SPOe.

[47] Czernetz, "Die Schulungsarbeit . . . ," *loc. cit.*

[48] Czernetz, responsible since 1946 for the work of the Central Education Office, was a leading functionary in the R.S. See his article "Die politischen Offiziere des Proletariats" (*Arbeiter Zeitung*, December 25, 1945), which puts almost exclusive stress on rigorous socialist education as the distinguishing mark of the cadre.

and for all of any inferiority feelings toward intellectuals and which was to provide them with thorough practical knowledge as well as character qualities of unyielding forthrightness and decency, a training aimed at enabling them to make decisions and accept responsibility in all situations.[49]

These goals were to be achieved by series of lectures and courses: nonintellectual though informative for the mass of members; systematic and organized at various levels of thoroughness for the functionaries.[50] Straight lectures were to be avoided as much as possible and replaced, for the mass membership, by propagandistically more effective means such as films; for functionaries, by discussion method (*Arbeitsunterricht*). It was recognized that indoctrination lectures failed to foster real understanding and independence of thought and action.

The SPOe has almost totally failed to achieve the educational objectives it set for itself. In the first place, the Party has failed to attract the regular or even occasional participation of more than a small fraction of its membership to lectures or meetings. Though Districts and Sections do not even attempt to schedule frequent meetings for the rank and file, attendance, by general estimate, usually hovers at about 10 per cent of the total membership, a 10 per cent which, as a rule, is composed of a hard core of "steady customers." [51]

Personal contact between the average member and the Party organization is, *de facto*, restricted to the monthly visit of the dues-collecting functionary. However, even this opportunity for "discovering the interests, moods, and emotions" of the masses and "spreading enlightenment and influence" is hardly ever utilized. Because of the limited time at the functionary's disposal, contact between him and the member consists usually of

---

[49] Czernetz, "Die Schulungsarbeit . . . ," *loc. cit.*

[50] Czernetz, "Der sozialistische Lehrplan," *SPOe-Vertrauensmann*, III (June-August, 1948), 123–26.

[51] A rough check of the—not very reliable—attendance figures in the Rudolfsheim District tends to corroborate this general estimate: of 616 meetings held in the District during 1948, 470 were limited to functionaries. The 96 political lectures and meetings open to the general membership were attended by a total of 6,349, an average of 66 per meeting. As the average strength of a section in 1948 was 445, attendance represents 15 per cent, including the 5 per cent functionaries. Cf. also the statement by F. Graczoll that "one has the experience again and again that in our Section meetings only a certain fraction of our membership participates and that it is always the same group. The larger part we have unfortunately not, so far, been able to pull in." (*SPOe-Vertrauensmann*, II [January, 1947], 24.)

little more than a minimum of casual conversation. In the words of a local report: "No time remains for personal political information, no time for discussion with the member, no opportunity for influencing the way of life of our comrades." [52]

The first conclusion we can therefore draw is that the great majority of Party members are not exposed to "socialist education" in any form. Lectures, courses, and meetings are, in fact, provided *by* Party functionaries *for* Party functionaries. But in the efforts directed at the education of the "cadre," achievement falls equally far short of expectation. The bulk of functionaries do dutifully attend the frequent talks aimed at them by the Education Office. But their apathy or even antipathy toward "systematic socialist education" has not been overcome. In response to their pressure, information lectures on the practical questions of everyday politics have increasingly replaced courses with theoretical content.[53] And comprehensive cycles of consecutive talks dealing with one subject have given way to separate and uncoordinated lectures ranging over a wide variety of topics.[54]

Contrary to the original intention, the straight lecture has remained the predominant form of presentation. In part this is due to the attitude of the audience itself. For the low-level functionaries, short on factual information, frequently painfully aware of their verbal inadequacy, are content to sit in silence and listen. In harmony with the Party's tradition they come to be told, to be briefed. To a considerable extent, however, it is the organization of the educational enterprise and the spirit pervading it which are responsible for this passivity. Trained Party speakers are handed centrally prepared *Redeanleitungen* ("speakers' guides") on centrally selected topics. Equipped with concise and dogmatic outlines, they travel the "circuit" of Party organizations, repeating mechanically the same lecture in each loca-

---

[52] *Die Nationalratswahl 1953*, Bezirksorganisation Neubau der SPOe, April, 1953, p. 74 (mimeographed).

[53] Cf. Czernetz, "Probleme der Schulungsarbeit," *SPOe-Vertrauensmann*, III (July, 1948), 229. Note also frequent references to demands that courses deal more with practical problems (e.g., *SPOe-Vertrauensmann*, VI [*February*, 1951], 93). See also the summary in *Report of PE*, 1956, pp. 126–37.

[54] Note the appeal by the Central Education Office that every local organization carry out at least two short cycles (three evenings each) per year. (*SPOe-Vertrauensmann*, VI [February, 1951], 95.) These cycles are disguised to appear as unconnected lectures, for it is feared that attendance will suffer if they give too educational an impression. (*SPOe-Vertrauensmann*, VI [August-September, 1951], 226–27.) During 1955 only 134 members participated in six short cycles of courses in all of Vienna. (*Report of PE*, 1956, p. 130.)

tion, a procedure hardly designed to stimulate the allegedly desired "independence of political thought" among the functionaries. In fact, the Party's tradition of preserving outward unity and discipline is not favorable to a spirit of free discussion and probing inquiry. Though adherence to Marxism as a faith has almost completely disappeared at the top, the Party "line" is still centrally determined and questions as to its rightness are unwelcome as signs of disunity.[55]

For a small number of functionaries—the speakers and future teachers of the Party—a more concentrated program of political education has been set up. It takes the form of training and agitation schools for selected functionaries, which usually last a week.[56] In addition, the Vienna Party School attempts to present a thorough introduction to social and political theory from the Socialist viewpoint in three-semester courses.[57] Though candidates are carefully selected,[58] as a rule more than half drop out before the end of the course,[59] and the total number of graduates between 1946 and 1952 was only 137.[60] The original intention to revive the Workers' University, which before 1934 had supplied an annual crop of working-class intellectuals instructed by Otto Bauer, Karl Renner, Max Adler, and others, has not been carried out.[61]

In the process of realization, the Socialist Party's educational scheme has simultaneously undergone a radical contraction and change of objective.

---

[55] Josef Hindels in "Für freie Diskussion in der Partei," *Die Zukunft*, VI (June, 1951), 165–67, provides examples of "tactics used to inhibit free discussion."
[56] These are organized by the Central Education Office. The students board at the Party School during that period. An average of 25 a year are held.
[57] For the full curriculum, see *Arbeiter Zeitung*, December 8, 1946.
[58] *Ibid.*
[59] In 1948 the number of graduates was 35 out of 80 who had initially been selected. (*Arbeiter Zeitung*, July 7, 1948.) Of 59 participants in the fourth series of courses started in 1950, 39 failed to finish the work. (*Report of PE, PTP*, 1951, p. 129.)
[60] The figure was compiled for me by the Secretariat of the SBZ.
[61] Among its graduates were some of the future leaders of the R.S.: Buttinger, Sailer, and Holoubek.

At present, no discernible effort is made by the Party to utilize the talents of the Party School graduates. It is significant that the Central Education Office has no record of their Party careers subsequent to graduation. The evidence here presented shows that the "training" requirement for Party functionaries—taken at face value by Duverger (*op. cit.*, pp. 141, 157)—is, in fact, almost pure fiction. By no means can it be said that training represents a prerequisite for leadership selection.

Comparing blueprint with reality, we find that the approach and objectives considered appropriate for the mass of party members have, in fact, characterized the efforts directed at the "cadre" of functionaries; and that the "systematic education" which was considered a prerequisite for the exercise of any party function has been limited to a very small and select group with sufficient time to attend the three-semester Vienna Party School. This concentric contraction of Party education is merely one aspect of the confrontation between Party myth and Party reality. According to the myth, the Party is the spiritual community of all its members. In reality, as our examination has shown, this community is almost exclusively made up of the core of functionaries who alone participate in its activities and who are forced to acquaint themselves, if only superficially, with its policies.

In spite of the merely passive and formal role which most members play, the need to "organize" continues to be stressed unrelentingly by the Party leadership. Growth of the organization in terms of numbers has become an end in itself, largely divorced from the rational objectives that were posited for it. In playing the traditional game, local organizations, striving to outdo each other in the number of new members, are willing to woo and hold members at almost any price. The rather rigid procedure adopted in 1945, by which prospective members were to be carefully screened and undesirables (primarily ex-Nazis) kept out, was not retained for long.[62] Promises and expectations of favors are widely used to gain new members. And frequently concessions regarding the payment of membership dues are made in order to hold wavering members.[63] The contribution asked by the Party is small—even by Austrian standards [64]—and organizations are authorized to reduce it in cases of real hardship. The plea most frequently advanced by those dropping their membership, that "they can't afford" to continue dues payments, must therefore be recognized for what it usually is—a sign of indifference rather than of poverty. The impression that the motives for joining the Party are in many cases purely opportunistic is bolstered by the frequency with which "nonfulfilment of material demands, such as for

[62] The special committees set up to screen each applicant were discontinued in 1949 through a change in par. 3 of the O.S.
[63] The reduced contribution which by statute is limited to old-age pensioners and unemployed members is actually collected from one-third of the total membership. (Report of PE, PTP, 1951, p. 77.)
[64] The full monthly dues are approximately the equivalent of three tram rides. The reduced contribution is half that amount.

apartments and jobs" are frankly admitted as reasons for decreasing membership.[65]

In view of the nonparticipation of the large mass of members in the Party's activities, the tenuous influence which the organization wields over them, and the frequency with which immediate personal desires of a material nature are given as reasons for joining or leaving the Party, one must conclude that the membership is, to a considerable extent, made up of political "drift sand," without strong ideological ties to its principles or traditions.[66] This conclusion is borne out by the previously mentioned fact that more than 60 per cent of the Party's members, while "new," are old enough to have joined the Party during the First Republic when it offered more fervor and fewer favors.

The Party as a "Democratic Community"

From its beginning, the commitment to "inner democracy" has been an essential part of the Austrian Social Democratic tradition, which it shared with other Socialist parties.[67] In accordance with this commitment, three broad principles reflecting the nature of the Movement as a "democratic community" have been officially accepted: decisions are to be reached democratically, i.e., through participation and free discussion by its members; these decisions are to be binding on the elected Party leadership; and those who are delegated by the Party to represent it in legislature or govern-

---

[65] *Report of PE, PTP,* 1952, p. 37. Though Sections are required to keep records as to members' "reasons for leaving the Party," such records are, in fact, only rarely maintained, perhaps because the impossibility of obtaining reliable data is recognized. Of the few District organizations which seem to maintain these records systematically, that of Wieden reported that of the 183 persons leaving the Party during the first six months of 1952, 76 left "because of the nonfulfillment of personal wishes" such as those made with regard to employment and apartments.

[66] Little concrete knowledge exists as to the members' motivation for joining. Hindels in "Probleme des Aufstiegs" (*Die Zukunft,* IX [January, 1954], 5–9) cites the case of two new, perhaps "typical" members. One, an engineer, joined the Party because he was convinced of the necessity for planning; the other— formerly a peasant, now an industrial worker—because he saw in it the strongest opponent of Communism. Neither, Hindels regretfully remarks, has any appreciation of the meaning of "Socialism."

[67] See Michels, *op. cit., passim.*

ment shall consider themselves entirely as the agents of the Party and subject to its continuous guidance.

Underlying this strict insistence on locating power at the bottom of the
Party pyramid is the egalitarian ethos of the Socialist Movement with its
wish to see equality become reality within the Movement's own ranks as
assurance of the future classless society.[68] Furthermore, as a "revolutionary"
party it has traditionally harbored profound suspicion of the existing state
power and of the corruption which power might bring to those coming into
too close contact with it. As the repository of the historical revolutionary
destiny, the Party had the duty to keep close watch in order to protect its
leaders from this threatening corruption. This doctrine of Party supremacy
was unconditionally expressed in 1918 when Austrian Socialist leaders were
for the first time called upon to accept responsible government offices:

We are a Party which has to fulfill great historical tasks and which must uphold
these tasks, perhaps uphold them in a struggle, as far as this is possible, against
its representatives in the government.[69]

The Party's "Democratic Constitution": The Organizational Statute

Apart from basic provisions for the election of Party functionaries at all
levels [70] and the convening of annual Party Conferences,[71] the ideal of
"inner democracy" has found expression in two clauses of the Organizational Statute. One aims to assure control of the Party and its elected
Executive Committee over those of its leaders who become members of
the government; [72] the second attempts to prevent concentration of power
in the hands of top leaders through the much-feared "accumulation of
offices." [73] In addition, committees known as "Control" (*Kontrolle*) [74] are

---

[68] Many symbolic expressions of this insistence on equality can be found: the reluctance to employ the term "leaders"; the use by members of the term *Genosse*
("comrade") and the familiar *du* ("thou") in addressing each other.
[69] Emmy Freundlich, *PTP*, 1919, p. 219. Cf. the excellent discussion of this
problem, common to socialist parties, by Duverger, *op. cit.*, pp. 192–97.
[70] O.S., 1945, pars. 19, 30, and 33.
[71] *Ibid.*, par. 22.
[72] O.S., 1919, par. 31, and O.S., 1945, par. 33. There is a significant difference in
the phrasing of these paragraphs that will be discussed below.
[73] O.S., 1945, par. 50, and O.S. 1926, par. 46, interpreted the decision of the
Party Conference of 1926. With one small but significant difference the formulation has remained identical.
[74] O.S., 1919, par. 35, and O.S. 1945, par. 37. Except for one unimportant
change, the formulations are identical.

elected at every organizational level alongside the Executive Committee. They are charged with the supervision of the Executive Committee in financial and political matters and are generally intended to serve as channels for criticism and complaints against the leadership.[75]

Adoption, in 1945, of an Organizational Statute which based itself, by and large, on its predecessor of 1926[76] marked the rejection by the Party Conference of the notions of "democratic centralism" which had prevailed in the organization of the Revolutionary Socialists.[77] In fact, no effort was made by surviving members of the R.S. to insist on reorganizing the Party along the lines followed by the underground movement.[78]

Some changes in the Organizational Statute—heatedly debated at the 1945 Conference—have had the effect of formally strengthening the position of the leadership compared to the Party rank and file. In 1919 the Conference had insisted on the inclusion of a clause which unequivocally provided that those members of the Central Executive Committee who accepted office in the federal government lost their votes and offices in the Party, retaining only advisory membership in the Executive.[79] Though he recognized that other socialist parties had not adopted such rigid procedures, Robert Danneberg put the case for the clause in terms which have lost nothing of their relevance:

One must say that today's government—a coalition government, not a purely social-democratic one—is by no means an organ of the Party . . . but of this

---

[75] O.S., 1945, par. 37: The Control "decides about complaints which have been lodged by Party members or organizations against the Executive." Cf. also *Die Verwaltung der Organization*, SBZ, 1946: "The Control is the organization's conscience, with two tasks: For one, it examines regularly and best without advance notice the financial operations of the organization. . . . Secondly, it sees to it that the decisions of the various bodies are executed in a timely and correct manner" (p. 4).

[76] "The provisional Party Executive issued the directive . . . according to which basically the old Organizational Statute, adopted at the 1926 Party Conference in Linz, remained in operation for the time being. Only a few timely clauses were added. Today I am putting before you a new draft. This, too, keeps in its main feature to the O.S. of the Linz Conference." (Franz Popp, *PTP*, 1945, p. 41.)

[77] Cf. Buttinger, *op. cit.*, pp. 367 ff.

[78] Among 18 speakers who participated in the debate on the new Organizational Statute, only one, a former functionary of the R.S., went so far as to ask that the final adoption of a new statute be postponed until the experiences of the illegal period had been thoroughly discussed. (Karl Mark, *PTP*, 1945, p. 50.)

[79] O.S., 1919, par. 31.

state which today even as a democratic republic remains a class state. The Party must control the policy of the government as well as the activities of the comrades whom it has delegated into the government and who are there overburdened with work.[80]

When the draft of the new Organizational Statute was presented to the 1945 Party Conference, this clause had been altered by the addition that "exceptions which are in the urgent interest of the Party could be made by decision of the Party Executive Committee." [81] In spite of considerable criticism, which in substance was a restatement of the argument put forth by Danneberg in 1919, the clause was adopted in this altered form, one indication, among many, of the fundamental change in the Party's attitude to state power, socialist or otherwise, and of the decreasing influence of the Party militants.[82] The qualification inserted in the clause which makes the loss of vote and office by holders of governmental positions exceptional and dependent on "urgent Party interest" has, in practice, turned out to be a mere formality. Dispensation has been granted automatically by the Party Executive and not a single case is on record in which it was denied. Resentment by militant lower-echelon functionaries has frequently focused on the clause and its application. Membership in the government, carrying with it power to grant numerous political favors, was felt to concentrate inordinate power in the hands of leaders theoretically subject to the Party's will.[83] But on every occasion when the question of amending the clause

---

[80] PTP, 1919, p. 188.

[81] O.S., 1945, par. 33.

[82] Cf. statement by Franz Jonas (PTP, 1945, p. 52), in which this change of attitude was expressly acknowledged. Duverger (op. cit., p. 192) correctly points out that the demand for subordination of the parliamentary representatives to the Party proper and to the Executive elected by the Party comes from the ranks of the militant elements who do not wish to see radical action sacrificed to parliamentary compromises.

[83] The following statement is a typical expression of this sentiment: "The mass of our members demand democracy in the Party. . . . What we demand is nothing more than the establishment of a situation whereby in the Party, too, legislature and executive are strictly separated. We believe that the Executive must lay down guiding lines for the members of the government and that the members of the government must follow these guiding lines. We believe that the members of the government, even if they do not possess the power of vote in the Executive, carry sufficient weight on the basis of their influence to persuade the Executive of the rightness of their views. It surely is no accident that so many identical motions [to deprive members of government of the vote in the Executive] have been submitted." (Josef Jackl, PTP, 1949, p. 120.)

was formally raised, the Party leadership firmly opposed change and was finally able to obtain the support of the Conference for total elimination.[84] By this action the Party has accepted the reasoning of its leaders—in complete contrast to the attitude prevalent before 1934—that personal identity of Party functionary and government official alone guarantees that "the will of the Party and the will . . . expressed in the political bodies of the state be identical." [85] Such reasoning avoids the main point at issue: on whose terms this identity of viewpoint is to be achieved and how much latitude the power holders are given in defining it.

Actually, there is no evidence that the reduction of Socialist ministers to nonvoting membership in the Executive would have materially increased the influence of the rank and file on government policy, or that the Executive is divided between holders of government positions and spokesmen for "the Party." Formally the supremacy of "the Party" remains assured, for the line which Socialist members of the government are to take continues to be discussed and decided by the Party Executive. And in the Executive members of the government form such a small minority that the weight of their votes—the only issue formally in question—is insignificant.[86]

The clause aiming at the prevention of "cumulation of offices" also has its roots in the traditional rank-and-file suspicion of powerful leadership. It was assumed that the democratic ballot would provide a remedy against accumulation of party functions. The offices referred to in the Organizational Statute thus are public offices, appointive and elective. The old Statute, as interpreted at the 1926 Conference, denied the compatibility of elective with higher administrative positions, or of membership in the federal parliament with that in the legislature of one of the *Länder*. Furthermore, it recommended that any doubling of elective public office be avoided. Exceptions to these provisions could be made only by decision of the respective Party Conferences in each individual case.[87] In a significant change, effectively strengthening the position of the leadership, the Organizational Statute of 1945 shifted the power of decision-making with regard to exceptions to the Executive Committees on the national and *Land*

---

[84] O.S., 1955 (in *Programm und Statut*, Zentralsekretariat der SPOe, 1955).

[85] Otto Probst, PTP, 1949, p. 117.

[86] According to the testimony of Dr. Bruno Pittermann (corroborated to me by another member of the Executive), so far no showdown vote in the Directorate has been decided by the votes of the members of the government. (PTP, 1949, p. 121.)

[87] *Anträge zum Parteitag*, PTP, 1926, p. 230.

levels, respectively.[88] This provision has hitherto remained unamended in the face of recurrent complaints against the prevalence of office accumulation.

In one more respect have formal changes in the Organizational Statute strengthened the position of the leadership and diminished its accountability to the rank and file. Until 1948 it was required that all written motions submitted to the Party Conference be published in the *Arbeiter Zeitung* at least one week prior to the Conference.[89] This requirement was eliminated on the motion of the Party Executive and replaced by a provision for their publication in a special folder to be sent to each Conference delegate. The effect of this change has been to restrict knowledge of these motions, containing the thoughts and criticisms of local Party organizations all over the country, to the small circle of Conference delegates.[90]

Oligarchic Tendencies

The Organizational Statute, in spite of the changes mentioned, remains ostensibly the constitution of a democratic community. The rights of election and free criticism, with the consequent accountability of leaders to the led, are still formally safeguarded by it. Because of the significant difference which exists between the concepts of direct and indirect democracy, we have to address ourselves to two separate questions: To what extent are decisions the result of a process of genuine collective deliberation by Party members outside the restricted leadership group making up the Central and *Land* Directorates? Or, in the absence of widespread participation in decision-making, how effective are the formal provisions of the Organizational Statute in enforcing accountability upon the leadership?

According to the theory of "inner-party democracy," the entire membership should participate in the discussion and determination of policy. The apathy exhibited by the mass of Party members reflected in their reluctance to play more than a passive role as dues-payers renders such an expectation

---

[88] *O.S.*, 1945, par. 50.

[89] *O.S.*, 1945, par. 28.

[90] Even prior to this official change, the provision was treated as little more than a formality. In 1946 and 1947 the *Arbeiter Zeitung* printed (in small type) only a few selected motions. (Cf. *Arbeiter Zeitung*, November 9, 1946, and October 1, 1947, respectively.) Hindels protested this violation of the letter of the *O.S.* (*PTP*, 1947, p. 99). An even more serious violation, according to Hindels, was the fact that the motion submitted by the SJ was published in condensed form in the special motion folder transmitted to the Conference delegates. (*Ibid.*)

entirely unrealistic. The problem of participation is thus limited reasonably to the core group of approximately 50,000 functionaries who, as active party workers, may wish to be consulted before decisions are taken. A large part of this group seems, however, content to react to decisions taken above by approval or criticism, humbly aware of their unpreparedness to participate in the solution of complicated issues; [91] a frame of mind which, in spite of avowals to the contrary, the Party leadership has done little to alter. Meaningful participation, as an insistent demand, is therefore restricted to that group termed the middle range of leadership, numbering perhaps 3,500 functionaries, who form the inner organizational cadre of the Party. The resolutions submitted by District organizations to the Party Conference protesting the lack of inner democracy on the part of the Central Executive are themselves as a rule the product of a small drafting committee whose draft was automatically approved by the District Conference.[92]

The regularity with which functionaries of this stratum complain about the failure to be consulted in important matters [93] is an indication of the absence of direct, or participatory, democracy even within the narrow scope made feasible by the realities of party structure. Specifically, the Executive has been accused of failure to have consulted or even to have properly informed functionaries outside its own narrow circle on salient issues such as the appointment of key officials in the Ministry of Interior, the redrawing of district boundaries,[94] and the wage-price agreement which vitally affected the nation's economic life.[95] While in matters of public policy government by coalition may have rendered widespread consultation difficult and the need for prompt action occasionally may have been genuine, the

---

[91] Cf., e.g., "Besser machen," *SPOe-Vertrauensmann,* II (February, 1947), 51–52. Attendance at meetings and lectures confirms this impression.

[92] This statement is based on personal observations which I have no reason to assume to be atypical.

[93] In 1946 five Vienna District organizations combined their motions demanding "deepening of inner democracy. . . ." In 1948 eighteen motions stressed the need for strengthening "inner democracy" (Paul Blau, *PTP,* 1948, p. 71). In 1950 the complaint that the functionaries were not being kept properly informed was voiced repeatedly and acknowledged by the spokesman for the Executive (Waldbrunner, *PTP,* 1950, p. 176). In 1951 four motions and three resolutions demanded more "inner democracy," or, in the words of one (Resolution X), that "political decisions in the coalition be not taken against the will of the functionaries."

[94] Eduard Weikhart, *PTP,* 1946, p. 119.

[95] Franz Poddany, *PTP,* 1949, p. 123.

extension of what has been cynically referred to as "secret democracy" [96] to inner-party affairs shows clearly the progressive concentration of decision-making power in the hands of the Party "peak."

In 1957, however, when the Party leadership prepared the new "basic program" of the SPOe, no attempt was made to impose a draft without consultation. The 1947 Action Program and the 10-Point Program of 1952 had been worked out by high-level commissions and merely submitted to the Conference delegates as motions of the Executive one week prior to the Conference, a procedure much criticized by some delegates.[97] For the "basic program" the leadership returned to the precedent of 1926, when the Linz Program had been adopted after prolonged inner-party debate. A small committee, headed by Dr. Benedikt Kautsky, submitted a draft (*Vorentwurf*) to the regular Conference. Another Extraordinary Conference was set for six months later to adopt the new program after the Party membership had had time to examine and criticize the draft. So lively was the debate, so sharp the criticism, that a new committee (including the members of the old, but adding several new ones, the Party chairman among them) completely rewrote the draft. The interest of low-level party functionaries is attested by the fact that 1,070 resolutions for changes and substitutions were submitted for consideration by the Extraordinary Conference.[98]

No formal machinery exists by which the process of consultation is institutionalized. The only body which meets frequently for deliberative and decision-making purposes is the Executive Committee, though informal discussions between its members and influential Party functionaries undoubtedly are a rule. The circle thus comprehended is exceedingly small and does not, for instance, include the approximately 70 Socialist members of Parliament—many also District chairmen—who therefore frequently complain about being kept in the dark on important matters.

Though we must conclude that regular consultation between the "peak" (the Party equivalent to the Cabinet) and the lower echelons does not exist, it must be realized that there is no lack of informal contact. The structure

---

[96] Emmerich Sailer, *PTP*, 1950, p. 72.

[97] E.g., Joseph Pöschl, *PTP*, 1949, p. 65; Marianne Lackinger, *ibid.*, p. 69; Ludwig Klein, *PTP*, 1950, p. 148.

[98] See *Zum Programmentwurf*, Ausserordentlicher Parteitag der SPOe 1958; also *Vorentwurf für ein neues Programm der SPOe*, Vienna, 1957; *PTP*, 1957, pp. 133–46; *Die Zukunft*, between January and June of 1958; and *Arbeiter Zeitung*, May 14, 15, 1958.

of the Party is such that most members of the top echelon are simultaneously active in *Land* and District organizations, where they are surrounded
by functionaries of the middle stratum. Thus, complaints, wishes, and
moods are readily relayed to them through Party channels. How much
weight these expressions of opinion will carry at the top depends, of course
—as in all pressure group situations—on the leaders' estimate of the power
of organized force standing behind any particular demand or criticism. The
effectiveness of pressure—consultation without solicitation—is clearly dependent on the degree of accountability enforceable on the leadership. We
will now turn to an examination of those institutions set up to enforce such
accountability.

The Party Conference (Parteitag)

In the democratic mythology of the Socialist Party, the annual Party
Conference is conceived as the "parliament" which, faithfully representing
the political community's will, combines the functions of constituent assembly, legislature, watchdog over the elected Executive, and last appeal
tribunal.[99] This view of the Conference's position and function—an almost
pure fiction—has been recently restated with solemn pretense by Dr. Schärf,
then Party chairman:

> As in every parliament part of its tasks is to watch over the activities of the bodies
> appointed by it, in other words: to receive reports about their work, and after
> thorough examination to approve, to criticize, or even to reject. Another task is
> the election of the Party Executive and Party Control. Furthermore, it is of
> course a task of the Conference to lay down for the executive bodies of the
> Party . . . guiding principles for their actions. . . .[100]

The following analysis will show that every one of the tasks mentioned by
Dr. Schärf is beyond the capacity of the Conference to perform adequately
and that its attempts to do so have, in fact, degenerated into a routine of
"going through the motions" in accord with the letter but not the spirit
of the Party's democratic constitution.

The Party Conference meets once a year, usually for three days. The
Executive Committee (and particularly some of its members) are in almost
daily contact throughout the year. The opportunity for constant observa-

---

[99] O.S., 1945, pars. 30 and 58.
[100] Adolf Schärf, "Nachwort zum Parteitag," *Die Zukunft*, VIII (November,
1953), 301–2.

tion and supervision of the Executive by the Conference does therefore not exist.

Two institutions are intended to serve the purpose of supervision. Neither, in fact, achieves it. The first is the "Party Control," [101] the other the supposedly binding nature of Conference decisions. As to the Control, it is elected on the same list as the Executive. Its personnel is—like that of the Executive—composed of top-level functionaries, most of them members of parliament. Its annual report to the Conference is limited to a statement of the financial accounts kept by the Party Treasurer. In no instance since 1945 has it voiced any criticism of Executive actions, nor has it reported a single case of a complaint reaching it from an individual member or local organization. This is sufficient proof that its function as watchdog over the Executive has atrophied and that its membership has in fact coalesced with that of the Executive and stands in the same relation to the lower-echelon functionaries and the Conference as the Executive.

In the absence of continuous supervision by an organ of the Conference, there is no assurance that decisions taken by the Conference will actually be implemented by the Executive. Until 1934 the annual report of the Party Directorate submitted to the Conference contained a brief summary of the action taken by the Executive on the motions adopted at the previous Conference. In spite of the specific requirements contained in the Organizational Statute,[102] this practice was quietly dropped after 1945, and the Conference at present receives no itemized report of this kind.

Even if both instruments of enforcing accountability—control and detailed reports—were used as intended, the Party Executive by its decisive influence over the formulation of motions and their disposal by the Conference would be able to escape effective supervision and retain for itself a wide area of maneuver. First, the wording of important motions is, on the insistence of the Executive, so modified as to make action not mandatory but merely a matter of recommendation.[103] Similarly, occasional demands

---

[101] See above for the formal description of its functions.

[102] O.S., 1945, par. 35.

[103] A good example is the successful fight that the Party chairman put up against a resolution which would have made it mandatory for the Socialist ministers to resign from the government unless certain specific conditions laid down by the Party were met by the coalition partner. ("Antrag Olah und Genossen," PTP, 1951, *Antragsheft*, p. 78.) In the form finally adopted, the Resolution merely required that the Party Directorate use "all appropriate means" to achieve the aims specified. ("Zusatzantrag zur Resolution XVIII der Parteivertretung," *Antragsheft*, 1951, p. 79.)

for compulsory consultation between leadership and low-level functionaries in specified instances have been uncompromisingly and successfully resisted by the Executive.[104] Second, the great majority of motions—usually the more controversial among them—are, in the official terminology, "passed on for action to the appropriate bodies," a method of disposition which is popularly referred to as amounting to a "first-class funeral." [105] The Party leadership maintains this extensive control over the fate of motions originating from the Conference floor in part through the institution known as "Committees for the Examination of Motions." [106] These committees, whose roll is made up in advance of the Conference, are largely composed of members of the Party "peak." [107] Toward the end of the Conference their spokesmen report to the Conference the method of disposal for each motion recommended by the committees. The vote on these recommendations, by a show of hands, has almost without exception become a mere formality. Not once since 1945 has the recommendation put forth by the *rapporteur* been turned down by the Conference; and in only one case does the record show a "fighting vote." [108] In many instances the result acceptable to the Executive is achieved by some diplomatic negotiations rather than by autocratic rule. The Executive attempts to work out its resolutions so as to "dispose" of those coming from the floor or attempts to negotiate formulations satisfactory to critics and criticized alike.[109]

---

[104] Such demands were contained, e.g., in Resolution III and *Antrag* No. 12, submitted to the 1951 Conference, and in the Motion (no number) by the District organization Alsergrund requiring that under certain specified conditions questions be submitted to a plebiscite by the membership. (*PTP*, 1949, pp. 123, 126.)

[105] Cf., e.g., Wilhelm Rosenzweig, *PTP*, 1949, p. 74. Resolution III (*PTP*, 1951, *Antragsheft*, p. 47) stated that "it is unbearable that motions . . . which for tactical reasons cannot be openly recommended for rejection are accepted to be passed on to the appropriate Party organizations."

[106] One committee scrutinizes motions pertaining to organization, the other motions on policy.

[107] The committee examining policy motions in 1951 included among its 18 members: 12 members of the Party Directorate; 1 Central Secretary; 1 Editor-in-chief of the *Arbeiter Zeitung*.

[108] A resolution, moved by the SJ delegation, was defeated by 111 votes in favor against 171 opposed (*PTP*, 1947, p. 123).

[109] As in the case of "Resolution Olah" (see footnote 103 above). Most critical motions, except where the language is too sharp or the conclusions too negative, are treated in this way.

Above all, however, it is the generally prevalent desire to preserve some show of unity as well as the absence, since 1945, of a coherent inner-party oppositional faction, which have prevented the Conference from seriously challenging the leadership.

The inability of the Conference, as constituted, to act as a legislature is shown on those rare occasions when the Executive, for reasons of its own, desires to shift the burden of responsibility for difficult decisions by throwing an as yet undecided issue into the Conference's lap. An example is the fate of the so-called "Hillegeist Plan." [110] Its author had widely canvassed the proposal that in cases where recipients had sufficient additional income, pensions should be accordingly reduced. Hillegeist had even submitted the plan to a plebiscite by the members of the trade union of which he was chairman.[111] The Executive, aware of the wide divergency of views on the proposal within the Party and of the political dangers it contained, referred the issue to the Conference for debate and decision.[112] The reaction of the Conference to having freedom and responsibility suddenly thrust upon it was one of helplessness. The debate was marked by apprehension that the revelation of division of opinion within the Party was harmful to it.[113] And vivid applause greeted the statement that "this question ought to be thoroughly discussed and thought through in a small circle; then we can come before you with a completely worked-out plan." [114] The explanation for the contradiction between the obvious reluctance or inability of the Party functionaries making up the Conference to decide a significant issue and their frequently expressed complaint at being invariably faced with accomplished facts has already been indicated. To enable an unstructured assembly of several hundred delegates, meeting for a few days once a year, seriously to debate and to decide a complicated and politically dangerous issue would have been possible only if the Executive had made every effort

---

[110] "Antrag Hillegeist und Genossen," *PTP*, 1951, *Antragsheft*, pp. 16–19.

[111] The Union of Employees in the private sector of the economy. (*Angestellte in der Privatwirtschaft.*)

[112] *PTP*, 1951, p. 122.

[113] Cf., e.g., the following statement by one of the Conference delegates: "One thing has depressed us deeply; we have immediately seen that this plan has not been issued as the common plan of the Party Executive and the Trade Unions, but as the individual action of a single representative. I believe that, when something is worked out, it always first requires the approval of the Party Executive." (Josef Greier, *PTP*, 1951, p. 118.)

[114] Robert Uhlir, *ibid.*, pp. 112–13.

to prepare the delegates by briefing them on the issue and stimulating prior debate. The traditional stress on an appearance of party unity as well as the centralization of the party machine have accustomed the delegates to receive the decisions which are handed down to them,[115] though there might be occasional grumbles.

The most important instrument—at least in theory—yet devised to render leaders accountable still remains to be discussed. The Central Directorate is elected by the Conference. Yet Party tradition, which aims at avoiding open contests which would disclose inner-party strife, as well as the method of voting, have done much to deprive this weapon of its effectiveness. The voting is done by striking out and substituting names on a list prepared for the delegates by a Conference-appointed Election Committee.[116] The true arena of contest is the Committee room rather than the Conference floor. For not a single candidate proposed by the Committee has been voted down by the delegates since 1945. The only means used by Conference delegates to show disapproval of a candidate has been a sometimes organized campaign to strike names off the list. A comparatively small number of strike-outs is then already considered a serious sign of a candidate's unpopularity.[117] The replacement of a candidate of the "platform" by one from the "floor" could only be the result of extensive prior caucusing by a strong faction. When this conditions exists [118] or when strong sentiment for a particular candidate is known to be felt, the Committee will

---

[115] The fate of the Hillegeist Plan at the 1951 Conference is significant and typical. On motion of the chairman, the Conference voted to send it back to the appropriate commission which, in turn, brought forward its own, noncommittal version (Resolution XX, *PTP*, 1951, p. 277), with a recommendation to "pass the question for consideration and clarification to the Party Executive who, in agreement with the Socialist fraction of the Trade Union Federation and the Socialist Parliamentary Club, will at the earliest moment work out appropriate proposals." This recommendation was duly approved by the Conference.

[116] Its members, as far as I have been able to ascertain, are drawn from the upper-middle range of Party officialdom (i.e., District chairmen, members of the *Länder* Directorates).

[117] The results of the voting are frequently not published. The highest number of such strike-outs on record is said to be 80 or 100. (The first figure was mentioned to me in conversation; the second was reported in *Der neue Vorwärts*, November 13, 1949.) This sign of unpopularity has not, however, prevented the annual renomination and re-election of the candidate concerned.

[118] Since 1945 it has not.

usually avoid a floor fight by anticipating the wishes of the delegates.[119] As the Committee merely acts as the spokesman for the Directorate, the method of election has, in fact, turned into one of co-optation, whereby new members are selected by the incumbent top leaders whose discretion is tempered by the necessity to make concessions to strong informal pressures.[120]

Even though we may accept the conclusion that the Party Conference is not exercising those functions which "constitutionally" are assigned to it, it would be erroneous to assume that it is merely tradition and custom that keep the institution alive. Rather would we suggest that the Conference fulfills certain functions for the Party which are significant even though they may be latent. Its continued existence is necessary to the maintenance of the myth of inner democracy, a myth which, though by now almost as nebulous as the proverbial Emperor's clothes, the leadership dare not discard. Furthermore, the Conference provides the lower functionaries with a feeling of "community" by bringing them into close contact with each other and the otherwise remote top leaders.[121] Finally, the Conference serves as a forum at which, however muted, the sentiments and wishes of the rank and file are brought out into the open. What is significant about the many utterances by local functionaries is not their specific content but the general current of opinion, the revelation of the kinds of problems which occupy their minds, the virulence and the targets of their criticism; these set for the top leadership the broad framework which circumscribes their area of maneuver. Pent-up emotions and the frustrations of the humble have been able to find an escape valve at the Conference all the more easily since 1945 because of the disappearance of such leaders as Bauer, Renner, *et al.*, who, before 1934, dominated Conference proceedings by their towering intellectuality.

The Composition of the Party Conference

Because the Party Conference is conceived as the central institution of the structure of "inner democracy," it is assumed to be the voice of the

---

[119] This is said to have happened in the case of Karl Czernetz, who was nominated for a position on the Party Directorate at the 1946 Conference in spite of sharply critical views regarding Minister Helmer which he expressed at the Conference.

[120] Cf. Michels, *op. cit.*, pp. 104 ff.

[121] On the basis of personal observation, gossip and lobbying are, on the whole, much more popular with the delegates than the often dreary and repetitive debates and formal reports of the Conference.

"people," i.e., of the mass of Party members. Thus the delegates are in theory supposed to be almost exclusively the representatives of the Party's territorial organizations, elected by, and therefore accountable to, the mass membership.[122] In fact, elected representatives of the District organizations have, as a rule, made up slightly less than two-thirds of the total Conference membership.[123] The remaining third is composed of the members of the Central and *Länder* Directorates as well as the appointed delegates of the "organizations with delegating powers," such as the SJ, Socialist fraction of the TU, and so on. In view of the fact that showdown votes hardly ever occur at the Conference, the presence of a sizable minority of non-elected delegates hardly can be said to affect significantly the nature of the Conference proceedings. Nevertheless, their number is frequently the target of criticism by District representatives who have the uneasy feeling that the democratic character of the Conference is being impaired and that the Conference is being manipulated by functionaries who are not representative of rank-and-file sentiment.[124] The District delegations themselves, however, are hardly qualified to play the role of grassroots representatives of the masses. As a rule, the chairman of the District organization heads the delegation while the remaining quota of seats is rotated among the members of the District Directorate and the Section leaders.[125] The re-

---

[122] See, e.g., Robert Danneberg, *PTP*, 1919, pp. 185–86.

[123] Before 1934 the situation was about the same. (Cf. *PTP*, 1920, p. 165; *PTP*, 1921, p. 170; *PTP*, 1926, p. 364; *PTP*, 1928, p. 36; *PTP*, 1929, p. 39.) The percentage of District delegates ranged from 65 to 68 per cent.

[124] This is attested by the disavowal on the part of the official *SPOe-Vertrauensmann*: "It is clearly apparent that the majority of the Conference is in the hands of the District delegates and not, *as is frequently assumed* [italics added] that the votes of the central organizations or the votes of the Party Directorate outweigh the others." (II [December, 1947], 334.) And again (III [December, 1948], 365): "[The figures] repudiate all arguments that the Party Conference is directed from above. . . ."

[125] At the 1948 Conference the delegates held the following Party offices (*SPOe-Vertrauensmann*, III [December, 1948], 366): District chairmen and vice-chairmen, 126; members of District Control, 18; leading functionaries in District organizations, 87; Section chairmen and vice-chairmen, 60; Trade Union and plant functionaries, 78; leading functionaries in the Central Organization and the Executive, 43; leading functionaries in *Land* organizations and the Party press, 62.

quirement that the delegates be elected by the membership is treated purely as a formality.[126]

Thus, Conference delegates come, by and large, from the upper and upper-middle strata of the Party hierarchy. The majority of them hold public office, elective or appointive.[127] They are mostly "old fighters," their political roots firmly embedded in the Social Democratic Party of the First Republic.[128] With few exceptions, delegates are not holders of jobs paid out of Party funds, for, as a rule, District Secretaries are not selected as delegates. The factors inhibiting the delegates' freedom of action and criticism concerning the leadership are therefore of a subtler kind than outright financial dependence. As holders of public offices they must obtain a minimum of central Party endorsement of their candidatures; as occupants of jobs in public or semi-public areas of the economy in which the Party wields great influence, their career chances are likely to be affected by a show of open opposition even when they hold secure positions. As long as the Socialist Party shares governmental power, its leaders must be sought out by lower Party officials for the political favors these are able to dispense; furthermore, in view of the co-optative nature of the process of recruitment for leadership positions, advancement within the Party is difficult in the face of opposition by top leaders.[129] In fact, it is the nonelected delegate from organizations not organizationally subservient to the Party

---

[126] Cf. Danneberg's criticism of this practice as early as 1919 (*PTP*, 1919, p. 186). In one of the Districts where I attended the election of delegates to the 1952 Conference, the chairman proposed a list headed by himself and including the vice-chairman, the head of the District women's organization, and two Section chairmen. The list was unanimously accepted without debate.

[127] In 1946, 47 were members of the Central or *Land* governments; and 233 held elective offices or positions of mayor or vice-mayor (71 members of Parliament, 83 members of provincial legislatures, the remainder in local legislative bodies). *SPOe-Vertrauensmann*, II (January, 1947), 11.

[128] At the 1953 Conference more than two-thirds of the delegates were over forty-five (*SPOe-Vertrauensmann*, VIII [December, 1953], 387–88); 80 per cent had been Party members before 1934. (*Ibid.*)

[129] The obstacles which Josef Hindels, the most outspoken critic of the leadership, has encountered—according to his own account—well illustrate this point. For several years Hindels was a paid functionary of the SJ. After leaving the SJ, Party chairman Schärf vetoed Hindels' employment by the Party publishing concern, *Konzentration*. When strong support for Hindels' nomination as a parliamentary candidate developed in one of the Lower Austrian District organizations, Minister Helmer made strenuous and successful efforts to prevent his nomination.

proper, resting on somewhat more independent centers of support, who enjoys greater freedom than the elected District delegate.[130] Although it would be misleading to assume that the factors of dependence have resulted in squashing criticism, they do make its expression an act of some political courage. Party Conferences are not, by any means, well-rehearsed cheering sessions. Indeed, serious criticism as well as a multitude of minor complaints have been voiced at many of the postwar Conferences.[131] Criticism from the floor may reflect divergent viewpoints within the ranks of the top leadership; furthermore, the traditional commitment to "inner democracy" makes it impossible to crush opposition overtly or even to "punish" severe and persistent critics.[132] However much top leaders may wish to escape what they consider factious or irresponsible criticism,[133] Party tradition militates against them:

A comrade who has become a minister must not thereby become immune against every criticism from the ranks of the organization, as he would like to. For it is we who have decided that comrades shall go into the government and therefore we have the right, if something does not suit us or when we believe that the comrades are following the wrong path, to tell them so, even when they are ministers.[134]

Stability of Leadership

As a consequence of the purely formal nature of the electoral process within the Party, leadership exhibits an extremely high degree of stability. Except for internal factional struggles which may lead to the elimination

---

[130] Thus Hillegeist, a powerful trade union leader, frequently has acted as the bête noire at Party Conferences. Significantly, it was in his union that Hindels found a position after having been denied one by the Party.

[131] The 1946 Conference was marked by a concentrated attack on Minister Helmer. In 1947 Erwin Scharf presented his extremely critical "Resolution of the 44." At the 1949 Conference much criticism was voiced as part of an election post-mortem. In 1951 "Resolution Olah" reflected a widespread feeling of dissatisfaction with the leadership.

[132] Karl Holoubek, e.g., formerly a leading functionary of the R.S., had made little effort to ingratiate himself with the leadership. Nevertheless he became a *Bundesrat* and, in 1953, *Nationalrat*, remaining chairman of his District organization since 1946.

[133] See, e.g., statements by Otto Tschadek (*PTP*, 1946, p. 140) and Max Neugebauer (*ibid.*, p. 141), attacking critics of the Executive.

[134] Holoubek, *PTP*, 1946, p. 148.

of the defeated faction from top positions, members of the Central Directorate enjoy practically lifetime tenure.

The composition of the Party Executive has undergone almost no change since 1946, except for its recent expansion and for the replacement of members who have died. Erwin Scharf, foremost spokesman of the Left, was dropped from the Executive in 1946. However, he retained the position of Central Secretary until 1947. At the same time, Scharf's close political and personal associate Hilde Krones moved from the Executive to the Control, remaining a member of the Directorate until 1948 (the year of Scharf's expulsion from the Party). At the 1948 Conference Hilde Krones was not renominated for a place on the Directorate. In addition to the elimination of Scharf and Krones from peak positions, only two other members of the Directorate lost their seats during the seven-year period from 1946 to 1953.[135] Leadership *in perpetuo* is not a new development in Austrian Socialism. The Executive of the Social Democratic Party similarly remained practically unchanged from 1920 to 1932.[136]

Automatic retention of leadership by the incumbent often leads to the assumption that these positions, once obtained, belong rightfully to the holder. In this way arrangements which originally may have been fortuitous or provisional are indefinitely perpetuated.[137] In consequence, top positions are held exclusively by old or aging persons and thus represent a bar to the advancement of younger men in the Party.[138] As the present leadership was newly recruited in 1945 and contains a considerable number of younger members, the problem of overaging has not as yet become pressing.[139] Since the failure to use the electoral process as a means of replenishing

---

[135] Karl Mantler and Franz Rauscher. They also failed to be renominated as candidates for Parliament in 1949. Personal rather than political reasons seem to have been involved in this shift.

[136] Except where death forced the replacement of the incumbent. Cf. also Michels (*op. cit.*, p. 99) for a description of the same phenomenon in the German Socialist Party as early as 1900.

[137] The outstanding example—though other factors undoubtedly play a part—is the retention by Dr. Schärf of the Party chairmanship from 1945 to 1957, although, by his own admission, his initial selection was purely provisional. (Adolf Schärf, *April 1945 in Wien*, p. 70.)

[138] See, for instance, complaints at the 1949 Party Conference (*PTP*, 1949, pp. 34, 80).

[139] In 1946 almost half of the members of the Party Directorate (18 out of 40) were under fifty, five were even under forty, and only four over sixty. (*SPOe-Vertrauensmann*, II [January, 1947], 11.)

leadership ranks extends to all levels of the organization, Sections and Districts as well as the central machine are subject to domination by an aging cadre whose habit of "sticking" is widely and unfavorably commented upon.

Accumulation of Offices

Socialists have generally considered it desirable to distribute public and Party positions, unpaid as well as paid, as widely as possible.[140] The principle was firmly anchored in the Organizational Statute, at least where public positions were concerned.[141] It reflects the traditional Socialist suspicion of *Bonzentum*, the fear that leaders will become "big shots" who will lose contact with the working class and cease to serve its cause. The rationale may be summarized in the statement that no Socialist should have too much power, too much money, or too much work.[142] All three negatives are violated by accumulation of offices.

The actual extent of office accumulation in the SPOe is not a matter of record. At the 1952 Conference the Executive was forced to accept a motion calling for a report on the extent of accumulation of offices, but action on the motion was successfully avoided.[143] The practice of combining a multiplicity of positions in the hands of a comparatively small group of high-level functionaries—whether as the result of the shortage of qualified personnel (the official explanation) [144] or of the functionaries' drive for increased power—clearly runs counter to the professed aversion to concentration of power, as well as to the insistence that a functionary should give adequate time to the performance of each function.

As an expression of the belief that service in the cause of the Party should not be the source of material rewards as well as of the insistence that members and leaders remain on a footing of equality, the Party long ago instituted a Party tax. Initially adopted by the *Land* organizations, it was put

---

[140] Cf. Danneberg (*PTP*, 1919, p. 180): "In the Party there arises a strong sentiment against the so-called accumulation of offices, against the accumulation of Party offices and public functions. This movement has a sound basis."

[141] O.S., 1945, par. 50.

[142] This represents a paraphrase of a statement made to me by Joseph Kratky of the Central Secretariat.

[143] The *Land* organizations were requested to supply a compilation of relevant data within six months. No reports were submitted.

[144] Cf. Danneberg in 1919 (!) using this argument (*PTP*, 1919, p. 180). Also, "Politik darf kein Geschäft sein," *SPOe-Vertrauensmann*, VI (December, 1951), 374.

on a unified national basis by a directive of the Central Directorate in 1931.[145] Subject to the tax, which was reinstituted in 1947, are all functionaries representing the Party in public bodies and Party employees earning more than a minimum income.[146] All other Party members earning comparable incomes are also expected to subject themselves voluntarily to it.[147] The rate is evenly progressive above the tax-free level.[148] For several reasons it is difficult to establish how effective the tax is in leveling the income of higher Party functionaries: no data or figures on collection are generally revealed; the collection itself is decentralized; [149] and no information exists as to the number or extent of exceptions made by the Executive.[150] Under the postwar regulation, two features of the pre-1934 directive were not revived; then all Socialist members of parliament suffered a 15 or 25 per cent deduction from their salaries,[151] and all holders of two or three elective offices had to surrender a large part of the second and all of the third salary to the Party.[152] Proposals put forth since 1945 aimed at putting a rigid ceiling on the incomes of all Party functionaries have failed to be accepted.[153]

In spite of the Party tax, the standard of living enjoyed by many Party leaders is considered "unsocialistically" high by many members. Spokesmen for the top have tried hard to explain to lower-level functionaries that legal provisions, apart from the Party tax, prevent holders of more than one position from enjoying more than one salary; that many public positions

---

[145] *Jahrbuch*, 1931, pp. 74–75.

[146] This includes nonparty organizations such as the Trade Union Federation, the Chambers of Labor, and public corporations. (See O.S., 1955, par. 48, for the most recent formulation.)

[147] "Parteisteuer," *SPOe-Vertrauensmann*, II (October, 1947), 269.

[148] In 1947 it was fixed at 2½ per cent for income from 600 to 1,000 schillings and another 2½ per cent for every additional 500 schillings (*ibid.*). In 1948 the rates were adjusted and the levying as well as imposition turned over to the *Land* Directorates (*Report of PE, PTP*, 1948, pp. 23–24). The exact rates have not been published since.

[149] I was assured, however, that the Party Control strictly supervises enforcement.

[150] The Executive is entitled to reduce or waive the tax in special cases. (*Report of PE, PTP*, 1948, p. 23.)

[151] Depending on whether they lived in Vienna or the provinces. For the latter the lower rate was probably based on the higher expenses they incurred in exercising their public function.

[152] *Jahrbuch*, 1931, pp. 74–75.

[153] Two motions to the 1948 Conference (*Report of PE*, Nos. 53, 54) were "passed on to the Directorate" and not heard of again.

are merely burdensome and unrewarded; and, finally, that the use of auto-mobiles is essential to busy officials.[154] This last item touches on a particu-larly sore point. Among a population where cars are still considered a lux-ury,[155] the use of shiny American limousines by their political leaders is a frequent source of adverse comment.[156] Even though use of a motorcar and the service of an attendant chauffeur may not actually estrange the Socialist functionary from the "people," these symbolize to many Party workers the gap that divides "top dog" from "the masses." By showing little discretion in this matter, leaders have given powerful impetus to the charge of *Bonzentum.*

Nomination for Public Offices

Since 1918, elections to Austrian legislative bodies have been conducted on the basis of proportional representation and the so-called electoral list system.[157] Under this system the voter is presented with a list of candidates prepared by the Party and is offered a choice only between competing party slates, not between candidates. We need not here be concerned with the merits of this as compared with alternate electoral systems, except insofar as the election and nomination process affects the inner structure of the Socialist Party. Party leaders, arguing for "Party responsibility," and a stress on "measures, not men," have in the past staunchly supported the list system.[158]

---

[154] "Politik darf kein Geschäft sein," *loc. cit.*

[155] In 1956 the total number of passenger cars registered in Austria was 189,632. (*Statistische Nachrichten*, XII/I [1957], p. 36.) Thus, fewer than 3 per cent of the population were car owners.

[156] See, e.g., the photograph of a row of cars parked in front of the hall where the Party Conference of 1952 was being held, with the malicious caption, "The 'Auto'crats of the SPOe." (*Das Kleine Volksblatt*, November 11, 1952.) A signifi-cant example of the traditional socialist attitude toward the possession of motor-cars is the letter to the editor of the *Arbeiter Zeitung* (November 5, 1953) by an old Party functionary asking for advice as to whether an occasional trip in his son-in-law's car was compatible with his own commitment to socialism.

[157] For the elections of November, 1945, the statute enacted by the Provisional Government (StGBl No. 198/1945) essentially re-established the system in use during the First Republic. In 1949 Parliament passed a revised electoral law set-ting up a system of "loose lists."

[158] Bruno Pittermann, *Stenographisches Protokoll*, 94. Sitzung des Nationalrates der Republik Oesterreich, December 10, 1948, pp. 2605 ff. (Hereafter cited as *Steno. Prot.*)

Such support has been a logical consequence of the historical role which socialist thought has assigned to the Party—a role before which individuals pale to insignificance. Paradoxically, it has also been a consequence of the commitment to "inner democracy." For this commitment implied policy determination by the whole Party or its elected organs, not by the parliamentary fraction or the electorate at large. Accountability was not conceived as a relationship between elected representative and local constituent, but between parliamentary delegate and the delegating body, the Party. Parliamentary "club discipline," by which members of the fraction are prevented from straying from the fold by speaking or—worse—voting against policy decisions taken by the Party leadership, is rigidly enforced.[159] This arrangement which permits management of the parliamentary force with military precision, is obviously convenient to the leaders so that no suggestions for change can be expected from them. There has been widespread popular dissatisfaction with the "remoteness" of representative from constituent resulting from the system. The representatives themselves have frequently expressed discontent at the rigid discipline to which they are subjected. Yet so far they have failed to dent the determination of the top leaders to maintain the traditional system.[160] The amended electoral law of 1949,[161] which provided for a system of "loose lists," was passed over official Socialist objections.[162] Though the law in theory gives the voter power to alter the order of candidates prepared by the parties, or even to substitute names for those presented, the practical effect of the change has been insignificant.[163] Aspirants to political office remain in fact as dependent as before on the party machines for nomination and election.

While the electoral law places the right to nominate candidates almost exclusively in the hands of the party machines, the Organizational Statute of the SPOe attempts to prevent nominating power from being concen-

---

[159] The SPOe and OeVP require of their candidates signed statements that in case of their expulsion from the Party they will relinquish their parliamentary seats.

[160] The suggestion by Karl Mark (*SPOe-Vertrauensmann*, VI [December, 1951], 366) that the German system might serve as a model for Austria has met with no official response.

[161] *Bundesgesetz vom 18. Mai 1949 über die Wahl des Nationalrates (BGBl* No. 129).

[162] Cf. Pittermann, "Listenlockerung," *Arbeiter Zeitung*, May 11, 1949; also Czernetz, as reported in *Arbeiter Zeitung*, February 11, 1949.

[163] See *Die Nationalratswahlen vom 9. Oktober 1949*, p. 21.

trated at the top of the leadership. The task of proposing candidates is, in the first instance, entrusted to local committees representing the District organizations.[164] While the Party Executive's agreement to the lists is required, final decision in case of disagreement between District and Executive lies with a special *Parteirat*.[165]

This formal arrangement has brought it about that candidates' lists result from a prolonged bargaining process that takes places between District organizations and the Executive. In this process certain rules have firmly established themselves. The Executive is allowed a limited number of *Parteinotwendigkeiten* ("Party essentials") whom it may require the Districts to include as candidates in prominent positions. These "Executive" candidates, on the other hand, accept the duty to "look after" their sponsoring Districts. Even in the case of these candidates an outright *Diktat* by the Executive is unknown; a candidate cannot be pushed through against the determined resistance of the District organizations.[166] Conversely, it appears out of the question that a District organization can succeed in nominating a candidate who is definitely *persona non grata* to the Executive or to a powerful member of it.[167]

The limitation on the power of the central leadership in the area of nominations is thus real and prevents the nominating process from becoming a manipulative tool in its hands. Even men known as strong critics of the central leadership can be barred from candidates' lists only with difficulty, particularly when they enjoy strong and undivided local organizational support.[168] The SPOe's parliamentary representation reflects geographically this degree of power decentralization. More than two-thirds of the Socialist *Nationalrat* members have their political roots in the elec-

---

[164] As the election districts (*Wahlkreise*) are larger than the Party districts, candidates' lists must be based on agreement among a number of Party District organizations.

[165] This *Parteirat* is composed of the Central and Land Directorates and the Central Women's Committee. (O.S., 1945, pars. 45, 48, as amended by O.S., 1955, par. 43.)

[166] I have been assured of this by a number of Party functionaries at various levels of the hierarchy.

[167] Cf. footnote 129 above. It should be noted, however, that the local leaders succeeded in replacing the unpopular incumbent with a candidate whose SJ background and affiliation with Hindels made him hardly an agreeable choice to the top leadership.

[168] Holoubek and Mark are examples of this.

toral district in which they are elected.[169] In spite of the electoral system of rigid party lists, which obviously furthers centralization of political power, the inner-party arrangement discussed has succeeded in giving considerable scope to the representation of local interests and has thereby diminished the dependence of aspiring or incumbent members on the "peak."

Party Discipline and Inner-Party Opposition

The insistence on party unity has long been an article of faith among Austrian Socialists. A division within Socialist ranks has been viewed as an ideological and organizational calamity of the highest order. The problem which the Party leadership has had to face—and has faced rather differently in the First and Second Republics—is the choice of means to maintain this unity. Was unity to be achieved by insistence on adherence to a clearly formulated "party line" or tolerance toward diverse viewpoints? Under Bauer's leadership in the First Republic, the Party adopted a policy of extreme tolerance toward the expression and propagation of divergent viewpoints. Bauer himself had risen to a position of dominance as the spokesman for a Left oppositional faction within the Party, and the well-defined groupings which during World War I had struggled for supremacy continued into the First Republic. Furthermore, the strength of radical sentiments in the Social Democratic Party, as well as the insignificance of the existing Communist Party, combined to create an atmosphere in which the notion of "deviation" found little support. In addition, the rank and file of the Party obviously shared Bauer's fervent commitment to the maintenance of proletarian unity in Austria and was persuaded by him that only tolerance of diversity could avoid a split similar to that which had divided and weakened German Socialism.[170]

---

[169] Cf. *Der österreichische Nationalrat und Bundesrat 1949*. The remainder are almost exclusively representatives of the Trade Unions or prominent Party functionaries whose reputation is more than local. With very few exceptions they are candidates on Vienna lists. Localism in Vienna is less pronounced, reputations are wider, and more positions are open. Significantly, when through reapportionment of seats Vienna lost some to the provinces, the provincial organizations insisted on filling them with local candidates, increasing, in the sarcastic words of a Vienna functionary, "the number of hicks in Parliament."

[170] The following impassioned affirmation of this conviction by Bauer was greeted with "stormy, minute-long, enthusiastic applause" (*PTP*, 1926, p. 128): "A hun-

Yet a line was drawn between "dissent" and "disloyalty" and the Party did not hesitate to punish, by immediate expulsion, those who were convicted of the latter. "Splitters" who failed to see the error of their ways were not allowed to continue their activities.[171] Free discussion and efforts to win adherents for honestly held opinions were not interpreted as potentially harmful to the Party.[172] But the expression of views likely to bring discredit to the movement—the washing of dirty Party linen in public—was severely discouraged. Any accusation reflecting on the honor of a fellow Party member was, so the Organizational Statute decreed, to be brought before special tribunals set up by the Party and not before the public courts.[173] The glorious name of the Party was not to be tarnished by unsavory revelations which would provide the "enemy"—the bourgeoisie— with easy targets and diminish faith in the Party's splendid historical role.

After 1945 the existence of an active Communist Party, small in size but known to possess the backing of the Soviet occupation army, greatly diminished the tolerance toward diversity of viewpoint within the SPOe. In view of the danger of forced merger and subsequent absorption by the Communists—the fate of Socialist parties in Eastern Germany, Poland, Hungary, and elsewhere, was never far from their minds—the leaders of the SPOe drew a rigorous demarcation line dividing Socialists from Communists. Thus the Party now not only "outlawed" actions clearly detrimental to its organizational interests but punished deviation from a set of principles. These principles, though nowhere officially enunciated, provide the framework within which free discussion is deemed permissible. As outlined by the foremost Left critic of the leadership, these principles are based on unquestioning acceptance of *democratic* socialism; they therefore acquire unconditional support of freedom as an absolute value and consequent condemnation of the so-called People's Democracies as dictatorships;

---

dred times rather walk the wrong road united—for mistakes can be corrected— than to split the Movement for the sake of the right road."

[171] See, e.g., the Conference discussion on the activities of Rothe and Frey, two leaders of pro-Communist *Arbeitsgemeinschaften* within the Party; particularly the statements by Fritz Adler (PTP, 1920, pp. 188–201) and Otto Bauer (*ibid.*, pp. 207–11).

[172] *Ibid.*, p. 208. In the case of Rothe and Frey, the Executive had even provided them with the paper required for the publication of their views in their own newspapers. In the words of Otto Bauer: "I consider it necessary to state that the freedom of expression, of opposition, even the freedom of organizing groups must not be touched, as long as the unity of action is not endangered" (*ibid.*).

[173] O.S., 1926, par. 59.

and, most important, the rejection of unconditional co-operation with the Communist Party or the Soviet bloc.[174] Attempts by spokesmen of the Left to establish an equally clear line dividing the Socialist from the bourgeois position has, however, remained ineffective. In view of the SPOe's commitment to coalition with an anti-Socialist party the delineation of Socialist Party principles could be effective only toward the Communist Left, not the bourgeois Right.

Party Discipline Enforced: The Case of Erwin Scharf

The expulsion of Erwin Scharf, Central Secretary of the SPOe from 1945 to 1947, represents the most dramatic instance wherein adherence to the Social Democratic principles put forth above has been enforced at the risk of a serious split. A brief recital of the facts in the case will illustrate the area of nonconformity enjoyed by Leftists within the Party and the measures by which the leadership has dealt with those who, like Scharf, became identified too closely with the Communist position.

In the unsettled days of April, 1945, Scharf, a little-known member of the Revolutionary Socialists, was appointed to one of the two Central Party Secretariats. It is not clear whether his appointment was due to an effort to give the R.S. equal representation on the Secretariat[175] or whether the impression that Scharf enjoyed cordial relations with the Russians and Yugoslavs was decisive.[176] He seemed a personable and talented young man and was accepted as a representative of the young Left.[177] In the years 1946–1947, Scharf, casting himself in the role of defender of Otto Bauer's heritage against the then-dominant "reformist" leadership,[178] became the figure around whom rallied all those who disliked the postwar course taken by the Party's leadership. Scharf's attempt to create an organized inner-party Left opposition reached a climax in the "Resolution of the

---

[174] Hindels, "Das Recht auf Opposition," *Die Zukunft*, III (December, 1948), 353–55.
[175] Scharf himself claims this to have been the reason. (*Der neue Vorwärts*, December 3, 1950.)
[176] Adolf Schärf, *Zwischen Demokratie und Volksdemokratie*, p. 63.
[177] Gabriele Proft, *PTP*, 1948, p. 50.
[178] Cf. his articles, "Neuorientierung des Bürgertums?" "Staat und Gesellschaft," and "Offene Fragen" in *Die Zukunft*, I, 1946. The theoretical issues will be more fully discussed in Chapter 4.

44," presented by him to the 1947 Conference. The Resolution criticized the leading men in the SPOe as partly responsible for the alleged breakdown of the Austrian economy and the deterioration of the working-class standard of living. By reviving the traditional slogan "the enemy is on the Right," it attempted to shift the weight of the political struggle away from the "ridiculously small Communist Party." And the SPOe's "unclear and compromising attitude in decisive political and economic questions" was scored as betraying the glorious tradition of Austrian Social Democracy and the Revolutionary Socialists.[179] This Resolution was sharply resisted by the Executive and defeated by the Conference. No disciplinary measures were taken against Scharf at the time. His position in the Party, however, was being gradually weakened. In 1946 a third Central Secretary was added in the person of the "strong" Karl Waldbrunner. As a consequence of sponsoring the Resolution, Scharf failed to be reappointed to his post as Central Secretary; in March, 1948, he ceased to act as co-editor of the *SPOe-Vertrauensmann*. In May of the same year the Party Executive prohibited his publication *Der Kämpfer*, a monthly intended to express the Revolutionary Socialist viewpoint,[180] and, in addition, instituted proceedings against him before a Party tribunal, which led to a one-year public-speaking ban.

Scharf's next step provided the Executive with the case it needed to rid the Party of the man whom many had come to consider a Communist agent.[181] In a move to arouse hostility to the incumbent leadership, Scharf, shortly before the 1948 Party Conference, published a pamphlet in which he accused the Party's leaders of betrayal of the traditional principles of Austrian Socialism by their relentless campaign against the Communist Party and their anti-Soviet attitude. He supported his argument by the use of confidential documents to which he, as Central Secretary, had had access.[182] The Executive moved without delay. One day after the *Arbeiter*

---

[179] *PTP*, 1947, pp. 250–51.

[180] This claim was publicly rejected by a number of former leading R.S. functionaries who dissociated themselves from the contents of *Der Kämpfer*. (*Arbeiter Zeitung*, May 21, 1948.) For the only detailed, though inevitably one-sided, account see Erwin Scharf, *Ich darf nicht schweigen* (Selbstverlag, Vienna, 1948), pp. 105–13.

[181] Cf. Adolf Schärf, *Zwischen Demokratie . . .* , pp. 64–67. Schärf's conviction was supported by Mrs. Jenny Strasser, wife of the chairman of the SJ, who had had close contact with Scharf. Scharf's activities subsequent to his expulsion lend further support to it.

[182] *Ich darf nicht schweigen, passim.*

Zeitung had first announced the news of Scharf's action—under the heading "A Communist Agent" [183]—it already reported to its readers that a Party tribunal had recommended his expulsion. There was some confusion as to the exact nature of Scharf's crime. The first announcement stressed his revelation of material which he had been pledged to keep secret, as well as his advocacy of unconditional co-operation with the Communist Party.[184] In a subsequent emendation, a spokesman for the Executive denied that Scharf's breach of confidence was the reason for his expulsion and listed his desire for unity with the Communists as the sole cause.[185] The Party Conference to which Scharf appealed his expulsion reaffirmed the tribunal's decision by a practically unanimous vote after a debate which showed that Scharf had lost the support even of those who had worked closely with him before he had come to reveal himself as an uncritical advocate of a pro-Soviet policy.[186]

Equally effectively, though less openly, the Party leadership proceeded against other manifestations of pro-Communist sentiment. The Socialist student publication *strom*, which had been under the influence of the "Scharfists," was cut off from Party subsidies and left to wither.[187] But so small proved the pro-Soviet appeal of Scharf that only an insignificant number of SPOe members followed him into exile, and no split or purge of any size took place in the wake of his expulsion.

Party Unity in the Face of the Communist Threat

The establishment of a war psychology concerning the Communist threat led to the intimidation of non-Communist Leftists by the occa-

---

[183] *Arbeiter Zeitung*, October 30, 1948.
[184] *Ibid.*
[185] Pittermann, *Arbeiter Zeitung*, November 4, 1948. It may perhaps be assumed that the rank and file did not consider the revelation of confidential discussions, if based on truthful accounts, a serious offense. Strictly speaking, the concept of "inner democracy" should have precluded the Executive's keeping secrets from the "sovereign" body of Party members.
[186] *PTP*, 1948, p. 52. One speaker expressed misgivings because of the obvious lack of independence of the committee which had reviewed Scharf's appeal from the Executive. (Robert Hutterer, *PTP*, 1948, p. 44.)
[187] Cf. *Der neue Vorwärts*, August 14, 1949. Two independent sources (Dr. Ernst Mayer, Mrs. Jenny Strasser) agreed that the students' organization had been infiltrated by Communists, who had taken over leading positions.

sionally indiscriminate use of the "Red smear" as well as the frequent institution of disciplinary proceedings against members suspected of pro-Communist leanings.[188] In the face of the Communist challenge, the insistence on presenting a united party front increased and contributed to the creation of an atmosphere markedly inhospitable to spirited discussion of inner-party problems. Mention has already been made of the decision to discontinue publication in the *Arbeiter Zeitung* of all motions submitted to the Party Conference.[189] Furthermore, in reporting Party Conferences, the *Arbeiter Zeitung* suppresses almost entirely all critical references and presents a propagandistic picture of party harmony and unshaken confidence.[190] In its "Letters to the Editor" column the *Arbeiter Zeitung* has never published a statement critical of Party policy, performance, or personalities. The boycott of Joseph Buttinger's *Am Beispiel Oesterreichs*, as well as the attempt to blot out his memory by rewriting the history of the illegal period, has already been mentioned. Thus, the tendency is to avoid public discussion of embarrassing issues with the argument that the Party's enemies alone would benefit by it. This results in the ludicrous and unhealthy situation whereby discontent and criticism are widely voiced in private conversation but not a breath of it is allowed to penetrate into the official Party literature. One must agree with the observation that the warlike "picture of defense" maintained by the Party vis-à-vis the political enemy is detrimental to free discussion and is consciously used by the leadership as a means to limit it.[191] In contrast to the tolerance shown by the Party in the First Republic to the formation of oppositional factions, the tendency now is to view with disfavor any attempts at their revival.[192]

---

[188] Cf. the protests by a spokesman for the SJ (Josef Handler, *PTP*, 1950, p. 148) and the students' organization (Hugo Pepper, *PTP*, 1949, p. 29) and the warning by Dr. Wilhelm Stammer against the habit of calling any dissenter a Communist. ("Mehr Mut zur Diskussion," *SPOe-Vertrauensmann*, II [October, 1947], 268.) See also *Der neue Vorwärts*, November 4, 1951.

[189] According to a critic, this change was defended as necessary to present a united front to the enemy. (Paul Blau, "Innere Demokratie," *Die Zukunft*, IV [February, 1949], 55–58.

[190] *Ibid.* Blau's criticism was corroborated by a comparison between the Conference protocols and the reports published in the *Arbeiter Zeitung*.

[191] Hindels, "Für freie Diskussion in der Partei," *loc. cit.*

[192] Benedikt Kautsky (son of Karl Kautsky) has stated the case for unity in "Parteiopposition" (*Die Zukunft*, IV [February, 1949], 44–48), arguing that the Party cannot afford the kind of factionalization that had prevailed in the First Republic. A similar reluctance to countenance the organization of factions within

It should not be assumed from the foregoing that all expressions of inner-party criticism have been suppressed. Criticism which remains impersonal, is not defeatist, and clearly marks itself off from the Communist position has been freely expressed in Party publications such as *Die Zukunft*.[193] Furthermore, the failure of a coherent oppositional faction to make an appearance since 1945 can hardly be ascribed to the repressive disciplinary measures taken by the Right-wing leadership. An attempt in 1945 to form a discussion group of former Revolutionary Socialists was discontinued because of lack of interest.[194] Scharf's attempted rally of radical discontent failed largely because of his own ineptitude, not because of bureaucratic repression. Josef Hindels, anxious to revive a Left Opposition similar to that which existed before 1934,[195] organized a *Sozialistische Arbeitsgemein-schaft* and maintained it in existence for one year.[196] The decision to dissolve it was taken on his own volition without pressure from above.[197]

The conclusion seems warranted that the failure of Left-socialist tendencies to find a common platform and to constitute themselves as an inner-party opposition [198] is not due, to any significant extent, to the oligarchic characteristics of the Party structure. The democratic machinery provided by the Organizational Statute, as well as the traditional commitment to inner democracy, assure that the impediments created by these tendencies could be overcome by a determined and effective oppositional group. The weakness of the Leftist critics has, above all, been their inability to offer concrete and appealing alternatives to the policies put forth by the official leadership. On one hand, the threat of the Communist rival organization seriously narrows their area of maneuver in the ideological sphere as well

---

the Party—a contrast to the position expressed by Bauer—is revealed by the report of the committee set up to inquire into Scharf's editorship of *Der Kämpfer*: "The publication . . . appears as a logical continuation of previous attempts by Comrade Scharf and his friends to create an organ for the expression of factional views within the Party as well as in public." (Quoted by Scharf, *Ich darf nicht schweigen*, p. 107.)

[193] Hindels, e.g., published eighteen articles in *Die Zukunft* in the years 1948 to 1951. The SJ publication (*Stimme der Jugend*, subsequently *Trotzdem*) has followed an independent line far to the left of the official *Arbeiter Zeitung*.

[194] Source: Dr. Ernst Mayer, in interview. No records exist.

[195] Cf. his "Reformisten und Linkssozialisten" (*Die Zukunft*, III [September, 1948], 263–68) and "Das Recht auf Opposition," *loc. cit.*

[196] *Der Sozialist*, No. 25, February, 1951, and Nos. 39/40, May-June, 1952.

[197] Sources: Hindels and Blau, in interviews.

[198] Hindels, "Das Recht auf Opposition," *loc. cit.*

as in the area of international politics; domestically, on the other hand, enthusiastic "Leftism" unsupported by thorough knowledge cannot contribute to the solution of difficult practical problems.[199] The trade unions, on the other hand, are able to develop concrete policy alternatives, since they have at their disposal research staffs of their own as well as those of the Chambers of Labor. The Socialist Party—not their equal in financial or scientific resources [200]—cannot easily brush their proposals aside.

Since 1945, the forces limiting the Socialist leadership's range of action have not so much been the ineffectively organized and poorly informed oppositional groups within the Party, as extraparty bodies such as the trade unions and, outside the labor movement, the rival party with whom the Socialists share government power. While these very real limitations of the power of Socialist leadership may be reassuring when viewed from the angle of the democratic state, they are irrelevant, nay opposed, to the concept of "inner democracy." For to the extent that the Party leadership is forced to share decision-making powers with nonparty organizations, the possibility for participation in these decisions by the Party rank and file, or even accountability of the leadership to the rank and file, is diminished.

---

[199] This conclusion is in agreement with the view expressed by Hans Müller, "Zum Problem der Parteiopposition," *Die Zukunft*, III (November, 1948), 323–25. This point will be developed at greater length in subsequent chapters.

[200] As long as the SPOe participates in the government, its ministers have the resources of their departments—their bureaucratic staffs—at their disposal, a somewhat doubtful source of strength for Socialists.

IV

The Ebbing of Marxist Theory

The Marxist Base

It would be tempting but misleading to picture the profound change which the Austrian Socialist Movement has undergone as the result of the present leadership's abandonment of Marxist theory. It is true that before 1938, in contrast to the present, the Party made extensive use of Marxist terminology and felt itself compelled to justify policies and actions, whether militant or conciliatory, by attempting to prove derivation from that theory. But the categories and concepts used by Marx—never free from ambiguity —had been subjected to subtle shifts, reinterpretations, and equivocations and had been deprived of their function as theoretical guideposts long before their abandonment by the present generation of Socialist "practitioners." Only as stereotyped and vulgarized slogans had they retained vitality. Thus they had often become shackles rather than stimulants to creative political inquiry.

Intellectually, Marx's writings were sufficiently ambiguous—even contradictory—to allow his disciples considerable leeway in applying his lessons to contemporary problems. By espousing "Marxism" the Socialist leadership was forced on the defensive by those who could appeal to the masses most convincingly in the name of certain simplified slogans. These slogans, allegedly representing the "true doctrine," identified Socialism with relentless class struggle, with a radical break with the existing system, with violence rather than peaceful achievement. By dispensing with the myth of Marxism—"myth" here used in the Sorelian sense—the post-1945 leaders of the SPOe deprived their radical critics of the possibility of charging them with treason to the principles of socialism. At the same time they

126

succeeded in forcing those critics into a discussion of practical problems not congenial to them. No drastic change took place in the substance of policies espoused, but the terminology and temper of discourse were drastically altered.

The person of Karl Renner may serve as a fitting symbol of the continuity within change which is so characteristic of the ideological development of Austrian socialism. Renner was *the* intellectual representative of the Party after 1945 in the same way that Otto Bauer symbolized the Party between 1920 and 1934. Yet Renner, though overshadowed by Bauer during the period of the latter's dominance, was already a prominent leader with a strong organized following in the First Republic. Even before 1918 he had belonged to the inner circle around Victor Adler—chairman of the Party from its founding to his death—which determined policy before the end of World War I. Without undue oversimplification, we may therefore describe the development since 1945 as resolving in favor of Renner's "practicism," the ambiguity and tension between revolutionary doctrine and practical social reform which had characterized Austrian Social Democracy from its inception.

Socialism and Democracy: The Austro-Marxist Discussion

Definition of the State

It was within a Party deeply committed to the heritage of Marx that the political thinkers collectively known as Austro-Marxists developed their ideas. The term Austro-Marxist is, in fact, misleading. It implies a degree of unity of thought which the representatives of this school never possessed. They all, Karl Renner, Otto Bauer, Friedrich Adler, Max Adler, and others, were aware of the tension between traditional Marxist theory and contemporary political reality. Yet they responded in profoundly differing ways.

Gulick's thesis, that in important respects the Austro-Marxist position, particularly if measured in terms of performance, approached that of Revisionism,[1] is not being contested here. But this approach did remain indecisive and theoretically ambiguous except in the case of Renner. Particularly with regard to the crucial complex of concepts—State, class struggle, and parliamentary democracy—the position adopted was equivocal. This ambiguity was due, in part, to the widespread habit of retaining the use of

---

[1] Cf. *Austria from Habsburg to Hitler*, Chap. 27, "Austro-Marxism."

terms while changing their meaning, a habit justified by Marx's dialectics as well as by considerations of political psychology. Thus Kautsky, as early as 1902, redefined the term "revolution" in such a way as to deprive it of any connotation of violence;[2] and in Renner's hands the same term was further transmuted by ceasing to characterize a general, fundamental social change.[3] Similarly, Renner was content to apply the term "class struggle" to any practical demand put forth by representatives of the working class on its own behalf, be it for shorter hours, better street lighting, or the construction of a public lavatory.[4] What appears to have set apart his "Rightist" use of the concept from that employed by the "Leftists" is not so much the nature of the actions—for the Party was generally united on the necessity of engaging in particular reform work—as the spirit in which they were performed. Max Adler, spokesman for the theoretical Left, countered Renner's broad definition thus:

This petty labor can only then be considered as socialist when it leads to the overthrow of class rule and if it is carried through by the individual *consciously in awareness of the great idea of socialism.*[5] [Italics added.]

Renner, though all his life insisting on being considered a Marxist,[6] early developed a concept of the state differing radically from that of traditional Marxism. Marxist theory defined the state as a coercive apparatus determined by the economic relations—the class-structure—of society. Since Marxism recognizes basically only two classes as historically significant in the present era, the state—with an occasional exception—can only be a bourgeois state, i.e., the means by which the bourgeoisie exercises its class domination. Renner never shared this position but rather viewed the state as a socially necessary device of organization and rule. While according to his view the state had served in Marx's time as the device of bourgeois class domination—Marx had thus correctly analyzed it *for his time*[7]—there was

---

[2] Noted by Ernst Glaser in "Soziologie heute," *Die Zukunft*, VI (August-September, 1951), 248–52.

[3] "One makes revolution in practice everywhere where the working class stands face to face with the class opponent." (*PTP*, 1919, p. 236.)

[4] *PTP*, 1917, pp. 120–21.

[5] *Ibid.*, pp. 123–24.

[6] This is another instance of Renner's habit of using old terms while giving them new meaning.

[7] Karl Renner, *Die neue Welt und der Sozialismus*, p. 12. The views expressed in this little book do not differ significantly from those Renner held earlier in his life.

no inherent reason why it could not be influenced and adapted to serve the needs of other groups and classes in society. Renner could develop this concept of the change of state function only because he also had already shed the rigid dialectical dichotomies of original Marxist theory. Society, for him, was not split into two irreconcilable camps but rather consisted of a multitude of groups each intent on using the state for its purposes.[8] The former "subject" was rapidly moving toward the status of equal citizenship within the bourgeois state. Renner was not inclined to disparage this development,[9] nor to qualify his enthusiasm for the concept of the *Rechtsstaat* in which every citizen enjoyed a sphere of anarchy which every state, under all circumstances, had to respect as inviolably his.[10] Socialism, in his view, would not overcome and dissolve the liberal state but would fulfill it by providing it with social content and by thus liberating the individual from oppression by irresponsible and arbitrary economic power.[11]

Max Adler, on the other hand, considered Renner's unqualified support for inviolable human rights and the *Rechtsstaat* incompatible with the principles of dialectical thinking. Renner, in his view, obviously failed to realize that rights and laws were mere expressions of class rule; that civil rights in a bourgeois *Rechtsstaat* were meaningless, "nothing else but one big hypocrisy" [12] as far as the proletariat was concerned. Bauer, always intent on arriving at a formulation which would avoid both the deductive rigidities of Max Adler and Renner's Revisionism, adhered firmly to the classical contention that each state was a class state serving the interests of the ruling class. But he rejected the view—put forth by the Bolsheviks and some Austrian Socialists—that this class *rule* was, under all circumstances, tantamount to class *dictatorship*.[13] For in a democracy, Bauer argued, the rule of the capitalist class could not assume the form of unlimited dictatorship. The capitalist class was small in numbers and needed the middle strata of economically dependent petty bourgeois businessmen, artisans, and small peasants to govern. Neither dictatorship nor complete domination, but manipulation, in which real and ideological levers were powerful

---

[8] *Ibid.*, p. 16.
[9] *Ibid.*, p. 13.
[10] PTP, 1919, p. 238; again in *Die Menschenrechte*, p. 28.
[11] "Vom liberalen zum sozialen Staat," lecture delivered to the 1st Conference of the OeGB (*Steno. Prot.*, Vienna, 1948, pp. 428–29).
[12] Max Adler, *PTP*, 1919, p. 254.
[13] Otto Bauer, "Kapitalsherrschaft in der Demokratie," *Der Kampf*, XXI (August-September, 1928), 335–44.

aids, was, in his view, the means of bourgeois class rule in Austria.[14] Thus Bauer, along with Renner, rejected the rigid dichotomy—here proletariat, there capitalists—and insisted (again in agreement with Renner) on the importance of the many "classes, groups, splinters," which became of great significance once government was based on the principle of numbers.[15]

Parliamentary Democracy and Proletarian Dictatorship

The socialist definition of the nature of the state has an obvious bearing on the socialist attitude toward democracy, particularly the parliamentary institutions of democracy. By 1901 Austrian Socialism had opted for parliamentarism as the best means of achieving its objectives. In 1918, when Austria became a parliamentary republic in which the labor movement was temporarily the strongest political force, the Party faced the crucial choice: to conserve and cherish the newly won form of government or to drive beyond it in an immediate attempt to establish socialist class rule—as Lenin had done in the Soviet Union. To put it differently: Should Socialists dedicate themselves to the preservation of the democratic state as an end in itself worthy of socialist effort and sacrifice? Should they renounce the use of violent means and rely exclusively on the ballot box for the achievement of their goal? Or should Socialists look at elections, parliaments, and civil rights as at least instruments to be used or discarded as the struggle seemed to demand?

Austro-Marxists did not answer these questions with unanimity. For a Socialist of Renner's cast of mind the answer was clear: Socialism would be the result of a prolonged process of sober, hard, detailed reform work in which the social and economic development itself would play a determining role. The terms "class struggle" and "revolution" were meaningful— once political equality for all classes had been achieved—only as references to practical work in state, municipality, co-operatives, and trade unions.[16] To believe that Socialism could be established at a single stroke, through an act of will, to him smacked of Syndicalism. And in opposing this notion he felt himself to be a more faithful disciple of Marx than those enthusi-

---

[14] Ibid.

[15] Ibid. Bauer early recognized the importance of the "middle strata" to Socialist success and attempted to attach them to the Party.

[16] PTP, 1917, pp. 120–21. He held even more strongly to this conviction after representative democracy had been established in Austria. (Cf. PTP, 1919, pp. 263–64.)

asts who endorsed direct action as the sole means of salvation.[17] To Renner, democracy was an "ideal form of government"; [18] in Lassalle's words, it was "like that wonderful mythical lance which healed the wounds while it inflicted them." [19]

Renner's view of parliamentary democracy as an ideal *per se* was not, however, shared by the dominant group in the Social Democracy of the First Republic. The fact that in 1918 the Party had not assumed full power in disregard of electoral results, establishing the "dictatorship of the proletariat," was the cause of explanations and apologies by the top leadership. They pleaded as the principal reason not its inherent undesirability but the dependence of Austria on the capitalist nations of the West for the essentials of life.

The planned rule of the dictatorship of the proletariat would have meant nothing else for us than that in eight days the hungry, starving mass of the proletariat would have become our greatest enemy. *Thus we had no choice left . . . we had to establish a democratic form of government.*[20] [Italics added.]

Bauer made common cause with Max Adler in criticizing those who "reduced questions of the historical situation, of the developments in the class struggle, to matters which could be disposed of by Sunday-school moralities (*Sittensprüchlein*),[21] a statement welcomed and supplemented by Max Adler with his usual straightforward radical formulation:

One must never allow the proletariat to get the erroneous view that we are opposed to the dictatorship of the proletariat. On the contrary, one must declare: We are, at present, not in favor of the dictatorship of the proletariat only

---

[17] *PTP*, 1917, p. 121.

[18] "Demokratie," *Arbeiter Zeitung*, November 19, 1948. The changelessness in Renner's position makes it permissible to refer to his views expressed at widely different times in his life without regard to their chronology.

[19] Renner, "Versagt oder bewährt sich die Demokratie?" *Der Kampf*, XXV (October, 1932), 401–5.

[20] Skaret, *PTP*, 1919, p. 144. This was echoed by Seitz: "The continuous suppression of one's passion was extremely painful . . . we had to be satisfied with what could be achieved: extensive democracy and social progress." (*Ibid.*, pp. 149–50.)

[21] *Ibid.*, p. 229. This statement is characteristic of Bauer's oscillations. That he was by no means free of the "bourgeois" preoccupation with individual freedom and had a deep hatred of violence is easily seen by the eloquent statement quoted below and many others in which he argued against Leftist extremists.

because we do not consider it possible at the moment. . . . We cannot imagine—Marx and Engels never did either—that the struggle of the proletariat is merely a legal one. Rather, it is carried on with all means at its disposal, therefore also violent ones where they are necessary and promise success. . . . Questions of violence are questions of the historical process. Violence used within the historical process is not violation of the rights of liberty but the foundation of new rights of liberty.[22]

From other statements, and even more from the actions of Bauer and the remaining top leaders of the Party, it becomes clear that they did not share Max Adler's lighthearted historical relativism with regard to the use of violence and his contempt for "bourgeois" civil rights. On the contrary, the major criticism directed at Bauer by the members of the revolutionary underground movement after the Party's bloody defeat in February, 1934, was that by his exaggerated regard for civilized forms of political relations and his lack of revolutionary ruthlessness he had brought about the ruin of the Party. Rarely indeed has the case against the achievement of socialism by violent means been put more eloquently than by Bauer himself when, at the Linz Conference in 1926 he launched an attack on the Party's "professional revolutionaries" (*Revoluzzer*):

Force means civil war; and more than that . . . force means foreign war! . . . We do not desire this road of blood-letting, or war! . . . Civil war means famine; civil war means the disintegration of the economy which forces the victorious socialist power to take on tasks which it cannot solve. Civil war means that socialism, even in case of victory, cannot bring improvement for a whole generation in the economic situation of the workers; only a worsening because the destruction of the economy outweighs by far the confiscation of surplus value. . . . From the experience of the great Russian revolution we have learned: He who uses force becomes the prisoner of force. . . . Civil war . . . creates so much hatred, rage, and passion that victors can hold down the defeated for a long time only through force. . . . We should understand that it [dictatorship] is not only a sacrifice for the other side but for the proletariat itself; that destruction of individual liberties for which the most precious blood

---

[22] *PTP*, 1919, p. 255. It is to be noted that in Max Adler's statement the identification of the "dictatorship of the proletariat" with the legal struggle for full political power has given way to the traditional and logical linking of dictatorship with violence and terrorism. (See Arthur Rosenberg's discussion of Robespierre's "Democratic Dictatorship" in *Democracy and Socialism* [New York, Knopf, 1950], pp. 13 ff.) What makes Adler's historical view untenable is its failure to distinguish between the use of violence to *achieve* political equality and its use to abrogate it for any group or class in society.

of mankind has been spilt for centuries does not merely affect the bourgeoisie but the proletariat itself which thus would sacrifice the main part of its liberty. That may be implacably necessary in a certain moment of history, but we wish to view it as a cruel necessity . . . not something we desire.[23]

On that occasion Bauer also found it necessary to redefine the concept "dictatorship of the proletariat," which had become increasingly ambiguous since Marx. Max Adler wished to revive its original definition as the legal rule by the proletariat as a parliamentary majority. Bauer responded by asking what difference then existed between dictatorship and democracy; and added that dictatorship—as the term was presently and generally understood—could not be divorced from the use of terror.[24] The more democracy was endangered by counterrevolution, the more precious did its preservation appear to Bauer. When some years later Parliament had been put out of action by the Dollfuss regime and the Socialist Left wing was pressing hard for violent action in order to establish the dictatorship of the proletariat, Bauer, in the face of strong criticism, wished to limit the Socialist objective to a struggle for the restoration of parliamentary democracy, a goal which he considered eminently worth the struggle.[25]

The ambiguity of the Party's position toward the democratic state found additional expression in the repeatedly voiced lack of confidence in the possibility that the bourgeoisie would allow a socialist triumph to be achieved by democratic means. It is impossible to determine whether the expectation of a resort to violence—either to block a socialist victory or to deprive the Movement of the fruits of victory—was a self-fulfilling prophecy [26] or rather an accurate forecast of the historical development. But it seems clear that a party which officially propounded the view that class contradictions were too great to be confined within the framework of parliamentary democracy had deprived the democratic structure of its most vital pillar: the unquestioning acceptance of a fundamental consensus, a basic will to community.

The leaders of Austrian Social Democracy were opposed to the destruc-

---

[23] *PTP*, 1926, pp. 267–68. Though free of "petty moralities," Bauer's argument could not hide the moral fervor he felt for the cause of individual liberty.

[24] *Ibid.*, p. 271. Adler revealed his own inconsistency when he variously identified "dictatorship of the proletariat" with its rule as a legal majority and (as in the statement quoted above) with the achievement of power by any means.

[25] Bauer, "Um die Demokratie," *Der Kampf*, XXVI (July, 1933), 269–76.

[26] Robert M. Merton, in *Social Theory and Social Structure* (Chap. 7), provides an excellent discussion of the mechanism of "self-fulfilling prophecy."

tion of parliamentary democracy and—at times even passionately—defended its value against detractors. Yet the fatalistic assumption that violence would be required to defend the Socialist achievement against its class enemies and the constant use of passionate diatribes against the "class enemy" contributed to the creation of a political atmosphere in which the mutual confidence and respect essential to democracy could not flourish. The well-known formulation adopted in the Linz Program spelling out this assumption, that the bourgeoisie would be tempted to overthrow the democratic republic and that in that case Socialists would have to resort to violence and to the establishment of the dictatorship of the proletariat,[27] reflected an outlook in which society resembled two armed gladiators facing each other in mortal combat.[28]

In accepting parliamentary democracy as the arena for this combat the Socialist leadership was faced with the necessity to define the extent to which the use of extraparliamentary methods was legitimate and feasible as a means of influencing political decisions. Bauer was careful not to rule out the use of such methods in principle, wishing to reserve them, however, for decisive occasions when it became necessary to defend the Republic. For the everyday struggle only the normal methods of parliamentary opposition were deemed appropriate.[29] Max Adler, on the other hand, concerned primarily with the increase of revolutionary fervor on the part of the proletarian masses, welcomed every sign of their political passion even if it took the form of undisciplined and destructive actions,[30] a position which, though rejected by the solid core of Party functionaries, apparently was popular, particularly with the young set of activists.[31]

During his entire political life Bauer viewed with horror the possibility

---

[27] PTP, 1926, pp. 175–76. In the original draft the clause did not read, "would be tempted" but, dogmatically, "would attempt." It was changed on the insistence of Friedrich Adler. (See "Unvollkommenheiten des Programmentwurfes," Der Kampf, XIX [November, 1926], 467.)

[28] I fully accept the view expressed by Robert M. MacIver (in The Web of Government, pp. 216–17), that class parties stressing the importance of the class struggle to the exclusion of wider community ties are harmful to the existence of a healthy democracy.

[29] PTP, 1921, pp. 97, 154.

[30] PTP, 1927, pp. 156–57. The occasion was the post-mortem on the fateful events of July 15, 1927.

[31] According to the official protocol, Max Adler's speech was received with hostility by the Conference delegates but with strong applause by the visitors in the gallery.

that exaggerated emphasis on peaceful reform might drive this "younger group" out of the Party. Even though it probably made up no more than a small fraction of the Party's membership, it was its most vocal, its most enthusiastic and most energetic part. It had acquired a certain amount of socialist education through attendance at Party schools which gave it facility in the use of Marxist terminology. To this Left, "socialization" was the act of a moment or, at the most, of a brief period of rule. Change was conceived of as cataclysmic. The Left accepted the abstract terms "socialist order" and "capitalist order" as representing two totally opposed systems. Only these two systems could be conceived of in the present historical period; and the socialist one would necessarily come into existence with the overthrow of the capitalist one.

Renner's view, that socialism grew within the womb of capitalist society, that capitalist society was being "socialized" gradually, imperceptibly, and inevitably, was anathema to the Left. Its own passionate approach to the task of social change was incompatible with Renner's patient, undramatic, and somewhat passive attitude. Reformism could result only in calming the political atmosphere, and an atmosphere charged with the excitement of battle was considered essential to arouse the class consciousness of the proletarian masses. Though Bauer at times accepted Renner's view that in the realm of reality—in contrast to the concepts of abstract thought—a long and complicated road with many traditional steps led from the bourgeois to the socialist society,[32] he nevertheless would not or could not use this recognition to counteract the prevalent view that, given a parliamentary majority, the Party would at once enact "Socialism." From this "one-day" concept of socialism the assumption followed that the "class enemy" would not peacefully accept the change; that the old body of administrators would have to be removed and replaced by a new one; and that, though the Party promised that its rule would be exercised "under all guarantees of democracy,"[33] it might be necessary to suppress capitalist agitation for a return to the previous system.[34] Viewing the change-over as a sudden rather than a gradual one, as one which would have to be imposed on society over the determined, perhaps violent, opposition of a considerable segment, the Left wing could argue that it was "necessary to learn from the Russians and

---

[32] See his remarks, *PTP*, 1921, p. 169.

[33] That is, if the bourgeoisie did not resort to violence, as predicted at Linz (*PTP*, 1926, p. 176).

[34] Cf. Otto Leichter, "Zur ökonomischen und machtpolitischen Theorie des Parteiprogrammes," *Der Kampf*, XIX (October, 1926), 435–42.

from all parties and classes who have managed to establish a lasting rule through the conquest of state power." [35]

In summary, the Austro-Marxist attitude toward democracy was one of ambiguity, personified in its foremost spokesman, Bauer, whose roots were deeply anchored in the nineteenth-century struggles for individual freedom and emancipation from oppression. He could uphold democracy and its values most eloquently,[36] while again and again affirming that "we are democrats for the sake of socialism." [37] In the oft-repeated phrase, Socialists favored democracy because it promised to be the "most favorable battleground on which the struggle for socialism could be carried on."

Thus the socialist attitude was destructive of democracy even where Socialists sincerely professed adherence to nonviolent methods. To view political opponents as enemies whose physical or political elimination was a prerequisite of one's own triumph, and thus to fail to recognize the important role which falls to a strong opposition in the democratic scheme; to assume that Socialists possessed a vision of absolute truth which was to be imposed on society upon the attainment of a bare majority of votes, was to uphold the letter while denying the spirit of democracy.[38] Among their opponents, lack of understanding of the conditions necessary for the success of a democratic political system was undoubtedly even more pronounced and was frequently accompanied by outright hostility to it.[39] Yet

---

[35] *Ibid.*

[36] As in the editorial "Wir Bolschewicken," *Arbeiter Zeitung*, October 23, 1932.

[37] "Die Zukunft der russischen Sozialdemokratie," *Der Kampf*, XXIV (December, 1931), 513–19.

[38] For discussion of the basis of a democratic policy, see MacIver, *op. cit., passim*, particularly Chap. 8; also Herbert McClosky, "The Fallacy of Absolute Majority Rule," *Journal of Politics*, XI (1949), 637–54.

[39] Gulick, *op. cit.*, convincingly analyzes the hostility toward democracy of Seipel and a growing section of the Austrian middle class. Nevertheless I cannot agree with Gulick's judgment that Austrian Social Democracy in the First Republic was unconditionally prodemocratic. My own conclusion is confirmed by Julius Braunthal, who was a prominent member of the Party's Left in the twenties, and until recently Secretary of the Socialist International: "The young generation which streamed into the Movement after 1914 soon learned to think in terms of force . . . in this struggle for the maintenance of democracy strangely enough the idea of democracy got lost. The principles of democracy were in these discussions mentioned at best parenthetically. Democracy was defined as the most useful, but by no means as the morally imperative form of the state. . . . Dictatorship of the proletariat was rejected with the argument that under existing power conditions every attempt at establishing a proletarian dictatorship would end in

the number of those in the anti-Socialist camp who were determined to destroy democracy was initially not large. By postulating a priori, however, that the class struggle was the most characteristic feature of social relations, and by maintaining through its propaganda an atmosphere charged with the threat of violence, the Socialist Party strengthened the hands of those opponents who denigrated parliamentary democracy as a system capable of adjusting competing political classes' claims. Renner continued to stress the need for exploring all opportunities for political conciliation as a prerequisite for maintaining a minimum of consensus, but his advice was ridiculed by the Party Left and went unheeded by the dominant leadership group around Bauer. Thus the Socialist Party of the First Republic never squarely tested its opponents' democratic convictions and contributed a share to the destruction of democracy in Austria.

Revolutionary Socialism

With the defeat of the mass party at the hands of the Dollfuss regime, Austrian socialist theory, now propounded by the revolutionary successors of the democratic leadership, swung to a radical position closely resembling Lenin's.[40] They dismissed past reliance on parliamentarianism as a "reformist illusion." This illusion, they claimed, had led Social Democratic leaders to overestimate the automatism of the historical process and to underestimate the importance of the active will to power. It was an illusion to believe that power could be conquered by attracting mass support. Stress on mass organization had merely detracted from the need for a trained cadre of revolutionary activists and had thus kept the Party from acting effectively in a crisis. The new aim of the Movement was unequivocally defined as the establishment of the dictatorship of workers and peasants (!), "to break the resistance of the exploiting class—capitalists, big landowners and their henchmen of priests, bureaucrats, and generals" in order to create the basis for a socialist society.

---

catastrophe, not because it would contradict the essence of socialism." (*Auf der Suche nach dem Millennium*, pp. 540–41.)

[40] Cf. "Prinzipienerklärung der R.S.," *Arbeiter Zeitung* (Brünn ed.), September 22, 1934. Some of the most influential new leaders (e.g., Karl Czernetz, Ilse and Leopold Kulczar) openly avowed their affinity to Leninism. (Cf. Buttinger, *In the Twilight of Socialism*, pp. 207–8.) The group of which they were members before joining the Revolutionary Socialists significantly was called *Funke* ("spark").

Bauer, now in exile, also endorsed the necessity of fighting for the overthrow of the present Austrian regime by revolutionary means but he perceived no inconsistency between his present and past positions. For the events of February, 1934, appeared to him as a fulfillment of the prophecy expressed at Linz: When the capitalists in their ultimate defense of property and profit overthrew the rules of the democratic game, the proletariat, too, had to emancipate itself temporarily from these rules.[41] But, understandably, Bauer did not view "the mistakes and illusions of the past" with the eyes of the new leaders. Parliamentary democracy had not, so he felt, been such an illusion. Rather, it had been a necessary stage through which the Socialist Movement had to pass.[42] Neither could he share even now the prevalent contempt for the values embedded in democracy. He had opposed use of dictatorial methods even when, as before 1934, they were used against the enemy of Austrian socialism, the National Socialists; and he had castigated those of his comrades who had been willing to applaud their application in that case.[43] For to Bauer, as to his opponent Renner,[44] individual liberty remained an essential aspect of that civilized life which the new generation of Socialists was in danger of rejecting. He revealed the gap which separated him from the totalitarian thinking which increasingly dominated the remnants of his Party:

The heritage of bourgeois democracy will be the precious heritage of every future social order. Secure liberty and dignity of the individual against the arbitrariness of the powerful, the free competition of all ideas for the judgment of all, the equal participation of all in the decisions about the fate and formation

---

[41] Neue Wege zum alten Ziel," *Arbeiter Zeitung* (Brünn ed.), March 18, 1934. Also, *Zwischen zwei Weltkriegen?* p. 206.

[42] The words "necessary" and "inevitable" occurred frequently in Bauer's arguments. For him the dialectical process of history necessitated and justified one mode of behavior at one time while requiring one totally different—equally right—at another. This observer cannot help but agree with the judgment voiced by one critic of Bauer's dialectical method: "As I listened to Bauer's speech in which everything was ordered into an inescapable chain of necessities which closed itself brilliantly from the days of the collapse [1918] to July 15, I had to put the question to myself whether this was not the case of a very enticing art of syllogism serving merely the attempt to picture something as inescapable necessity which, basically, was still lack of human foresight." (Leuthner, *PTP*, 1927, p. 170.)

[43] Bauer, "Um die Demokratie," *loc. cit.*

[44] Renner could not accept liberty as being based on any "natural rights"; he viewed it as an "acquisition of culture." (*Die Menschenrechte*, p. 39.)

of the community—all this no society of cultured human beings will ever be able and willing to do without permanently.[45]

In 1936 Bauer's affirmation of democratic values appeared to be little more than the retrospective sentimentalism of a discredited leader intellectually rooted in the nineteenth century. Yet the events of the next few years brought about a shift which carried the Austrian Socialist Movement well beyond the position adopted by Bauer toward a belated acceptance of the opinions consistently expressed by Renner.

The Disappearance of Theory

Before we enter a discussion of the changed viewpoint which postwar Austrian Socialism exhibits, it is essential to point out the most conspicuous change of all: the total disappearance of a comprehensive socialist theory and the almost complete loss of interest on the part of those calling themselves Socialists in the re-establishment of a coherent system of socialist thought.[46] The reasons responsible for this change must remain a matter of speculation. Some of the reasons are obvious: The physical elimination of the preponderantly Jewish intellectual element in the Party; the heavy demands on the time and energy of Party functionaries caused by their participation in the administration of the country; the predominant role which Renner's disciples, the professed "administrators," play in the postwar Party; and finally, the apathy accompanied by a notable "privatization of values" which the masses, including the young, now exhibit toward political causes of all sorts.

However, disintegration of socialist theory is not confined only to Austria.[47] And even those who are not overburdened with administrative tasks, and opposed to the prevailing trend of practicism, have failed to lay even a groundwork for any theoretical structure. Hence, the obvious explanations

---

[45] *Zwischen zwei Weltkriegen?* pp. 108–9.

[46] This "loss of ideology" is widely commented on in Austria inside and outside the SPOe and forms the basis for the book by Karl Bednarik, *Der junge Arbeiter von heute—ein neuer Typ.*

[47] The Declaration of the Socialist International, adopted at Frankfurt in July, 1951 (cf. *Die Zukunft*, VI [July, 1951], 177–80), is evidence for the international nature of this development. For recent comments on this development, see Seymour M. Lipset, *Political Man,* and Daniel Bell, *The End of Ideology.*

proffered above cannot entirely satisfy us. (In part they are effects rather than causes.)

"Scientific socialism" was an ideological structure which contained the seed of disintegration in its own internal contradiction. The positivist and scientific element could not continue to be reconciled with the eschatologic and dogmatic total doctrine of historical salvation. Its failures—failures to foresee historical developments or to comprehend social forces accurately; failures also taking the form of disappointments with achievements (such as nationalization and central planning) [48]—forced a choice between faith and science, between a doggedly doctrinal reassertion of obsolete part-insights and a "rethinking" of both future goals and the means of their achievement. The beginning of this rethinking process is marked by loss of direction, by disintegration and confusion, and inhibited by a novel realization of the imperfectibility and at least partial irrationality of man. Thus there is a new awareness—reinforced by Soviet experience—of the network of unintended consequences which planned social change inevitably brings and which thus makes rational planning never quite rational. At its best this results in the reassertion of the humanitarian core of Socialism coupled with undogmatic willingness to search for ways to improve human conditions.

The new program which the Party gave itself in the spring of 1958 was originally intended to be the expression of a newly achieved theoretical position as well as of its implications for political action. But the final version which emerged from the draft [49] fully deserved the label—"premature program"—which one of its critics gave it.[50] It denied *ab initio* any intention to commit the Party authoritatively to a scientific interpretation of contemporary social developments,[51] thus cutting the ground from under any common socialist theory. It demonstrated that the policies and institutions advocated did not derive from a set of theoretical concepts. Nor had they emerged from a careful inquiry into the problems facing Socialists at present—such as the nature of "socialist planning," organization of public enterprises, or workers' control, but instead represented a grab bag of trite, ambiguous, and occasionally contradictory demands.

---

[48] These will be discussed in Chapters VI and VII.

[49] *Vorentwurf für ein neues Parteiprogramm der SPOe*, Vienna, SPOe, 1957 (hereafter cited as *Vorentwurf*).

[50] Karl Czernetz, "Das verfrühte Programm," *Die Zukunft*, XIII (February and March, 1958), 39–44, 69–73.

[51] Benedikt Kautsky, PTP, 1957, p. 135.

The members of the drafting committee attempted to use the occasion to draw a clear line between the Party's present position and its Marxist past.[52] But in the discussion aroused by this attempt it became clear that such an open repudiation continued to be obnoxious to the small but vocal minority of "orthodox" Marxists [53] as well as to a larger number of those who saw in this a dishonorable concession to opportunistic considerations; and the offending clause and section were not retained in the program as adopted. The ambiguity of the very term "Marxism" is indicated by the fact that the final version succeeded in assuaging self-declared Marxists and anti-Marxists alike [54]—though any comparison of the 1958 Program with the Linz Program of 1926 will show the abandonment of the terminology and temper of radical Marxism which marked the earlier effort.

We can now turn to the question of what continuities, if any, exist between past Austro-Marxist positions and present views, noting in passing the Party's reluctance to surrender openly the mantle of Marx.

Democracy Triumphant

With the destruction of the R.S. cadres by the Gestapo and the retreat from political life of the uncompromising revolutionaries who had come to lead them, the commitment to dictatorship of the proletariat was replaced by a remarkably unanimous and unequivocal enthusiasm for parliamentary democracy. Many Austrian Socialists had unconditionally enlisted in the war against fascism; many had personally experienced the terrible results

---

[52] The draft contained the following passage: "Modern society has developed quite differently from Marx's anticipation in the Communist Manifesto." (*Op. cit.*, p. 10.) In his speech introducing the draft to the Conference, Benedikt Kautsky stated: "In the modern welfare state in which we live not much can be done with Marx's theories and Marx's concepts." (*PTP*, 1957, p. 137.)

[53] See particularly Josef Hindels, "Das vierte Programm und der Marxismus" (*Die Zukunft*, XIII [January, 1958], 11–16) and his "Kann der Sozialismus Menschen verändern?" (*ibid.*, XIII [April and May, 1958], 123–27).

[54] The following utterances will illustrate the point: (1) *Hindels:* "The final program is a good document, a socialist document, a document permeated by the Spirit of Austro-Marxism" (*Arbeiter Zeitung*, May 14, 1958, p. 2); (2) *Dr. Neugebauer:* "I, in contrast to Comrade Hindels, find that it, to a very large extent, severs the tie with Marxism" (*ibid.*); (3) *Dr. Broda:* "The formulation that the Socialist Party fights for a classless society and wishes to remove classes is prime Marxist heritage, prime Marxist ideological treasure" (*ibid.*).

of dictatorship; many had spent years in close contact with the democratic labor movements of Britain and Sweden and the German émigré Socialists, who had gained new appreciation of the ethical core of Socialism.[55] Thus even those who continued to consider themselves as "Revolutionary Socialists" at the end of World War II affirmed the integral connection between socialism and democracy. A multiparty state, a recognized opposition, elections and civil rights all were unequivocally accepted.[56] Thus they not only failed to resist but actively participated in the reformulation of the revived Party's attitude toward democracy. As expressed officially in 1946, the pre-1934 "instrumental" view of democracy as the most favorable arena for the socialist struggle was still accepted. But it was supplemented by a novel appreciation of the *intrinsic* value of democracy.[57] Subsequently, when it became increasingly imperative to distinguish the socialist position beyond any possibility of misunderstanding from that of the Communists, this commitment to democracy was made even more explicit: "There is no dictatorial, no terroristic way to socialism. *The democratic way may be long and difficult, but it is the only way to socialism.*"[58] [Italics added.] Thus the Party came to accept officially the position consistently expounded by Renner. And Renner, whose understanding of democracy was basically liberal and English, for the first time spoke for the Party as a whole when he praised political democracy as that system which permitted maximum social change at minimum social cost.[59]

This unquestioning endorsement of political democracy has been accompanied by a rejection of the distinction—accepted without question before 1934—between "political" and "social" democracy as alternate types. When Otto Leichter, for several years closely associated with the Scharf group, revived the dichotomy between "formal" democracy as it existed in the

---

[55] Cf. Erich Matthias, *Sozialdemokratie und Nation*, pp. 250–56, for a discussion of "practical humanism," developed by German socialist émigré groups, and its influence on Austrian Socialists abroad.

[56] Cf. Manifesto of KZ-Socialists, reprinted as Appendix No. 1 in Kautsky, *Teufel und Verdammte*, pp. 299–304; also, Czernetz, "Der Neuaufbau der Sozialistischen Partei in Oesterreich," in *Die Zweite Republik in Oesterreich* (Londoner Büro der österreichischen Sozialisten, London, 1944).

[57] Cf., e.g., *Merkblätter*, Serie I, No. 2, "Was ist Demokratie?" (SBZ, 1946).

[58] *Redeanleitung* "Volksdemokratie und KPOe" (SBZ, 1950). This is in complete contrast to Bauer's insistence on the "two roads."

[59] Cf. *Arbeiter Zeitung*, October 27, 1945, reporting Renner's speech; "Die Menschenrechte und der Staat" (*ibid.*, November 23, 1947); "Demokratie" (*ibid.*, November 19, 1948); also Renner, *Demokratie und Bürokratie*, pp. 25 ff.

United States and "economic" democracy as it was being established in the "People's Democracies," [60] Oscar Pollak heatedly castigated Leichter. Pollak claimed that Leichter failed to realize that the development could take place only from political democracy—a system in which everyone was free to fight for reforms and against what he recognized as evils—toward social democracy, and not the reverse.[61] By drawing the traditional distinction, Leighter had challenged the central dogma of the new creed: that socialism was not possible without democracy; that by its very definition, socialism contained within itself the concept of political democracy. So great was Pollak's enthusiasm for political democracy that he even failed to mention the existence of economic inequality as vitiating the premises of political democracy.

Since the liquidation in 1948 of the Scharf faction, the only group which continues to qualify its endorsement of political democracy with classical Marxist arguments is the Left wing of the SJ, with Josef Hindels as its (former) spokesman. Hindels, who has been strongly influenced by the ideas of Rosa Luxemburg, shares the view, now generally accepted, that socialism and political freedom are inseparable; that even in a future socialist society functional differences and thus the need for freely organized parties will continue to exist; [62] that, indeed, with nationalization of the means of production democracy becomes even more important than in the past in order to counteract the dangers inherent in bureaucratic power; he even shares the view expressed by Oscar Pollak in the controversy with Leichter, that political without economic democracy was possible, but not the reverse.[63] Yet, while citing Rosa Luxemburg to the effect that "freedom is always only freedom for those who think differently," [64] Hindels' adherence to rigid concepts of classes and class struggle forces him into a contradiction: the freedom to differ shall be reserved for "the working people"

---

[60] "Politische und soziale Demokratie nach dem zweiten Weltkrieg," *Die Zukunft*, II (September, 1947), 263–67.

[61] "Kein Sozialismus ohne Freiheit," *Die Zukunft*, II (October, 1947), 287–92.

[62] "Was ist demokratischer Sozialismus?" *Die Zukunft*, III (June, 1948), 168–71; also *Lehrbriefe der SJ-Akademie*, 1. Semester, pp. 53–55. How much following Hindels' views command in the SPOe it is impossible to estimate. He exerted considerable influence on a circle of young members which formed around him. His views also received general, though critical, support in *Der Sozialist*, a mimeographed "underground" publication put out by disgruntled Leftists.

[63] Hindels, *Von der Urgesellschaft zum Sozialismus*, p. 205.

[64] *Lehrbriefe der SJ-Akademie*, p. 69.

(*arbeitende Menschen*), not for the former bourgeois exploiters who cannot be converted to Socialism. They are to feel "the iron fist of the ruling proletariat." [65] That Hindels likes to toy with the concept of the dictatorship of the proletariat is confirmed by the praise he lavishes on the institution of the "soviets" during the Russian Revolution as representing "opinions and moods of the working masses more clearly, more openly, more immediately than they have ever been expressed in a bourgeois parliament." [66]

Austro-Marxism Today

Hindels' Left position may be briefly summarized. (1) He continues to stress the class nature of society and the historic role of the class struggle. (2) He therefore rejects class conciliation and reformism, and thus any prolonged coalition between the parties of the bourgeoisie and the proletariat. (3) In the international sphere he agitates for a policy of independence from capitalist America.[67]

Between Hindels' position and the "Leftism" expounded by Erwin Scharf there were many points of contact. Scharf also stressed the class nature of Austrian society, scored the weakness of the "reformist" leadership in fighting against reviving capitalist influences, and—at least publicly—demanded neutrality in the struggle between East and West. Scharf and Hindels alike professed faithful adherence to Marx's teaching and Bauer's concept of "integral socialism." What separated them in the realm of theory was Scharf's unqualified acceptance of Marx's two-class dichotomy and the definition of class in terms of ownership or lack of ownership of the means of production. Hindels, on the other hand, accepted as the major revision in Marx's system what might be called "the theory of the third solution." This theory, elaborated by Paul Sering,[68] has its origin in James Burnham's prediction of the "managerial revolution." [69] Briefly, its

---

[65] *Ibid.*, p. 63.

[66] *Von der Urgesellschaft zum Sozialismus*, pp. 167–68.

[67] Cf., e.g., the 7-point program formulated by him, as quoted in *Der Sozialist*, No. 25 (February, 1951).

[68] Paul Sering, *Jenseits des Kapitalismus*, pp. 68 ff. and pp. 214 ff.

[69] James Burnham, *The Managerial Revolution*. Stress on the increasing importance of the managerial stratum is not Burnham's original contribution. Max Weber, Joseph Schumpeter, and Karl Renner had previously pointed to the phenomenon. Burnham's significance for socialist thought lies in the fact that he adapted this insight to a modified Marxist scheme which appealed to Socialists by its use of familiar concepts and categories.

argument is that the transfer of the means of production from private hands to state ownership does not automatically lead to a classless society, as Marx had argued, but rather to the development of a new class consisting of those who do not own but through their manipulative skill control the means of production and thus the state. For reasons not far to seek, this theory has been widely publicized in Austria [70] and is frequently adopted by Austrian Socialists. Yet the theory of "managerial revolution" is, of course, a two-edged sword for Socialists. While it provides a pat and superficially plausible explanation for the puzzling and disappointing turn which the Soviet experiment has taken and thus allows Socialists to escape the Communist argument which permits only a choice between a "socialist" Soviet Union and a "capitalist" West, it also appears to destroy the socialist case for replacing private by public ownership. To escape this dilemma, Burnham is criticized for "vulgar Marxism" and for exaggerating the determining role of economic factors.[71] All that is needed "to change Burnham's 'managerial revolution' into a socialist one," it is asserted, "is the introduction of political democracy." [72]

This mixture of "Burnham-cum-Democracy" and its acceptance as the theoretical revision of Marx's class analysis illustrates eloquently how Marxist theories are emptied of content and replaced by eclectic and undigested formulations adjusted to immediate political requirements. It destroys the Marxist definition of class without replacing it by a new one; it questions the relationship between economic base and political superstructure without attempting to clarify it; [73] it divorces political power from its social

---

[70] Burnham's book was published in German translation, in an inexpensive edition, by the Austrian Trade Union Federation. Renner, by implication, pursues parallel ideas. (*Die neue Welt und der Sozialismus*, pp. 24–25.) The term is frequently on the lips and pens of Austrian Socialists. The argument has more recently been refurbished by Milovan Djilas in *The New Class* (New York, Praeger, 1957).

[71] Bauer and Renner also were criticized by the Revolutionary Socialists for undue reliance on "historical automatism." Cf. Matthias, *op. cit.*; also Sering, *op. cit.*, pp. 276–77, and Buttinger, *op. cit., passim*.

[72] Jacques Hannak, "Die Revolution der Manager," *Die Zukunft*, II (December, 1947), 360–64. The quotation is actually ascribed by the author to Léon Blum.

[73] Engels' modification of the one-way determining relationship between the former and the latter in his letter to J. Bloch obviously opened a large breach in the superficially firm structure of Marxist philosophical thought. (*Marx-Engels, Selected Works* [London, Lawrence & Wishart Ltd., 1950], II, 443–44).

base; and it denies the inevitability of the historical process, depriving the observer of belief in his powers of prediction. In fact, it raises the question how Leftists who accept these formulations can call themselves Marxists. The reconciliation—psychological rather than philosophical—is achieved, equally superficially, by accepting a definition of Marxism which, in the past, has been characteristic of the Revisionist Right. Renner, for example, who long ago revolted against the Marxist habit of deducing consequences and expectations from rigid definitions, had always insisted that Marxism was not a doctrine but an empirical science, which provided the tools for the examinations of the relation between the conditions of social existence and the institutions of the "superstructure." [74] The present-day Left has made its own definition of Marxism as a "method" or as a "science." It consciously set itself apart from the "orthodox"—in fact, Communist— Marxists, for whom Marxist formulations were dogmas to be repeated and a faith to be implicitly believed.[75] But the specific nature of this Marxist "scientific method" has so far not been elaborated or concretized by its exponents. For Renner it was his continued acceptance of the determining role which economic functions played in shaping social and political institutions, though he was aware of the varied forms which economic functions would assume under the impact of the differentiating influences of geography and history. This insistence on the specific, nontransferable nature of economic developments in each country led him to reject the assumption of uniform laws of capitalist development toward a uniform concept of socialism.[76] The relation between the term Marxism as used by Renner, who declared that there would be "as many socialisms as there are states in the world," [77] and the traditional meaning of the term is obviously tenuous. It becomes even more so, however, when the determining role of the economic base in relation to the superstructure of ideas and values is abandoned. Yet one of the criticisms of the Left was specifically directed

---

[74] Cf., e.g., Renner, "Ist der Marxismus Ideologie oder Wissenschaft?" *Der Kampf*, XXI (June, 1928), 245–56.

[75] Cf., e.g., Czernetz, "Für und wider den Marxismus," *Die Zukunft*, IV (April, 1949), 113–17; also Oscar Pollak, "Marxismus: Vergangenheit oder Zukunft?" *Die Zukunft*, I (September, 1946), 5–7. Pollak notes that the Marxist idea has made its way from "prophets to professors, finally to parrots."

[76] See "Ist der Marxismus . . . ?" *loc. cit.*

[77] *Ibid.*

against the acceptance by Austro-Marxist writers of a one-way determinism and of "fatal automatism." [78]

Aware of the gap between "objective" conditions and "subjective" consciousness, the present-day Austrian "Marxists" recognize that an important link has been broken which, in the past, gave them assurance to analyze tendencies of development and to predict their future direction. Thus Hindels, the most determined protagonist of classical Marxist formulations, admits that Marxism must be supplemented by and integrated with the findings of modern science, particularly psychology.[79] Karl Czernetz has gone a step further in eviscerating the meaning of the term Marxist while retaining its use. Although for Hindels the notion of "Marxism as a science" still means the *modified* use of Marx's own categories, particularly of his concepts of class,[80] Czernetz—now following in the theoretical footsteps of Renner—applies the term to any study of the relation between economic and ideological factors which proceeds on an empirical basis. Strangely, he combines this view of Marxism as "nothing else but a system of modern sociology" with a conviction that "this does not mean a general revision of Marxism." [81] Dr. Ernst Glaser, almost alone among Austrian Socialists in seriously adopting the empirical methods of sociology, has criticized these efforts, shared by him at one time, to retain the name of Marx at all costs, in the following way:

One can, of course, describe the inclusion of new realms as "further development," as I myself have tried. Thereby one stresses a certain intellectual tradition. Whether one gains anything factually thereby is, however, questionable. . . . From a certain point on in sociology one could simply speak of modern scientific sociology in which the lasting elements of Marxism have been accepted. . . .[82]

---

[78] Cf., e.g., Czernetz, "Wissenschaft und Politik," *Die Zukunft*, I (March, 1946), 14–16, which retains much of the old R.S. criticism.

[79] "Krise des Marxismus," *Die Zukunft*, IV (February, 1949), 49–51.

[80] Ibid.; also Kautsky, "Eine Marx-Kritik," *Die Zukunft*, VII (April, 1952), 128–29. Kautsky adhered to the view that Marx indicated only tendencies of development which are valid under certain conditions.

[81] "Wissenschaft und Politik," *loc. cit.*

[82] "Soziologie heute," *Die Zukunft*, VI (August-September, 1951), 248–52. As late as 1949 Glaser agreed with Czernetz in describing Marxism as "a scientific theory and method of research into certain problems of human society." ("Eine Kritik am Marxismus," *strom*, V [March 25], 1949.)

Similarly, Dr. Adalbert Duschek, one of the "new" academic socialist intellectuals, has favored discontinuance of the use of the term Marxism if it is not intended to describe the substantive sociological, economic, and political teachings of Marx and Engels.[83]

That this criticism is justified is shown by the fact that when challenged to produce examples of Marxism as "science" or as "a branch of modern sociology," its protagonists are shown to be fighting primarily for continued acceptance of some of Marx's specific *findings*. Thus Hindels conceives the core of Marxist scientific *method* to lie in the recognition that "history is the history of class struggles." [84] And Czernetz similarly defines Marxism as the science which discovered the class struggle just as other scientists in the natural sciences discovered existing facts.[85] Also Marx's unearthing of the "laws of capitalist concentration" and even the concept of surplus value are cited by Czernetz as parts of present-day Marxist "methods." [86]

Much of the discussion, the haggling over the use or abandonment of the term Marxist by the SPOe has been carried on in a vacuum. The most important leaders of the Party have publicly ignored the issue and refused to participate in the debate. And whatever the discussion's outcome—it is unlikely that it can be neatly and permanently resolved—the Party's tactical line is not affected by it. Apart from Hindels' writings, it is only in the area of inner-party education that Marxism in its traditional and less attenuated form has found expression. Thus the *Merkblatt* on "scientific socialism," [87] published in 1946 by the Socialist Education Office, had not as yet got around to defining Marxism as a method but rather described it as a discovery of the "lawfulness" of human development, involving the materialist interpretation of history, the class struggle as the motor of history, and the developmental tendencies of capitalism. And two years later "essential parts of the Communist Manifesto," such as its analysis of early

[83] Dr. Adalbert Duschek, "Noch einmal: sind wir noch Marxisten?" *Die Zukunft*, IV (May, 1949), 151–53. Yet the fervor with which continued adherence to Marxism is espoused by a minority in the Party (cf. *Die Zukunft*, IV [January and April, 1949], 32, 127–28 for readers' letters) provides an indication why the Party finds it so difficult to endorse the views expressed by Glaser, Duschek, and Kautsky.

[84] "Krise des Marxismus," *loc. cit.*

[85] Czernetz, "Der alte Anti-Marxismus," *Arbeiter Zeitung*, January 18, 1949.

[86] Czernetz, "Für und wider den Marxismus," *Die Zukunft*, IV (April, 1949), 113–17.

[87] Serie I, No. 3 (SBZ, 1946).

capitalism, the discovery of the class struggle, and the dialectical view of historical development were considered "to have retained their validity to the present day and to be undisputed in the socialist camp." [88] Another *Merkblatt* repeated the Marx-Lenin definition of the state as "the political executive instrument of the economically ruling class," which is not changed in essentials by the admitted growth of welfare functions benefiting the ruled classes.[89] And in the educational pamphlet prepared for the use of SJ instructors, the state is declared, in the most uncompromising terms, to be "the product of the irreconcilability of class contradictions . . . in reality a machine of suppression in the hands of a ruling class against a suppressed class"; [90] while the Revisionist approach of "soft words" is castigated as a "great, most dangerous and fatal error" for believing that the "beneficiaries of capitalist exploitation will voluntarily withdraw." [91]

The explanation of the continued existence of this stream of almost unadulterated "gospel" terminology is probably to be found in two factors: the domination of the education sections, both of the Party proper and the SJ, by the Leftists Czernetz and Hindels, respectively; and the fact that the views expressed in these instruction pamphlets are couched in far more radical and traditional language than their authors otherwise use. The attempt to convey coherent socialist theory forces the otherwise more sophisticated authors to return to the simple, clear, and rigid formulations of classical Marxism as traditionally interpreted.[92] The simplification and vulgarization involved are apparently accepted as the only means to convey what is still considered the core of socialist theory. In spite of the weakening of the Marxist grip, the tendency of Party members to screen themselves off against "bourgeois ideas" is still very pronounced.[93]

---

[88] *Redeanleitung*, "Hundert Jahre Kommunistisches Manifest" (SBZ, 1948).

[89] "Staat, Staatsform und Verfassung," Serie I, No. 4 (SBZ, 1946). It may be significant that the instruction pamphlets cited are all dated 1948, or earlier. At that time Czernetz still clung to a far more radical position than he came to occupy subsequently. Instruction pamphlets with theoretical content do not appear to have been published by the Education Office after 1948.

[90] *Lehrbriefe der SJ-Akademie*, 1. Semester, p. 45.

[91] *Ibid.*, 2. Semester, p. 33.

[92] Hindels and Czernetz have not only been formally responsible for the publication of these pamphlets but are actually the authors of the majority of them.

[93] My own impression is confirmed by Peter Maier in "Theoretische Revision," *Die Zukunft*, IV (May, 1949), 147–51. The way in which nonsocialist views are dismissed with scorn and abuse in the reports on parliamentary debates, not only by the *Arbeiter Zeitung* but in the *SPOe-Vertrauensmann* (which is intended

"Humanitarian Socialism"

The 1958 Program opens with the central definition of a socialist order as one in which "the goal is the free development of human personality" and ends with the expression of faith in a socialist world in which "the free development of the individual person is the fruitful development of all mankind." The slogan "democracy only for democrats," widely accepted at the war's end as a justified limitation on the grant of democratic rights to former or potential enemies of democracy, is no longer voiced. Instead, special pain is taken to underline the Party's insistence on the protection of minority rights as a basic feature of democracy. Thus, the Party deliberately places the individual—not the Movement or the proletariat—in the center of its programmatic concern.

The difference between this document—as well as the "Declaration of the Socialist International" of July, 1951 [94]—and the theoretical section of the Linz Program of 1926 is obvious and striking. Fervor is replaced by conciliation; anticipation of catastrophic power struggles is absent and the qualified acceptance of the necessity for dictatorship of the proletariat is replaced by the rejection of dictatorship in any form. Theoretical analysis, however superficial, of historical tendencies is absent. Equally absent is the use of such terms as pauperization and exploitation. And in the center of the new declaration stands the individual man, his dignity and freedom.

This changed emphasis, this stress on personal freedom, security, and dignity, is viewed as a logical response to the experiences of Fascism and war.[95] Whether the original Marxist inspiration was humanist or not is irrelevant to our discussion. There can be no doubt, however, that due to the insistence on the theory and practice of class struggle, the core of humanism—acceptance of every other human being as a person whose dignity and worth are to be respected—had in the past been obliterated.[96]

---

for the information of the Party functionaries), expresses and reinforces this tendency.

[94] Reprinted in *Die Zukunft*, VI (July, 1951), 177–80.

[95] Cf. Oscar Pollak, "Humanistischer Sozialismus," *Die Zukunft*, VII (July-August, 1952), 201–5.

[96] Cf. Michels, "Die Psychologie der antikapitalistischen Massenbewegung" (in *Grundriss der Sozialökonomie*, II, Part 2 [1926], 244–81); also the testimony of Julius Braunthal that through the concentration on the class struggle and on ex-

The Marxist dialectic which considered the rigid system of "bourgeois" ethics hypocritical and rejected it on philosophic grounds replaced, at least temporarily, a general humanitarianism with a proletarian class ethic. Division of society into "progressive" and "declining" classes and exclusive identification of acts done by or on behalf of the "progressive" class with the morally good are incompatible with humanism.

Austrian Social Democracy, dominated by Bauer and subsequently the Revolutionary Socialists, was much slower than the German Socialist Movement in moving toward a reappreciation of the humanitarian heritage of the West.[97] Bauer's concept of "integral socialism," which involved acceptance of the dictatorial road to Socialism as one possible approach, inhibited the move until after his death and the start of World War II. Even after the move was made, Austrian Socialists generally failed to examine the theoretical implications of this "humanist socialism." [98] It has remained a slogan, a title for a treatise which as yet remains to be written. It nevertheless symbolizes the new temper that distinguishes the present Party from its prewar predecessor. In establishing the doctrine that "man is the measure of all things," the humanitarian Socialist must reject the attempt to think exclusively in class terms. He must refuse to elevate the proletarian man over bourgeois man [99] and must refuse to accept or propagate the inevitability of the class struggle.[100] Furthermore, he necessarily rejects the dogmatic assumption that socialization of the means of production and planning will automatically redound to the happiness of the individual. Sering,[101] Duschek,[102] and Marianne Pollak [103] all agree that planning and socialization become of value only when and if they serve

---

propriation of the means of production "the social and moral idea of socialism had been generally lost sight of." (*Op. cit.*, II, 661.)

[97] Matthias, *op. cit.*

[98] Pollak, who has used the term freely in discussions with me, disavowed any theoretical profundity in his understanding of it. It represents an attitude rather than a theory; a stress on "softness" rather than on ruthlessness; on conciliation rather than on struggle; on "decency" in the most general sense.

[99] Duschek, "Mensch, Staat und Gesellschaft," *Die Zukunft*, VI (May and June, 1951), 133–38, 167–72.

[100] Oscar Pollak (in "Humanistischer Sozialismus," *loc. cit.*) cites *Socialism—A New Statement of Principles* to this effect.

[101] *Op. cit.*

[102] "Mensch, Staat und Gesellschaft," *loc. cit.*

[103] "Jenseits des Kapitalismus," *Arbeiter Zeitung*, November 1, 1947.

the free development of the human personality and therefore must be critically examined as to their effect on it.[104]

In assigning central importance to the free individual and in rejecting the traditional socialist identification of freedom with absence of capitalist exploitation, the Marxist order is reversed: the economic relations, the ownership of property, become secondary and independent of the political and ethical superstructure. Thus Jacques Hannak, admitting that in questions of property distribution "progressive forces" [105] and Communists are in close agreement, stresses that *"where the most essential factor—human rights—are concerned . . . the uncrossable border of freedom separates them forever."* [106] [Italics added.]

Changing Attitudes Toward Soviet Communism

In breaking with dialectical Marxism and officially adopting the slogan of "socialist humanism," ambiguous as it was, the Party succeeded in escaping from the dangerous traps which Soviet Bolshevism had continuously set for it.

Adherence to Marxism had, in the past, prevented Austrian Socialists from flatly condemning the Soviet Union or local Communist parties for the use or advocacy of proletarian dictatorship with its corollary of terror and suppression of civil rights. Though the Austrian Socialist Party was aware that it was carrying on a struggle to the death against its Communist rival,[107] it had to fight in an atmosphere of uncertainty. As the spokesmen of the Party, by and large, accepted the Marxist premises shared by Communists, the differences which they stressed as dividing Socialists from Communists appeared less fundamental than tactical.[108] Thus, Otto Bauer,

---

[104] This attitude finds expression in the Declaration of the Socialist International.

[105] The use of the term "progressive forces" is significant as facilitating alignment between Austrian Socialists and the United States.

[106] "Zwischen Plutokratie und Despotie," *Die Zukunft,* V (February, 1950), 39–42.

[107] See, e.g., Fritz Adler's pronouncement in 1920 that, "where a party has been centrally ordered to carry on a fight to the death [against us] there is no room for sentimentality." (*PTP,* 1920, p. 194.)

[108] Thus, Max Adler stated that, "as a matter of course, we are the party of Communists; that, of course, we do not fight Communists because they are Communists but because they weaken by their senseless 'Putsch' tactic, the unified power of the proletariat." (*PTP,* 1921, p. 164.)

though by no means uncritical of the methods employed by the Soviet regime and of the "new, terrible despotism" it represented, refused to condemn the regime on this account. For he accepted the contention that in the Soviet Union a *socialist* society—albeit of a despotic nature—was coming into existence.[109] It was this faith as well as his preoccupation with the preservation or restoration of proletarian unity which caused him, and the Austrian Party as a whole, to refuse to forsake the Soviet Union and to denounce it openly. In spite of all the differences between the despotic socialism of the East and the democratic socialism of the West, Bauer insisted on perceiving "socialism there as here" [110] based on a community of interests which he expected would grow closer as the efforts of the Soviet regime at industrializing their country succeeded. The prevalent position was expressed by Friedrich Adler when he apprehended the possible failure of Stalin's experiment as "a catastrophe for the Socialist Movement in all countries." [111]

Following the suppression of the legal party in 1934, the appeal of the Soviet Union as "the socialist fatherland," particularly to the rank and file of the Revolutionary Socialists, became even more powerful. Having long held parliamentary democracy in low esteem, they were not inclined to cavil at the Soviet regime for its use of terror and violence. For Otto Bauer, the international developments of the thirties deepened the dilemma, increased his anxiety, yet strengthened his conviction that the Soviet state was the main bulwark of the world proletariat.[112] In spite of the deep shock of the Moscow purges and trials, he could not bring himself to take the side of those—as the Trotskyites were doing—who denied that the Soviet Union was either socialist, proletarian, or historically progressive.[113] The leaders of the Revolutionary Socialists—the self-proclaimed New Men —less fortified by "historical optimism" than Bauer, turned against Soviet

---

[109] Bauer, *Bolschewismus oder Sozialdemokratie?* p. 62.
[110] "The Bolsheviks are . . . undoubtedly supported by part of the proletariat, are undoubtedly revolutionary, undoubtedly a socialist party. Certainly their socialism is not ours. . . . But whatever the contrast between their despotic and our democratic socialism may be, yet it is socialism there as here." (Bauer, "Der Kongress in Marseilles," *Der Kampf*, XVIII [1925], 281–85.)
[111] "Das Stalinische Experiment und der Sozialismus," *ibid.*, XXV (1932), 4–16.
[112] "Der Trotzkysmus und die Trotzkystenprozesse," *Der Kampf* (Brünn ed.), IV (1937), 84–93.
[113] *Ibid.*; also "Grundsätzliches zu den Hinrichtungen in Moskau," *ibid.*, III (1936), 294–99.

Russia not because of its nondemocratic nature but because, in the words of their leader, they had acquired the insight that the spirit and political world of Russian Communism represented the ugliest distortion of their ideals.[114] As far as the bulk of the Party was concerned, severance of the terms "Soviet Russia" and "socialist" had by no means been accomplished.

After 1945, when the Party was faced with heavy ideological pressure from a native Communist Party supported by the physical presence of powerful Soviet occupation forces, it became essential to escape the traditional ambiguities. It was now necessary to develop a position which the Communists could not exploit and which would not make it possible for them to accuse the Socialist leadership of "betraying" the "socialist ideal" by their hostility toward the Soviet Union. The clarification of position was, in fact, made easier by the very presence of the Soviet troops and the policies pursued by the regime which rapidly alienated the traditional sympathies accorded them by the Austrian proletariat.

During 1946 the *Arbeiter Zeitung*—though strongly criticized by the Party Left—shifted decisively toward a pro-Western and anti-Soviet line.[115] A small group, with Erwin Scharf as its foremost spokesman, continued to expound openly a pro-Soviet viewpoint, reiterating propositions, generally accepted before 1938, attempting to establish the socialist nature of the Soviet regime, the legitimacy of terroristic methods in the service of Socialism, and the overriding necessity for eventual reunification within the "socialist camp." [116] The less extreme bulk of Leftists merely desired the maintenance of equidistance between East and West; [117] a position which became increasingly difficult to maintain by 1948, when the Soviet Union forced a choice by her pressure against acceptance of Marshall Plan aid and the communization of Czechoslovakia. The last defenders of a pro-Soviet course—now isolated by identification with a hated power—were

---

[114] Buttinger, *op. cit.*, p. 386.

[115] Throughout that year the *Arbeiter Zeitung* carried on a vigorous campaign against the kidnapping of Austrian civilians and their secret trials by Soviet authorities. For criticism of the change in editorial policy, see, e.g., the speeches of Weikhart, Krones, and Mark delivered at the 1946 Party Conference. (*PTP*, 1946, pp. 117–18, 154, 203, respectively.)

[116] E.g., Otto Leichter, "Balkanprobleme—einst und Jetzt," *Die Zukunft*, II (August, 1947), 226–29; and "Die grosse Gefahr," *Der Kämpfer*, I (April 5, 1948).

[117] Weikhart, *PTP*, 1946, pp. 117–18. See also motion to the same effect proposed by several Vienna District organizations (*PTP*, 1946, p. 235).

eliminated from the Party [118] and its ideological unity established on the basis of total rejection of the Soviet model.

Leftists found the justification they needed for the outright repudiation of the Soviet Union in the continued use of terror within the Soviet orbit not only against "class enemies"—which could have been excused on the basis of dialectical considerations—but against the proletariat itself.[119] They came to view democracy as the only safeguard against the solidification of dictatorial managerialism.[120] Gone was the day when these Austrian Leftists had refused to join "the reactionary agitation" against the Soviet Union.[121] They, too, unequivocally condemned the Soviet system as that of a managerial dictatorship based on a noncapitalist class structure, thus once and for all breaking the fatal identification of "noncapitalist" with "socialist." The new position, freed of the anguish of ambiguity and unburdened even by subtlety of historical interpretation, found drastic expression in the description of the Soviet Union by the drafting committee of the 1958 Program as "a planned economy directed solely at war and armaments . . . glued together by the blood of millions of murdered peasants, workers, and intellectuals." [122]

The "Capitalist West"

Austrian Socialists thus succeeded in erecting a seemingly unscalable wall between themselves and the terroristic forms of Communist dictatorship. But their position toward the democratic West was harder to define and necessarily had to remain more ambiguous. "Equidistance"—equal hostility toward "American capitalism" and "Soviet dictatorship"—seemed ruled out once acceptance of American aid and of NATO's military power was considered essential. Yet how could socialists reconcile it with their

---

[118] Erwin Scharf was expelled; Hilde Krones died soon after; Otto Leichter re-emigrated to the United States; Karl Mark lapsed into silence.

[119] The bloody repression of the Hungarian uprising represents the ultimate justification for this position. (See, e.g., the speech by Oskar Helmer, *PTP*, 1957, pp. 98–100.) The past position had been exemplified by Otto Bauer when he declared: "Terror has its historical justification as far as it is necessary and unavoidable to accomplish the historical deed." ("Der Diktator in der Diktatur," *Der Kampf*, Brünn ed., II [1935], 457–61.)

[120] Hindels, "Volksdemokratie und Sozialismus," *Die Zukunft*, IV (June, 1949), 173–77; and "Nicht zwei—sondern drei," *Arbeiter Zeitung*, August 8, 1950.

[121] *Stimme der Jugend*, III, August 9, 1947.

[122] *Vorentwurf*, p. 6.

convictions to be integrated into a "Western camp" led by "capitalist" America? In order to identify themselves with the West in the name of "democratic unity," it became necessary to revise the socialist appraisal of the United States. For as long as the United States was viewed as the "fortress of monopoly—capitalist imperialism," a sympathetic tie with the Western bloc, whose mainstay the United States was, remained quite unthinkable.

Up to the end of 1947 it was possible to avoid open alignment in the cold war and the official party line remained that of "equal criticism." Thus, while it was admitted that the New Deal had brought about changes in American capitalism, the "basic laws of capitalist development" were still assumed to apply to the United States; indefinite avoidance of severe economic crises was considered impossible and the Marshall Plan was originally viewed as primarily a device to solve the otherwise insoluble problem of capitalist overproduction.[123] Subsequent to the acceptance of Marshall Plan aid—and in view of the absence of a depression in the wake of the war—the firmly held belief that such a depression was inevitable in the United States sooner or later was abandoned.[124] The usual explanation provided for this change was that the United States, borrowing socialist techniques, had learned to plan. This explanation, however, presented Austrian Socialists who had come to define socialism as "democracy plus planning," with a dilemma: By this definition the United States, paradoxically, would have to be classed as a socialist state. The way out of this dilemma was to insist that the United States, although not yet socialist and, for historical reasons, at present prevented from developing a specifically socialist mass movement, had been undergoing an essentially socialist transformation.[125]

---

[123] E.g., Stefan Wirlandner, "Blockpolitik und Washington," *Die Zukunft*, II (April, 1947), 106–8; Peter Anders, "Kapitalismus in einem Lande," *ibid.* (August, 1947), 230–35; OP (Oscar Pollak), "Europa und der Dollar," *Arbeiter Zeitung*, June 17, 1947; Julius Deutsch, *PTP*, 1947, pp. 180 ff.

[124] See OP, "Das Gerede vom Kriege," "Was jetzt?" and "Amerika," *Arbeiter Zeitung*, August 12, 1947, December 17, 1947, January 8, 1950, respectively.

[125] Cf., e.g., j.h., "Warum gibt es keinen amerikanischen Sozialismus?" *Arbeiter Zeitung*, March 10, 1949; Alfred Migsch, "Auf dem Wege zur sozialistischen Wirtschaft," *Die Zukunft*, V (October-November, 1950), 273–83; also the speech by Benedikt Kautsky to the 1950 Party Conference (*PTP*, 1950, pp. 196–98). It should be pointed out that a very large number of Socialist Party functionaries and Trade Union Federation officials were given the opportunity of visiting the United States for prolonged periods under the auspices of the U.S. Department of State.

The New Deal is depicted as a decisive break with America's fully capitalist past, starting the country on the road to a planned welfare state.[126] Such projects as the TVA, farm price supports, Point Four, and the role which "progressive circles," particularly the trade unions, play in influencing and realizing projects such as these, are cited as evidence for the contention that American capitalism, as the term used to be understood, is dead.[127]

If this analysis is accepted, it ceases to be necessary to apologize for close co-operation between socialists and the United States by pointing to tactical necessities. Rather, by increasingly identifying "socialist" with "progressive" goals in general, the close link to the United States which for twenty years was under the leadership of "progressive" Presidents has been rendered ideologically acceptable.[128] As a corollary of this theoretical change, the socialist view of American motives in extending Marshall Plan aid was also rapidly modified and the description of the United States as an "imperialist power" forcefully rejected.[129] Karl Czernetz, who, in November, 1947, had still seen Austrian Socialism as tied "for better or worse" to the fate of the Soviet Union, in 1950 viewed the cold war as a combat between democracy and dictatorship, between law and terror, freedom and slavery, in which nonparticipation was tantamount to cowardly and suicidal neu-

---

[126] In addition to articles quoted above, see j.h., "Aufstieg in Freiheit," *Arbeiter Zeitung*, July 4, 1951, and interview with Dr. Schärf after his return from a visit to the United States. ("Amerikanische Eindrücke," *Arbeiter Zeitung*, May 10, 1952.)

[127] The title of a lengthy article in the *Arbeiter Zeitung*, April 23, 1950, read: "In America, too, capitalism is dead." A hasty correction in the next day's issue insisted that the title should have read: "In America, too, the *old* capitalism is dead."

[128] In 1947 Oscar Pollak had already begun to speak in one breath of "the progressive forces" and the "socialist forces" (see "Was jetzt?" *Arbeiter Zeitung*, December 17, 1947) and no distinction was drawn at later dates between an American non-Socialist Left (ADA) and European social democracy. (WH, "Amerikanische Linke," *Arbeiter Zeitung*, June 1, 1952.) Note also the statement by Dr. Schärf (in *Arbeiter Zeitung*, May 10, 1952): "much of what we Socialists had to wrest from bourgeois parties is in the United States accepted as a matter of course in the minds of non-Socialist parties."

[129] Kautsky, *PTP*, 1950, pp. 196–98; Migsch, "Auf dem Wege zur sozialistischen Wirtschaft" (*loc. cit.*); Oscar Pollak, "Der Krieg in Asien und wir," *Die Zukunft*, VI (January, 1951), 3–4. In late 1947 Pollak had, by implication at least, still classed the United States among the "imperialist" powers. ("Zwischen den Blöcken, gegen alle Blöcke," *Arbeiter Zeitung*, October 9, 1947.)

tralism.[130] Even acceptance of neutrality as part of the State Treaty, which formally restored Austria's sovereignty and secured the withdrawal of all occupation forces, does not mean ideological neutrality, as Socialist spokesmen never tire of repeating, nor does it imply refusal to side with the democratic West against Communist dictatorship.[131]

Yet it must be recognized that the degree of sympathy which Austrian Socialists bring to the evaluation of the non-Socialist West, and above all, the United States, is largely dependent on the degree of "progressivism" which prevails there. Signs of a depression in the United States, or an emphasis by the American government on "capitalist" as well as "democratic" goals in the struggle against Soviet Communism, tend to result in "alienation of affection." Thus the replacement of the Roosevelt-Truman administrations by a Republican one and of the British Labor government by a Conservative one led to a renewed tendency toward equidistance. Fearful to be confounded in the Western sea of "more or less progressive welfare-statism," Austrian Socialists have found it necessary to re-emphasize, at least verbally, their division from the camp of Western capitalism, declaring "democratic socialism to occupy a position between capitalism and dictatorship" and "incapable of reconciling itself either with Communism or capitalism." [132] Yet whenever a choice is necessary, in view of the reversal of the relative significance attached to the political and economic spheres the affinity felt for democratic political systems outweighs the distaste for societies in which the capitalist "remnants" are still powerful.

---

[130] Czernetz, "Korea, Europa und der Friede," *Die Zukunft,* V (October-November, 1950), 273–78. In 1949 Czernetz had already expressed similar sentiments. ("Die Bedingungen des Friedens," *Die Zukunft,* IV [June, 1949], 161–65.)

[131] See *Vorentwurf,* p. 9.

[132] 1958 Program (*Arbeiter Zeitung,* May 15, 1958, p. 12).

V

The Permanent Coalition

Coalition and Opposition in the First Republic

Principle or Tactics?

The problem of what attitude should be adopted toward participation in government—a problem common to socialist parties in general—became of urgent importance in Austria with the end of World War I. Until then the existing state had appeared too uncompromising an opponent, the opportunity for affecting the course of decisions too remote to necessitate serious consideration of this tempting possibility. In some ways and for some sections in the party the war itself had begun to change the Socialist attitude toward the governing power. Though no Socialists were invited to enter a government of "national concentration," the official leadership, and in particular its Right wing (Renner, Pernerstorfer), in giving qualified support to the war effort, was drawn closer to a government which showed itself capable of a measure of directing and planning the economy.

This "proximity to the government," interpreted as a desire to participate in the administration of a bourgeois state, was violently criticized by the Party's Left faction. The Left saw in it a betrayal of the principles of the class struggle and showed its own hostility to the existing state by declaring:

We reject unconditionally every lasting alliance with bourgeois parties, every bloc policy, every vote for budgets of the class state, every participation in bourgeois governments.[1]

---

[1] Gabriele Proft, PTP, 1917, p. 116.

The same Left faction, propelled into Party leadership a short time later, had to face the question whether its hostility toward bourgeois institutions extended also to the newly established Republic. The Socialist leaders of the Left as well as the Right realized that an attempt to push beyond parliamentary democracy toward dictatorial rule by the proletariat would inevitably end in disaster. Austria was at the mercy of the capitalist Western powers in military matters and dependent on them for the bare necessities of life. Furthermore, Otto Bauer saw Austrian society so evenly balanced (in class terms) between the urban working class on one side and the peasantry allied with the middle class on the other that peaceful rule of one over the other seemed impossible. He recognized that a division of Austria into two hostile camps would lead to the disintegration of the Republic through civil war.[2]

Under Bauer's leadership, the Party therefore concentrated on the limited objectives of preserving its gain, i.e., the democratic republic as "the most favorable battleground for socialism." But in order to save it in the chaotic period after the war, not only the passive support of the working class but its positive efforts on behalf of the new state were needed. Furthermore, the power of the proletariat seemed in the ascendance and a voice in public decision could be expected to bring to it some immediate benefits. In the face of this situation—so full of promises and threats—theoretical doubts were suppressed, and the Social Democrats entered the government together with representatives of the Christian Socials as an almost entirely united party. Yet to the majority of its functionaries and leaders, this decision appeared only as a "bitter necessity," [3] and a temporary one at that. Karl Seitz, one of the most popular figures of Austrian Socialism,[4] expressed the reasons for the disquiet which was so widely felt within the Party at the decision to join the government:

As our votes were not numerous enough to allow us to exercise power in parliament alone, it was logical to take the second step and to form a coalition with other strata of the population. . . . You only need to know the life history of each of us to realize what an effort this cost us. . . . Since the day when we first were capable of thinking politically and engaged in the class struggle we knew only one thing: fight to the death against the bourgeois parties. . . . We

[2] For a lengthy discussion of the question of coalition, see Otto Bauer's speech at the 1920 Conference (*PTP*, 1920, pp. 136 ff.).
[3] Bauer's words (*PTP*, 1919, p. 158).
[4] Mayor of Vienna, sometime chairman of the Party, he combined a strong practical sense of administration with temperamental radicalism.

must not forget for a moment that when a Social Democrat belongs to a ministry in a capitalist society, this can only be due to the requirements of emergency, only a temporary measure. Social Democracy cannot identify itself permanently with a bourgeois state.[5]

The conviction that a radical socialist party's right place was in opposition was very strong. When it appeared to Bauer, after the Party had suffered some losses in the 1920 elections, that the Socialists could not hope for easy and immediately tangible benefits from participation in government, and that the bourgeois parties were now capable of governing the state without causing its ruin, he insisted that the Party break loose from the coalition. In this he was apparently supported by a Party majority.[6] Foremost in Bauer's mind was the consideration that continued coalition threatened the unity of the labor movement. By forcing the Socialist Party to take responsibility for decisions also acceptable to the bourgeoisie, the masses might lose confidence in the Movement. Thus the natural role of a socialist party in a bourgeois state, even in its representative parliamentary form, was, according to Bauer, that of opposition.[7]

Bauer continued to impose this view on the Party even after its mood changed and the advantages of sharing power came to seem increasingly alluring.[8] Karl Renner, whose views on coalition differed fundamentally from those of Bauer, failed in his attempts to convince the conscience of the Party that it was advisable to exchange the "purity," fervor, and free-

---

[5] PTP, 1919, pp. 150, 155. It is ironic to note that Oscar Helmer, at the same Conference, severely criticized the Party's coalition policy (PTP, 1919, p. 157). But not even Max Adler doubted the temporary necessity for coalition. He only warned against any subordination of the class interests of the proletariat to the interests of the state as a whole. (Ibid., p. 164.) The mood of many functionaries was reflected by one speaker, Dr. Justiz, who exclaimed: "I believe he [Bauer] smells now too much of coalition. We would prefer the earlier Bauer." (Ibid., p. 222.)

[6] In the speech in which he explained the decision to leave the coalition, Bauer noted: "I believe there are no differences of opinion anymore in the Party that we have done right in leaving the government." (PTP, 1920, pp. 136–37.) The absence of criticism of this decision at the conference and several statements approving it (e.g., Maurer, p. 154; Binder, p. 162; Ferencz, p. 163; Klement, p. 166) testify to its general popularity.

[7] Ibid., p. 143.

[8] In 1921 and 1922 Bauer noted that many who in the past used to condemn the coalition were now eager to resurrect it. (PTP, 1921, pp. 151–52 and PTP, 1922, pp. 146–47, respectively.)

dom of opposition for the responsibility, influence, and sedateness of shared government. In contrast to Bauer, he conceived the natural role of the working class not as an oppositional but as a participating force in the state's affairs—a role which he believed was its due.[9] Renner's position may thus be described as the "policy of permanent coalition." His motives in advocating such a policy were not limited, however, to a desire to obtain the maximum of state power, or at least influence, for the working class. He was gravely concerned lest the hostility of two increasingly rigid political blocks lead to the eventual destruction of the Republic.[10]

In spite of their profound differences, Bauer's and Renner's views had this in common: neither professed to consider entry into the coalition a violation of socialist principles but primarily a tactical consideration. Contrary to the usual assumption, Bauer saw no necessary relationship between readiness to participate in coalition government and reformism. Intent on maintaining an area of unhampered tactical maneuver, Bauer insisted that a good case *for* such participation could be made out by a revolutionary socialist aware of the necessity to put the hands of the working class on all levers of state power. The true criterion for or against the decision was whether those levers were used to serve as instruments of the class struggle.[11] And that, according to Bauer, depended entirely on the concrete class relations prevailing.

Renner's Argument for Coalition

From 1920 to 1934 Bauer successfully exerted his influence against Socialist re-entry into a coalition government. For several years the disagreement on this issue between him and the Renner wing of the Party was confined to debates within the Executive.[12] But following the bloody events of July 15, 1927, the debate erupted into the open. At the 1927 Conference, Renner restated his views in more forceful terms: The state was not an abstract definition but an organization comprising concrete power positions; it was the right and duty of the working class to occupy as many of these power positions as possible; the all-or-nothing view of political power was childish and dangerous and, by leading to events such as the July riots, was pushing Austrian society down the road to civil war.[13] Bauer and the Left wing,

---

[9] PTP, 1923, pp. 168–69.
[10] Ibid.
[11] Ibid., p. 198.
[12] Karl Renner, Oesterreich von der Ersten zur Zweiten Republik, pp. 42–43.
[13] PTP, 1927, pp. 130–50.

however, neither accepted Renner's social theory nor his pessimistic view of the future.[14] They saw no urgent need for coalition or conciliation. Only when the Socialist Party was the stronger, when it could extract concessions from the bourgeoisie would Bauer consider the occasion suitable for entry into a coalition government.[15] Bauer, as usual, maintained a middle position in this debate. Max Adler insisted that no policy of coalition, however concretely rewarding, should be allowed to diminish the proletariat's revolutionary fervor. Renner, on the other hand, saw the cause of Socialism served wherever workers fought for their class demands. To Bauer each of these views seemed one-sided, "ideological," and destructive of that balance which alone, so he believed, could preserve a socialist party as an effective mass movement.[16] Yet in the concrete situation of the First Republic Bauer, after 1920, sided with the Left wing, not because he entirely accepted Max Adler's argument but because the advantages of a coalition seemed to him to be outweighed by the drawbacks: the loss of fighting spirit, the dangers of an internal split, and, internationally, the widening of the gap between the Second and Third Internationals.

The "Permanent Coalition"

In the First Republic the socialist attitude toward coalition was dominated by apprehension, by fear of the dangers it held for the Party's spirit, and by fear of the political consequences of coalition. In this atmosphere Renner's insistence on coalition between the genuinely democratic forces as a means of extending proletarian influence as well as of furthering this desirable conciliation could not make much headway.[17] Many Socialists

---

[14] PTP, 1927, pp. 109–30; also Julius Braunthal, "Untaugliche Argumente für die Koalition," Der Kampf, XXI (February, 1928), 49–53; Max Adler, "Neueinstellung unserer Partei?" ibid., pp. 53–59; Oscar Pollak, "Einige Erfahrungen des internationalen Klassenkampfes," ibid. (May, 1928), pp. 209–12.

[15] Bauer, "Klassenkampf und Ideologie," Der Kampf, XXI (July, 1928), 281–88. Under the conditions stipulated by Bauer the other side obviously had no incentive to enter into a coalition. The notion of coalition as "give and take" was unacceptable to any but the Renner group within the Party. See also Bauer's statement on the principles of coalition at the 1923 Conference. (PTP, 1923, p. 196.)

[16] "Klassenkampf und Ideologie," loc. cit.

[17] Renner has blamed the dogmatism both of Bauer and of his opponent in the anti-Socialist camp, Monsignor Seipel, for the failure to achieve the conciliation between the two great blocs. (Oesterreich von der Ersten zur Zweiten Republik, pp. 42–43.)

measured the effectiveness of the Party's fight in the class struggle by the hatred of other groups in society.[18]

In 1945 the Party's position in this respect was dramatically reversed. In spite of the civil war of February, 1934, and the subsequent period of "revolutionary socialism," the generally accepted form of exercising political power at the end of World War II was by the joint government of all "democratic forces." The intervening years had brought about a remarkable change in the Party's temper. The mortal enemies of 1934 had both suffered equal cruelty at the hands of the Gestapo. Among those who went abroad to escape the Hitler regime the most uncompromising revolutionaries refused to return to Austria at the war's end, perceiving the hopelessness of their efforts. In the leadership of the revived party Renner and his circle, though sharing office with representatives of the former R.S., played the dominant part. Above all, the obvious need for unity in face of the four-power occupation and the immediate tasks of physical reconstruction created unanimous agreement that Socialist participation in the government was a matter of course. Now there was no talk of the "bitterness" of this decision. On the contrary, when after the elections of November, 1945, the SPOe emerged once more as the second strongest party, its new chairman, Dr. Schärf, propounded the theory which we have previously characterized as that of "permanent coalition." He rejected any notion that the Socialist Party's natural role was that of an oppositional force and expressed his conviction that only its influence exercised *within* the government could guarantee the country's democratic future.[19] The "Left" position toward coalition, an echo of Bauer's views, was put forth at the 1945 Conference by the former R.S. leader Karl Czernetz: only emergency justified coalition. With the passing of the emergency the Party would have to free itself in order to carry on the forceful struggle for total power.

Criticism from the Left

By 1947, when the four-power occupation seemed likely to go on indefinitely, the temporary emergency had turned into a typical Austrian state of "provisional permanence." It was then that a radical Left group, led by Scharf and Hindels (but *not* Czernetz), which included factions within the youth and student organizations,[20] began to press for an immediate end to

---

[18] See, e.g., Braunthal, "Untaugliche Argumente für die Koalition," *loc. cit.*
[19] *PTP,* 1945, pp. 85 ff.
[20] Cf. resolution of the *Verband der Sozialistischen Studenten, PTP,* 1948, p. 159; also *Trotzdem,* II (November 19–December 2, 1949), report of debate in

the coalition. In their view the coalition gave the lie to the Marxist concept of the class struggle [21] by causing the Socialists to accept the proposition that in decisive questions class enemies shared economic interests. Furthermore, the Party was losing its fighting spirit and was inhibited in the use of those extraparliamentary methods which would create a higher pitch of combativeness and allow it to wrest concessions from its opponents. Finally, the charge went, continued coalition forced the Party into acceptance of responsibility for decisions which did not advance the cause of Socialism.[22] They criticized Czernetz—who had abandoned his earlier position and now wished to see continued coalition combined with an absence of soft "coalition spirit"—as unrealistically desiring to eat his cake and have it too.[23]

The Scharf-Hindels group's contention that the possession of ministerial positions and participation in governmental decisions did not outweigh the loss of enthusiasm caused by the continuous need for compromise and conciliation was never widely accepted in the Party.[24] The twin arguments of the four-power occupation and the tangible benefits derived from the occupancy of governmental and administrative positions proved too persuasive. While the more radical critics rejected class conciliation implied by coalition, a large majority of the Party apparently accepted the claim that "in spite of differences between the parties it has been possible to reach agreement in the decisive questions and thus to avoid political and economic crises which would have led to serious disruption." [25]

---

the Executive of SJ on attitude toward coalition. No agreement was reached and the SJ delegates to the Party Conference were allowed to formulate their position individually. These show the persistence of the anticoalition sentiment within the youth organizations.

[21] E.g., Josef Hindels, "Die Linken auf dem Parteitag," *Die Zukunft*, II (December, 1947), 358–60.

[22] Hindels, "Gefahren der Koalitionspolitik," *Die Zukunft*, IV (December, 1949), 345–48; for an expression of the radical viewpoint, see "Koalition um jeden Preis oder konsequenter Klassenkampf?" (anonymous), *Der Sozialist*, No. 38 (April, 1952).

[23] Hindels, "Gefahren der Koalitionspolitik," *loc. cit.*

[24] Hindels' motion at the 1949 Conference asking that the Party leave the government was supported by only one delegate. (See editorial note introducing "Gefahren der Koalitionspolitik.")

[25] *Resolution of the Party Executive*, PTP, 1948, p. 30. Paul Blau, a representative of the Left-wing SJ, criticizing the resolution, asked: "How can we reach agreement in decisive questions with the People's Party? We were merely able to wrest concessions from the class enemy." (*Ibid.*, p. 114.)

The Lack of an Alternative

The radical argument for withdrawal from the government would have had greater appeal if a realistic hope had still existed that such an oppositional role would be a comparatively brief prelude to the Party's achievement of a decisive electoral majority. But the realization emerged that class and party lines were apparently firmly fixed in Austria and that, for an indefinite period, the Socialist Party would be faced by a political opponent of roughly equal power.[26] As a glance at the election results since 1945 show, the Party has failed to make decisive headway among the peasantry or the urban middle class, except in Kärnten and Burgenland.[27] True, the SPOe has succeeded in becoming "respectable" even in the traditionally anti-socialist rural areas, and also in attracting a considerable number of ex-Nazis and *Volksdeutsche* who, because of the nature of their work or of their anticlericalism, have shown themselves open to its appeal. These successes, balanced by the defection of that section of the working class which went over to the Communists, fall far short, however, of the realization of the "grand alliance" of all working people (including the smaller peasants) which had traditionally been firmly expected to arise as the social basis on which a socialist system could be erected.

The major advance into the rural areas had been achieved by 1945—an indication that not the policies and propaganda of the SPOe but the changes brought about during the past dozen years were primarily responsible—and has since continued only at a slow rate. Furthermore, most of the gains made since then have been achieved at the expense of the heterogeneous League of Independents (VdU) and have therefore failed to weaken seriously the SPOe's major opponent, the People's Party.

The argument on behalf of "permanent coalition" has furthermore been strengthened by the Party's change to unqualified support for the democratic state. Because government is still conceived as inevitably "over and against" the opposition, the move to an oppositional role is identified with freeing the Party for an all-out struggle against the governing majority with little regard to the requirements of responsible democratic opposition.[28]

---

[26] Otto Tschadek, *PTP*, 1948, pp. 116–17; Benedikt Kautsky, *Geistige Strömungen im österreichischen Sozialismus*, p. 26; also Max Opravil's retort to Hindels' anticoalition argument, "Keine Experimente," *Trotzdem*, II (November 5–18, 1949).

[27] See Appendix 1.

[28] This is made clear by Hindels' criticism of coalition as inhibiting "extraparliamentary" actions.

Because it is widely assumed that a majority government would rule without regard for the minority party and the social forces it represents, the breakdown of the coalition is pictured as necessarily a severe trial for the state and for the democratic system. Oscar Pollak has shrewdly pointed out that in a well-established democracy such as England the peaceful alternation of governments represents, in fact, "a projection of coalition in time." Austria, on the other hand, is not considered mature enough to live by the rules implicit in such a system and therefore requires the existing "one-beside-the-other" form of coalition.[29] The practice of *packeln*, of reaching compromise decisions, is thus defended as the basic safeguard of the minority's living space against an unbearable use or abuse of the majority's power.[30] The conception of the polity as divided into two power blocs which will, unless immediately checked by each other, use their power to the fullest against each other regardless of consequences—the continued denial of consensus sufficiently strong to support a democratic community —is part of the traditional Marxist outlook. The existence of a radical theory of coalition acceptable to that element in the Party which requires a theoretical underpinning for its political actions helps to unify the organization in support of the present leaders' determinedly pro-coalition course.

More recently, however, the concept of democracy in which government and opposition alternate in rule, and which was based on an acceptance of the British model as superior, has been replaced by a novel one which daringly views the present coalition as a "new working method of parliamentary democracy." [31] The permanency of the coalition combines, it is now argued, the common concern for the general welfare with continued healthy competition of the two parties within the government. Each party is necessarily committed to the maintenance of political freedom as the guarantee against domination by the other. Although the coalition government seemingly represents an overwhelming power concentration in the

---

[29] "Koalition und Opposition," *Die Zukunft*, VII (February, 1952), 33–36.

[30] Adolf Schärf, "Das 'Packeln' in der Politik," *Arbeiter Zeitung*, January 27, 1952. The argument here advanced is reminiscent of John Calhoun's advocacy of a "government by concurrent majorities," which, characteristically, was put forth in a society lacking fundamental consensus.

[31] Bruno Pittermann, *PTP*, 1957, p. 94. See also Otto Kirchheimer's excellent analysis, in which the Austrian situation is viewed as a prototype ("The Waning of Opposition in Parliamentary Regimes," *Social Research*, XXIV/2, 1957, pp. 127–56).

view of the average citizen, this power is weakened by the government's internal dualism. Elections no longer decide fundamental changes in the political and social system but merely weight the scales of government toward more "progressive" or more "conservative" policies.[32]

The "Ghost of February, 1934"

The unflinching acceptance of Herr Julius Raab as head of the coalition government was a particularly significant reflection of this eagerness to maintain the coalition. For Raab, in his person, represented all those forces in the People's Party which the SPOe in the past had most uncompromisingly rejected. When the People's Party was first organized in April, 1945, it disclaimed any connection with either the old Christian Social Party of Seipel or the near-Fascist Dollfuss-Schuschnigg regime. It was then led by men who, together with some prominent Socialist leaders, had suffered in Nazi concentration camps; some had been active in the resistance movement. Raab, the representative of business, a former leader of the Fascist *Heimwehr*, untouched by Nazi persecution, was relegated to a back seat.[33] To some Socialists the People's Party's leadership, make-up, and program in 1945 indicated that it was a "strongly Left-oriented bourgeois party." [34]

Obviously as a means of keeping the OeVP on the defensive, the SPOe pretended to fear a repetition of the developments which led to the events of February, 1934, and frequently voiced doubts as to the OeVP's sincere acceptance of democratic principles. Above all, it demanded of the People's Party an explicit dissociation from the authoritarian regime of the 1934–1938 period and a clear admission of historical guilt for the events of February, 1934.[35] The People's Party, on the other hand, desired to have these events accepted as the result of tragic errors committed by patriots on both sides and expressed the hope that old wounds would not be reopened, a

---

[32] *Ibid.*

[33] In 1945 Julius Raab was only Third Vice-Chairman of the People's Party. Its chairman was Dr. Figl, a long-term inmate of Dachau and a prominent functionary of the Peasants' League; the posts of First and Second Vice-Chairman were held by representatives of the Christian Trade Unions and the Resistance, respectively. (Adolf Schärf, *Zwischen Demokratie und Volksdemokratie*, pp. 83–84.)

[34] *Ibid.*

[35] Cf., e.g.: "Das Gespenst," *Arbeiter Zeitung*, October 3, 1945; "Nicht wieder so," *ibid.*, November 30, 1945; "Die Versuchung des Bürgertums," *ibid.*, December 12, 1945.

hope which the Socialist insistence on a monopoly of historical righteousness again and again disappointed. For in the Socialist version the fight had been exclusively one between democrats and Fascists in which all the guilt was to be borne by the latter:

Our mistake was that we did not fight well and were beaten. The mistake of the others, the "patriotic" forerunners of the OeVP, consisted of breaking their oaths, destroying the sworn constitution, and establishing . . . their gallows regime. . . .[36]

Long before 1953 and the acceptance of Raab as Chancellor, this tone of aggressive ferocity with regard to the People's Party had been greatly modified, in spite of the fact that developments in the OeVP ran counter to Socialist hopes. In 1951 the "KZ" (concentration camp) leadership identified with the name of Figl had been replaced, and Raab, chairman of the Chamber of Business, had taken over the leadership.[37] The reason for the SPOe's sudden moderation in tone is clear: reference to the People's Party as "Fascist" had become a weapon in the hands of the "Scharfists" and Communists who wished to undermine the coalition and who were using the hallowed battle cry, "The enemy stands Right." It would have been impossible for the SPOe to insist on sharing governmental power with a party which it seriously suspected and publicly accused of harboring Fascist tendencies. Thus from 1948 on there is a sudden, almost total, cessation of references to the OeVP's unsavory political past in official Socialist publications. The bitterness previously so prominent in any reference to the events of 1934 is now muted into sorrow.[38] Only Hindels, speaking for that group in the Party remaining intractably hostile to continued coalition, does not cease to link the bourgeois leaders of today with the Fascist executioners of yesteryear.[39]

The SPOe's sensitivity to the events of 1934 has not abated, but it has taken on a primarily defensive note; the Party's version of the authoritarian period must not be publicly challenged; rehabilitation of those prominently responsible for the Fascist course of those years is still considered intoler-

---

[36] Karl Czernetz, *Der Sozialismus und seine Gegner*, p. 19.
[37] See *Wiener Zeitung*, June 15, 1951; *Keesing* (1951), 2983-F. Figl remained Chancellor but Raab became chairman of the Party and, according to all accounts, its true leader.
[38] Cf., e.g., "Gedenktag," *Arbeiter Zeitung*, February 12, 1948.
[39] "Sie haben sich nicht geändert," *Stimme der Jugend*, February 11, 1948.

able, precisely because it implies a reassertion of the conservative claim that they too "were honorable men." Testimony to this attitude is the violent reaction with which the Party leadership met a court decision early in 1952, restoring his extensive properties to Prince Starhemberg, the leader of the *Heimwehr* fight in February, 1934. The more radical elements represented in the Executive wished to use the case as reason to break the coalition and fight an election, a demand which was successfully resisted by Chairman Schärf and the moderates.[40] But impressed by the heat the issue was engendering, particularly among the former R.S. element and the older body of functionaries, and fearful of a repetition of the undisciplined riots of July 15, 1927, the Executive itself responded by a campaign of protest demonstrations in the plants in support of a political solution which would prevent the "criminals of 1934" from benefiting by a court decision designed to help the "victims of Fascism." [41]

In the case of Raab's rise to the leadership of the People's Party, this symbolic challenge to socialist "face" was absent. He was not prominently connected in the popular mind with the Dollfuss-Schuschnigg regime. Furthermore, Raab's ascent in the OeVP had been gradual, giving the socialist negotiators opportunity to get used to dealing with him as the most powerful man in the conservative camp. Proving himself a tough but apparently honest bargainer, he had convinced the SPOe leadership that his former commitment to Fascism had been no more than an episodic expression of the *Zeitgeist* and that he was now sincere in his readiness to abide by democratic rules.[42] Thus there was little inclination to allow the "ghost of 1934" to torpedo the re-establishment of the coalition so much emphasized by the Socialist Party. Contrary to the expectations of many of the Party's functionaries, its leaders declared themselves completely disinterested in the personal history of the prospective Chancellor and resolutely

---

[40] Interview with Dr. Bruno Kreisky.

[41] Interview with Karl Czernetz; also *Arbeiter Zeitung*, January 6, 1952, and January 8, 1952. As in 1927, the Party this time, too, found itself in the unhappy position of fighting a legal decision. The law subsequently passed (see *Arbeiter Zeitung*, March 6, 1952), though carefully avoiding mention of Starhemberg's name, nevertheless bears the taint of running counter to the principles of the *Rechtsstaat* by embodying a retroactive measure and in amounting, in fact, to a bill of attainder.

[42] Address of Minister Waldbrunner to Conference of Works Councilors, 1953. (Author's notes.)

suppressed all stress—even countering Communist propaganda efforts—on Raab's past activities in the Fascist movement.[43]

The tenacity with which the SPOe has fought against any alteration in the conditions of the coalition can be explained by its fear of being faced once again by a "bourgeois bloc" such as had been organized by Chancellor Seipel in the twenties.[44] The two-party coalition between the Socialist and People's Parties provides the Socialists the opportunity to share equally in the administration of the state, though they received less than half of the total vote at the polls. The closer the People's Party is tied through binding agreements, the more difficult is the establishment of this feared "anti-socialist majority" as a political force in the country and in parliament. The People's Party, unlike the SPOe, though also short of controlling an absolute majority of the votes, has the choice of forming, if necessary, a "little coalition" with the League of Independents.

In 1949 the Nazi taint of the Independents was as yet too strong, the internal situation as yet too unstable, and the People's Party too apprehensive of foreign, particularly Russian, reaction to make feasible such a "little coalition," or, for that matter, any grouping including the Independents. The intervening years, however, have given the VdU (now FPOe) respectability and have made it *koalitionsfähig*. Raab's desire to strengthen his position vis-à-vis the SPOe by taking the VdU into the coalition—backed by the tacit or overt threat of a coalition from which the Socialists would be altogether excluded—was therefore quite natural.[45] The Socialist leaders were aware that they lacked a parliamentary majority but were unwilling to gamble on taking the Party into opposition. They clung to the concept of

---

[43] Cf., e.g., O.P., "Krise in der OeVP," *Arbeiter Zeitung*, March 24, 1953. This was in sharp contrast to past policy. In 1946 the *Arbeiter Zeitung* had attacked Raab as representative of the Fascist element in the OeVP who had signed the "Korneuburg oath" in which the *Heimwehren* pledged themselves to reject the democratic parliamentary system and to fight for a Fascist order. ("Linz und Korneuburg," *Arbeiter Zeitung*, February 17, 1946.)

[44] For a recent expression of this apprehension see the speech by Party Chairman Pittermann at the 1957 Conference. (*PTP*, 1957, p. 85.)

[45] See *Die Presse* of March 6, 7, 10, 11, 13, and 15, 1953, for reports on OeVP-VdU negotiations. It is quite possible that Raab, a very shrewd political bargainer (see the Profile in *The Observer* (London), June 13, 1954), merely used this threat as a lever to reduce Socialist demands called forth by their success at the polls; if this was his tactic, he succeeded admirably, for in the end the SPOe was happy to have achieved the continuation of the coalition under roughly identical conditions.

permanent coalition, though they realized that a coalition in which they could be outvoted on crucial issues by an anti-Socialist majority would be useless. Hence they found their area of maneuver seriously restricted. If the Socialist leaders had taken the risk and forced the People's Party to rely for a governmental majority on the support of the internally unstable and, in part, anticlerical League of Independents, the result, in the long run, might have been highly favorable to the SPOe: there were indications that such a course would have seriously disaffected certain sections of the People's Party and might have weakened, perhaps split, the none too cohesive ranks of the VdU.[46] The Socialist leadership, however, preferred to sacrifice gains promised by the electoral success and the chance of a more decisive victory in the future to the continuation of the *status quo*. All efforts of the People's Party to achieve a loosening of the coalition tie were frustrated by Socialist insistence on maximum continuity.

The Coalition Pacts

The relations of the Socialist Party to its partners in the government have been regulated through a series of agreements defining the degree and nature of co-operation to be established. The Provisional Government, set up in April, 1945, was described as a *Vereinbarungsregierung* in which, in theory at least, no decision was to be taken except by unanimous agreement.[47] In fact, however, Renner assumed unanimity to exist when none of the parties in the government was ready to carry its objections to a proposed measure to the point of resignation, and several decisions were taken "unanimously" though over the strong objections of the Communist representatives.[48]

Three-party government was resumed after the elections of November, 1945. But it was changed in composition and also in the manner in which decisions were arrived at. In the Provisional Government agreement had been reached not only through cabinet decisions but also through the prin-

---

[46] The "Catholic Action" group, as well as the Catholic trade union groups, was reported to be strongly opposed to any intimate ties with the Independents. The lack of stability in the VdU was clearly shown by the numerous resignations and removals which have occurred. The first vote when the newly formed parliament elected the three presiding officers gave evidence that the Independents were by no means agreed on supporting an alliance with the OeVP. (*Arbeiter Zeitung*, March 19, 1953.)

[47] Renner, "Vereinbarungsregierung," *Arbeiter Zeitung*, September 25, 1945.

[48] Schärf, *Zwischen Demokratie und Volksdemokratie*, p. 31.

ciple of three-party administration, institutionalized by means of multiple under-secretariats in each department. In the words of Dr. Schärf, it had been a "concentration government which had synthesized parties into a 'higher unity.'" [49] The subsequent structure, on the other hand, was described as being based simply on party "*Proporz*": the cabinet decided unanimously on the legislation which was to be submitted to parliament; it formulated foreign policy and agreed on the appointment of high civil servants. In other matters, particularly of administration, each department was independent. Furthermore, this "*Proporz*" government was characterized by an absence of written party agreements, interparty contact committees, or, with few exceptions, interparty *ad hoc* negotiations.[50] The system of under-secretariats was maintained only in two crucial departments [51] which the parties considered too important to leave to the uncontrolled command of the other.[52] The Communists, as a consequence of the defeat suffered at the election, were relegated to a single department, losing control over the Ministries of Interior and Education. In 1947, upon the withdrawal of the Communist representatives from the government, the Socialist wish for a more integrated form of partnership was realized.[53] The parties reached an agreement which provided for a common parliamentary working program, common wage-price policy, and a date for the next election.[54] This agreement set the pattern for the subsequent Coalition Pacts which considerably extended the area of co-operation.[55]

The Pacts have served to establish the *methods* of party co-operation

---

[49] "Konzentrationsregierung oder Proporzregierung?" *Die Zukunft*, I (September, 1946), 4.

[50] *Ibid.*

[51] Ministry of Interior and Ministry of Planning.

[52] The existence of these under-secretariats did not prevent the Socialist Party press from again and again attacking the Ministry of Planning. These attacks put the Socialist under-secretary in that Ministry in an embarrassing position; he had either to admit complicity in the Minister's actions or accept responsibility for failure to represent his Party's interests effectively. Only on one occasion did he come openly to the Minister's defense. (See Karl Mantler's statement on planning, *Solidarität*, No. 49, March, 1948, p. 7.)

[53] Schärf, "Konzentrationsregierung oder Proporzregierung?" (*loc. cit.*), where the author criticizes the "*Proporz*" form as too weak for effective action in periods of emergency such as the present.

[54] *Keesing* (April 3, 1948), 1447-F.

[55] Though the Pacts of 1949 and 1953 were nominally secret, their provisions were well known. In 1956 the new Coalition Pact was published by agreement of the two parties. (*Wiener Zeitung*, June 27, 1956.)

(and competition) as well as to ratify agreement on certain major points of substantive policy. The main clauses of the 1956 Pact may serve to illustrate both functions. The two parties pledged themselves to form a government for whose actions they would accept joint responsibility and from which they would exclude all other parties. New elections would be called only by joint agreement. A two-party "contact" committee, consisting of ten members, equally divided, would meet regularly to assure smooth cooperation. Unanimous agreements reached by the government would bind the two parties in parliament, though the government could give the parliamentary parties freedom in dealing with governmental draft legislation. The Pact officially confirmed the principle of *"Proporz"* by agreeing that executives and directors of the nationalized industries and banks should be selected by the parties in proportion to their respective electoral strengths. Substantively, the gains made by the OeVP in the 1956 elections forced the Socialists to concede a major reorganization of the Ministry supervising the public sector of the economy. In 1949 the SPOe had been able to insist on the creation of a Ministry for Nationalized Industries and Transport under the SPOe leader Waldbrunner. This "Waldbrunner empire" had long been a thorn in the side of the OeVP; and the possibility that the nationalized oil industry suddenly freed by the withdrawal of the Soviet occupation forces would accrue to Waldbrunner's power sphere had unsettled the precarious balance between the parties and forced arbitration by elections. Thus it was natural that the OeVP exploited its electoral success by forcing Socialist agreement to a reorganization of that Ministry. Its area of competence was restricted to transportation and public power, while all other public enterprises (except the nationalized banks) were subordinated to the federal government as an entity. Agreement was also reached on the Ministry of Defense—to be newly established—assuring that it would not become the power instrument of any single party.

The "Proporz"

From the very beginning of the Second Republic the determination to fill the maximum number of public positions with its members has been a preoccupation of the Socialist Party. This determination, the result of ideological considerations as well as of the simple hunger for jobs by a large number of its followers, has been shared by all groups within the Party.[56]

---

[56] Schärf (*April 1945 in Wien*, pp. 80 ff.) tells some amusing stories of the wild job-hunting spree which the downfall of the Nazi regime set off among its political opponents.

The exigencies of jointly-held power, as well as some restrictions embodied in the legislation adopted after 1945, and—as some critics claimed—the weakness of some of the SPOe's leaders in pushing their followers' claims, have proved obstacles to the achievement of anything like a Socialist monopoly in the sphere of public administration.

Originally the claim for such a monopoly had been based on the demand that the Austrian civil service and police force be fashioned into a reliably republican and democratic instrument of government; a demand, so the Socialists felt, which eliminated from consideration employees who had served either "Black" or "Brown" Fascist masters and freed the vast majority of jobs for occupancy by persons affiliated with the SPOe. The notion that a neutral civil service was an essential part of a modern *Rechtsstaat* had no place in Socialist thought.[57] Right and Left could unite, for different reasons, on this objective, though the latter warned against overemphasis of this method of peaceful permeation.[58] In the Socialist view, the traditional civil service was the product of a class society, a privileged caste incapable of meeting the demands made on it by the positive or future socialist state. To become truly democratic and reliable, class privilege in entrance and promotion would have to be eliminated.[59]

These early hopes and the demands flowing from them, linked to expectation of speedy conquest of political power by the Socialist Party, had to give way to more modest and realistic claims once "permanent coalition" was widely accepted as the Party's most favorable prospect for the indefinite future. This process of scaling down, accompanied by considerable bitterness and tension in the Party, led to the establishment of the principle of "*Proporz.*" [60]

When Nazi power collapsed in Austria, a host of public positions were suddenly thrown open for new appointment, partly through the precipitate flight of the former occupants—as in the case of the Vienna police force which had almost in its entirety "moved West"—and partly through the provisions of the Civil Service Transition Law (*Beamtenüberleitungsge-*

---

[57] Planke, *PTP*, 1945, p. 124.

[58] Cf., e.g., Czernetz, "Verwaltung und Macht," *Die Zukunft*, I (October, 1946), 19–22.

[59] *Ibid.*; also "Demokratie in der Verwaltung," *Arbeiter Zeitung*, January 7, 1947.

[60] Exact information and figures are not available in this field. Our discussion of the nature of "*Proporz*" represents merely as accurate a sketch of its main features as could be assembled.

setz).[61] Only those civil servants who had never been active National Socialists and had suffered deprivations for political reasons (*"gemassregelt"*) between 1933 and 1945 were automatically taken over into the federal civil service of the Second Republic. Furthermore, the law provided that in forming the new personnel organization an undoubted "Austrian democratic attitude" was to be more important than expert qualification.

From the Socialist viewpoint, the most serious drawback of this arrangement—inevitable under the prevailing political circumstances—was that Austro-Fascists who had suffered persecution at the hands of the Nazi regime were treated as the legal equals of Socialists who had been persecuted by these very former Austro-Fascists. Worse, this nominal equality amounted, in fact, to an initial disadvantage for the Socialists. The number of their federal employees had been small in the First Republic, and of those—due to the longer period of interruption—only a small fraction was available for service in 1945. The public offices, much to the chagrin of socialist functionaries, seemed to be rapidly filling up with "men of the past" drawn from the Catholic Conservative camp. The frustration felt at having been prevented from settling the old accounts of February, 1934, was now channeled into violent criticism of their own Party leaders for permitting these hated enemies to creep back into high public office.[62] The Party leadership found itself between inner-party charges of weakness and treason on the one hand, and violent attacks for alleged disregard of the law by the coalition partner and the non-Socialist press on the other. Yet according to the Party chairman, the SPOe was able "to place almost everyone who applied." [63]

---

[61] August 22, 1945, *StGBl*, No. 134.

[62] See the discussion at the 1946 Conference (*PTP*, 1946, *passim*). Weikhart stated: "Truly a storm of outraged disapproval swept over Vienna. No meeting, no assembly could take place without the question being put on the agenda." (*Ibid.*, p. 119.) In the debate the former R.S. functionaries (Czernetz, Holoubek, Weikhart, Wedenig) took a particularly prominent part. The debate had overtones of antagonism between Left and Right as well as between Vienna and Lower Austria.

[63] Schärf, *Der geistige Arbeiter in der Zweiten Republik*, p. 12. Note his assurance that, though he could not speak openly about these matters, Socialist influence on personnel questions existed even where the departments were not controlled by the SPOe. (*PTP*, 1946, p. 208.) And Minister Helmer, replying to his critics, stated: "I have made appointments recently to the police force which have greatly favored former trade unionists and Socialists—I cannot give more detailed information on the subject." (*Ibid.*, p. 194.)

The system of *"Proporz,"* intended to regularize and formalize the appointment procedure, has been officially established only in the nationalized industries. Its operation in other public offices is veiled by administrative autonomy, the provisions of the civil service law, and understandable reluctance to discuss it in public. In the absence of a central, neutral personnel agency, the individual department heads, in the *Land* governments as well as in the federal government, enjoy considerable autonomy in appointments, dismissals, and promotions, making it possible for them to surround themselves largely with men of their own parties.[64] Whether, however, the SPOe has been able to match the advantages of the OeVP derived from its more favorable initial position, as well as from the continuing requirement—modified only slightly in the Socialist-controlled Ministry of Interior [65]—of formal educational qualifications as prerequisites for appointment and promotion is uncertain. What is clear is that no action involving a public position, however low in the administrative hierarchy, can be taken without party affiliation playing a major role in the decision. Even generally recognized merit cannot compensate for a person's failure to affiliate himself with one of the two large parties. In the words of a prominent Catholic spokesman: "He who tried to escape the profession [of party loyalty] must bear the consequences: political and thus frequently economic passivity." [66]

The area to which party personnel policy extends is not limited by the bounds of public office. It is particularly pronounced, as previously mentioned, in the sphere of the economy under public control either through nationalization or because of its status as former German property. In addition, the self-administering public law institutions such as the Social Security Board and Chambers of Labor, Business, and Agriculture, with their

---

[64] Dr. Karl Lugmayer, "Der wirtschaftlich-politische Proporz," *Oesterreichische Monatshefte,* VI (1950), 661–65.

[65] According to the Report of the Party Executive to the 1948 Conference, a certain number of nonjurists were employed in the *Bundespolizeidirektion Wien* and several medium-level appointments were made on the basis of an efficient record and an upright attitude during the Nazi period, waiving the educational requirements. (*PTP,* 1948, p. 13.)

[66] Lugmayer, *op. cit.* Two headmasters of Vienna *Gymnasia*—one appointed on the OeVP, the other on the SPOe *"Proporz"* quota—agreed in conversation that the man best qualified for a high position then open in the educational service had no chance of promotion to it since he had consistently refused to solicit Party endorsement.

extensive administrative and research staffs, fall within the party personnel domain. In the latter the *"Proporz"* does not operate—as it does in the nationalized industries—on the basis of shared power but rather on that of a "balance of powers." Each of the Chambers is almost exclusively the preserve of one of the two large parties. In the social security boards the two sides, employees and employers, are represented in varying proportions fixed by law. Needless to say, in selecting the delegates who, on the employee side are proposed by the trade unions and the Chambers of Labor, Socialist Party affiliation is generally a requirement. Similarly, the administrative staff positions of these institutions are largely the perquisites of the respective parties.

When soon after the war an article appeared in the Socialist monthly *Die Zukunft* warning against the prevailing rejection of the ideal of a neutral, expert civil service, it represented a lone voice. The anonymous author warned that in a state in which several parties contributed to the formation of the political will, the increase of party influence on all levels of administration would inevitably lead to the disintegration of the *Rechtsstaat*; would confuse the notions of legal right and wrong, and end all predictability in matters of law, bringing about, as a substitute, the "more or less exact knowledge of the prevailing social power relations." [67] Whether due to belated recognition of the dangers thus depicted, to dissatisfaction with the results actually achieved, to an awareness of the widespread disgust aroused by the total "politicization" of the public service, or to a decline in radical temper, there are indications that thinking on the subject is beginning to change within the SPOe. The formulation included in the 1958 Program,[68] and the pronouncement of an editorial published by the *Arbeiter Zeitung* unequivocally calling for a system of competitive examinations as the basis for entry into the public service,[69] were public indications that the thinking of the Party was changing. That they do not at present represent much more than a change in temper is made evident by the complete absence of any concrete proposals (or discussion regarding them) to implement this objective, as well as by the fact that the principle of *"Proporz"* was reaffirmed in the new Coalition Pact. Yet the fact that some

---

[67] "Ueber die Demokratisierung der Verwaltung" (from a government report), I (December, 1946), 16–19.

[68] "Public offices are to be made accessible to all citizens by means of public announcements and awarded on the basis of objectively established qualifications." (*Arbeiter Zeitung*, May 15, 1958, p. 10.)

[69] OP, "Schach der Protektion," *Arbeiter Zeitung*, March 5, 1953.

of those who formerly were most insistent on a radical "socialist" personnel policy now are, if only academically, interested in a change leading to the establishment of a "neutral, expert" civil service signifies another step from the Marxist to the liberal concept of the democratic state.

Problems of Church and School

Sources of Traditional Conflict

Prolonged co-operation between the Socialist Party and the OeVP would have been impossible had the hostility which the Socialists and the Catholic Church felt for each other in the past continued into the Second Republic. The People's Party as the successor of the former Christian Social Party still claims the role of "defender of the faith"; and definition of the exact sphere of the Church's influence over such areas as marriage and education has remained a persistent bone of contention between the coalition partners. Though some of the issues involving the Church have so far defied solution, relations between the SPOe and the Catholic Church have undergone a fundamental change.

The change is not due to any formal alteration in the Party's position. From Hainfeld to the present it has officially adhered to the position that religion was to be considered a matter of private conscience and has insisted on strict separation between Church and State.[70] The change was caused, above all, by the decision on the part of the Church to abstain from overt participation in Austria's political life. This decision was in part responsible for the disappearance of antireligious agitation in the Socialist Movement. For in the past a wide gap had existed between the Party's official pronouncements and the sentiments and actions of its members toward the Church.

For reasons of principle, as well as out of tactical considerations, the Party had always refused officially to adopt an antireligious position and had always insisted on distinguishing between religion and clericalism. Thus Bauer, eager to build a bridge between the extremes of militant freethinkers and religious Socialists, used the Marxist analysis to stress the priority of the economic base and assigned religion to the superstructure. Religious problems were not therefore of primary concern to Socialists since their solution depended on the prior establishment of a rational eco-

---

[70] *Aktionsprogramm*, PTP, 1947, p. 14.

nomic system. Antagonism between socialism and religion appeared to him not inherent in socialist theory but the result of historical configurations which, while typical of the history of Continental Europe, were quite alien, for example, to English Socialism.[71] Although Bauer's opposition to the militant freethinkers in the Party was in part genuinely based on principle, the most persuasive argument seemed to him the tactical one: a militantly antireligious attitude, while fulfilling a vital function for the emancipated section of the working class, would, if adopted officially, thrust great masses of the rural population and even of the supposedly "enlightened" Vienna proletariat back into clericalism and thus prejudice the cause of Socialism.

The Party refused to adopt "enlightenment of the masses" in the sense of antireligious propaganda as part of its political task, except where it felt that religion was consciously being used as a means of obscuring class rule. But as the political struggle in the First Republic was mainly carried on against a party claiming to represent Christian tradition and receiving the active support of the Church and its clergy, against a party whose leader was a prominent member of the Catholic hierarchy, the fine distinction between an anticlerical and an anti-Christian position was easily lost. Though the Party officially declared its indifference to the metaphysical problems of religion, organized agitation for defection from the Church was widely advocated among its members by a flourishing organization of militant freethinkers. Most fundamentally, the Party's stress on critical rationalism, its commitment to the ideal of "progress," and its advocacy of values and a way of life antithetical to those endorsed by the Church [72] were the source of profound antagonism. To the extent that the Party was a "spiritual community" and not merely an instrument of economic or political emancipation, loyal membership in one precluded sincere adherence to the other.

Attempts at Conciliation

At the end of World War II, as mentioned before, the Church took the first important step to remove some of the most obvious sources of hostility between it and the Socialist Party. Cardinal Innitzer, Archbishop of Vienna, issued an order to the effect that members of the clergy were to refuse to accept public office; refuse to interfere in public affairs; refuse to

---

[71] *PTP*, 1926, pp. 319 ff.

[72] The values of the Socialist Party were entirely secular. Implicit in them was a spirit of irreverence toward tradition, an almost pagan naturalism, a defiance of traditional standards of sexuality, and advocacy of contraception and legalized abortion.

give recommendations for worldly positions; and limit their sermons to matters of a religious and charitable nature.[73]

This commitment to noninvolvement in political matters—at every point a departure from the Church's practice in the First Republic—was met by the determination on the part of the Socialist leadership to refrain in the future from any expression of hostility not only toward the Christian religion but toward the Catholic Church as well.[74] The organization of Socialist freethinkers, suppressed in 1934, was not revived after the war. What made it easier for the Party to live up to its promise was the fact that militant anticlericalism or even atheism apparently had lost its hold on any sizable sector of the Movement.[75] As in other spheres of socialist ideology, indifference had replaced former fervor.

Austrian Socialists, in several statements, have gone further than merely to acknowledge and reciprocate a changed attitude on the part of the Catholic Church. Attempts at *rapprochement* have involved efforts at proving that, when historically inevitable misunderstandings and frictions have been apparently rendered obsolete by recent events, a socially oriented Catholic Church and the Socialist Movement are no longer separated by any fundamental differences. And these attempts are bolstered by many different and frequently incompatible arguments. Some insist on the strict separation of the spiritual and temporal realms, asserting that Christianity proper has no social content;[76] others view Socialism and Christianity as both temporal and spiritual institutions which belatedly are discovering their common roots in the values of humanism. They consider socialist theory, Marxist or otherwise, quite compatible with the doctrines of the Church.[77]

It would be misleading, however, to convey the impression that the

---

[73] Schärf, *Zwischen Demokratie und Volksdemokratie*, p. 111.

[74] a.p., "Brief an Freidenker," *Arbeiter Zeitung*, December 4, 1948; also Schärf, "Sozialismus und Kirche," *ibid.*, September 13, 1949.

[75] From personal conversations it is my impression—confirmed in interview with Oscar Pollak—that only a small group of old functionaries continues to feel strongly on the subject and suffers from the Party-enforced silence.

[76] Alois Piperger, "Sozialismus, Religion, und Kirche," *Die Zukunft*, II (May, 1947), 131–32.

[77] Ernst Mayer, "Kirche und Sozialismus," *Die Zukunft*, I (July, 1946), 13–15; Max Neugebauer, *Wir wollen den inneren Frieden*. The 1958 Program formulates it thus: "Among the great religious communities, the Christian Churches in particular recognize the need for social reforms. Socialism and Christianity as the religion of neighborly love are perfectly compatible with each other." (*Arbeiter Zeitung*, May 15, 1958, p. 9.)

conciliatory tone adopted by the Party in the Second Republic marks a break with its fundamentally lay tradition. There is no indication that its gestures go beyond superficial pronouncements of mutual compatibility, or that they involve any positive appreciation of the Church's role in contemporary life or a sympathetic attempt to understand the intellectual assumptions of its teachings. The occasional admission that the inability of science to provide answers to some of the "ultimate questions" [78]—an echo of the antifreethinker position taken by some Socialists in the First Republic [79]— would always leave room for religious belief hardly amounts to a sustained effort at comprehending the basis of religious principles. What the Party aims at is a tactical adjustment with a powerful opponent made easy by the prevalent indifference, and not the exploration of a possible synthesis between Socialism and Christian religious belief.

The Continued Struggle Against Clericalism

That the Socialist determination to avoid a *Kulturkampf* goes hand in hand with continued sensitivity to the extent of clerical power is shown by the stubborn fight which the Party has put up to restrict Catholic influence on education and marriage. It indicates the strength with which the Socialist leaders concerned in these negotiations cling to the ideal of a state in which human relationships would be subject to regulation solely by secular political authorities.

With regard to the questions of marriage and divorce, the SPOe has been satisfied to stand pat on the position established by the introduction of German law subsequent to the *Anschluss*.[80] Under German law a civil ceremony is required and must precede the church ceremony. The latter is a matter of voluntary choice and by itself has not the force of law. In talks between representatives of the Church and the Socialist Party carried on immediately after the war, agreement was reached on this basis, the Socialists, in turn, recognizing the "sacramental character" of marriage.[81] Agreement in this was only one aspect of a much wider settlement of outstanding issues at a time when a swing toward socialism or even communism seemed

---

[78] Piperger, *op. cit.*
[79] Dr. Ellenbogen at 1926 Party Conference (*PTP*, 1926, pp. 335–37).
[80] JS, "Ehegesetze," *Arbeiter Zeitung*, November 25, 1950; Schärf, "Die kirchliche Trauung—verfassungswidrig," *Die Zukunft*, V (August, 1950), 211–13.
[81] Schärf, "Bischofsworte über Eherecht und Schule," *Die Zukunft*, V (April, 1950), 89–90.

likely and the Church was therefore willing to adopt a conciliatory position.

One of the fundamental assumptions on which this settlement was based was that the Concordat which the Dollfuss government had concluded with the Vatican in 1934 had ceased to be in force. Under the Concordat, the Catholic Church was granted a position of superior authority; the civil authorities pledged to support the Church's institutions and to enforce its rules.[82] The Socialist reaction to attempts, however veiled, to assert the continued validity of the Concordat [83] makes it clear that the Party would consider such a claim as an open declaration of war on the part of the Church.[84] For the modus vivendi reached between the Catholic bishops and the Socialist Party was considered by the latter to represent a kind of new Concordat.[85] By 1949, however, when it had become clear that the earlier fears of the Church in Austria had been unwarranted, Catholic spokesmen were less inclined to regard as permanent the position established in 1945. In his *Hirtenbrief* (pastoral letter) read from the pulpits in 1949, Cardinal Innitzer, though not openly repudiating the former position of nonintervention in political matters, nevertheless abandoned the attitude of strict neutrality by declaring that the Church would not be indifferent into whose hands public authority was entrusted; and that Christians should examine candidates for office with regard to questions which they as Christians considered crucial, such as marriage and religious education. This was an open attack on the SPOe which was unwilling to meet the Church's new demands.[86] The SPOe proved its determination not to be provoked into an open struggle with the Church by the restraint with which it met this challenge but remained firm in its unwillingness to alter the 1945 agreement.[87]

The Party's determination to avoid a *Kulturkampf* was reaffirmed in the Coalition Pact of 1949 but the interparty talks provided for in the Pact

---

[82] Schärf, "Gilt das Konkordat?" *Die Zukunft*, V (May, 1950), 117–25.

[83] As by Stephan Verrosta, *Die internationale Stellung Oesterreichs, 1938–1947*

[84] Schärf, "Gilt das Konkordat?" *loc. cit.* Dr. Schärf's argument against the validity of the Concordat is twofold: Austria's annexation by Germany in 1938 caused a break in its legal continuity and a lapse in all treaties previously entered into; the Concordat, enacted by the Dollfuss regime, had failed to receive a two-thirds majority in Parliament as specified in the Constitution.

[85] *Ibid.*

[86] "Der Hirtenbrief," *Arbeiter Zeitung*, March 1, 1949.

[87] a.p., "Antwort auf den Hirtenbrief," *ibid.*, March 3, 1949.

have so far not led to a final resolution of the outstanding differences.[88] In the marriage question the outlines of a possible compromise were sketched by Dr. Schärf when he implied that the Socialists would be willing to recognize the religious ceremony as valid if the Church, in performing the ceremony, recognized the civil law as binding.[89]

The issue of the marriage ceremony is likely to be settled only in connection with another question of much more fundamental importance: the new school law. Here the important issues which divide the Socialist Party from the Catholic Conservative camp fall roughly into two groups: questions affecting the relation of religion to education; and questions of equal educational opportunity and of educational method.

Specifically, the issue of religion and education has revolved around two major questions: the conditions under which religious instruction is to be administered in state schools, and the position and method of financing parochial schools. With regard to the former, the SPOe accepted religious instruction as a "means of education toward moral values" and was therefore ready to re-establish the position prevailing in the First Republic: religious instruction was to be a regular teaching subject presented on the premises of the state schools.[90] Parents of children under fourteen and the pupils themselves above that age were to have the right to declare their objection to attendance at the beginning of the academic year. The issue was settled on this basis, accepted by the Catholic bishops in 1945 and embodied in an act of parliament in 1949.[91]

---

[88] In 1955 the Catholic bishops formally stated their demands in a White Book. They may be summarized as follows: (*a*) Recognition of the Concordat of 1934; (*b*) marriage ceremony to be based on the Concordat, though the Church would not insist on a religious ceremony as a necessary prerequisite to valid marriage; (*c*) repeal of the right of pupils above 14 years of age to decide whether or not to attend religious instruction in school; and (*d*) maintenance of private Catholic schools by public funds, allocated in proportion to the number of students attending. (*Wiener Zeitung*, June 2, 1955.) Needless to say, these demands proved unacceptable to the SPOe.

[89] "Die kirchliche Trauung—verfassungswidrig," *loc. cit.* This would, for example, prevent a priest from marrying a couple where one partner was still legally married under civil (but not canon) law.

[90] F. Popp, "Schulforderungen der Sozialisten," *Arbeiter Zeitung*, April 18, 1948.

[91] Leopold Zechner, "Der Religionsunterricht," *Arbeiter Zeitung*, July 19, 1949. Originally the SPOe had demanded that students would have to register for courses of religious instruction. (Wilhelm Stemmer, "50 Jahre Schulkampf," *Arbeiter Zeitung*, April 10, 1948.) The Party continues to oppose introduction of religious instruction at vocational continuation schools for older students.

A more serious stumbling block in this area has been the second question, the position of parochial schools. After the Nazi government had suppressed them entirely, permission to re-establish them was granted immediately at the war's end by the Communist Minister of Education, with the reluctant consent of his Socialist under-secretary.[92] For the Socialist position has remained fundamentally hostile to any school system which is not unified under public control. The Socialist educational ideal is the education of citizens as rational, democratic, human beings who, in sharing a body of basic knowledge, would be equipped to form their own judgments and beliefs.[93] It is therefore hostile to any measure which would weaken the unitary public system of education, especially when this would involve handing over influence to groups which the Socialists assume to be inherently antiprogressive, anti-Socialist, and even antidemocratic.[94] The official Catholic position—embraced in the draft law prepared by the OeVP-controlled Ministry of Education—demanded a public subsidy for private schools where attendance met a stipulated standard figure, thus providing for a double school system, both state supported, of which only one was open indiscriminately to all children and fully accountable to the public authority. Socialist arguments against such a state subsidy have followed the obvious lines: that those who do not desire to take advantage of the educational services supplied by the state should bear the cost themselves; and that private schools should not be allowed to weaken the public-school system by dividing the student body.[95] Furthermore, it is argued, an extensive system of parochial schools would lower educational levels, decrease tolerance, and necessarily aim at the indoctrination of the students.[96] Just as Socialists are basically opposed to *any* church-controlled schools,

---

[92] "In a real democracy private schools have—except perhaps for experimental purposes—no justification." (*Arbeiter Zeitung*, October 25, 1945.)

[93] Anton Tesarek, "Erziehung zur Demokratie, zum Republikanismus, zum Pazifismus," *Die Zukunft*, I (May, 1946), 17–19. This involves stress on learning by discussion (*Arbeitsunterricht*) rather than by the traditional method of lecture; also a de-emphasis on mere learning of facts. (Cf. Hans Fischl, *Schulreform, Demokratie und Oesterreich, 1918–1950*, pp. 140 ff.) Gloeckl's slogan, "*Von der Lernschule zur Arbeitsschule*," is frequently cited.

[94] Cf., e.g., Stemmer, "Schulreform ohne Kulturkampf," *Die Zukunft*, III (September, 1948), 271–75, where the Church is assailed for its past connection with capitalism and all anti-Marxist forces.

[95] Ibid.; also Zechner, "Schulfragen und Schulverhandlungen," *Die Zukunft*, IX (February, 1954), 41–43.

[96] Zechner, "Schulgesetz," *Arbeiter Zeitung*, December 18, 1951.

whether publicly financed or not, they suspect the Catholic Church of the desire ultimately to bring the *entire* school system under its control.[97]

Equality of Educational Opportunity

Apart from this major issue of the position of private (really Catholic) schools, there is one other educational question which seriously divides the Socialist from the People's Party: that of the so-called "common high school" (*Allgemeine Mittelschule*). Put briefly, it is the Socialist aim, realized experimentally on a small scale in the First Republic (and endorsed as a Party objective in the Linz Program) to replace the division between the present *Hauptschule* and the various types of *Mittelschulen* by a "common school" for all students between the ages of eleven and fifteen. Pupils in the *Hauptschule* at present generally are expected to terminate their education at the age of fourteen while the *Mittelschulen*, in theory, serve as preparation for advanced study.[98]

According to the Socialist plan, all students would share a common curriculum up to the age of fifteen. After that age the best qualified would go on to the preprofessional *Obermittelschulen*. By means of this "philosophical and social coeducation," Socialists hope to break the still-existing "educational privilege" of youths from nonworking-class homes. The present system of eight-year *Mittelschulen* forces pupils (or rather their parents) to make a career decision at the age of ten, long before an accurate estimate of the child's true inclinations and abilities has been gained. The *Mittelschulen*, endowed with superior prestige and frequented largely by children from middle-class homes, thus foster elitism and class distinctions.[99] For in the present *Mittelschulen*—the only avenues to advanced education and the positions rewarded with higher prestige and more money—the working class and peasantry are seriously underrepresented: in 1948, only 13.5 per

---

[97] Zechner in "Sehen wir Gespenster?" (*Die Zukunft*, VII [May, 1952], 152–54), quotes the Lenten pastoral letter to the effect that the public *Simultanschule* should be allowed to remain only as an emergency solution. It is Zechner's conviction that a school system completely dominated by the Church remains for it the ideal to be striven for. Everything else is merely a concession to existing power relations, at best a truce until revocation.

[98] In fact 40 to 50 per cent of its students also leave school at the age of fourteen. (Fischl, *op. cit.*, p. 177.)

[99] Stemmer, "Einige Gedanken zur Einheitsmittelschule," *Die Zukunft*, I (August, 1946), 10–11; also Fischl, *op. cit.*, p. 178.

cent of the students of the Vienna *Mittelschulen* came from working-class families; [100] and at the university level the percentage of students maintained by manual workers is only 9 per cent.[101]

The reasons for this situation are admittedly not primarily financial. The fees for attendance at *Mittelschulen* and institutions of higher education alike are hardly more than nominal and exemptions are easily obtainable. Furthermore, the occupational groups such as white-collar employees and civil servants, from which almost 60 per cent of the students at the *Mittelschulen* are drawn, are today financially in no better position than manual workers to provide for the prolonged education of their children.[102] The main reason, accepted even by Socialists, appears to be the traditional insistence on "good" (i.e., high-prestige) education on the part of those who themselves benefited by it.[103] The Socialist plan, by allowing the parents to make the decision at an age when the child's abilities have been more fully revealed, is intended to make this choice easier for working-class parents who by habit seem unwilling to take educational risks. Furthermore, by reducing the number of years which gifted working-class children would spend in the "class-alien" atmosphere of *Mittelschulen*, the danger of their cultural and political estrangement from their class would be lessened.[104]

In the field of education the SPOe is content to fight old battles—battles which may well be still worth fighting—and to fall back on the ideas of its pioneers.[105] There is a marked absence of a searching examination of the Socialist reform measures in the educational field. Any thought of fundamental reform in the *Obermittelschulen* and the universities—the most tradition-bound sector of the Austrian educational system—has been largely

---

[100] Manual workers made up 55 per cent of the Vienna population. (Stemmer, "Kein Bildungsprivileg mehr?" *Die Zukunft*, III [July, 1948], 212–16.)

[101] Cited by *Salzburger Nachrichten*, July 11, 1953. As another 7 per cent are listed as "self-supporting," of whom undoubtedly a major proportion come from working-class families, the difference between universities and *Mittelschulen* seems insignificant.

[102] Stemmer, "Kein Bildungsprivileg mehr?" *loc. cit.*

[103] Fischl, *Warum allgemeine Mittelschulen?* p. 13.

[104] Cf. Fischl, "Mittelschulreform und Sozialismus," *Der Kampf*, XV (November, 1922), 337–41; also Fritz Kurz, "Welche Schule sollen Arbeiterkinder besuchen?" *Arbeiter Zeitung*, February 15, 1951, p. 5.

[105] "All observations . . . make one realize that generally little is today left of the *élan* and dynamism which carried the reform movement in Glöckl's time." (Fischl, *Schulreform* . . . , p. 119.)

neglected by the Party.[106] This neglect is a reflection of the continued weakness of the Party's position in the academic community, the feeling of hopelessness toward the prospect of breaching this conservative stronghold; and the spirit of "practicism" which refuses to engage in speculation on far-reaching changes which are not related to pressing needs or Party advantage.[107]

By viewing the school as an instrument for training independently thinking, democratic citizens, respectful of human dignity and freedom, Austrian Socialists have placed themselves in the main stream of modern liberal education with little relation to specifically socialist goals. Equality of educational opportunity and "philosophical and social coeducation" of all members of the community are general liberal objectives. Only under conditions where the working class has been the exclusive bearer of the ideas of the Enlightenment have they become identified as specifically socialist aspirations.

---

[106] Occasional Socialist suggestions for changes in university education are limited to stress on increased professional (i.e., technical) training and on participation by Parliament in the selection of teachers and determination of curricula. (Cf. Duschek, "Zur Frage der Hochschulreform," *Die Zukunft*, V [February, 1950], 45–49; and Wolfgang Speiser, "Für eine radikale Hochschulreform," *Die Zukunft*, II [April, 1947], 117–18.)

[107] In 1957 the Socialist slate received only 11 per cent of the votes cast at university elections. (*Wiener Zeitung*, January 26, 1957.) This marks a decline from the immediate postwar period, when it polled 20 to 25 per cent. (Cf. *strom*, June 5, 1949; *Arbeiter Zeitung*, January 25 and 26, 1951.)

VI

Toward a Socialist Economy? (Part I)

Some Questions of Economic Principle

The Marxist Heritage

Marx left to his intellectual disciples a heritage in which faith in the inevitable economic collapse of the capitalist system was coupled with a conscious refusal to draw a blueprint of the emerging socialist society. "Sufficient unto the day . . ." was the feeling of the early generation of Marxist Socialists. Provided the breakdown of the capitalist order took place, the specific arrangements characteristic of socialism would automatically take shape. Though Marx himself was not too clear on the exact causes of the eventual breakdown, and divergent schools of socialists therefore expended much intellectual energy in formulating theories as to the economic reasons for the inevitable collapse of capitalism,[1] the *fact* of such an inevitable catastrophe was for them beyond doubt. It formed, indeed, the core of the structure of scientific socialism on which their faith in the inevitability of the socialist triumph could be based. They therefore viewed every economic crisis with eager anticipation and every sign of recovery with puzzled disappointment, finding ever new explanations for the delay in the overdue total collapse of the capitalist economies. Only the Revisionists, who had broken with the belief in the iron law of capitalist development which their fellow Socialists devoutly believed Marx to have laid bare, were freed of the necessity of explaining away periods of capitalist expansion and prosperity or of discovering complex sets of "countertendencies" which rendered the Marxist laws "temporarily" inoperative.

---

[1] Cf. Paul M. Sweezy, *The Theory of Capitalist Development*, *passim*, for a summary of the various "collapse" theories.

Revisionists also avoided the dilemma which was the lot of every socialist who was faced with the opportunity of participating in the governing of his society, whether as a politician or trade unionist: the dilemma between the desire to hurry the system on its way to the "inevitable" demise, and the duty to accept the responsibility to work for the well-being of that society within the framework of the existing order.[2]

The logical consequence of the assumption that the capitalist system suffered from an incurable internal disease—and it was one that was widely accepted—was that socialism, the system which should supersede it, would have to be animated by economic laws radically different from those operating under capitalism. In its most extreme form this notion led to a vision of a moneyless, incentive-free, and competitionless economy in which all hierarchies—those created by the productive process as well as by private ownership—had been destroyed.[3]

As Socialists in many countries began to penetrate into positions of responsibility and power following World War I, a speedy clarification of their hitherto vague expectations was forced upon them. Particularly those who rejected the Leninist solution of imposing a political revolution on a society which was not, in Marx's sense, ripe for Socialism—and to this group belonged all European Social Democrats, Right and Left [4]—had to pay close attention to the distinction between those aspects of capitalism which were inherent *in the system*—thus evil and to be removed with the advent of socialism—and those aspects which were part of the industrial method of production. The latter would, by and large, have to be retained under any subsequent social and economic arrangement aiming at an abundance of goods.

The group of political thinkers lumped together under the name "Austro-Marxists" were free of economic utopianism. The success of Otto Bauer's

---

[2] For a pithy expression of this dilemma, see Adolf F. Sturmthal, *The Tragedy of European Labor*, 1918–1939, pp. 83 ff.

[3] The period of War Communism (1918 to 1921) in the USSR, with its radical economic experiments and the subsequent return to more traditional forms of production, illustrates the lack of concrete preparation for the task of constructing a socialist economic system. According to Valentin Giterman (*Die historische Tragik der sozialistischen Idee*), Marx had no sympathy for such utopian expectations. However, his refusal to concern himself with the ultimate characteristics of the future socialist society and Engels' cryptic and utopian remarks on the subject in the *Anti-Dühring* left the field free for enthusiastic speculation.

[4] It was this criterion of historical maturity with all its implications which primarily served to divide the "Leftist" Kautsky from "Leftists" like Lenin.

Der Weg zum Sozialismus [5] was in part due to the fact that it provided concrete and apparently feasible solutions to economic problems which until that time, had been dealt with largely in abstract slogans. The stress which Bauer put on the necessity for maintaining production, his belief in the continued need for material incentives and appropriate financial rewards for better or harder work, his opposition to any large measure of outright "workers' control" demonstrated his realistic refusal to envision Socialism as a system in which all the economic features of capitalism would simply be reversed. His vision was that of a society in which all the means of production would be owned or controlled by organs of the community. Proceeding from industries whose ownership was already strongly concentrated to those which would become "ripe" through appropriate rationalization measures—and which in the meantime would be under public supervision—socialization would eventually pervade all areas of the economy down to the small craftsman and peasant.

Karl Renner, though differing from Bauer in points of principle, tactics, and temper, shared with him two basic assumptions: opposition to any form of utopian experiment which might disturb the productive process; [6] and the anticipation of a system which, though gradually, would become entirely socialized.[7]

The attempt to take a middle road—so characteristic of Austro-Marxism —between the extremes of Revisionism and believers in "catastrophic socialism," [8] to devise a picture of the capitalist world which would comfort the faithful while taking realistic note of observable tendencies, took shape

---

[5] Published in Vienna in 1919.

[6] "Do interventions exist which do not put out of action any agent of circulation still functioning? That is obviously the main point." (Renner, *Die Wirtschaft als Gesamtprozess und die Sozialisierung*, p. 371.) Note also his insistence that socialism would not be "completely different" and his rejection of certain concepts of Socialism as "wish dreams of the future . . . the ancient idea of paradise, even if now turned into the social and established in this world." (Renner, *Wege der Verwirklichung*, p. 14.)

[7] Renner conceived this process as the result of diverse measures and institutions which would, through different methods in diverse areas, render the owners of capital functionless, thereby eliminating them and thus socializing the surplus value formerly appropriated by them. "For each special form [*Teilform*] of exploitation practice finds special institutions." (*Wege der Verwirklichung*, p. 97.)

[8] Though Leninist "voluntarism" would seem to be able to dispense with it, it yet put great emphasis on the automatic elements leading to the inevitable downfall of capitalism.

in the economic formulations of the Linz Program of 1926.[9] Devised at a time when the American economy was booming and the capitalist economies of Europe seemingly had recovered from the consequences of World War I, the Linz formulation accepted a theory of increasing concentration and alternating depression-prosperity cycles in place of the expectation of outright collapse and disappointed those who desired to be comforted by eschatological certainties.[10] Although the eventual triumph of Socialism was still viewed as inevitable by Austro-Marxists, the conditions of this triumph had become not so much the inherent developmental tendencies of capitalism as the Party's conscious struggle for political power.[11] According to them, the fully socialized society was the only answer to exploitation, alienation, and recurrence of crises believed inherent in capitalism. In the transition period socialized and capitalistic enterprises would continue to coexist, with the socialized sector consciously fostered at the expense of the capitalist one.[12]

The Acceptance of a Mixed Economy

Under the theoretical impact of Keynes's teachings and the practical demands of the American "alliance," the view that capitalism and crises were twins has, since 1945, been largely given up. Or, more correctly, it is admitted by Socialists that reforms and planning measures within an essentially capitalist framework—leaving aside the scholastic question whether it thereby ceases to be capitalist—can secure a crisis-free economy. The anti-theoretical frame of mind characteristic of the postwar leadership is clearly observable in the field of economic theory. With the exception of fewer than half a dozen professional economists who as individuals have con-

---

[9] PTP, 1926, pp. 169–71, Section: "Der Kapitalismus."

[10] See, e.g., Otto Leichter, "Zur ökonomischen und machtpolitischen Theorie des Parteiprogrammes," *Der Kampf*, XIX (October, 1926), 435–42. Leichter proposed inclusion of a paragraph pointing to *ever deepening* crises and *falling* wages. The Linz Program spoke only of recurring crises and a widening gap between the rising productivity and more slowly rising wages.

[11] This does not apply to Renner's ideas. In his view Socialism did not require for its realization strenuous efforts—harped on by the Party Left—to arouse the proletariat's class-conscious will to power. His Revisionist inevitabilism obviously did not require a breakdown theory.

[12] Cf. Section 5 of the Linz Program (PTP, 1926, pp. 189–93), "The Transition from the Capitalist to the Socialist Order."

cerned themselves with economic theory,[13] the Party's attitude in this sphere seems exclusively determined by tactical considerations and internal pressures.

The new position has been popularly expounded as that of the "middle way," [14] which found its authoritative formulation in the 1958 Draft Program. For there the maintenance of full employment through a variety of countercyclical measures was put forth as the very heart of a future socialist economic policy.[15] This exclusively Keynesian approach did not, however, recommend itself equally to various Party economists for technical and ideological reasons. For by implication it clearly slighted the need for control and planning of production in a largely collectivized economy, formerly central to the socialist economic concept.[16] Meeting this criticism with evasion rather than genuine reappraisal, the final version of the 1958 Program vaguely reaccepted the distinction between Keynesian and truly socialist policies (which the Draft Program had slighted) and limited its espousal of Keynesianism to a transition period.[17]

In practice, the SPOe's economic policy has not followed any particular economic theory. It has been much more radical than Keynes by stressing the traditional socialist objective of nationalization of industry. On the other hand, while avowing the fiscal methods advocated by Keynes, it has failed to utilize the required budgetary and monetary tools. Faced with a slowly rising price level and the realization that stable prices, stable wages (under conditions of free collective bargaining), and full employment apparently were incompatible,[18] the Party tacitly revised its main objectives

---

[13] Primarily Stefan Wirlandner, the late Benedikt Kautsky, and Karl Ausch. Their names will frequently recur in the following pages.

[14] KA, "Der dritte Weg," *Arbeiter Zeitung*, January 24, 1953.

[15] *Vorentwurf*, p. 20.

[16] For recognition of the changes in basic socialist thinking required by acceptance of Keynesianism, see Stefan Wirlandner, "Vollbeschäftigung in unserer Zeit," *Die Zukunft*, VI (May, 1951), 127; and Introduction to Karl Forchheimer, *Keynes' neue Wirtschaftslehre*, 1952. The most outspoken criticism of the Draft Program's departure from traditional socialist concepts was voiced by Peter Anders in "Der Sozialismus und die Wirtschaft," *Die Zukunft*, XIII (January, 1958), 5–8.

[17] The crucial paragraph in the Draft Program had stressed the merely *corrective* role of state intervention. The final version reads as follows: "As long as ups and downs of the economy have not been eliminated through socialist planning, full employment will have to be assured through anticyclical measures."

[18] KA, "Probleme der Vollbeschäftigung," *Arbeiter Zeitung*, September 21, 1952.

of "full employment." Fearful of the opponents' charge that it favored policies leading to inflation,[19] the Party disavowed an "extreme full employment policy" and reduced its aim to the achievement of "almost full employment." [20]

The present economic concept of the SPOe is clear only in a negative point: its opposition to unregulated market capitalism. In every other respect—the nature of planning and controls, the extent of the public sector, the role of the market and its corollary of prices and incentives—the Party has failed to work out an unequivocal position. On one hand it is still committed to a truly socialist economy, i.e., one in which the principle of profit is replaced by production for the general welfare.[21] On the other hand, it now accepts a "mixed economy" not merely as a transitional phase on the way toward full socialization but as the ultimate goal—even promising in its new program wide scope to private entrepreneurial initiative. Although many of the Party's leaders and members appear satisfied with the present limits of the size of the public sector, the conviction that the transfer of privately owned property into collective possession represents the core of socialism is still sufficiently widespread to prevent open acceptance of the *status quo* and results in continued equivocations.[22]

---

[19] Wirlandner, the Party's most outspoken Keynesian, accepts a slight inflationary trend as a necessary part of a full-employment policy. See his "Planung, Vollbeschäftigung und Währungspolitik," *Arbeit und Wirtschaft*, V (January, 1952), 1. Benedikt Kautsky's "Das Ende des billigen Geldes" (*ibid.* [March, 1952], 1–3) contained a strong criticism of this view which, so Kautsky argued, was disastrous for an economy relying on exports as much as the Austrian did.

[20] "Extreme full employment," or "overemployment," has been defined as a situation in which less than 3 per cent of the employable labor force is out of work; "almost full employment" exists when fewer than 5 per cent are unemployed. (Cf. KA, "Der dritte Weg," *Arbeiter Zeitung*, January 24, 1953; "Kampf der Deflation," *ibid.*, January 27, 1953; and "Keine Inflation, Keine Arbeitslosigkeit," *ibid.*, October 23, 1952.) It should be noted, however, that in the 1958 Program (and this includes the more extensive Draft Program) no recognition is given to the possible conflict between the goals of full employment and currency stability. The Program emphatically advocates both.

[21] 1958 Program (*Arbeiter Zeitung*, May 15, 1958, p. 10).

[22] The Draft Program contained the controversial statement that nationalization had "largely fulfilled its purpose in Austria." (*Vorentwurf*, p. 27.) In response to criticism (e.g., Friedrich Scheu, "Die Verstaatlichung im neuen Parteiprogramm," *Die Zukunft*, XIII [January, 1958], 8–11), the offending sentence was eliminated and replaced by the noncommittal assertion that "considerations of

By being merged into the concept of "mixed economy" in which the principle of welfare planning has replaced the autonomy of the market, the concept of a "socialized economy" as a precisely defined type has disintegrated. The new boundary lines betwen "capitalist" and "socialist" economies are all the vaguer because the role of public ownership in the planning process has been left undetermined.[23]

Cartels and Competition

As long as part socialization was merely considered a transitional phase, the concentration process going on in the capitalist sector of the economy was watched by socialists with equanimity, not to say benevolence. For it was one way in which the capitalist economy was "socializing" itself from within, and provided a measure of an industry's "ripeness" for public ownership.[24] The acceptance of a mixed economy has logically led to a fundamental change in the socialist attitude toward "combinations in restraint of trade." As free markets are now accepted as essential parts of a "socialist economy," it becomes the interest of the community to assure in the private sector economic freedom in its purest form—perfect competition.

The establishment of a Monopoly Commission by the British Labor Government was watched with considerable interest by Austrian Socialists, among whom thoughts had begun to run along parallel lines.[25] The significant relationship between the general development of socialist thought and

---

the general welfare would alone be relevant to future transfers of private enterprises into public ownership."

[23] Ranking the United States among the "mixed economies" implies that extensive public ownership is not a prerequisite. (See "Der dritte Weg," in which the United States is cited as an example of a society planning for "almost full employment.")

[24] Otto Bauer in *Der Weg zum Sozialismus* argued not for destruction of cartels but their utilization for the general welfare. The cartel law, whose enactment was demanded in the Linz Program, was clearly not intended to lead the economy back to competition but to prevent monopoly abuses during the period of transition. On the traditional view, see Wirlandner, "Konkurrenzsozialismus," *Die Zukunft*, IV (May, 1949), 145–47.

[25] *Ibid.* In June, 1948, Wirlandner pointed out that "once control measures are lifted, unhindered competition must take their place." ("Vor der NEP," *Die Zukunft*, III [June, 1948], pp. 175–78.) Party propaganda, in defending controls, reiterated constantly that in a highly cartelized economy such as the Austrian, the vaunted law of supply and demand would fail to operate to the advantage of the consumer.

the problem of an anticartel policy was thus dramatically put by the social-ist economist Dr. Wirlandner:

If the transition to a totally planned economy were, so to say, at the door, it would hardly be worth while to develop a special cartel policy. But if we must reckon with the fact that in the second half of our century no decision in this direction will be taken, but that Western Europe and the United States will at best exhibit features of a mixed economy, then it becomes important to solve the question of cartels and monopolies.[26]

Wirlandner's remarks reflected the line which the Party had adopted in the pages of the *Arbeiter Zeitung* since the middle of 1948.[27] The SPOe's de-termined campaign, supported by the Central Executive of the Trade Union Federation,[28] led to the passage of an anticartel law in July, 1951. This law, though eventually greatly strengthened[29] and thereby made ac-ceptable to the Socialists,[30] represented little more than a weak first step in the direction of a truly competitive economy.[31] According to an unbiased

---

[26] "Bemerkungen zur Kartellpolitik," *Die Zukunft*, V (December, 1950), 326. Note that Franz Domes, a veteran Austrian trade union leader, had already (in 1928) put forward a stringent anticartel policy. His views then found no echo in the Party. (See "Zur Frage des Kartellwesens," *Die Zukunft*, VI [July, 1951], 203–4.)

[27] See *Arbeiter Zeitung*, June 18, August 10, October 1, October 2, and October 7, 1948. The editorial of August 21, 1949, in calling for new and strong anti-cartel legislation referred to cartels as "public enemy number one."

[28] "The OeGB begins a publicistic struggle against the cartel evil and will not cease from it until an effective law has been passed." (*Solidarität*, No. 87, Octo-ber, 1949, p. 1.) In this struggle the Executive encountered resistance from some of the affiliated trade unions. (See *Solidarität*, No. 89, November, 1949, p. 3.)

[29] The original draft had been prepared by the Ministry of Trade—traditionally a clientele department of the Austrian business community; the revised act as eventually passed, *BG #173 vom 4. Juli 1951 (Kartellgesetz)* of August 27, 1951, contained the following major provisions: (*a*) All cartel agreements must be regis-tered and approved by a Cartel Commission; and (*b*) registration is to be refused on some specific grounds (par. 12, clauses 2–4) and whenever the agreements tend "to raise prices or prevent their lowering; or if it limits the production or distribution of goods" (par. 12, clauses 2–5).

[30] Cf. KA, "Mit dem Kartellgesetz gegen die Kartelle," *Arbeiter Zeitung*, July 6, 1951. For criticism of the ministerial draft, see KA, "Ein unzulängliches Kartell-gesetz" (*ibid.*, June 24, 1950); and "Kartellgesetzgebung" (*Arbeit und Wirt-schaft*, III [January, 1950], 16).

[31] See the appraisal of an outside observer in "Wirtschaftsordnung im Zeichen des Pluralismus," *Neue Zürcher Zeitung*, June 8, 1952.

source, the economic concentration process has progressed so far in Austria that about one-third of all goods is produced by industries comprising a single enterprise; another third by industries made up from two to five firms; for one-sixth production is divided between six and twelve producers per industry and only another sixth comes from industries with over a dozen enterprises.[32] In addition, restraint on competition through legal regulations, public law functions of self-governing bodies (the Chambers), interlocking directorates, and concentration of investment banking is so deeply entrenched that only a veritable social and economic revolution could eliminate it.[33] The Austrian Socialist Party is fitted neither by temperament nor by political interest for the role of antirestrictionist Hercules. Benedikt Kautsky has spelled out the implications of a determined anti-cartel policy in which consumer choice would be effectively realized. It requires the abandonment of all attempts at controlling and directing the private sector, consequently elimination of the bureaucratic control apparatus, a complete liberalization of the nonnationalized part of the economy.[34] These ideas are obviously too strange, too unsettling, and too much at odds with Socialist tradition for outright Party endorsement. Yet by its willingness to see central planning machinery weakened, by its acceptance of the return to dear money and a private capital market, and by its own campaign for the repeal of the so-called *Untersagungsgesetz*,[35] the SPOe has

---

[32] Franz Nemschak, *Der Weg zu einem gesamtwirtschaftlichen Konzept*, p. 29.

[33] Cf. Harry W. Johnstone, *The Restraint of Competition in the Austrian Economy, passim.* The violence of reaction to Johnstone's strictures coming from the (usually pro-American) Conservative camp is indicated by the following paragraph: "Austria's economy does not need any advisers from Texas, especially not when they view everything through red spectacles." (*Das Kleine Volksblatt,* May 1, 1952, p. 4.)

[34] Benedikt Kautsky, "Kartelle und Trusts," *Die Zukunft,* VI (May, 1951), 131–32; also "Kapitalskonzentration und Monopolkapitalismus," *ibid.* (February, 1951), 46–51.

[35] Under this law, entry into any trade was made dependent on approval by the established members. This holdover from the medieval guild system has now been repealed. The result of this "liberalization" is likely to be the opposite of that desired by the SPOe: to reduce, through increased competition, the excessively high middle-men margins. As these high margins are due to the already overblown middle-men apparatus, a further influx of new units will mean further division of the already small market, requiring even higher margins for each unit. Because of the political importance of the stratum—to the SPOe as well as to the People's Party—it is unlikely that, once established, it will be left to the ruthless forces of an unregulated market, in the name of free competition.

tacitly and in piecemeal fashion moved in the direction indicated by Kautsky.[36]

Equality, Efficiency, and Incentives

The anti-utopianism characteristic of Austro-Marxism led its foremost spokesmen, Bauer and Renner, to insist strongly on the necessity and the virtue of economic efficiency under socialism. In their discussions of the economic features of a future socialist society, the vague yet appealing dreams of transforming the repressive industrial system into a community of free and equal brothers, for whom work would be joy and discipline freedom,[37] met with little sympathy. Thus there is in Bauer's *Der Weg zum Sozialismus* no expectancy that at any time, however remote, a man will receive from society compensation according to his needs rather than his contribution. On the contrary, Bauer considered it a particular merit that in this future socialist society, rewards for the first time would be received strictly on the basis of the contribution which the worker made rather than on any extrinsic grounds.[38] This severely practical approach, so reminiscent of the Webbs,[39] also has dominated Austrian Socialist thought in the Second Republic. The principle of efficiency (*Leistungsprinzip*) as the basis of reward, and consequently the endorsement of money incentives and thus of income differences, are generally accepted and highly valued. Some critics insisted that the socialist goal could not merely be "equality of opportunity" but was that of "minimal economic and social differentiation" between members of a socialist society.[40] But the Party, in its 1958 Program, modestly limited its objective to the "right to a working income proportionate to personal effort" obtained on the basis of equal career chances.[41] Thus it simply endorsed the classical formulation of "from everyone according to his ability; to everyone according to his labor."

---

[36] The Socialist attitude toward planning, money policy, and private saving will be further discussed in Chapter VII.

[37] These expectations are inherent in the Marxist conception of socialism as ending "alienation" and the replacement of government over men by the administration of things.

[38] *Der Weg zum Sozialismus*, Chap. 1.

[39] Bauer pays tribute to the Webbs in the Introduction to his *Der Weg zum Sozialismus*.

[40] Christian Broda, "Was ist Sozialismus?" *Die Zukunft*, XIII (January, 1958), 2–5.

[41] *Arbeiter Zeitung*, May 15, 1958, p. 10.

The question whether a rigorous system of industrial efficiency based on equality of opportunity and appropriateness of reward is identical with the traditionally held view of socialism—or whether it is designed to create a more truly and ruthlessly competitive society—has been generally ignored. Yet socialist practice and, infrequently, socialist thought also acknowledge the alternate principle at the opposite pole from that of "to everyone according to his contribution":

Education, health, pensions for the disabled and old are recognized as total costs of industrial society which must be borne by the public treasury . . . *this principle of regulating society according to human needs* instead of automatic laws of the market represents a breach in the system of capitalism.[42] (*Italics added.*)

The incompatibility of the values of efficiency and humanism has created for socialism its most profound dilemma which, so far, it has attempted to escape rather than face. For it should be quite clear that the establishment of "efficiency" as the paramount value can only mean man's continued subjection, potentially—as in the Soviet Union—far more ruthless than under capitalism for being clothed in the mantle of communal welfare.[43]

Terming the values of productive efficiency and humanism incompatible in theory is not tantamount to declaring them irreconcilable in practice. Just as Socialism historically was largely motivated by the revulsion against the subjection to the impersonal efficiency of the capitalist market—the degradation of the individual to an interchangeable and expendable cog in the economic machine—in the same way workers, in a free society, rebel against the abstract efficiency of a planned economy which continues to subject them to a superior force outside themselves. The significance of this conflict in helping to shape that system known as the welfare state will become evident as we turn to some of the more important concrete economic policies pursued by the SPOe.

---

[42] Paul Sering, *Jenseits des Kapitalismus*, pp. 53–54. It hardly need be pointed out that the definition of socialism as a system in which society is regulated according to human needs is incompatible with one which puts foremost stress on equality of opportunity (and therefore on social utility).

[43] Occasional extreme formulations pointing in the same direction can even be discovered among Austrian Socialists committed to "humanism": "Work-shy parasites and saboteurs of the plan will have to be dealt with through the force of law . . . a democratically planned economy means voluntary labor free of hunger." (Josef Hendrych, "Freie oder demokratische Wirtschaft?" *Solidarität*, No. 35, July 15, 1947, p. 13.)

These policies may be broadly divided into two areas: those affecting the ownership of the means of production, taking the form of transfer of ownership into public hands (or merely of modification of the terms on which such ownership continues to be exercised); and those policies which intentionally or as a by-product create a more egalitarian society through redistribution of income. Under the former heading, traditionally considered more "genuinely" socialist, we shall discuss such questions as nationalization, planning, and workers' codetermination; under the latter, subsidies, taxation, social services, and public housing.

Socialization in the First and Second Republics

Bauer's Scheme

When Otto Bauer developed his concept of economic democracy through socialization, his foremost thought was to devise a system which would be guarded against two opposite dangers: syndicalism, destructive of efficient production; and centralized bureaucratization, threatening the people's liberty and economic efficiency as well. The core of Bauer's proposal was that the industries taken over by the state should not be administered by regular government departments; rather that, in the form of *Gemeinwirtschaftliche Anstalten*—a modified form of public corporation—they should be run by boards composed equally of representatives of labor, consumers, and the state, the last to be selected in part by Parliament and in part by the Minister of Finance.[44] To ensure against political influence in the selection of managers, they were to be chosen on the basis of proposals made by impartial boards consisting of technical experts. Compensation to the previous owners of the industries taken over would be financed through a steeply progressive capital levy amounting to one-sixth of the total national wealth.

Bauer's scheme, though not universally accepted by Austrian Socialists,[45]

[44] For some of the ideas underlying his scheme Bauer acknowledged himself indebted to the English guild socialists, particularly G. D. H. Cole's *The World of Labour* (G. Bell & Sons, London, 1913), the plans worked out by various contemporary socialization commissions as well as the (presumably negative) experiences of the first phase of Soviet Russian War Communism. (Bauer, *Der Weg zum Sozialismus*, Introduction.)

[45] Renner criticized the concept of the tripartite boards, particularly the inclusion of the state's representatives in day-to-day decisions. (*Wege der Verwirklichung*, Chap. 7.)

was the most comprehensive and representative expression of Austro-Marxist thinking on the subject of organizing socialized industry; the proof of this was its embodiment in the abortive socialization act passed in the early days of the First Republic.[46] Though the failure of the Social Democrats to achieve a significant degree of nationalization after World War I precluded any conclusion on the working of Bauer's scheme, the distinction between nationalization and socialization which was at its heart was taken over by the Party in 1945 and with it, theoretically at least, the concept of Bauer's tripartite *Gemeinwirtschaftliche Anstalten*.[47]

History and Scope

In 1945 the SPOe was united in the desire to achieve a maximum of socialization. This desire was not based on a carefully worked-out socialist theory. Its impetus came rather from three sources: the traditional, matter-of-course identification of socialism with the removal of the means of production from private ownership; the urge to put the Party's hands on important levers of power, thereby weakening the power position of the traditional anti-Socialist forces; [48] and—most frequently referred to in public discussion—the need for public direction in the reorganization of the chaotic, denuded, and largely ownerless industrial machine.[49]

The history of Austrian nationalization measures since 1945 is tortuous and the legal situation extraordinarily complicated by the international position in which Austria found herself as a consequence of the war. Be-

---

[46] BG No. 389 of July 29, 1919.

[47] See, e.g., Franz Rauscher, "Die Sozialisierung und die öffentliche Wirtschaft," *Die Zukunft*, I (June, 1946), 8–10; K.C., "Heraus mit der Verstaatlichung," *Arbeiter Zeitung*, May 10, 1946; Anton Proksch, "Probleme der Verstaatlichung," *Solidarität*, No. 28, January, 1947, p. 6; and AP, "Wie steht es mit der Verstaatlichung?" *Arbeiter Zeitung*, October 27, 1946.

[48] In 1946 the official speakers' guide of the SPOe demanded "the achievement of a maximum degree of nationalization even under present electoral conditions" possible because of the weakness of contemporary capitalist power. (*Die politischen Aufgaben der SPOe*, SBZ, p. 2.) Alfred Migsch ("Die Sozialisierung als politische Aufgabe," *Unsere Arbeit*, September 25, 1945), pointed out that the favorable attitude of the victorious powers, Britain and the Soviet Union, would facilitate maximum socialization in Austria.

[49] Cf. Rauscher, *Die Verstaatlichung in Oesterreich*, *passim*; the speeches by Anton Proksch and Karl Krisch (*Steno. Prot.*, July 26, 1946, pp. 697 ff.); and *Oesterreichs Grundindustrie Verstaatlicht* (Bundeministerium für Verkehr und Verstaatlichte Betriebe, Vienna, 1951).

cause the circumstances under which nationalization was carried out have had some influence on our central issue—the changing Socialist attitude toward nationalization—a brief discussion of these circumstances is indicated.

At the end of World War II the outlook for socialization was indeed favorable from the Socialist viewpoint. Whatever the reasons,[50] the People's Party did not object to immediate and extensive nationalization measures. On September 5, 1945, on the motion of Minister Heinl, the People's Party's Minister for Trade and Reconstruction, the Provisional Government decreed the transfer of a considerable number of enterprises to public ownership.[51] The Soviet occupation authorities—at the time the sole occupying power in Vienna—forbade, however, the publication of the decree and thus prevented it from becoming law.

In November, 1945, the three legal parties all agreed on the principle of nationalization, though significant differences existed on the nature of implementation.[52] Following the election of that year, Chancellor Figl of the People's Party, speaking on behalf of the coalition government, still included "nationalization of a number of key industries" as part of the government's program.[53] After interparty negotiations lasting more than

---

[50] E.g., the chaotic condition of the Austrian economy, the flight of former owners, stagnation of private initiative, the presence of Russian occupation troops, belief in a Socialist victory at the forthcoming elections.

[51] *Report of the Parliamentary Club of the SPOe, PTP, 1946*, pp. 33 ff. The list included electric power, mining, oil production, iron and steel production, electrical machinery, locomotive and railroad car construction.

[52] The electoral proclamation of the People's Party spoke of "affirming socialization of enterprises necessary and vital to society." (*Ibid.*) The Communist Party's proclamation, after calling for the nationalization of certain specific industries, concluded with the ambiguous sentence: "Private property is and remains what honest Austrians possess; national property must be what was German and Fascist." (*Ibid.*) This position was completely reversed when the Soviet authorities objected to precisely what the KPOe had demanded: nationalization of former German and Nazi property.

[53] *Steno. Prot.*, December 21, 1945, p. 24. The election victory had, however, strengthened sentiment in the People's Party against extensive socialization. This change was made evident when Chancellor Figl interpreted the election result as proving that "the overwhelming majority of the Austrian population has decided for maintaining private initiative, the idea of private property, and the principle of reward for achievement." (*Ibid.*)

half a year, the First Nationalization Act was passed.[54] By it a number of enterprises, designated in the law, became the property of the Austrian state.[55] It provided for future compensation to the former owners, but left the problem to be dealt with by further legislation. Similarly, apart from specifying that administration of the nationalized enterprises should be organized from "the viewpoint of comprehensive economic planning," all organizational provisions were left to be determined by future legislation.[56]

The list of enterprises—considerably longer than the one originally proposed by the Provisional Government—included the entire coal and ore mining industry, almost the entire metals industry, the venerable Danube Shipping Company (DDSG), the Austrian branches of some large enterprises of the German electrical industry (AEG-Union, Siemens-Schuckert Werke A.G., Siemens-Halske A.G.), Austria's largest nitrogen plant (Oesterreichische Stickstoffwerke, Linz), various units of the transport and construction industries, the entire oil refining industry, and—hailed as a particular success by the Socialists—the three large investment banks (Creditanstalt-Bankverein, Länderbank Wien A.G., and Hypotheken Creditinstitut A.G.).[57]

In a letter to the Austrian Chancellor, the Soviet government had made it plain that it viewed the nationalization of those enterprises which it considered to be German property as contrary to international agreements and insisted on their exclusion from the law.[58] When the Austrian Parliament decided not to give in to this Soviet demand and all attempts by Soviet

---

[54] BG No. 168 (*Verstaatlichungsgesetz*) and BG No. 169 (*Werksgenossenschaftsgesetz*) of July 26, 1946, published in *BGBl* No. 50, September 16, 1946.
[55] BG No. 168, par. 1, clause 1.
[56] *Ibid.*, par. 1, clauses 2 and 3.
[57] The complex problem of regulating the transfer of the electric power industries was dealt with in the Second Nationalization Act. (*Bundesgesetz über die Verstaatlichung der Elektrizitätswirtschaft—2. Verstaatlichungsgesetz—vom 26. März 1947, BGBl* No. 81, published May 10, 1947.) What had delayed its passage was the issue—on which the SPOe was by no means in unity—of the powers which federal, provincial, and municipal authorities, respectively, should wield in the administration of the industry. Much to the chagrin of some Socialist-controlled municipalities, the SPOe Executive favored a maximum degree of centralization in the hands of a federal authority. (See Franz Rauscher, "Fragen der Verstaatlichung," *Arbeiter Zeitung*, October 3, 1946.) Also *Steno. Prot.*, March 26, 1947, pp. 1361 ff.
[58] *Steno. Prot.*, July 26, 1946, pp. 696–97.

occupation authorities to prevent the passage of the law were frustrated [59] because the Allied Control Council could not reach the unanimous agreement necessary to veto the Act,[60] the Soviet authorities acted to prevent the law's application in those parts of Austria which they controlled. The result of their action was that almost half of the enterprises nationalized, among them the entire oil-producing industry, remained outside the reach of the Austrian government until the end of the occupation. It is estimated that about 22 per cent of Austria's industrial output is produced in the nationalized sector; [61] if those firms controlled by the nationalized investment banks are included, the enterprises potentially accountable to the public amount to about 70 per cent.[62]

Organization of the Nationalized Industries [63]

As previously mentioned, the Socialist leadership in 1945 adopted Otto Bauer's distinction between "nationalization" and "socialization." The legal framework within which the transfer took place, the political balance prevailing, and experiences with the working of publicly run industries, make it unlikely, however, that the present form of nationalization will, in fact, be modified in the direction of "full" socialization.

As pointed out, the First Nationalization Act made no provision for the organization of the enterprises taken over by the state. In 1956 these enterprises were formally organized into a newly founded holding company, the Austrian Industrial and Mine Administration Corp., Ltd.,[64] whose shareholders were identical with the members of the government. They are supervised by a six-man ministerial committee, under the chairmanship of the Chancellor, which in turn appoints a three-man board of executive directors. As long as the coalition lasts, all these bodies are composed of the

---

[59] Rauscher in *Die Verstaatlichung in Oesterreich* (p. 12) presents a brief summary of these attempts.

[60] Ironically, it was the United States spokesman who "recognized the right of the Austrian government to nationalize private property in Austria including the property of foreign owners." (*Ibid.*)

[61] *Oesterreichs Grundindustrie verstaatlicht*, p. 11.

[62] Estimate by Director Tambornino. According to the estimate of the author of "Wirtschaftsordnung im Zeichen des Pluralismus" (*Neue Zürcher Zeitung*, June 8, 1952), the figure should be 80 per cent.

[63] My sources for the brief discussion following were primarily interviews with which I supplemented the very scanty published material.

[64] With the exception of public power and transport and the nationalized banks, which remain under separate ministries.

representatives of both parties and must act by unanimous agreement.[65] Directorial and supervisory positions in the individual enterprises are filled on the basis of *"Proporz."* This transfer of legal power to the Austrian government as a whole marked the end of the period (1949–56) during which the SPOe Minister for Nationalized Industries had exercised these same functions—circumscribed, however, by a bipartisan Committee of Six, which wielded final authority in personnel matters as well as in questions involving major organizational changes.[66]

In filling the positions apportioned to the SPOe, Minister Waldbrunner drew heavily on pre-1934 members of the Socialist student organization, of which he himself was an active member. At that time this organization was divided into students at the philosophical faculties, the university proper— mostly Jews—and those at the engineering colleges (*Technische Hochschulen*), predominantly gentile, and out of sympathy with the Jewish-left leadership of Otto Bauer. Waldbrunner belonged to the latter group, many of whom were employed during the period of German occupation in occasionally important technical positions, and some of whom even joined the Nationalsozialistische Deutsche Arbeiterpartei (NSDAP). They returned to the Socialist Party after 1945 to become part of the growing stratum of "socialist managers" significantly affecting the image of the postwar labor movement.[67] Experience with the majority of these "socialist managers"

---

[65] *Wiener Zeitung*, June 24, 1956. For a hostile Socialist reaction to the reorganization, see Paul Blau, "Genosse Direktor vor der Prüfung," *Die Zukunft*, XI (December, 1956), 346–49. Following the Socialist election success of 1959, the nationalized industries were administratively subordinated to the Socialist Vice-Chancellor and a (Socialist) section chief appointed by him. (*Die Presse*, August 20, 1959, p. 3.)

[66] See Karl Waldbrunner, "Verstaatlichte Industrie," *Arbeiter Zeitung*, October 3, 1951. In 1952, by rough count, 34 out of 75 positions on executive boards or as public administrators were occupied by persons nominated by the SPOe; and 116 of 250 directors' positions on boards of directors. (Source: unpublished list maintained in the Ministry for Nationalized Industries.)

[67] This account is based on statements made to me in interviews and informal conversations, which lack authoritative confirmation. Their inherent plausibility, as well as the fact that several persons gave me identical accounts independently of each other, in my opinion justifies the inclusion of this brief presentation.

See *Welt der Arbeit*, September, 1950, p. 19, for a report of an investigation into the charges against the General Director of the VOEST—charges which were based on the Director's performance under the Nazi regime. It was confirmed to me that he is not untypical of the managers appointed by Minister Waldbrunner.

appears to have confirmed Marx's saying of "being determining consciousness," as well as Michel's hypothesis of the irresistible impact of bureaucratic functions on personal attitudes. Though the dilemma inherent in the concept of "socialist manager" may well be insoluble, the smoothness with which many of these new managers adapted themselves to the traditional ways in the exercise of their official functions, as well as their private style of life, reflects the lack of depth of their socialist convictions. The workers, by their suspicion of "management," make it difficult even for those who had close ties with the working class to retain these ties after the change of function. In preference to being left to dangle between the worlds of management and labor, most men choose to bring their mode of life and outlook into harmony with their new functional position, and thus resolve the problem by becoming unequivocally "managers." By its stress on "efficiency in management" and "need for responsibility," the Party gives strong support to this tendency.

In spite of the initial endorsement of Bauer's tripartite scheme, the principle has not been followed in filling the supervisory positions in the public enterprises. Certain limited aspects of it were accepted. Thus the directorates of the holding companies were composed of representatives of the federal and provincial governments as well as of trade unions and the private sector of the economy.[68] But no specific consumer representation has been instituted, nor is the diverse representation based on any principle of parity; labor is represented according to the provisions of the Work Council Act,[69] while the remainder is made up wherever possible of men having knowledge of the particular branch of industry, of whom some may represent important consumer interests (e.g., the railroads vis-à-vis the coal industry; the city of Vienna vis-à-vis the electrical power industry). The ultimate consumer has not been specifically given a voice in the administration of the nationalized enterprises and all arrangements described are based on informal agreements, not on binding law.[70] It should also be emphasized that the Executive Committees, though also divided on the

---

[68] Fritz Matzner, "Eisenholdung," *Arbeit und Wirtschaft*, II (December, 1948), 1.
[69] In the holding companies, labor representatives are delegates of trade unions; in the other public enterprises, they are work councilors drawn from the working force. They are included on the basis of party membership in the list maintained for purposes of assuring "*Proporz*."
[70] Except where the Work Council Act or the Second Nationalization Act requires specific representation.

basis of party *"Proporz,"* do not include members representing workers' or consumers' interests as such.

Principles and Spirit of Administration

The enterprises in the public sector of the economy have legally retained their separate identities and therefore also their separate and parallel administrative organizations. Their capital needs have been met by means of self-financing out of profits and ERP credits.[71] On the insistence and under the supervision of the government and the Court of Accounts, they are run along commercial lines identical with those prevailing in the private sector. Each enterprise must prove itself *independently* economically viable. Deficits and subsidies are ruled out. By being "ruthlessly purged of inefficiency" they are to make their contribution to Austria's position in the world market.[72] Since productive efficiency has been adopted as the main goal, nationalized industries can be only an indirect instrument of planning for social welfare by rendering the Austrian economy healthily competitive. Being required to operate on the profit principle, they cannot disregard economic imperatives in order to assure their workers job security or other benefits not also extended by private industry. That this acceptance of the principle of economic rationality ill accords with rank-and-file expectations of the meaning of "socialization" is revealed by an occasional outraged public protest such as the following:

However important the careful consideration of the public interest is, it seems that consideration of the workers' interest stands higher. . . . Minister Waldbrunner will and must weigh all circumstances. That is clear. But it is quite certain that regard for the human being, the worker, comes first, and only then regard for the enterprise. *Were we to act otherwise we would not be different*

---

[71] Cf. Waldbrunner, "Verstaatlichte Industrie," *Arbeiter Zeitung,* October 3, 1951; *Die Presse,* April 9, 1953, citing report of Court of Accounts. According to a statement by Minister Waldbrunner (reported by Austrian Information Service on April 10, 1954), of the investments required in 1954, approximately 70 per cent were to be supplied by the nationalized industries themselves while the remainder was to be covered from ERP funds. (The state railroads and the post office, however, rely on budget appropriations to provide for their investment needs.)

[72] "Not everywhere has administration been carried on in the *proper business spirit* [italics added] . . . not everywhere has effort been properly rewarded . . . no deficit must exist." (From speech by Minister Waldbrunner, reported in *Der sozialistische Akademiker,* III, February, 1950.)

from the capitalist principle of production; we would then be no socialists.[73]
[Italics added.]

Even if we dismiss the protest expressed in the demand for *primary* consideration of the human element as the reflection of utopian expectations, it must be admitted that the present organization and the spirit in which the nationalized industries are administered prevent even the acceptance of a concept of "social efficiency" which would take social cost into account in striking the balance of efficiency.[74] Although the Ministry occasionally has used its influence to convey to the managements a spirit less narrowly commercial in character and has assisted them in working out solutions to economic problems which will cause the minimum of human hardship,[75] the self-imposed requirement that *each* enterprise separately be commercially viable precludes any wider application of the "social cost" concept. The lack of central co-ordinating power, furthermore, makes it impossible to treat the entire nationalized sector, or even a major segment of it, as an organizational or economic whole. The working out of a common standard of wages and benefits for the workers in the nationalized industries—so strongly insisted on by the Socialist Party as a means of unifying the working class—has proved impossible.[76] And rationalization through the co-ordination of such common and frequently overlapping functions as sales, advertising, research, statistics, and cost accounting has been prevented by the present form of organization.

In spite of the improvised and limited nature of control which the state exercised over the public sector through the Ministry for Nationalized In-

---

[73] Rudolf Holowatij, *Die Welt der Arbeit*, Nos. 17–18, August, 1950, p. 20. The occasion was the planned shutdown of an obsolete rolling mill, required by the rationalization of the steel industry.

[74] The plea for consideration of the over-all balance rather than of profit-loss in bookkeeping terms contained in Alfred Mikesch's "Sind die verstaatlichten Betriebe rentabel?" (*Die Zukunft*, V [July, 1950], 194–96), was obviously doomed in the light of Minister Waldbrunner's categorical statement: "No deficits!"

[75] Sometimes "strict business principles" were violated in the process. In such instances the Ministry took it upon itself to shield the responsible management against criticism by the Court of Accounts, usually by an advance "gentleman's agreement" with the Court. It is this practice which may have accounted for the Socialist demand, following the election of 1953, that a member of the SPOe become head of the Court of Accounts.

[76] Nationalized enterprises favored by the market situation, in spite of opposition on the part of the Ministry, instituted more attractive housing and pension programs for their work force.

dustries, the leaders of the SPOe seemed willing to discard the old Bauer blueprint and accept the temporary organizational form as permanent.[77] The reorganization in 1956 appears, however, to have caused a revival of the concept of public enterprises less directly dependent on governmental organs which might not always be under Socialist control. In their search for an alternative, the drafters of the 1958 Program simply fell back on the old Bauer scheme, whose glaring deficiencies—cumbersome administrative structure, lack of accountability, syndicalist "plant egoism"—they ignored without examination.[78] The superficiality of their efforts is demonstrated by their reliance on pious formulas attempting to reconcile contradictory principles. Thus, while the *Gemeinwirtschaftliche Anstalt* institutionalizes a decentralized, consciously enterprise-directed form of public ownership, managers and workers are exhorted to "subordinate plant egoism to the general welfare," and to concern themselves simultaneously with the economic interest of their enterprise for which they are held responsible, and that vague entity, the common weal.

Uncertainty about the proper "socialist" organization of publicly owned enterprises,[79] the difficulties encountered in running those already taken over, and disappointment, not often publicly admitted, with some of the results,[80] have combined to weaken drastically the Socialist insistence on further nationalization. The ideological urge which in 1945 was the source of the Party's advocacy of maximum socialization has been in part satisfied and in part emptied of its utopian content. Lacking clear-cut economic cri-

---

[77] See, e.g., Waldbrunner, "Sozialisierung und Verstaatlichung—wie und wie weit?" *Die Zukunft*, VII (February, 1952), 36–42.

[78] The failure to inquire carefully into experiences with the administration of public enterprises in other countries was criticized by Karl Czernetz, "Das verfrühte Programm," *ibid.*, XIII (February, 1958), 69–73; and Ernst Zipperer, "Unsere Rechte in den Betrieben," *ibid.* (March, 1958), 86–87.

[79] Chairman Schärf, in the speech previously referred to, readily admitted this uncertainty. See also Waldbrunner, "Sozialisierung und Verstaatlichung . . . ," *loc. cit.*, for a similar admission.

[80] The disappointment of rank-and-file hopes for a truly "humanitarian" industrial system have been mentioned; also the failure of the new "socialist managers" to live up to expectations. But there is also disappointment on the part of old Socialist functionaries in the effect of nationalization on the workers. Instead of an improvement in spirit and morale, they too often observe a slackening of working morale as a consequence of increased job security. This observation, regretfully expressed in conversation with me, is generalized into a sociological theory by Karl Bednarik in *Der junge Arbeiter von heute—ein neuer Typ*.

teria which could serve as determinants of the desirable scope of a socialist program of public ownership,[81] the Party has refused to list specific enterprises in addition to those already taken over by the state.[82] As far as extent of public ownership of the means of production is concerned, the type of "mixed economy" envisaged by Austrian Socialists will differ but little from that at present established.

Planning of Production

Public ownership of industry, which was the feature most characteristic of socialist thought at the close of World War I, gave way to "planning" as the core of socialist aspirations at the end of World War II. In Bauer's *Der Weg zum Sozialismus*—as in socialist and communist literature of the time in general—the concept of a comprehensively planned economy had as yet found no prominent place. The identification of socialism with planning is thus a rather recent feature, the result of two wars and the Soviet experience, as well as a reflection of the "temper of the times" pervading nonsocialist as well as socialist regimes.[83]

It must be recognized that this unequivocal endorsement of the principle

---

[81] In Socialist arguments "key industries," industries with a monopoly character, and industries "controlling the commanding heights" were indiscriminately mentioned (e.g., Waldbrunner, "Sozialisierung und Planwirtschaft in Oesterreich—wie und wie weit?"; Wolfgang Speiser, "Solidarismus, Planwirtschaft, Sozialismus," *Die Zukunft*, II [July, 1947], 200–202), as criteria defining the desirable scope of nationalization. For a criticism of the looseness of this terminology, see Ernst Kübler, "Verstaatlichung—Form und Inhalt," *Die Zukunft*, III (September, 1948), 269–71.

[82] The Action Program of 1947 still listed a considerable number of industries the Party intended to transfer to public ownership. But the 10-Point Program of 1952, which, according to Karl Czernetz, was nothing but a boiled-down and modernized version of the 1947 Program ("Vor der Entscheidung," *Die Zukunft*, VII [December, 1952], 325–30), omitted all reference to further nationalization. The 1958 Program limits itself, as previously mentioned, to vague hints at future nationalization required by "the general welfare."

[83] Though the concept of a "rational" socialist economy as contrasted to the chaotic and contradictory capitalist system always *implied* the idea of planning, a formulation such as Paul Sering's—echoed by the SPOe—that "Socialism *is* planning plus democracy," is definitely new. After World War II socialization was primarily stressed as a means required to make planning possible. (See KA, "Die Wirtschaft im Aktionsprogramm," *Arbeiter Zeitung*, October 31, 1947.)

was, however, based on hardly more than vague notions as to the concrete scope and measures demanded by socialist planning. Austrian Socialists, pressed to counter charges that planning would lead to bureaucratization and enslavement, followed Anglo-American lines of thought in rejecting a totally planned and centralized system;[84] visionary features such as the elimination of the price mechanism were also eschewed.[85] The goal was defined as a crisis-free, expanding economy, which was to be achieved by the co-ordination of centrally determined over-all production priorities with plans for individual branches of industry.[86] Doubts were expressed by some Party economists about the feasibility of extensive planning in Austria, a country whose population, it was held, lacked the trained experts, as well as the spirit of self-discipline and self-sacrifice, required for successful planning.[87]

The memories of the Great Depression, the Soviet example, and the chaotic state of the economy, however, gave to the concept of comprehensive planning a profound appeal which made it impossible for the Socialist Party to accept openly the validity of practical objections.[88] Further-

---

[84] Cf. Sering, *op. cit.*; also Peter Anders, "Planwirtschaft und Demokratie," *Die Zukunft*, I (December, 1946), 7–13, who consciously espouses the ideas put forth by Barbara Wootton in *Freedom Under Planning* (University of North Carolina Press, Chapel Hill, 1945); j.h., "Plan und Zwang" and "Planwirtschaft und Freiheit," *Arbeiter Zeitung*, May 4, 1947, and April 5, 1947, respectively. Also KA, "Die Wirtschaft im Aktionsprogramm," *loc. cit.* The TVA frequently is cited as an example of how planning and democracy can be combined.

[85] E.g., Peter Hilferding, "Die Organisation einer sozialistischen Planwirtschaft," *Die Zukunft*, IV (January, 1949), 14–19; also Albert Lauterbach, *Planung und Freiheit*, who abjures any utopian hope of changing human personality by stressing that "every realistic kind of planning . . . must use the individual and possessive instincts of the little man" (p. 67).

[86] Julius Deutsch, *Was wollen die Sozialisten?* (1949).

[87] Hans Müller, "Ein Generalplan für die österreichische Wirtschaft?" *Die Zukunft*, II (March, 1947), 47–79, and "Plan ohne Basis?" *ibid.* (August, 1947), 235–38. Particularly telling was Müller's reminder that an over-all plan required agreement on the carefully worked-out details of such a plan rather than mere general objectives expressed in forms of slogans like "raising the living standard"; and, furthermore, that any plan would require sacrifices from some group, sacrifices for which no section of the population had been prepared by the political leadership.

[88] Cf. K. J. Tambornino, "Ist Planung teilbar?" *Die Zukunft*, II (May, 1947), 135–36, and Franz Rauscher, "Planwirtschaft oder Wirtschaftsplanung?" *ibid.* (April, 1947), 110–11, rejoinders to Müller's two articles attacking overambitious planning schemes.

more, in its own propaganda it had identified economic planning as the most characteristic feature of socialism. Yet the Party was never in a position to implement its sweeping slogans, and the degree of economic planning achieved was definitely limited in time and scope. The Ministry for Economic Planning, in which the SPOe occupied an under-secretariat, produced a number of group plans of which the four most important ones (coal, steel, electric power, and metals) were completed by the end of 1948 and put into operation for the nationalized industries.[89] Because of the political balance and the legal situation, similar production plans could not be attempted for the private sector, and the plans designed for nationalized industries had to stop short of major organizational changes.[90] Paradoxically, it was as the result of an outside impetus coming from the United States that a comprehensive plan roughly along the lines originally contemplated was eventually drawn up. The "long-term program" which the Austrian government had to submit as a prerequisite for obtaining Marshall Plan aid, hurriedly put together, defined the major areas for proposed investments in the private as well as the public sector of the economy for the period from 1949 to 1953.[91] The *Kreditlenkungskommission* (Credit Direction Commission), originally set up as a high-level planning instrument [92] which had subsequently lost all effective power over credit direction to the banks,[93] was now reactivated as the central authority allocating Marshall Plan funds.[94] Thus, for a limited period the Austrian economy was subject to central, high-level planning.

---

[89] Tambornino, "Der österreichische Kohlenplan," *Arbeit und Wirtschaft*, II (December, 1948), 3–5; Rauscher, "Der österreichische Eisen–und Stahlplan," *ibid.* (October, November, December, 1948), 3–6, 13–15, and 6–8, respectively.

[90] The People's Party apparently was opposed to any extension in the Ministry's power or change in the present legal situation. The provisional arrangement keeps open the possibility of reprivatization and assures a high degree of continuity with the past both in personnel and business spirit. The large banks, taken over by the state and administratively supervised by the Ministry of Finance, have not been used as planning instruments but have been allowed to conduct business largely as before. (The post of Finance Minister has always been occupied by a non-Socialist.)

[91] Cf. "Das österreichische Investitionsprogramm" in *Jahrbuch der Arbeiterkammer Wien*, 1948, pp. 351 ff.; also K. W., "Ein österreichischer Wirtschaftsplan," *Arbeiter Zeitung*, January 6, 1949.

[92] *Neues Oesterreich*, July 29, 1945, and August 2, 1945.

[93] Interviews with Dr. Wirlandner and Karl Ausch.

[94] Korp, "Die Kredite aus der Marshall-Plan Hilfe," *Arbeiter Zeitung*, March 18, 1952.

The dwindling of American aid and the termination of the phase of massive capital investments, however, have once more caused the government's planning functions to atrophy. Power to use such planning tools as investments, taxation, budgeting, and controls over foreign trade is not concentrated in any one directing agency. It is politically and administratively divided, with the most important functions in the hands or under the control of an anti-Socialist Finance Minister committed to the "liberalization" of the Austrian economy. The *Wirtschaftsdirektorium* (Economic Directorate), established in 1951 to co-ordinate all economic policies, was not intended to act as a planning agency and thus lacks the staff and powers to fill that role. Representing the major competing political and economic forces and requiring unanimity for its decisions,[95] it is merely an extension of the coalition cabinet capable of discussing economic policies in a general way and of resolving issues as they arise.

The Socialist Party did not resist this dismantling of the economic planning machinery. The Party is cognizant of the change of the term "planning" from one which possessed a semantically positive ring to one which carries the threatening overtones of Orwell's *1984*. The leadership has therefore decided to play down the planning theme, a decision reflected in the formal 1958 Program. There both size and comprehensiveness of the proposed planning machinery are defensively minimized; and the planning function—in a proposal of doubtful feasibility—is to be assigned to a body independent of the government and accountable directly only to Parliament.[96] While still committed to the maintenance of "almost full employment" the Party in practice attempts to achieve this goal by pressure, particularly on the Minister of Finance, to continue to finance large investments out of budget funds, if necessary by accepting a temporary budget deficit.[97] Although the existence of a large publicly owned sector, as well

---

[95] It consists of a cabinet committee enlarged by representatives—limited to advisory roles—of the National Bank, the three Chambers, and the Trade Union Federation. Cf. Ausch in *SPOe-Vertrauensmann*, VI (March-April, 1951), 106.
[96] The Draft Program proposed a "small planning commission not accountable to the government." (*Vorentwurf*, p. 26.) The final program speaks of a planning commission "directly subordinate to Parliament." For inner-party criticism of this suggestion, see "Der Programmentwurf und die österreichische Wirtschaft," *Die Zukunft*, XIII (February, 1958), 46–49.
[97] In 1954 the coalition government agreed on a ten-year investment program "for the purposes of ensuring full employment and increasing the productivity of public enterprises and services." The SPOe-controlled railroads and postal serv-

as the plurality of well-organized and powerful economic groups which operate in, and in part control, the capitalistically organized "free" sector, prevent us from defining Austria's economy as a "free economy," it is yet—with Socialist connivance—moving away from, rather than toward, a centrally planned system.[98]

---

ices would, under this plan, obtain the funds necessary for their expansion and modernization. (*Austrian Information*, June 19, 1954.) Although this represented a success for Minister Waldbrunner, the provision that implementation of the program would depend on the availability of funds, and that an insufficiency of funds would proportionately slow down the projects contemplated, appears to have deprived the program of its countercyclical potentialities.

[98] For corroboration of this appraisal, see "Wirtschaftsordnung im Zeichen des Pluralismus," *Neue Zürcher Zeitung*, June 8, 1952, and "Wirtschaftliche Stabilisierung," *ibid.*, June 14, 1952.

VII

Toward a Socialist Economy? (Part II)

"Plant Democracy"

The Work Council Acts

The Work Council Law of the First Republic was enacted as a concession
to strong syndicalist feeling which, in the wake of the Soviet revolution, led
to demands that all industries be turned over to administration by those
who worked in them.[1] Otto Bauer, who, in spite of his acknowledgment of
indebtedness to the guild socialists had no sympathy with syndicalism,
was determined that "economic democracy" in plants would have to stop
short of interference in technical and economic direction; "socialization"
involved administration not for the benefit of the workers of the plant
taken over but for that of the entire community.[2] For Renner, too, Socialism implied more, not less, discipline and submission of the individual
economic unit to the planned needs of society.[3]

Though a similar wave of radical demands was lacking in 1945, the Socialist Party, without explicitly repudiating the ideas of Bauer and Renner
on the subject, attempted to push "plant democracy" beyond the limits
which Austro-Marxist antisyndicalism had imposed on it. The aim of the
new Work Council Bill which the SPOe drafted was to give the workers,
through their elected councils, a voice in the over-all management of the
enterprise. The draftsmen of the SPOe may have seen in it primarily a

---

[1] Gulick, *Austria from Habsburg to Hitler*, pp. 204–5.
[2] Bauer, *Der Weg zum Sozialismus*, Chap. 4.
[3] Renner, *Wege der Verwirklichung*, pp. 67 ff.

means for extending Party control to the part of the economy remaining in private hands;[4] they hoped to keep the councils under Party or trade union control and thereby to counteract syndicalist tendencies. Bauer had developed his scheme in the expectation of a fully socialized economy and was concerned with the maintenance of its productive efficiency through expert and fully responsible management. The Socialist Party in 1945, on the other hand, was interested above all in permanently reducing capitalist power in an economy which was not expected to become fully socialist within the foreseeable future.[5]

The new Act[6] differs from its predecessor in the First Republic in the following significant points, all of which extend the scope of the Work Council's powers or strengthen the councilors' legal position:

(1) It contains a specific declaration that the workers' representatives have the task of "participating in the leadership and administration" of the enterprise,[7] and that the Work Councils must be kept regularly informed on the firm's policies.[8]

(2) The Work Council is entitled to participate in the drawing up of business plans (production, investments, etc.) through suggestions and concrete proposals. In case these are disregarded, the council, in enterprises with a work force of more than 500, may lodge a complaint with the State Economic Commission, which is to be set up.[9]

(3) Work Councils receive strengthened powers of appeal against dismissals of any employee. They may use these to prevent dismissal where it "imposes a social hardship and is not justified by conditions in the enterprise."[10]

(4) Work Councilors themselves receive increased protection against

---

[4] Cf. Bruno Pittermann, "Betriebsdemokratie," *SPOe-Vertrauensmann*, I (September, 1946, and October, 1946), pp. 20 and 48, respectively.

[5] Another reason may be found in the admission that the Nazis apparently had succeeded in increasing the worker's interest in, and feeling of responsibility for, the plant he worked in. (Erna Fischer, "Betriebsdemokratie," *Unsere Arbeit*, No. 8, SBZ, November 15, 1945, p. 10.) Under no circumstances could the Socialists afford to provide the workers with less scope for "participation" than they had enjoyed under National Socialism.

[6] BG No. 97 vom. 28. März (*Betriebsrätegesetz*), BGBl, June 2, 1947.

[7] *Ibid.*, par. 3.

[8] Ibid., par. 14.

[9] *Ibid.*

[10] *Ibid.*, par. 25.

dismissal. The grounds on which a member of a Work Council can be dismissed are enumerated and narrowly circumscribed; and in every case approval must first be obtained from an arbitration office (*Einigungsamt*).[11]

The Act, which became law only after protracted interparty negotiations,[12] failed to go as far toward increasing the Work Councils' powers as the Socialist Party had demanded.[13] It excluded agricultural laborers and retained separate councils for manual and white-collar workers. The veto power against dismissals was considerably weakened.[14] The qualification that councils in enterprises employing fewer than 500 men had no recourse to the State Economic Commission was inserted in spite of Socialist objections. And, most stubbornly fought, the councils' voice in the hiring of new employees was reduced to the mere right to be notified. The People's Party was determined not to legalize "closed shops" in which Socialist-dominated Work Councils would be able to discriminate against non-Socialist workers.

The Failure of "Codetermination"

The powers of the Work Councils may thus under the law be exercised in three distinct spheres: implementation of collective agreements, personnel questions, and participation in the formulation of business policy. The major innovation of the new act consisted in adding the third sphere aiming at the establishment of "codetermination." Though no careful study of the workings of the act has so far been undertaken, the degree of workers' participation in policy decisions effected by it appears to have been

---

[11] *Ibid.*, par. 18.

[12] The ministerial draft which represented the Socialist view was completed by midsummer 1946. In February, 1947, the Cabinet decided to present the draft to Parliament though no interparty agreement had been reached on certain points. (*Arbeiter Zeitung*, February 26, 1947.) It became law on March 28, 1947.

[13] See *Steno. Prot.*, March 28, 1947, pp. 1378–401, where the SPOe spokesman lists the points in which the Act fell short of Socialist demands.

[14] This invalidated the expectation expressed by Pittermann (in "Betriebsdemokratie," *loc. cit.*) that the Act would make workers "practically safe against dismissal except in cases where they were at fault or in the event of a major crisis." Retrospectively, the SPOe leaders may congratulate themselves on their failure to establish this principle in law, for it was based on an obviously naïve assumption about the workings of a dynamic economy. Recently, for example, the nationalized steel industry went through a period of readjustment that required the layoff of many workers.

negligible.[15] Two reasons seem responsible for this failure. In some instances, particularly in larger firms where councilors are freed of all other duties, contact between the workers on the shop floor and their elected representatives is lost; this has happened all the more frequently because Party considerations have played a more important role than personal qualifications in the selection of the councilors. Even more important is the failure of the Work Councils to take advantage of the power to make concrete suggestions.[16] Lack of training and expertise, combining with and in turn causing indifference toward problems of general business policy, have led them to neglect the information which the employer is required to supply. By providing that councilors are to be *recipients* of *information*, remaining on the outside of the decision-making process, the law has made meaningful participation difficult. Lacking the day-to-day involvement in business policy, Work Councils are rarely able to provide concrete, effective proposals which can be taken seriously by the employer. This is borne out by the complete absence of complaints from Work Councils to the State Economic Commission, whose very existence seems to have been forgotten. Only where management has considered it desirable to commit its labor force to business policies—as was frequently the case in the immediate postwar period of chaotic production conditions—has a measure of genuine participation been achieved. Where this has taken place, it has been due not to the law but to the exigencies of the situation. For the law's provisions which require management to hold monthly consultation meetings and to supply the councils with current information are widely disregarded with the apparent connivance of the Work Councils.[17]

Consultation in Nationalized Industries

Because of the legal position of the nationalized enterprises, the Work Council Act applies to them in the same way as it does to private firms. The Ministry for Nationalized Industries, aware of the great distance by which performance has fallen short of expectation, took the initiative in supplementing the law with institutional devices intended to realize a degree of workers' participation in certain policy decisions. It established a central

---

[15] "Das betriebliche Mitspracherecht," *Solidarität*, No. 150, October 22, 1951, p. 2. The opinions there expressed were confirmed to me by an official of the Ministry for Nationalized Industries.

[16] This point was stressed to me by Dr. Wirlandner. It is also implicit in the increasing recognition that further legislation is not really needed.

[17] "Das betriebliche Mitspracherecht," *loc. cit.*

consultative body, the Social Advisory Council (*Sozialbeirat*, SAC), whose task it is to discuss all welfare and personnel questions arising in the nationalized sector.[18] The council's membership was equally divided between management and labor representatives.[19] In limiting the SAC to the consideration of personnel and welfare problems, the Ministry has been careful to refrain from delegating any substantial measure of power to the body which, in addition, has advisory functions only. The SAC is furthermore precluded from considering those matters dealt with by collective agreements.

In addition to the central council, the Ministry for Nationalized Industries initiated a program of setting up consultation machinery on the level of the individual firms [20] as a means of giving the workers a "deeper feeling of belonging and influence." [21] In its recommendations for the establishment of this machinery, the ministry advised that the consultative committees, whose membership should be equally divided between labor and management, were to avoid discussion of controversial issues such as wages and working conditions but should regularly receive information "concerning the commercial, technical, and personnel situation and of the projects in all fields of activity within the plant." [22] Though it is stressed that these committees are not to replace the Work Councils, it is difficult to see a clear dividing line between their functions. Under the law the Work Councils receive the same information which is to be provided for the consulta-

---

[18] *Standing Orders of the SAC*, a circular prepared by the Ministry of Transport and Nationalized Industries.

[19] The labor representation consists of Work Councilors and delegates of the trade unions—not necessarily the unions concerned directly with the nationalized industries. In 1953, of the eight labor representatives three were elected Work Councilors, four officials of Trade Unions within the nationalized industries, and one represented a union with hardly any members in the nationalized sector. Five of the eight belonged to unions organizing manual workers; the other three represented salaried employees. (*A Social Advisory Council for the Nationalized Industries*, prepared by the Ministry of Transport and Nationalized Industries, p. 2.)

[20] A visit to England to study consultation machinery set up by the Labor Government by members of the Ministry is said to have been influential in introducing the committees in Austria.

[21] As pointed out, the Ministry could not legally order the establishment. The following account is based on the circular, *Consultative Machinery*, issued by the Ministry in June, 1952.

[22] *Ibid.*

tive committees. The difference is that the latter's voice, unlike that of the Work Councils, is to be purely advisory. It would therefore seem that the full activation of the Work Councils within the scope of the law would do even more toward bringing about workers' participation than the Ministry's device.

Explanation for the need to establish additional machinery is probably found in the fact that, contrary to expectations, Work Councils have remained almost exclusively grievance committees concerned with immediate interests and individual complaints rather than broad policy. They thus face management inevitably as complainants. The Ministry is primarily concerned with improving relations between management and the work force in a way which will create a more tranquil atmosphere and lead to increased productivity. It may be asked whether this represents a move in the direction of genuine workers' codetermination or merely a device on the part of management—this time public management—to create a "happy" climate by giving labor the appearance rather than the substance of participation in decision-making. The respect shown for labor's traditional fighting instruments, trade unions and work councils, differentiates this approach from that commonly known as "human relations" in industry. The latter has come under sharp attack from Austrian Socialists [23] as a form of "psychologically refined exploitation" [24] which, by fostering plant-egoism and anti-trade unionism, destroys working-class solidarity.[25] Yet the manipulative element [26] is present—and privately acknowledged—in the public sector as well. As in the Party itself, democratic machinery is merely used to improve communication. Action cannot be compelled from below; the ultimate power of decision remains unshared.

The disappointing experience with the new Work Council Act and the

---

[23] See Ernst Glaser, "Die zwischenmenschlichen Beziehungen im Betrieb," *Arbeit und Wirtschaft*, V (September, 1951), 15; also, Dr. Hans Bayer, "Die menschlichen Beziehungen in Betrieb und Beruf," *ibid.*, IV (July, 1951), 12–14.

[24] Glaser, *op. cit.*

[25] *Ibid.* The charge can be easily substantiated. See, e.g., Elton Mayo, *The Human Problem of an Industrial Civilization* (Cambridge, Mass.: Harvard University Press, 1933), *passim*. Glaser cites approvingly an article to this effect by Walter Pahl, published by the *Gewerkschaftliche Monatshefte*, (DGB), April 1951. (See also Reinhard Bendix and Lloyd H. Fisher, *The Perspective of Elton Mayo*, University of California, Institute of Industrial Relations, Berkeley, Calif., 1950.)

[26] For a useful discussion of this widely used term, see Philip Selznick, *TVA and the Grass Roots* (Berkeley: University of California Press, 1953), pp. 220 ff.

increasing awareness of the psychological and economic complexity of the problem of codetermination have created uncertainty in Socialist ranks about the nature of the next steps toward the goal of "economic democracy." The approach followed by the German labor movement—codetermination at the top of the management hierarchy—has been officially rejected as leading to managerialism and as failing to give workers genuine participation.[27] On the other hand, the shortcomings of the Austrian solution are recognized and the need for new forms appreciated.[28] But apart from the realization that the problem has ceased to be primarily one of new legislation,[29] no indication of the direction of future development is provided.

We may thus be observing a retreat on the part of Austrian Socialists to the more "realistic" position put forth by Otto Bauer, the position that "economic democracy" could not mean participation of the working force in decisions affecting not only the firm in relation to its workers but to the economic system and the community as well. For Bauer, as for the Webbs, "economic democracy" meant representation of the working class on different levels in a functionally appropriate manner, through trade unions, through political leaders—thus the Socialist Party in Parliament—and not merely or primarily through plant councils. The Party and the trade unions are by no means willing to leave determination of important questions exclusively to Work Councils, for they strongly feel the need for a corrective to the councils' necessarily narrower field of vision.[30] In view of the fact that Party, trade unions, and Chambers occupy positions in which they can influence economic decisions on various levels and because of the existence of powers in the Work Council Act hitherto not fully utilized, it may be doubted whether a strong impetus for extension of "workers' control" will

---

[27] KA, "Der Betriebsdemokratie entgegen," *Arbeiter Zeitung*, June 4, 1950.

[28] "Die Mitbestimmung im Betrieb," *Die Zukunft*, VII (March, 1953), 96.

[29] *Ibid.* The shift of position compared to 1947 is obvious.

[30] The frequent criticism of "plant egoism" in the trade union press reflects the annoyances caused by Work Councils, which at various times have taken positions running counter to the national policies advocated by the unions and the SPOe. The most serious occasion was the general strike call issued by the Communists in 1950 when Work Councils in many plants proved useless as weapons to combat Communist action. Attempts to eliminate illegal barter and compensation deals during the period of strict controls, anticartel measures, and efforts to obtain price reductions all met with tacit or overt opposition from various Work Councils. The 1958 Program demands succinctly: "Plant egoism must be subordinated to the solidarity of the totality of workers and employees." (*Arbeiter Zeitung*, May 15, 1958, p. 11.)

come from the leaders of the labor movement. They are dedicated to a "responsible" policy. A multiplicity of powerful and hard-to-control Work Councils might create obstacles in the path of an efficient and broadly conceived national economic policy. It must therefore be suspected that the intention, expressed in the 1958 Program, to give the workers of an enterprise formal representation on its management board—a solution rejected by the British labor movement[31]—represents an empty and superficial reiteration of a traditional slogan rather than the result of a careful determination of a desirable line of socialist action.[32]

The Wage-Price Agreements

From its inception at Hainfeld, the Austrian labor movement has always put equal emphasis on the ultimate establishment of socialism and the immediate struggle for a maximum share of the national income. The "glorious period" of the twenties brought the Party little opportunity for truly "socialistic" achievements, but in Red Vienna it boldly redistributed income in working toward a "welfare city." This tradition of practical work, the leadership of Karl Renner, and, above all, the demands of political reality, combined in 1945 to bring to the fore the task of defending and improving the material position of the working class. The most immediate aspect of this struggle for "social justice" was to prevent the diminution of the workers' share in a period of economic disorganization, extreme scarcity of consumer goods,[33] and inflationary pressure. The Party tackled this problem—effectively, on the whole—by means of central wage-price agreements once it recognized that no continuation of wartime controls would solve the problem.[34]

---

[31] See Kurt L. Shell, "Industrial Democracy and the British Labor Movement," *Political Science Quarterly*, LXXII (1957), 515–39.

[32] This observation is echoed by Czernetz, "Das verfrühte Programm," *loc. cit.*, p. 71.

[33] "Insufficient raw material supplies and lack of stocks, causing frequent hold-ups and constant below-capacity working, cross-transportation to barter scarce commodities, an undue amount of repair and maintenance work . . . out-of-date machinery, and a decline in skill and labour owing to bad housing and productivity." (K. W. Rothschild, *The Austrian Economy Since 1945*, p. 41.)

[34] For an analysis of the first period of wage-freeze and its administration by a Central Wage Commission, see Franz Olah, "Um die künftige Lohnpolitik," *Arbeit und Wirtschaft*, I (October 1, 1947), 8.

By means of a general wage-price freeze and rigid production and consumption controls, the government attempted strenuously during the first two postwar years to keep prices low and steady and to assure even the lowest income group the essentials of life. However, under the chaotic conditions then prevailing, controls were being rendered largely meaningless by wholesale evasion and the ubiquitous presence of a black market. By July, 1947, wages had fallen well behind prices—even when the official and not the black-market prices were considered [35]—and the farmers, in turn, were demanding higher prices to compensate them for increasing costs. [36]

It was under these conditions that the representatives of labor attempted to combine a kind of "parity principle" for labor with a semipermanent stabilization of the economy. The attempt took the form of a central wage-price agreement—later to be known as "the first"—which was intended to anticipate the next turn of the inflationary spiral (rather than force the recipients of wages and salaries to fall behind and subsequently catch up) and then, with the help of a currency reform, to stabilize the economy on the higher level. [37]

In spite of their recognition that the national income had been approximately halved since 1937, the Socialist spokesmen rejected any similar reduction in real wages as long as other groups in the population—especially farmers and businessmen—had not proved their willingness to reduce their own standard of living accordingly. [38] This refusal by all groups to face economic facts and make the necessary sacrifices inevitably rendered any hope for speedy stabilization chimerical. The all-round wage and price increases decreed by this first agreement allowed for a drop to 90 per cent of "parity," for living costs were expected to rise from 8 to 11 per cent. Yet from labor's point of view it had the advantage of eliminating the limping-

---

[35] The price index—unrealistically figuring the price of rationed goods at official, not black-market prices—stood at 261 (1945, 100), that for wages at 210. (Rothschild, *op. cit.*, p. 46.)

[36] *Ibid.*

[37] *Ibid.* It should be pointed out that this far-reaching agreement affecting all groups in the Austrian population was negotiated by the Trade Union Federation and the three Chambers and only subsequently "ratified" by Parliament. (See *Arbeiter Zeitung*, July 12, 19, 22, 1947.)

[38] Stefan Wirlandner, "Das Stillhalteabkommen," *Arbeit und Wirtschaft*, I (August, 1947), 3; also KA, "Keine Rechentricks," and "Wer zahlt's?" *Arbeiter Zeitung*, June 20 and 29, 1947, respectively.

behind process and of safeguarding the economic position of disadvantaged groups, particularly of those who through dependence on fixed incomes or because of inferior bargaining power would be likely to fall behind in any upward movement of prices initiated by strongly organized trade unions.

The currency reform which, it had been hoped, would accompany the agreement and reinforce its stabilizing effect was not enacted until half a year later. When it materialized it proved less effective than anticipated, partly because the delay imposed by the requirements of the occupation statute between enactment and date of taking effect had deprived the measure of the vital element of surprise. The SPOe, which had been the most insistent advocate of currency reform,[39] left itself open to criticism for permitting the reform to violate seriously principles of social justice. As enacted, the reform failed to take into account the needs of the poorest sections of the population, failed to deprive of their gains those who had profiteered during the period of wartime and postwar emergency; and it penalized almost exclusively those who had trusted the old currency and had heeded the government's advice not to transform their savings into nonmonetary values.[40] Surprisingly, the idea of a rigorous capital levy which would have counteracted the inequities of the currency reform and could have served as a major instrument of a socialist policy of property redistribution never caught the imagination of the SPOe leadership. Though the Party insisted that a mild levy be enacted as part of the currency reform, it admittedly lacked confidence in its efficacy [41]—with justification, as the results showed. With rising prices and dragging collections, the levy turned out to have been little more than an empty gesture.[42]

---

[39] Cf. Wirlandner, "Löhne, Preise, Währung," *Die Zukunft*, II (September, 1947), 255–57. Business spokesmen argued frequently against its urgency. (Cf. *Denkschrift der Leiter der Spar- und Kreditinstitute*, quoted by Dr. Wirlandner in "Das Währungsschutzgesetz," *ibid.*, December 1947, pp. 349–52.)

[40] Rothschild, *op. cit.*, p. 53. These facts, exploited by Communist propaganda to the embarrassment of the SPOe, were admitted by Socialist spokesmen (see Wirlandner, "Das Währungsschutzgesetz," *loc. cit.*), who pleaded, however, that People's Party opposition and lack of trained administrators made a more socially discriminating law unattainable.

[41] Wirlandner, "Die Vermögensabgabe," *Die Zukunft*, III (March, 1948), 72–5.

[42] This was anticipated by Rothschild (*op. cit.*, p. 53), and confirmed to me by Dr. Wirlandner. The government securities, which through the collection of the levy were eventually to be converted into cash, had by 1950 fallen from 100 to 40 schillings.

As could be anticipated, the wage-price agreement of 1947 did not succeed in completely stemming the inflationary movement. Price-control laws, loosened as part of a trend away from a tightly controlled economy, could not prevent increased costs from being passed on to the consumers. The 10 per cent rise in the cost of living allowed for in the first agreement was exceeded long before the standstill period had expired.[43] The SPOe probably realized that general agreements like the first were factors contributing to the inflationary trend and that neither price reductions nor any other means could, in the short run, do much to increase the real income of the population,[44] yet, for obvious political reasons, the Party could not allow this realization to deter it from demanding a new all-round agreement to restore the workers' position to that of July, 1947. The second wage-price agreement began the process of allowing the prices for certain basic items (e.g., milk and potatoes) to find their natural level by ending subsidies out of ERP and tax funds.[45] Another important new feature of this second agreement—characteristic also of the subsequent ones—was that new cost increases were to be compensated by a fixed bonus to each wage earner irrespective of income level. The cost of these bonuses was to be borne in part by the employer and in part by the state.[46] Once again it was piously assumed that prices would not be allowed to reflect the increased wage bill.

No attempt will be made here to analyze the economic development of the years from 1948 to 1951, which led to a third, fourth, fifth (and final) wage-price agreement. Many causes combined to prevent the stabilization

---

[43] The exact level of the standard of living was an issue of furious political dispute throughout the period of wage-price agreements. The Communists usually claimed that prices had risen far more than wages, while the Socialists defended their own claim that each agreement exactly balanced the wage gains against price rises. Though the index figures my not have shown it, the *real* standard of living rose dramatically in the years 1947–1949 because goods, for the first time since the war, were generally available at official prices. Currency reform and Marshall Plan aid succeeded in rapidly ridding the Austrian economy of the black market.

[44] The *Arbeiter Zeitung* tacitly accepted this point in reporting the conclusions of the Institute for Economic Research. ("Lohnerhöhung auf Kosten der Unternehmergewinne," September 10, 1948.)

[45] Wirlandner, "Ein Stabilisierungsversuch," *Die Zukunft*, III (October, 1948), 291–96.

[46] Each wage earner was to receive from his employer a cost-of-living bonus of 34 schillings and from the state a childrens' grant of 23 schillings per dependent.

which each agreement aimed at. Most important among them was the delay in establishing a balance between wages pegged at their 1937 level of
"parity" and production which only slowly crept back to the prewar level.
Another cause as well was the sudden impact of the Korean War, which
dramatically worsened the terms of trade for Austria, a country which re-
lied heavily on the import of commodities put in short supply by American
stockpiling.

The Socialists did not view the wage-price agreements—sometimes considered the most characteristic feature of Austria's postwar economy [47]—as
an attempt to bring about planned and possibly permanent income distribution among the Austrian population. These agreements had evolved in
1947 not on the basis of plan but as an *ad hoc* solution to problems faced
by practical bargainers. The Socialist leadership saw in them merely the
least objectionable way of eventually reaching a stabilized adjustment, a
way which possessed some real advantages, such as protection of all segments of the population depending on wages and fixed incomes; [48] the grad-
ualness with which the necessary painful adjustments could be brought
about; and the resulting atmosphere of comparative labor peace which provided the Communists with a minimum of opportunity to fish in troubled
waters. [49] These advantages appeared to them to outweigh some drawbacks. Most serious among these drawbacks was the dissatisfaction of the
stronger unions at being prevented from obtaining for their members as
much as they could have through a process of free bargaining; the apathy of
union and party members and the lethargy of officials engendered by the
substitution of negotiations at the top for rank-and-file struggles; [50] and the
leveling of wage differentials as the result of fixed-money grants and restraint on free bargaining. Listing the leveling effect of the price-wage
agreements among the drawbacks is a reflection of the Party's curious position: leveling was accepted not on the basis of socialist principle but only

---

[47] "Kaufkraftschöpfung und Vollbeschäftigung," *Neue Zürcher Zeitung*, June
11, 1952.

[48] The most notable exception was the civil servants, particularly those in the
middle and higher classification categories who were not covered by the agreements and whose union failed to receive anything approaching full "valorization."

[49] Cf. Alfred Migsch, "Das Fünfte—musste es sein?" *SPOe-Vertrauensmann*,
VI (August-September, 1951), 193–94; also Fritz Klenner, "Lohnpolitik am
Scheideweg," *Arbeiter Zeitung*, December 13, 1949.

[50] *Ibid.*

defended as inevitable though undesirable.[51] It is clear that the wage-price agreements thus represented not a consciously socialist wage policy but the attempt to re-establish the working-class standard of living prevailing in 1937.

The wage-price agreements obviously were dictated by sound political considerations (in which the Communist threat played a large role) rather than by purely economic ones, a fact admitted by Socialist spokesmen [52] as well as by some critics.[53] The agreements, invariably followed by price rises beyond the supposedly compensating wage increases, were decidedly unpopular with those whom they were intended to benefit.[54] The SPOe was forced to take full responsibility for these agreements. To it fell the unaccustomed and unpopular task of explaining, over and over, that the achievements guaranteed by the agreements represented the best obtainable solution for labor; that, in fact—appearances to the contrary—no real worsening of the living standard had taken place.[55] Acceptance of responsibility for the prevailing economic policy created for the Socialist Party and Trade Union Federation—traditionally "malcontents" demanding a larger share for the working class—a paradoxical situation. They now attacked any statement purporting to show that wages had not kept up with rising prices, however unbiased the source, as an irresponsible utterance playing into the hands of Communist propaganda.[56] The strictures against the Socialist policy which came from persons thinking exclusively in economic

---

[51] *Ibid.*; also Wirlandner, "Zur Preis-Lohn-Diskussion," *Die Zukunft*, IV (July, 1949), 207–11. This apology did not, of course, extend to the leveling-up of the lowest-income groups, such as old-age pensioners, whose standard of living the Party intentionally raised.

[52] Cf. Migsch, *loc. cit.*

[53] "Kaufkraftschöpfung und Vollbeschäftigung," *loc. cit.*

[54] Communist agitation against them—culminating in the general strike attempted as a protest against the fourth agreement—as well as the People's Party's tendency to hold the Socialists responsible for them, is testimony to this fact. In computing their living standard the citizens of the Austrian welfare state have the habit of counting only the cash contained in their pay envelopes and failing to consider the social welfare benefits they receive in return for the high pay deductions, a fact unscrupulously exploited by Communist propaganda.

[55] Cf., e.g., Wirlandner, "Zur Preis-Lohn-Diskussion," *loc. cit.*

[56] See, for instance, the criticism directed at a report of the nonpartisan *Institut für Wirtschaftsforschung* by the president of the Trade Union Federation. (Johann Böhm in *Arbeiter Zeitung*, July 9, 1949.)

terms [57] missed the central point. True, the SPOe failed to take the coura-geous course of the British Labor Party of advocating a policy of "auster-ity." But in view of the low civic morale—made evident by the universal black market—the Party's position as a junior partner in a coalition, and the readiness of the Communist agitators to turn popular discontent to their advantage, the Party's unheroic line may have been the only feasible one.[58]

Surprisingly, the SPOe also failed to follow the example of the British Labor Party in embracing a policy of subsidies as a useful tool of social engineering and income redistribution. Though subsidies were used in Austria and their effect understood, the Party's position toward them was marked by uncertainty.[59] In part this uncertainty flowed from the aware-ness that subsidies contradicted the commitment to efficiency on the basis of "true" prices. More important than those theoretical doubts may have been the fear that the presence of an anti-Socialist Finance Minister made a social subsidy policy difficult to achieve and to maintain. Furthermore, the Party accepted the contention that the taxload had almost reached the limit of feasibility and was unable to discover the large revenue sources that an extensive program of subsidies would have required. Finally, the tactical point was recognized that in fighting for low agrarian prices, labor could count on the co-operation of industry and urban consumers in gen-eral while a subsidy policy based on higher taxes would have destroyed this co-operation and allowed the peasantry to gain advantages at the ex-pense of the consumers.

Private Versus Public Saving

By early 1952 inflationary pressure had abated and the defense of labor's living standard had to take the form of antideflationary measures. Com-

[57] As, for instance, Dr. Franz Nemschak in *Der Weg zu einem gesamtwirtschaft-lichen Konzept.*

[58] The term "austerity" was avoided by the SPOe. No determined efforts were made to level high incomes or large fortunes, cut off luxury imports, or maintain rationing beyond the time when it seemed absolutely essential.

[59] Cf. "Für oder gegen Subventionen" (*Die Zukunft*, VI [March, 1951], 91), where it was stated that the question arouses "uncertainty in socialist circles." Rothschild, *op. cit.*, p. 56, remarks: "The government and most of the Austrian economic press have taken it for granted that price subsidies are something un-healthy which should be removed as quickly as possible."

bining Keynesian theory with sound class politics, some Socialist spokesmen argued vigorously against the stimulation of private savings and the return to a private capital market, both advocated by the People's Party, and insisted that capital formation had become a public function entirely.[60] Acceptance of the primary role of private saving, they argued, would once again place economic power in private hands. It would imply recognition of the social function of capital interest, thus justifying the claims of savers to a larger share of the national income, and it would force the state to treat the "saving strata" as a favored group in such matters as taxation.[61]

In spite of the persuasiveness of this argument, the Party leaders lacked the political strength and political conviction to take the radical measures it required. Why endanger the comfortable position achieved by policies which might undermine the coalition as well as prove electorally unpopular? Fearful of the impact of the charge leveled against the Party that it favored inflationary policies, it fought the election campaign of 1953 cautiously, carefully abstaining from advocacy of deficit financing or budgets not annually balanced.[62] No effort was made to spell out the "flexible budget" policies endorsed as part of the "third way"; a strong contrast to the bold Keynesian language of 1945, when the danger of inflation had been discounted as long as the creation of real new values balanced the issuance of budget advances.[63] And thus no strong effort was put up to stem the return to the notion of investment as largely a function of private saving.[64] In fact, the Draft Program of 1958 went so far as to put into the foreground the "fight against inflation" and the "cultivation of the capital market." [65] These formulations proved somewhat too "bourgeois" to some inner-party critics and were softened in the final version of the Program,

---

[60] Wirlandner, "Oeffentliche und private Kapitalsbildung," *Die Zukunft,* VII (October-November, 1952), 294–96.
[61] Wirlandner, "Sparmittelbildung und Investitionspolitik," *ibid.* (December, 1952), 374–79.
[62] Cf. KA, "Keine Inflation, Keine Arbeitslosigkeit," *Arbeiter Zeitung,* October 23, 1952.
[63] Ausch, "Die neue Wirtschaft im neuen Oesterreich," *op. cit.,* pp. 10–11.
[64] See, e.g., "Geld für Strom" (*Arbeiter Zeitung,* March 2, 1953), in which the SPOe wished to take credit for introducing the idea of financing expansion of electrification by means of loans floated on the capital market. The Party also agreed to the enactment of the *Sparbegünstigungsgesetz (Bundesgesetz über die Begünstigung des Sparens,* April 24, 1953; BGBl No. 51, s. 254, May 30, 1953), which was intended to stimulate and reward private saving.
[65] *Vorentwurf,* p. 22.

which nonetheless still retained the assertion—doubly doubtful from a socialist as well as Keynesian viewpoint—that intense savings by broad strata of the population were the prerequisite for sufficient capital formation.[66]

Tax Policy

Occasional reference has been made to acceptance by the SPOe of the present level of taxation as the maximum achievable. The Party takes a conservative view of the present tax structure, considering it in essence as socially just,[67] and has given up any idea of instituting major changes affecting either the distribution of the tax load or its weight. The traditional Socialist demand for direct and progressive taxation [68] was met by the introduction of a progressive income tax at the time of the *Anschluss*.[69] In addition, the Germans imposed a "business tax" (*Gewerbesteuer*), which now serves as the main revenue source for local governments.[70] This tax too, though its incidence eventually falls on the consumer, is fully accepted by the SPOe. Where additional revenue had to be found, Socialist policy has been to meet the need by across-the-board percentage increases of the income tax.[71] Though progression levels off markedly in the very high brackets—a fact significant for social rather than fiscal reasons—it has not been part of the Socialist program to press for increases but merely for

---

[66] *Arbeiter Zeitung*, May 15, 1958, p. 11.

[67] "We have a generally just tax system which we must defend against unrealistic and unjust attacks by enemies of the working population." (Migsch, "Ist unser Steuersystem gerecht?" *SPOe-Vertrauensmann*, VI [February, 1951], 71.)

[68] *Ibid.*; also "Direkte und indirekte Besteuerung," *Solidarität*, No. 136, April 9, 1951, p. 2.

[69] In Austrian terminology, a distinction is made between *Lohnsteuer* ("wage tax"), which is withheld from wages, and *Einkommensteuer* ("income tax"), in which the taxpayer makes his own return.

[70] For a brief discussion of this tax and the position of the SPOe with regard to it, see Robert Bechinie, "Die Gewerbesteuer," *SPOe-Vertrauensmann*, VI (January, 1951), 27–28.

[71] Cf., e.g., "Die Besatzungesteuer," *Die Zukunft*, IV (March, 1949), 94–95. The Finance Minister's draft had provided for a much less progressive tax, by which 5 s. (schillings) were to be added to a present tax of 2.6 s. and 41.60 s. added to a present tax of 1,166 s.—a 300 per cent increase at the lowest level compared to a 4 per cent increase at the higher one.

elimination of minor hardships and inequities for the low-income wage earners.[72]

Socialist enthusiasm for the progressive income tax appears to have cooled noticeably in recent years. Its obvious unpopularity with the masses of the population—who perversely prefer the traditional hidden turnover taxes [73]—the ease with which payment of the income tax can be evaded precisely by those groups in the population who are most hostile to the SPOe,[74] and, finally, the structure of the Austrian income pyramid with its exceedingly broad base and thin peak—a fact which deprives the tax of most of its redistributive effect [75]—have combined to put the Party on the defensive and to create disenchantment. This defensiveness is made apparent in the formulations of the 1958 Program, which read more like an appeal for understanding by the working class than a challenge to the possessing classes.[76] Having found that "soaking the rich" was an insufficient policy to raise the large funds needed for the maintenance of an extensive welfare state, the SPOe discovered that its members and sympathizers were developing a petty bourgeois "tax payers' outlook," accepting services as a matter of course, grumbling freely about them, and complaining about the high tax burden imposed on them.

---

[72] Cf. Pittermann, "Steueränderungen zugunsten der Arbeiter und Angestellten," *Arbeiter Zeitung*, July 17, 1951. For a criticism of the Party's willingness to see taxes level off at a less than confiscatory rate at the top, see Müller, "Das Steueränderungsgesetz," *Die Zukunft*, IV (June, 1949), 165–68. The 1958 Program contains no demands for significant changes in the tax structure.

[73] The unpopularity of the direct taxes was exploited by the Communists in their prolonged propaganda campaign for repeal of the "Nazi wage tax."

[74] As is true in other countries, the peasantry in Austria fails to contribute its share of the revenue, a fact which is the source of frequent castigation by Socialist spokesmen. (Cf., e.g., *Arbeiter Zeitung*, April 27, 1951, p. 2; "Direkte und indirekte Besteuerung," *Solidarität*, No. 136, April 9, 1951, p. 2; KA, "Steuerhinterziehung," *Arbeiter Zeitung*, December 18, 1948.)

[75] See Ernst Kübler, "Um ein soziales Steuerprogramm," *Die Zukunft*, II (November, 1947), 335–37.

[76] "The SPOe is aware of the fact that the modern state cannot meet its manifold tasks merely by collecting direct taxes from high incomes, capital gains, and properties. . . . The burden imposed on the population by certain excise taxes is justified if the revenue is used to secure the achievements of the welfare state." (*Arbeiter Zeitung*, May 15, 1958, p. 11.)

Welfare Services

In the field of social welfare the Socialist Party at the war's end set itself a double objective: to restore the pre-1938 system—with appropriate modifications and some improvements—and, in the long run, to extend its coverage, hitherto limited to wage-and-salary earners, into a "general people's pension" (*Volkspension*). The Party modestly acknowledged that the ambitious program for a universal old-age pension could not be realized within the near future.[77] Though the "people's pension" still forms an important part of the Socialist program and propaganda, the Party has failed to implement its demand with any concrete plans for financing the scheme, which must therefore be considered primarily a piece of rhetoric.[78]

The short-term goal of restoration was largely realized by the end of 1947. The rapid pace of social legislation initiated in the first years could not be maintained subsequently,[79] partly because the bulk of measures demanded had been enacted, and partly because the remaining pieces of legislation met with strong resistance from employer groups.[80] Though in contrast to the First Republic, the business community abstained from agitation for relief from the "social burden"—the political effects of any cut in social services served as a deterrent [81]—it insists that labor pay attention

---

[77] Cf. Karl Mantler, "Die soziale Frage und die Sozialgesetzgebung," *Unsere Arbeit*, June 21, 1946.

[78] In the speech accompanying the 10-Point Program, Chairman Schärf declared: "The people's pension is a demand which we shall insist on until it is realized." (*Die Aktion der Sozialistischen Partei Oesterreichs*, p. 17.) This plank in the Party program represents one of the foremost attempts to attract the votes of the "marginal," nonworking class strata of the population.

[79] With monotonous regularity the annual report of the Vienna Chamber of Labor repeated the complaint that "the furtherance of social welfare policy has bogged down." (*Jahrbuch der Arbeiterkammer Wien*, 1948, p. 5; ibid., 1949, p. 5; *ibid*, 1951, p. 5.)

[80] E.g., land workers' law, hour law, labor exchange law. Of these the first was enacted after prolonged negotiations.

[81] In the election campaign of 1953, SPOe propaganda stressed the alleged intention of the Finance Minister to cut the state contribution to the old-age pension fund, thereby reducing services, an allegation that was violently denied by the People's Party.

to the postulate it itself had set up: a high level of productivity as a pre-requisite for an extensive and expanding system of social services.[82]

Among the major pieces of social legislation embodying the ideas of the SPOe, the first to be passed after the end of the war was the Workers' Vacation Act.[83] By increasing the length of paid vacations granted to manual workers, one of the Socialist objectives—the equalization of working conditions for manual and salaried workers—was considerably advanced.[84]

The main issue which delayed the Collective Bargaining Act—it became law in 1947 [85]—was the question of the organizations which should be recognized as legally entitled to act as responsible parties in bargaining procedures. On demand by the Trade Union Federation and the Chambers of Labor, the SPOe had originally requested that the Federation and Chambers alone be recognized as bargaining agents on the labor side.[86] This demand was eventually withdrawn when the opposite side countered with the parallel request that the powerful Chamber of Business be the sole bargaining partner on the employer side. In defending the final settlement,[87] the SPOe took the position that it represented an improvement over the original draft, and that the Party had all along felt uneasy about the prospect of two monolithic power blocs covering the whole of Austrian industry in its negotiations.[88]

---

[82] *Jahrbuch der Arbeiterkammer Wien*, 1947, pp. 23–25. As the subsequent brief discussion will show, welfare provisions are very generous in Austria, particularly when the relative poverty of its economic resources is taken into account.

[83] *BG No. 142 vom 12. Juni 1947 (Arbeiterurlaubsgesetz)*, BGBl, August 7, 1947.

[84] Paid time-off rises from one week per annum after nine months' employment to 24 working days after 15 years. Under the provisions of the old law, workers were entitled to a one-week paid vacation after 12 months' employment and to a maximum of two weeks after 5 years. ("Arbeiterurlaubsgesetz," *SPOe-Vertrauensmann*, I [September, 1946], 10–11.)

[85] *BG No. 76 vom 26. Februar 1947 (Kollektivvertragsgesetz)*, BGBl, May 6, 1947.

[86] Karl Maisel, "Das Kollektivvertragsgesetz—gut oder schlecht?" *Arbeiter Zeitung*, February 21, 1947.

[87] Under the law as finally enacted, individual unions (except "company unions") were given the right to act as bargaining agents. From 1947 to 1951, because of the policy of settling wage questions through general wage-price agreements, individual unions played only a minor role in determining wage rates; their role merely supplemented that of the Federation.

[88] Maisel, *op. cit.*; also Pittermann, as reported in *Arbeiter Zeitung*, February 20, 1947. In the parliamentary debate, however, Socialist speakers stressed the advan-

The enactment of a law regulating the working conditions of rural laborers [89] represented a major success for the Socialist Party. Though, contrary to Socialist demands, the act merely set up a framework within which the *Länder* were required to pass their own implementing legislation and fell short of SPOe hopes in other ways,[90] it nevertheless represented a comprehensive codification of labor law for agricultural workers, which put them, *mutatis mutandis,* on a level of rough equality with workers in industrial labor.

In connection with the second wage-price agreement, the principle of fixed food and children's grants—the latter from public funds—was established.[91] This constituted an important step toward recognition of maintenance of the existence minimum as a public duty. A fixed housing grant based on the same principle was also a part of the Rent Act passed in 1951.[92] And as a step toward the equalization of manual workers and salaried employees, the basis of computing insurance payments for the two groups (though not the amounts paid) was made identical.[93]

Preparation for the enactment of the complex Social Insurance Transfer Act (*Sozialversicherungsüberleitungsgesetz,* SVUeG) took more than eighteen months. While largely favoring a return to the administrative arrangement existing before 1948, the SPOe demanded reform in two directions: [94] establishment of a unified administrative authority comprising *all* aspects of social insurance, combined with a high degree of geographical decentralization; and maximum influence for the representatives of labor in the self-governing bodies which under the law were re-estab-

---

tage which, because of its centralized power, the Chamber of Business would have derived from such an arrangement. (Böhm, *Steno. Prot.*, February 26, 1947, pp. 1260–261.) The entire argument may represent merely a "sour grapes" attitude and a defense against Communist charges of weakness.

[89] BG No. 140 vom. 2. Juni, 1948 (*Landarbeitergesetz*), BGBl, August 12, 1948.

[90] The Party criticized it as deficient with regard to the regulation of agricultural child labor, apprentice training, and the narrow scope given to Work Councils.

[91] The charge for children's grants was put on the public treasury to avoid discrimination by employers against workers with large families.

[92] For a more detailed discussion of the Party's housing policy, see below.

[93] Edward Stark, "Die sozialpolitische Durchführung der Lohn-Preisregulierung," *Die Zukunft,* IV (June, 1949), 168–70.

[94] See Robert Uhlir, "Das SVUeG," *Die Zukunft,* II (April, 1947), 112–16, and "Neuordnung in der Sozialversicherung," *SPOe-Vertrauensmann,* II (May, 1947), 171.

lished to administer the system.[95] The inevitable compromise in which functional unification was rejected while simultaneously the People's Party's counterdemand for a multiple system of insurance institutes along occupational lines was also buried, left the administrative setup largely unchanged.[96] Labor representation on the self-governing bodies was set as ranging from two-thirds to four-fifths. This provided a large number of patronage positions which the Chambers of Labor and the Trade Union Federation filled [97] after protracted negotiations.[98]

The Socialist Party has continued to adhere tenaciously to the insurance principle as the basis of financing welfare services in theory while modifying it in practice. It has insisted that the fact of federal contributions supplementing employer-employee payments represented neither a violation of the "strict insurance basis" nor its replacement by a welfare (*Fürsorge*) system.[99] Thus the trend toward the view of social security as a right of citizenship and away from the insurance principle—characteristic of the concept of the welfare state and humanitarian socialism [100]—was disregarded in the reconstruction of the Austrian system.

Political considerations, apart from the mere irrational carry-over of traditional ideas and institutions, are probably responsible for this Socialist position. The insurance principle guarantees that claims will be met—barring economic or political catastrophes—as "vested rights" which cannot be denied. A system relying on budget appropriations for its financing is always at the mercy of a penny-pinching or hostile Finance Minister. Fur-

---

[95] In this latter demand, full backing from the Ministry (occupied by the Socialist Karl Maisel) apparently was lacking. The draft worked out by the Ministry allowed the employer side one-third of the delegates to the Health Insurance Institutes (*Krankenkassen*) as compared to one quarter before 1934, a concession which was criticized by Uhlir (*ibid.*).

[96] The final arrangement was described as an unsatisfactory compromise by Uhlir. A complete recasting of the complex law, partly because it still retains features derived from the Nazi occupation, was subsequently undertaken.

[97] It was decided for the time being to substitute appointment by delegating bodies for election by the members.

[98] *Jahrbuch der Arbeiterkammer Wien*, 1947, p. 46.

[99] Uhlir, "Das SVUeG," *op. cit.*

[100] The National Health Service adopted by the British Labor Government is an outstanding example which is in strong contrast to the system of contributory *Krankenkassen* established in Austria. For an elaborate criticism of the insurance principle, see Abraham Epstein, *Insecurity, a Challenge to America* (New York: H. Smith and R. Haas, 1933).

thermore, payment under the insurance system is automatic once certain formal conditions are fulfilled and does not require examination of need through a means test.[101] The inequities and drawbacks of the insurance system—severely criticized by all groups of the population, including those whom it is supposed primarily to benefit—though undoubtedly recognized and occasionally exposed by Socialist spokesmen,[102] have not impressed the Party leadership sufficiently to bring about a change in position. Foremost among these inequities is, of course, the financing system itself, which requires high and nonprogressive contributions [103] and which still falls short of guaranteeing a desirable level of payments to the insured. The absence of reserves and the rising amount of expenditures (overaging, increase of "bad risks") have made the financial outlook for the insurance institutes very insecure. By greatly complicating the process of computing benefits due, the system has made it impossible for the beneficiary to check the justice of the award and has thus undermined his confidence in its equity. It has also fostered a large bureaucratic apparatus. The principle of "democratic self-administration," harped on by the SPOe, has failed to counter this process of bureaucratization. The mass of the insured have shown little interest in the self-administering bodies which have become patronage preserves for the large labor and employer organizations. But the SPOe leadership has shown no enthusiasm for the principle that need and not previous contributions should become the decisive criterion in extending support. This was demonstrated most clearly when it failed to back the Hillegeist plan, which would have required that old-age pensions be withheld from persons receiving a full income after reaching the statutory age

---

[101] This consideration played an important part in the Socialist struggle to replace the system of unemployment relief (*Arbeitslosenfürsorge*) in force after 1934 with the pre-1934 system of unemployment insurance.

[102] Hans Winter's "Die Lage der österreichischen Sozialversicherung" (*Die Zukunft*, V [August, 1950], 222–25) contains the most outspoken public criticism of the present system to come from the Socialist camp. The writer, however, does not seem to represent official thinking. For criticism of the present system of health insurance, see Karl Rom, "Sozialärztliche Gedanken zur Neuregelung in der Sozialversicherung," *Die Zukunft*, II (January, 1947), 19. The following points are based on these sources.

[103] In 1953 22 per cent of the total amount of wages went for social service contributions. Of this, 12 per cent was contributed by the employer and 10 per cent deducted from wages.

level.[104] This tentative step toward an egalitarian welfare concept away from an insurance principle already punctured by inflation [105] was apparently considered as too radical and politically explosive by the leadership [106] to be adopted as the official Party position.

Public Housing and Tenants' Protection

In the First Republic the Socialist position on the housing question was characterized by two principal policies: tenant protection through a system of rigid rent controls, and extensive building with public (at that time municipal) funds.[107] After 1945 the SPOe simply resumed these prewar policies and continued on the same course without major deviation. Those principles, however, which had been passionately fought over in the twenties were now lifted out of the realm of partisan controversy; the passage of time and lack of feasible alternatives had made dead issues of them.[108]

Tenants' protection, applying to all houses built before 1917, has kept

---

[104] See Friedrich Hillegeist, "Was der 'Hillegeist Plan' wirklich will," and Fritz Koubek, "Die Rentenreform—kritisch betrachtet," *Die Zukunft*, VI (October, 1951), 274–79.

[105] Koubek, a leading inner-party opponent of the "Hillegeist Plan," had to admit that inflation, by wiping out capital reserves, had in practice already eliminated the basis of the insurance principle.

[106] The inner-party opposition was headed by the Union of Public Employees, whose members benefit most from the present arrangement and are most insistent on retention of "vested rights." Their considerable strength, as well as the potentially politically disastrous charge that the SPOe favored reduction of old-age pensions, prevented the Party from endorsing the principle contained in the "Hillegeist Plan."

[107] For a sympathetic and extensive analysis, see Gulick, *op. cit.*, Chap. 14.

[108] The SPOe admits that the People's Party is reconciled, verbally at least, to tenants' protection and considers it untouchable. (*Arbeiter Zeitung*, September 18, 1951.) The reopening of the issue ("Fragen an Herrn Raab," *ibid.*, January 18, 1953) was clearly election propaganda. The following quotation is taken from a speech by a member of the government belonging to the Christian Trade Union wing of the People's Party: "An apartment today does not represent a commodity. Rather it is the right of the human being to a decent home; a social need which also in future will not be dealt with on the basis of supply and demand." (Fritz Bock, "Wohnbau—Sache der Allgemeinheit," *Arbeit und Wirtschaft*, IV [February, 1951], 22.)

rents at a level intended to assure maintenance but no return to the owner of the property.[109] It was, however, recognized at various times that the destruction of the capitalist market in the sphere of house ownership required that the market's function be taken over by public authorities and that the community would henceforth have to provide for all housing needs in the absence of any incentive to private capital.[110]

Between 1918 and 1933 the city of Vienna had constructed 58,668 apartments and 5,257 one-family houses, over the violent opposition of the federal government and the Christian Social Party which controlled it.[111] Rents for these dwellings, which were financed exclusively out of current taxes, were kept on the same level as those covered by the tenants' protection law, providing for almost nominal payments sufficient to cover running expenses of these new buildings.[112] One of the obvious consequences of this policy was to accustom large parts of the Austrian population to accept nominal, noneconomic rents as a right of citizenship; another result was that the wage structure was geared to a living standard in which housing played almost no part in a family's budget.

With regard to the housing problem, the Socialist objective in the Second Republic has been described as "raising financial means for new building, reconstruction and maintenance of old houses without further increase of the financial load for low-income groups and unconditional preservation of tenants' protection." [113]

So thoroughly accustomed had the masses of the population become to the view of housing as a free service—the result of decades of Socialist propaganda—that the Party leadership met with fierce resistance by its members whenever it was forced to accept modifications in the existing

---

[109] In 1951 about 65 per cent of all houses were covered by the law (in Vienna 78 per cent). (*Wohnungsfrage und Mietengesetz,* SBZ, October 1951.)

[110] Cf., e.g., KA, "Mietenschutz und Wohnungsnot," *Arbeiter Zeitung,* December 24, 1946.

[111] Gulick, *op. cit.,* p. 450. The heavy preponderance of apartment buildings over one-family houses was not only due to the lower cost of construction for the former and the habits or preferences of the tenants. Large apartment buildings with their collective laundries, nurseries, playgrounds, etc., were considered more appropriate to the political and social requirements of the proletariat and the future socialist society.

[112] The average monthly rent for a small apartment amounted to approximately 7 schillings, i.e., 2 per cent of an average worker's income.

[113] Kurt Heller, "Die neuen Wohnungsgesetze," *SPOe-Vertrauensmann,* VI (February, 1951), 62–69.

rent structure. In order to preserve older houses from falling into a state of disrepair,[114] rents obviously had to be increased (unless the requirements were met out of general taxation) at least to a level sufficient to keep up with increased costs of maintenance and repair. Indeed, the increase had to go beyond this level because of the growing decrepitude of these houses, brought on by war and prolonged neglect. In 1951 the leaders of the SPOe agreed to a "valorization" of rents. The bitter pill of greatly increased rents [115] was sweetened by the introduction of fixed housing grants which, for the smallest apartments, were deemed high enough to balance the higher rent bill.[116] Nevertheless, the explanations of the top leaders were met with a near revolt on the part of the lower-level functionaries who saw in this measure a betrayal of Socialist tradition and a sign of political weakness.[117] The law, as a concession to Socialist demands, also contained clauses to assure that these increased rents would actually be used for repair and maintenance work.[118] The idea that rents should be turned over not to the landlords but to a general public repair fund, though apparently widely favored by the rank and file of Party functionaries,[119] had been rejected by the leadership as "too bureaucratic" [120] (and probably impos-

---

[114] One of the consequences of tenants' protection is that it gives the owner no incentive to make any repairs or do maintenance work. On the contrary, as rents are frozen for five years (previously three) in a repair fund, it is to his interest to postpone necessary repairs beyond this time limit.

[115] The new rents were based on a uniform rate of one Austrian schilling for one so-called "peace-crown" (*Friedenskrone*) that had formed the basis of the pre-1934 calculation. This amounted roughly to a quadrupling of rents over their 1945 level. ("Wohnungsfrage und Mietengesetz," p. 8.)

[116] Almost 72 per cent of all apartments in Vienna were assumed to belong to this category. As these grants were to be borne by employers it must be assumed, however, that they were passed on to consumers in the form of higher prices.

[117] See report on "Wiener Konferenz der SP Vertrauensmänner und neues Mietengesetz" in *Arbeiter Zeitung*, September 21, 1951. The meeting, in spite of the toned-down reporting characteristic of the *Arbeiter Zeitung*, appears to have been very stormy. Though a motion to instruct the Vienna delegation to the annual Conference to vote against the draft was defeated "by a considerable majority" (no figures given), Bruno Pittermann's motion to approve the draft and thus to express confidence in the Party leadership was accepted by a vote of only 244 against 132. The heavy negative vote was a remarkable and rare public exhibition of dissatisfaction.

[118] *BG No. 227 vom 21. September 1951. BGBl*, October 31, 1951.

[119] Speakers at the "*Wiener Konferenz*" repeatedly returned to the demand.

[120] "Instandhaltung," *Arbeiter Zeitung*, July 14, 1951.

sible to achieve within the framework of the coalition). Yet in the absence of some such provision, it is questionable whether the means of enforcement envisaged by the act [121] can be effective in assuring adequate maintenance when the landlord has no incentive to obey the law while receiving a premium for evading it.

In continuing to back unreservedly the principle of tenants' protection, the Party is perpetuating an arrangement which should never have been anything but a temporary and transitional solution. To leave house ownership in private hands and at the same time to deprive the owner by law of most of the benefits of such ownership is to make of him a resentful and necessarily ineffective administrator. It is to combine the evils of the capitalist and socialist worlds without the advantages of either. Rents have lost all rational relation to size, location, or facilities offered. No incentive exists for apartments too large for occupants' needs to be exchanged for smaller ones—on the contrary. As a consequence, a new, exploited high rent-paying class—the subtenants—has vastly increased. The Socialist mayor of Linz, in a rare public burst of frankness, aptly described the situation:

Here social justice frequently ends. The word "tenants' protection" has really lost its meaning: sense becomes nonsense, welfare a plague.[122]

Yet official pronouncements give little indication of how the Party intends to solve the problem. It is committed to a level of rents which will cover maintenance costs and to the establishment of an equalization fund to alleviate hardships caused in individual cases.[123] But it is not clear how the present crazy-quilt pattern is to be straightened out as long as the Party

---

[121] Sanctions of increased severity, the right of tenants and municipalities to enforce the use of rents for repairs, etc. The SPOe's request that rents be permanently accumulated so as to be available for repairs was defeatd.

[122] Ernst Koref, "Das Wohnbauprogramm und die Gemeinden," *Der Aufbau*, V (January, 1950), 3–9; also "Mietzins und Wohnraum," *Arbeiter Zeitung*, February 17, 1948. The latter, appearing anonymously as coming from an "expert," contained sweeping criticism of the irrationality and circumventions of the current law and suggested radical changes. The editors of the *Arbeiter Zeitung* took the unusual step of introducing this leading article with the statement that the opinions were the author's own and had not been examined by the Party. It must be added that Koref coupled his courageous criticism with a fervent disavowal of any intention to undermine the principle of tenants' protection.

[123] 1958 Program, p. 12.

uneasily accepts both the concepts of "socialized" and "private capitalist" building [124] and the shortage of adequate housing is perpetuated. Unlike the British Labor Party, which proposes to cut the Gordian knot by "municipalization" of all nonowner-occupied rental housing and apartments, the SPOe does not advocate—even in its long-range policy statement—a radical socialist solution of taking over housing into public ownership and coherently planning the allocation of living quarters.[125]

Extensive early plans for large-scale reconstruction of cities—influenced by the British Labor Party's Town and Country Planning Act and New Towns Act—have not been implemented. The need to meet the immediate housing demand, the difficulty of raising the necessary funds in the face of rising costs and a Finance Minister unsympathetic to Socialist objectives, made it necessary to concentrate on the continuation of the more traditional housing activities. While the Socialists thus devoted themselves to the construction of low-cost housing out of public funds,[126] the OeVP developed a long-term loan program to help applicants who desired to rebuild their bomb-damaged houses. The rivalry of the coalition partners thus extends into the housing field; and charges that the other party uses control over the funds it administers to benefit almost exclusively its own followers are frequently voiced on both sides.[127]

The "rationing" of the available supply of housing by the authorities [128] and the uneven and irrational rent structure have made the entire question a focus of political power struggles. These conflicts today do not center

[124] The Draft Program stated that housing needs "cannot and must not be met *solely* [italics added] by private capital"; shortly after it declared that elimination of a financial return to the landlord "makes housing construction based on the principles of private capitalism impossible"; and shortly after that it admitted that the present situation in the housing market was totally obscure. (*Vorentwurf*, p. 31.)

[125] See the section *"Bauen und Wohnen"* in the 1958 Program, *loc. cit.*, p. 12.

[126] The tapping of the income tax revenue for public housing was claimed as a major success by Socialists. See *Arbeiter Zeitung*, April 20, 1950, and December 16, 1950; also, "Der österreichische Arbeiterkammertag zur Wohnbaufrage," *Arbeit und Wirtschaft*, III (June, 1950), 24.

[127] See KHS, "Das Wohnungseigentum," *Arbeiter Zeitung*, July 23, 1950; KA, "Wohnungseigentum," *ibid.*, November 29, 1952; "Wohnungseigentum," *SPOe-Vertrauensmann*, V (June-August, 1950), 91–92.

[128] In Vienna each apartment that falls vacant must be registered with the City Housing Office, which has the right—under certain circumstances—to requisition it for needy cases and which must approve each change of occupancy.

primarily on the issue of public versus private housing, but rather around the controversy as to which of the two major parties shall control access to the available apartments, new and old. In the absence of the automatic criteria of the market or of an airtight system of allocation of available space according to need, political "pull" rather than genuine need has become the decisive factor in obtaining an apartment.[129] Though the Socialist Party considers housing projects built under its auspices a major source of organizational strength,[130] the embarrassment of continuous harassment and the opportunism bred by turning Party membership into a vehicle for preferred treatment admittedly more than balance the organizational gain.[131]

Thus, while carrying on the public housing policy with which the Socialist Party of the First Republic became identified, the luster which surrounded the large building projects of Red Vienna today appears dimmed. For at mid-century, large-scale public housing has ceased to be a radical innovation. It has become commonplace and essentially noncontroversial. In fact, it has taken its place among the services which the citizen of the welfare state expects from his government and which arouse in him less a feeling of political pride and gratitude than a tendency to criticize the authorities for their failure to provide more for less.[132]

---

[129] The "point system" that has been established as the basis of allocation is frequently circumvented. I cannot share Gulick's complacency on this point (op. cit., p. 454). The jealousy and bitterness that inequities in the housing field arouse are hard to exaggerate. Money still plays a part, not in the form of bribes but because under the law it is possible for landlords to "sell" apartments to the highest bidder.

[130] I have heard Party District chairmen discuss the growth and decline of membership in terms of how many housing projects the city had carried out in their districts.

[131] It is ironical that the SPOe hardly dares to allocate a new municipal apartment to one of its officials, prominent or otherwise, because of the furor and envy this would arouse. District Party secretariats, which were considered as local housing offices by Party members, have in many places been forced to refuse categorically to handle housing questions, though applicants are still given (and require) recommendations by the local SPOe leader. I am convinced that the establishment of an airtight and equitable allocation system based on priorities of need would help the Party by far more, internally and externally, than it would lose by such a move.

[132] My own observations confirm the general conclusions to this effect reached by Bednarik (op. cit., passim).

VIII

Socialism in the "Age of Fulfillment"

The Feeling of Uneasiness

The previous chapters have attempted, above all, to fix as accurately as possible the position of the Austrian Socialist Party since the end of World War II; to establish its structural features; and to plot the areas of change in policies, actions, verbal expression, and temper. In the pursuit of this task, the causal relations inherent in the historical transformation to which the Party has been subject could be touched on only briefly. Because so many relevant data are unavailable, and because the subject is such a contemporary one, any attempt to clarify the causes of change will be necessarily speculative. For the following assessment of the transformation and crisis of modern socialism, the impressions gained from a study of the SPOe will be used primarily as illustrations of a process which is assumed not to be limited to the Austrian political scene.

The foremost impression which the observer of Austrian Socialism gains is the cooling of its political temper, the replacement of its former spirit of militancy by a widespread feeling of indifference, disenchantment, and frequently expressed uneasiness.[1] Underlying this change in temper, and

---

[1] The existence of *Unbehagen* ("uneasiness") and the lessening of enthusiasm have been widely noted and commented on in the SPOe. See, e.g., Hans Müller, "Vom Unbehagen in der Partei," *Die Zukunft*, II (November, 1947), 320–22; Karl Czernetz, "Selbstbesinnung," *ibid.*, V (June, 1950), 151–55; Anton Tesarek, "Ueber die geistige Haltung der österreichischen Arbeiterklasse," *ibid.*, V (May, 1950), 133–36; OP, "Das Zeitalter des Unbehagens," *Arbeiter Zeitung*, September 19, 1951; JS, "Kein Schwung?" *ibid.*, November 7, 1948; Fritz Klenner, "Mangel an Kampfgeist?" *ibid.*, September 26, 1950; Wolfgang Speiser,

largely responsible for it, is a more fundamental development, the increasing uncertainty about the Socialist Movement's future objectives. This uncertainly extends to the features of the socialist society desired—the ultimate goal—and consequently to the institutional devices intended to achieve this end. "Scientific socialism," in the past the source of confident thought and action among the leaders and a messianic dogma for the masses, has disintegrated or—what in effect amounts to the same thing—has been transformed into empirical attempts to discover what institutional means will bring about certain desired limited social ends. Socialist theory, whether the explicit Marxist structure or the implicit assumptions held in common by all socialists about the main features of the future "good society," has given way to vague and generalized assertions of humane sentiments and concern for the national welfare. As a result, "practicism"—hailed by some as statesmanlike realism and damned by others as treacherous opportunism —is today the acknowledged approach to questions of socialist policy.[2]

There can be little doubt about the reality of the Party's change in temper. It is, however, necessary to examine in some detail how this change affects various groups within the Socialist Movement and whether the change represents indeed as profound a break with the past as is—perhaps too readily—assumed. The shrillness with which the fact of disenchantment is proclaimed by speakers at Party Conferences may be misleading. For it may represent a projection of these speakers' disappointments and frustrations rather than a changed mood in the Party as a whole. What appears on closer observation is that those who suffer most acutely from the feeling of disenchantment, of "unease," are the lower-echelon functionaries. In the past they eagerly accepted the Party's truculent and messianic slogans and looked at organizational activity as the implementation of a fighting faith. Though they were and are vocal in criticizing the leadership's policies, they represent no more than a fraction of the present Party's functionaries or membership. Most of the leaders, high and low, have accepted

---

"Volksbildung und Apathie," *ibid.*, July 7, 1949; Karl Bednarik, *Der junge Arbeiter* . . . , and "The Central European Worker in the Ideological Vacuum," *Confluence* (June, 1953), 57–68; and SPOe Party Conference Protocols 1947 (pp. 95, 99, 175); *ibid.*, 1949 (pp. 26, 28, 31, 32, 34, 39, 43, 55, 57, 99); *ibid.*, 1950 (pp. 96, 101, 124, 128, 148, 149).

[2] Leftists like Hindels and Czernetz deplore this development (e.g., Czernetz, "Selbstbesinnung," *loc. cit.*), while the followers of Renner see in it the necessary and inevitable application to the problems of "here and now" that the period of "socialist fulfillment" demands (e.g., JS, "Kein Schwung?" *loc. cit.*).

the passage from the phase of struggle and propaganda to that of practical and routine work with satisfaction or at least equanimity; with satisfaction if they had identified themselves in the past with Renner's position and saw in the change a belated justification of their own convictions; with equanimity where the opportunities for practical work and the novel tasks facing the Party met their powerful need for political activity of some kind. With some exceptions, even former members of the Revolutionary Socialist cadre—generously provided by the Party in 1945 with full-time positions— have so completely immersed themselves in these new practical tasks that they have come to accept, without overt protest and apparently even without inner struggle, the failure of their former revolutionary aspirations and ideals to determine or significantly influence Party policy.[3]

That large and increasing section of Party functionaries who, because of their youth or former indifference, do not share the memories of militant thought and action, must also, by and large, be reckoned among those who cannot share the much talked-about feeling of loss and frustration. Furthermore, the retrospective view of Social Democracy in the First Republic as having been imbued with a "miraculous spirit" of selfless enthusiasm and devoted uprightness [4] and of the Party as a closely knit spiritual community [5] is, to some extent, an idealization of the past by middle-aged men sentimentalizing their own youth. That bureaucratization, "practicism," and opportunism were not absent in the Social Democracy of the First Republic is proved by the Revolutionary Socialists' repudiation of the old Party's tradition on these very grounds [6]—though they were then counter-

---

[3] Examples of prominent ex-R.S. functionaries who today again fill important Party positions without any apparent feeling of frustration are: Czernetz, Kratky, Kreisky, Probst, Proksch, Olah, Wedenig, Weikhart.

[4] See, e.g., Tesarek, op. cit.

[5] Ibid.; also, Julius Braunthal, Auf der Suche nach dem Millennium, II, 492.

[6] Braunthal confirms this judgment when he notes that "the glow of enthusiasm which had pervaded it in the day of my youth [prior to World War I] had somehow cooled, I felt . . . [by 1934]. . . . After the World War [I] . . . a period of disappointments" began. (Ibid., II, 538–39.) Braunthal ascribes this reaction to the Party's growth in breadth, the resulting bureaucratic superstructure, the increasing contacts and ties with existing institutions and vested interests. Charles Gulick's massive opus (Austria from Habsburg to Hitler) is devoted to the attempt to prove that Austrian Social Democrats of the First Republic were essentially practical men, Revisionists, good democrats and parliamentarians who used radical slogans merely as a tactical device to pacify the Party Left. Though I myself cannot accept his analysis (see Chapter 4, passim), Gulick mar-

acted by an influential and vocal radical wing and largely veiled by the prevalent commitment to revolutionary phraseology. The old Party contained Renner as well as Bauer, revolutionary zealots as well as the subtreasurers of the Sections. But, to paraphrase one of Marx' bons mots, the ideas of its ruling elite are the ideas of the Party. Just as Bauer's fervent faith overshadowed Renner's sober spirit in the First Republic and thus imparted to the entire Party a characteristic hue of radical enthusiasm, so Schärf's nonideological and unimaginative approach has given the Party of the Second Republic its characteristic features. Before World War II, practical work, to be acceptable to the Party Left (and such leaders as Bauer, who simultaneously feared it and felt an affinity for it) had to be cloaked in the mantle of the revolutionary phrase. It is now pursued proudly in the serene knowledge that it will receive the backing of the most powerful men in the Party.

The Change of Objective

More easily demonstrable than the exact nature of the shift in Socialist temper is the change in the Party's goals and methods. In the past a fully socialized society, however vague its outlines, was the goal toward which the Party's thought and effort were directed, while the immediately feasible demands were considered mere transitional steps toward its achievement. The SPOe's programs since 1945 reveal that advance toward a fully socialized society is neither anticipated nor even desired. In fact, no radical transformation of the existing economic and social order, even as a distant goal, is contemplated. Thus the Party's "basic" Program of 1958 limits itself to the conservation and extension of established gains—social security, public housing—and to such objectives as full employment, increase of the country's productive power, and improvement of the standard of living; [7] objectives which can, according to the Party's present thinking, be achieved within the existing framework of a mixed economy. This change from a radically reforming to an essentially satisfied and conserving party is underlined by the pride with which the Party's former chairman viewed its stabilizing role. The establishment of a constitutional democracy and its success-

---

shals ample evidence to show that the SPOe of the present does not differ as radically from the Party under Otto Bauer as speakers of the Left or emotionally involved participants wish us to believe.

[7] *Arbeiter Zeitung*, May 15, 1958, pp. 9–12.

ful defense against the Communist threat are hailed by him as the Party's most outstanding achievements.[8] In his system of values the traditional socialist relationship between the political structure and socialist goals is reversed. No longer is the democratic state viewed as a favorite means for the achievement of specifically socialist objectives; socialist policies are acclaimed as assuring the stability and viability of the Austrian democratic state.[9]

This phenomenon is by no means restricted to Austria and the Austrian Socialist Party. The "loss of momentum," as to the present meaning of Socialism and consequently as to the next steps in the direction of the ultimate goal is equally pronounced—and more honestly admitted—in the largest social democratic party, the British Labor Party.[10] The group of British Socialists known as "Socialist Union," re-examining socialist fundamentals, expressed a widespread sentiment when it found that "the easy confidence of the past is gone and our way forward is beset with uncertainty." [11] And the Frankfurt Declaration, which expresses the tenets of belief agreed on by Europe's social democratic parties, lacks the vision of a socialist system differing in any fundamental way from the welfare state already largely realized in several European countries.[12]

That this dulling of the socialist edge, this transformation of a once radical movement into a basically conservative force, is not restricted to one country, leads us to the assumption that we are dealing here with a broader historical process rooted in the nature of the socialist doctrine rather than in any incidental cause or set of causes—as asserted by some Austrian Social-

---

[8] Adolf Schärf, "Rückblick auf 8 Jahre sozialistischer Politik," *Die Zukunft*, VIII (January-February, 1953), 1–4.

[9] "If a retrospect is made of the politics of the past years one must not forget to mention that the Socialist Party through nationalization and expansion of social services has essentially contributed to the pacification of the country's social development." (*Ibid.*)

[10] See, e.g., R. H. S. Crossman, ed., *New Fabian Essays*, particularly the contribution by Crossman, "Toward a Philosophy of Socialism," in which the author notes "symptoms of a . . . serious ailment, a failure of the sense of direction" (p. 1).

[11] *Socialism—A New Statement of Principles*, Lincoln-Prager Press Ltd., London, 1952, p. 1.

[12] *Die Zukunft*, VI (July, 1951), 177–80. C. A. R. Crosland views the Declaration as identifying Socialism with what he has described as "statism" and has defined it as a *transitional* step toward socialism proper. ("The Transition from Capitalism," in *New Fabian Essays*, p. 60.)

ists—such as the impact of Fascism, the elimination of the Jewish intellectual element, the smallness of the country, or the four-power occupation. Those apologists, mostly spokesmen of the Movement's moderate wing, who view the change as a necessary reflection of socialism's entrance into its "period of fulfillment" are coming to realize that socialism, in a fundamentally changed environment, has largely outlived the inspiration which gave it birth.

The Sources of Socialist Inspiration

Socialism everywhere, even where its message was expressed in Marxist terms, was a broad stream fed by several tributaries. Though "social justice" represented the goal of all the diverse groups and individuals who professed themselves to be socialists, the meaning of the term varied with the motives and values of those who made up the movement. What was common to all, what may be described as the specifically socialist element which gave unity to this diversity of belief, was the identification of the socially just system with one in which the exploitation of one man by another within a class society—a society in which one group derived power over another from its position in the class structure—would be eliminated.

The "Felt Needs" of the Proletariat

Even this common core of socialist belief, however, obscures existing ambiguity and diversity. For the term "exploitation" was neither felt nor understood identically by all those who agreed that it would have to be eliminated. It is possible retrospectively to distinguish four broad interpretations of the term and thus also four differing versions of the socialist goal. These differing concepts of Socialism should not be identified with specific historical figures or groups. Rather, they represent the basic social and psychological elements found to have combined in varying degrees in creating the modern socialist movements known to us. The first is derived from the workers' experience of economic misery and insecurity, lack of power compared to the "boss class" and inability to extract a "just wage" from employers. The mass of industrial workers, rendered capable of organized political effort by the institutions of the new factory civilization,[13]

---

[13] For a discussion of the relation between the growth of the factory system and the development of proletarian class-consciousness, see Robert Michels, "Die Psychologie der antikapitalistischen Massenbewegungen," in *Grundrisse der Sozialökonomie*, II, Part 2 (1926), 244–81.

was drawn into struggles whose foremost aim was the alleviation of these most pressing hardships: grinding poverty and the threat to existence through loss of work.

Equality of Opportunity

While the first view identified the ending of exploitation with the fair distribution of the national product to all individuals and classes, the second concept, which might be termed that of "humanitarian socialism," aimed at the political and economic emancipation of the working class primarily for ethical reasons. The postulate of individual self-development and of the inherent equality of men appeared denied by a class system in which economic and political power were monopolized by one class and used to limit the life chances of the members of the industrial working class. What distinguished upholders of "humanitarian socialism" from such liberals as John Stuart Mill was the stress they put on the recognition that a certain degree of economic security was a prerequisite for a fully developing personality; and that in modern society state power was needed to curb private economic power and enforce measures (including collectivization of part of the economy) which would establish the necessary degree of economic equality. Equality of opportunity was an intrinsic part of their faith. And equality of opportunity was deemed incompatible with gross economic inequalities.[14] Though they accepted collective means and rediscovered the worth of community and the state, their instincts and values were individualist, libertarian, essentially middle-class.

"Scientific Socialism"

The most characteristic feature of the third approach, that of Marxist "scientific socialism" was its combination of the egotistical and ethical aspirations—expressed by and on behalf of the proletariat—into a theoretical system closely related to the historical process. It put responsibility for the attack on the existing system squarely on the working class itself, endowing

---

[14] It is characteristic that L. T. Houbhouse's "New Liberalism" (L. T. Houbhouse, *Liberalism*, Holt and Co., New York, 1911) is closely related to the socialism of the British Labor Party. British socialists have freely acknowledged their intellectual indebtedness to John Stuart Mill and T. H. Green, who bridge the gap between Liberalism and Socialism. Even the "radical" pamphlet, *Keeping Left* (London, *New Statesman and Nation*, 1950), uses as its point of departure Colonel Rainboro's famous assertion of the inherent equality of men and the consequent claim to equal opportunity.

the aims of that class with historical (and, therefore, to Marxists ethical) justification, and linked it to a promise of an otherwise undefined future of social justice, one in which "the last shall be first." The political effectiveness of Marxist doctrine lay in its ability to concentrate resentment and to inspire it by a message of historic mission.

The theory of "scientific socialism," though in essence a working hypothesis about the relation between economic institutions and social organization, was put forth, and widely received, as the prophecy of inevitable developments deducible from the definition of existing class relations. The deceptive clarity lent to the theory by its use of lapidary definitions and of dialectical dichotomies—and those were the aspects of the theory which gave it such wide appeal—corresponded to a fighting mood engendered by the misery and turmoil of emerging industrial capitalism and proletarian impotence. In its forecast of the future socialist society, only the negatives stand out clearly: capitalism will *collapse*; exploitation of man by man will *cease*; the state will *wither away*. Beyond the fact that all the means of production would be collectively owned—the term "collectively" itself was left undefined—and that thus, by definition, economic classes as well as the state as a machine of repression would disappear, the positive features of the future socialist society were left to the imagination of individual Socialists. For Marxists the war was more important than its aims. Speculation about the concrete outlines of the future society was discouraged, in part because it was assumed that a profound change in the economic relations would create its own forms of social life inconceivable to men raised and confined in bourgeois society; [15] in part, because preoccupation with the features of the future society would detract from the proletariat's concentration on the present struggle and would create divisions where hatred of the existing system had created a feeling of solidarity. Three tacit assumptions underlay the Marxist theory: that the future society, being proletarian—or, more correctly, classless—would inevitably represent an improvement, materially and spiritually, over the existing bourgeois one; that the correct ordering of the economic relations of society would inevitably free mankind from the problem of power as well as want; and that man, free for the first time in history, would use this freedom rationally and beneficially in the service of his happiness and spiritual growth.

---

[15] Valentin Giterman, *Die historische Tragik der sozialistischen Idee*, pp. 92–93.

The Utopian Vision

The gap which "scientific socialism" refused to fill could not, however, remain unfilled. For some socialists at least, the negative stimulus of class antagonism had to be supplemented by a more definite vision of a just society. The vague hints put forth by Marx and Engels needed amplification if men were to give of their generous best. Socialism, for these utopians, became the "new Jerusalem," where abolition of private property was a means to the transvaluation of all values, to the release of all that was highest in human nature. With the elimination of material self-aggrandizement, all the dross of human selfishness would be discarded. Honesty instead of hypocrisy; co-operation instead of selfishness; spirituality instead of materialism; rationality instead of irrationality—these qualities would distinguish socialist man and socialist society from their capitalist predecessors. Spontaneity and equality would replace the hierarchy and alienation characteristic of capitalist industrialism. In every instance the features of the envisioned socialist society contrasted with those of the existing one. As the institutions and values of bourgeois capitalism were those of individualism, socialist utopianism was frequently linked to the contrasting notion of a collectivist order. Class and Party, unity, fulfillment of the individual through his submergence in the collectivity, these came to be viewed as values worthy to replace the existing bourgeois ones. An attempt, favored by the warlike mood of the political struggle, was made to realize the ideal within socialist parties before it could be implemented within society at large. Out of this attempt came the emphasis on "socialist honor," on *Haltung* in socialist ranks; a demand for ruthless frankness and unselfishness in the relations of party members toward each other; and, in addition, a seemingly irrelevant stress on such modes of behavior as love of nature and abstinence from smoking and drinking. These attitudes could be identified with socialism only because they were conscious protests against, or deviations from, the "corrupt" bourgeois way of life.[16]

In the Continental socialist parties this love of nature was linked, however, with a rejection of everything that was consciously "folksy," such as the cultivation of rural folk traditions. Such cultivation was considered to be regressive, irrational, and intended to lull the population into a neglect of the class struggle. These socialist movements were proudly urban, cosmo-

---

[16] Tesarek, *op. cit.*, cites as an example of the miraculous spirit of the Party in the twenties the fact that "more than half of the Socialist members of parliament declared themselves as teetotalers."

politan, rational. Even though, particularly in their nature worship, they were strongly influenced by romanticism, they fully accepted Marx's anti-romantic sneer at the "idiocy of rural life."

These main streams of socialist inspiration may be summed up in four capsule formulations: the drive by the proletariat against poverty and insecurity; the aspiration for a society in which irrational inequalities would be eliminated by conscious economic and political action; the utopian vision of a co-operative society embodying values and motives opposed at every important point to those of the bourgeois order; and "scientific socialism," which analyzed the movement away from the existing capitalist system as an inevitable economic and historical process in which the industrial working class was to be its own liberating force.

The Rise of a Class

The growth of socialist ideas and socialist organizations is rooted in the failure of the liberal revolution to implement its own ideals, and in the nineteenth-century assignment to the industrial working class of the role of economic, political, and social pariah. The revolt against this pariah position gave energy to the proletarian movements of Europe, a revolt simultaneously directed against the power of a ruling class and the economic misery which was deemed to flow from this class dominance. Every explanation of the slackening of socialist energy must first take into account the emancipation of the working class from this former pariah position. Anyone contemplating the industrial proletariat's condition of a century ago and comparing it with its present condiion finds sufficient reason to explain the transformation of the political organizations which served as vehicles for proletarian aspirations.[17]

The physical environment in which the modern worker moves—the plant, his home, his community—has been transformed. The taint of social inferiority has been largely removed and equality of opportunity has been realized to a considerable degree. The voice of industrial labor, organized in massive trade unions and large political parties, is heard powerfully in the

---

[17] The SPOe in an exhibit entitled "The Rise of a Class" (Der Aufstieg einer Klasse), has proudly acknowledged the emergence of the working man from pariahdom to power. This contrasts with its attitude during the twenties, when one of its leading publications was entitled "The Discontented" (Die Unzufriedene).

land. Representatives of labor participate in the government and administration of domestic and foreign affairs. The improvement in working-class living standards—reflected not only, or even primarily, in higher wages, but in shorter work weeks, longer paid vacations, and an extensive system of social welfare—has done more than merely alleviate the most pressing miseries of the past. It has, in many instances, progressed far enough to create a problem novel to the working class: how meaningfully to dispose of the surplus of time and money accruing to it.[18] Under the impact of working-class power incomes have been equalized to the point where admittedly further measures in the same direction would have no significant redistributive effect;[19] and social services have been extended to the point where they, too, are ceasing to act as an equalizing element between classes and come to resemble merely a collective self-insurance system or a highly desirable means of securing the aid of more fortunate *individuals* (as distinct from classes) for their less fortunate fellows. And in response to the widespread demand for economic security through continuous and full employment—a demand rendered effective by the power of political organization— the autonomy of the economic sphere, the market's claim for self-regulation, has been superseded by the acknowledgment of the community's right to judge the economy in terms of its results for the nation's welfare and to regulate it accordingly.

This "major social revolution"[20] which has transformed the face of Austrian society along with that of other European nations has made of the industrial working class a segment of the population "at home in the existing state" and one sharing a feeling of responsibility for its fate instead of

---

[18] I do not wish to suggest that poverty in the old-fashioned sense has ceased to exist, even in states with extensive welfare features. As a series of articles by Norman MacKenzie in the *New Statesman and Nation*, Vol. 47 (May 29, June 12, June 26, 1954), indicated, the problem continues to be of significance to certain groups, such as old-age pensioners and large families with one breadwinner, but has ceased to be typical of the working-class situation. On the other hand, neither is the "Americanization" described by Bednarik, *op. cit.*, with its attendant problems of increasing leisure and multiple choice of objects for expenditures, as yet typical.

[19] See Chapter 7, above; also Jenkins, "Equality," in *New Fabian Essays*.

[20] For a systematic enumeration of the features in which this new system of "statism" differs from nineteenth-century capitalism, see Crosland's "The Transition from Capitalism" (*loc. cit.*); also, Bruno Seidel, "Wesen und Wandlung des Sozialismus und seiner Sozialkritik vom klassischen zum heutigen Sozialismus," *Zeitschrift für die gesamten Staatswissenschaften*, CIV (1951), 660–97.

one committed to its overthrow.[21] This process of transformation has led many Socialists—to the evident disgust of their more radical comrades—to speak of the present age as the "period of socialist fulfilment."[22] Their rise to respectability and importance, the negative impact of the Soviet Union's course of development, so contrary to socialist expectations and hopes, and some recently gained disappointing insights into the complexity of human nature and the economic system, have all but destroyed the pillars which traditionally supported the socialist structure of thought and aspiration.

Causes of Disappointment

All socialist theories, non-Marxist as well as Marxist, assumed that the collective ordering of the economy, the abandonment of private profit, and the elimination of economic classes were the primary, perhaps the sole, prerequisites for meeting the demands of economic and social justice.[23] The specifically Marxist assumption was that economic and historical forces alike—the two were identical for Marx—were driving toward the probably violent replacement of the bourgeois capitalist state by the proletarian collectivist order. These assumptions were found wanting in a number of respects: capitalist economics failed to collapse as inevitably and rapidly

---

[21] This is acknowledged again and again by Austrian Socialists (except Hindels and his followers). See, e.g., Tesarek, "Es gibt kein Zurück," *Welt der Arbeit*, VII (July 22, 1949); Oscar Pollak, "Die Aufgaben der Sozialistischen Partei," *Die Zukunft*, I (November, 1946), 1–3; "Koalition und Opposition," *ibid.*, VII (February, 1952), 33–36.

[22] Braunthal, *Auf der Suche nach dem Millennium, loc. cit.*; Oscar Pollak, "Koalition und Opposition," *loc. cit.*; Pollak, "Von Geschichtsperioden, Kampfmitteln und Bündnissen," *Die Zukunft* (April, 1952), 116–17. The acceptance of Renner's views of socialization as a gradual and continuous historical process makes the attempts at dating the phases of development irrelevant. They are significant only as ideological attempts to deduce "correct" policies and justify them by reference to history. (See, e.g., Hindels, "Die übersprungene Periode," *ibid.*, VII [March, 1952], 78–83.)

[23] "The central belief of socialism was that through some form of collectivism the just and good society would be established. . . . All socialists were united in proclaiming the moral and historical necessity of some form of common ownership of the means of production, distribution, and exchange. Indeed this became the accepted definition of socialism." (*Socialism—A New Statement of Principles*, pp. 14–15.) This judgment clearly holds true, as shown by an examination of Austro-Marxist literature and the Linz Program, for Austrian Socialism prior to World War II.

as anticipated;[24] the polarization of the social structure into a mass of exploited proletarians and a small minority of exploiting capitalists failed to take place;[25] and the subjective feeling of class consciousness which was expected to correspond to the "objective facts" of class position failed to emerge as predicted.[26] Lastly, where capitalism was superseded or severely modified as in the Soviet Union or Nazi Germany, the emergent collectivist system did not exhibit the features anticipated by Socialists. These factors undermined socialist theory, and Marxist theory in particular, in three fundamental points: they destroyed the clear-cut concept of the working class as the bearer of historical destiny; they raised a question as to the inevitability of historical progress toward socialism; and, most significantly, they exposed as a fallacy the assumption that the subordination of private economic power automatically brought in its train a society of free and happy men.

In the past, socialist theory had combined certainty about the goal—the collective ownership of the means of production—with a set of definite philosophical and historical assumptions about the approach toward this goal. While the theory was ambiguous enough to leave ample room for disagreements, for a long time these were, or were asserted to be, merely disagreements on tactical questions. In this we find the explanation why the socialist parties of Britain and Austria, differing from each other profoundly in tradition and spirit, nevertheless felt in the past a high degree

---

[24] That the teachings of Keynes and the success of the non-socialist economic system of the United States have forced Socialists everywhere to re-examine some of their premises is affirmed by Andrè Philip ("Die Krise der sozialistischen Doktrin in Europa," *Rote Revue*, XXXI, 215–27), Crosland (*op. cit.*), and John Strachey ("Tasks and Achievements of British Labour," in *New Fabian Essays*).
[25] The stabilization of the size of the industrial proletariat and the increase of the white-collar class through the growth of service occupations and bureaucracy are generally acknowledged features of a maturing industrial society. (See, e.g., Sering, *Jenseits des Kapitalismus*, pp. 70 ff.; Renner, *Die neue Welt und der Sozialismus*, p. 16; Crosland, *op. cit.*, p. 42; Bednarik, *op. cit.*) The characteristic result is not the consolidation of the proletariat—anticipated by Marx—but the increasing functional fracturing of the mass of wage and salary earners.
[26] Cf. Reinhard Bendix and Seymour Lipset, "Karl Marx's Theory of Social Classes" (in Bendix and Lipset, *Class, Status and Power: A Reader in Social Stratification*, Chicago, Ill., The Free Press of Glencoe, Illinois, 1953.) The "lack of psychology" in Marx's class analysis has been frequently commented on. In Austria Max Adler and the Revolutionary Socialists criticized the "automatism" inherent in the Marxist theory of historical development.

of affinity for the Soviet Union.[27] For the Soviet Union was noncapitalist and it was proletarian. The historical process—this was Bauer's lifelong faith—would eventually and inevitably eliminate those vices which at present still marred the nascent proletarian socialist society.

The most significant feature of the postwar period is that the socialist goal itself has become uncertain. A collectivist economy was recognized as merely a stepping-stone toward other goals. These ultimate goals could only be vaguely described as human dignity and happiness. But the abolition of private ownership was not the only means of achieving them: in fact, it was a possible means of frustrating them. The strength of Marxist theory had been its specific assumptions about the relation between economic organization, social power, and human freedom (as well as between human freedom and human happiness). The uncertainty of present-day socialists is the result of their loss of confidence in the correctness of these assumptions. Socialism, engaged in *exploring* these relations instead of *assuming* them, is for the first time becoming truly "scientific" instead of merely ideological, but thereby is subordinating itself to the findings of the social sciences. It gives up a theory providing its approach with definitude and is left only with a set of values, idiosyncrasies, and verbal and organizational commitments. The result, optimistically termed "practical humanism," [28] is indecisiveness and conservatism in the realm of practice, and a profession of only vaguely defined ideals which socialists share with most "men of good will" whatever their party.

Socialist Ideals

These "socialist" ideals may be broadly summarized as "freedom," "equality," and "participation." [29] To discuss in any detail the difficulties

---

[27] The Austro-Marxist position toward the Soviet Union has been discussed earlier (see Chapter 4); for a retrospective view of the British Labor Party's attitude, see Roy Jenkins, *Pursuit of Progress* (William Heinemann, Ltd., London, 1953), pp. 10 ff.

[28] Erich Matthias, *Sozialdemokratie und Nation*, p. 254.

[29] I have selected these three goals on the basis of such diverse sources as Matthias' references to "practical humanism," Socialist Union's *Socialism—A New Statement of Principles*, the *New Fabian Essays*, and such Austrian statements as Oscar Pollak's "Linkssozialismus von heute" (*Die Zukunft*, III [October, 1948], 285–88), "Humanistischer Sozialismus" (*ibid.*, VII [July, 1952], 201–5), "Was hat sich geändert?" (*Arbeiter Zeitung*, November 10, 1953), and Czernetz'

and confusions besetting attempts at exact and agreed-on definitions which would make these terms a usable basis for a concrete socialist policy would go beyond the scope of this study. Some of the most obvious and fundamental problems may, however, be reviewed.

Socialists have habitually linked freedom to economic security. With the realization of a full employment economy and the maximization of output, the *framework* for individual freedom has been established. What specifically socialist measures are required beyond these economic achievements? Does the concept of freedom have a distinctly socialist meaning which sets it apart from its traditional liberal connotations? If the socialist answer to this question is to link freedom to the need for economic planning and public ownership—and socialist enthusiasm for both has considerably abated—it must be asked: Is the intermediate goal of efficient planning compatible with the increase of individual liberty? Can planning, whose main goal is the most effective use of a society's resources, dispense with an extensive bureaucratic apparatus? If Socialists today have come to see in the managerial society rather than in capitalism the enemy of human freedom,[30] can Socialists unequivocally commit themselves to any measure involving the extension of state power?

This socialist stress on freedom, which, although implicit in socialist tradition, has at times been obscured by preoccupation with more immediate economic and political goals, is admittedly a reaction to the suppression of freedom in modern totalitarian regimes. Freedom has come to appear so unquestionably, so supremely desirable that neither its relation to other socialist values nor the peculiar problems inherent in it are carefully examined. The fallacy embodied in the traditional assumption of man's potential perfect rationality has been discarded and with it the naïvely opti-

---

"Bilanz eines halben Jahrhunderts" (*Die Zukunft*, V [January, 1950], 1–5). Austrian references to these goals are even vaguer, if possible, than those contained in British sources. There is a tendency to equate "socialist" with "social" and with "decent" and to identify every ordinarily decent human relationship at work or in the home with "socialism." (E.g., Marianne Pollak in a lecture entitled "Gibt es sozialistische Lebensformen?" June 15, 1953; author's notes.)

[30] "Today the enemy of human freedom is the managerial society." (Crossman, *op. cit.*, p. 12.) Crossman accepts the challenge, declaring that "the test of socialism is the extent to which it shapes a people's institutions to the moral standard of freedom—even at the cost of a lower standard of living." (*Ibid.*, p. 15.) This position is not only politically unfeasible; it also contradicts one of the major socialist claims of the past: that socialism contains the assurance of material plenty.

mistic view of human nature.[31] But socialists have failed to grapple with the opposite view which regards freedom as a mental burden and a potential source of political and social aberration.[32] There is a dim awareness that "freedom to develop personality fully" as conceived by socialists must differ from the bourgeois "freedom to develop personality fully," whose results are by no means approved by socialists. To be "socialist freedom" it must have a social dimension.[33] But an answer beyond the vague assertion of the necessity for "fellowship" [34]—the fulfillment of an individual through his identification with others—is lacking.

In fact, some of the institutional devices generally accepted by present-day Socialists increase individual freedom in the traditional sense, but, by failing to encourage the members of society to think in social rather than individual terms, are likely to hamper development of that sentiment of fellowship which would provide the background for "socialist freedom." I am referring primarily to two features of socialist policy: the insistence that differential incentives and material rewards would remain indefinitely part of any socialist society; and the intention to leave the largest possible share of spendable surplus in the hands of individual consumers.[35] This maximization of "consumer freedom" represents a radical departure from the traditional socialist vision of a society in which individual needs would be met by social services and in which personality would find expression in

---

[31] Matthias, *op. cit.*, notes the abandonment by German socialists of the faith in human rationality and perfectibility considered to be a vulgarization of the heritage of the Enlightenment; and Crossman, *op. cit.*, p. 8, declares: "There is far more to be said for the Christian doctrine of original sin than for Rousseau's fantasy of the noble savage, or Marx's vision of the classless society."

[32] The problem is briefly touched on in *Socialism—A New Statement of Principles* (p. 25); and Crossman (*op. cit.*, pp. 14 ff.) has acknowledged the ambiguity of the relationship between socialism and freedom. Bednarik (*Der junge Arbeiter von heute*) has attempted to show that some of the most undesirable features (from the socialist viewpoint) characteristic of the new generation of workers— their indifference, lack of social conscience, materialism—are the result of the newly gained freedom from want and insecurity. Oscar Pollak and other Austrian socialists, however, when confronted with this warning, refuse to be seriously concerned with the prospect, which seems remote to them; instead they merely bewail the lack of "traditional spirit" among the young.

[33] *Socialism—A New Statement of Principles*, p. 35.

[34] *Ibid.*

[35] E.g., Barbara Wootton, *Freedom under Planning*, Chap. 3, particularly pp. 52 ff.; Crosland, *op. cit.*, p. 63; Jenkins, "Equality," p. 76; Renner, *Die neue Welt und der Sozialismus*, pp. 36–37.

ways other than material acquisition, of a society in which the importance of material possessions for man's development was diminished rather than increased.[36] Such a society could not have avoided the problem of establishing a hierarchy of values, a system of priorities on which the national surplus would be expended, thereby restricting the ways in which individuals were able to express their preferences. By increasing consumer freedom and thereby reducing any taint of potential totalitarianism inherent in the collective determination of private wants, socialists have abdicated the determination to "remake" man through a new set of economic institutions. In the past, socialists had few doubts that in the "new Jerusalem" social and collective values would rank higher than "petty" personal and material ones. Yet the naturalness, the self-sufficiency, the Puritanism which characterized traditional socialist *Haltung* are unlikely to resist corrosion through a greatly increased capacity to spend funds for personal purposes. So great has been the recoil from collectivist values, caused by the Nazi and Soviet example, concentration camps, and war, that "rugged individualism," deprived of its exclusively economic connotations, has been newly appropriated for the cause of present-day socialism.[37]

Stress on the value of equality rather than freedom in the abstract has traditionally been charactertistic of socialism. Yet the implementation of

---

[36] R. H. Tawney has stated the traditional aspiration: "The ultimate goods of human life, which belong to the realm where to divide is not to take away, may more easily be attained when its instruments and means are less greedily grasped and more freely shared." (Quoted in *Socialism—A New Statement of Principles*, p. 31.) There can be little doubt that in the past the choice between collective and individual spending of the surplus would have been resolved by socialists in favor of the former; that, once poverty had been relieved and a decent minimum standard of living achieved, such communal projects as city planning, museums, parks, libraries, subsidization of the arts, would have been given preference over increasing individual living standards and the resulting ability of each person to spend increasing amounts for perhaps trivial things. In other words, compulsory "uplift" was definitely a part of socialist thinking.

[37] Crossman, *op. cit.*, stresses the role of the socialist as a critic and heretic, upholding freedom against managerial oppression. In a forum on the topic "The Use of the Word Socialism" (*Dissent* [Summer, 1954], pp. 285–89), Sebastian Frank sees as the specific task of socialism the defense of the individual against the managerial machine and the pressure of conformism. Marianne Pollak (in "Gibt es sozialistische Lebensformen?") clearly expressed the socialist recoil from collectivist ideals of living; the trend in socialist town-planning from "proletarian" blocks of apartment houses to individualistic garden suburbs has been previously mentioned.

this goal through social institutions has also encountered difficulties brought about by socialism's failure to clarify its exact meaning and to explore its compatibility with other socialist objectives. Socialists have failed to re-solve the conflict between the goal of equality of opportunity, with its corollary of rewards as widely different as the difference in the "marketable" qualities possessed by individuals, and the goal of equal distribution, a true community of equals. The recognition that material incentives would con-tribute some part of the future socialist system and that wages, like prices, would have to be retained as a means of allocating labor in a com-plex industrial economy has led Socialists generally to restrict the meaning of equality to "equality of opportunity." [38]

Yet, the utopian spark in socialism, the vision of a noncompetitive so-ciety of equals in which men will not be valued and rewarded according to their economic usefulness, has not been completely extinguished. A feel-ing of unease remains at the thought of identifying with socialism the type of society in which each individual would be *strictly* rewarded accord-ing to his deserts. The urge for justice—central in the socialist inspiration—is not one-dimensional. It is not exhausted by the distributive concept which in its crudest form is expressed by the slogan, "He who does not work shall not eat." The concept of the "equal dignity and worth of all men" which socialism shares with Christianity has radical implications. These find their clearest expression in the Sermon on the Mount's refusal to value men according to any accepted temporal standard. It implies a pure broth-erhood founded on love which refuses to judge, representing a revolt against the injustice of fortuitous natural endowments as much as against those of the man-made social order. However noble, it is clearly utopian. For valuing is an intrinsic human activity and part of every social structure known. Furthemore, refusal to value implies refusal to discriminate, an end, therefore, to the recognition of, and striving for, excellence in all fields of human endeavor. The noble ideal of brotherhood therefore con-flicts with the equally noble ideal of striving for perfection (which depends on the recognition of a hierarchy of values); not to mention the more mundane requirements of maintaining a working industrial system on at least a nominal level of efficiency.

---

[38] The Declaration of the Frankfurt International recognizes (as do the authors of the *New Fabian Essays*) "the claim of the individual for reward corresponding to his achievement" as basic. The same is true, of course, of wage policy in the Soviet Union.

Thus, the ideal of a socialist equality of fraternal association appears to many contemporary socialists as a dream which is not even desirable. More importantly, all the practical exigencies of the existing political and economic structure combine to inhibit any approximation to it. The ideal of a brotherhood of equals now remains in socialist thought merely as a vague aspiration, a weak trace. It still finds expression in the socialist (and by no means exclusively socialist) insistence on maintaining at a decent level the weak, ineffectual, and useless; [39] in a tendency to diminish the span between top and bottom incomes; in the demand for simple and unostentatious living by Party leaders; and in the quest for a meaning which would carry equality of opportunity beyond that of a race in which all are encouraged "to scramble up the ladder of ambition, with the strongest and most unscrupulous winning all the prizes." [40]

In Austria, where large accumulations of wealth have been generally destroyed by the political and economic upheavals of this century, the problem of redistributing property—which, as distinguished from redistributing income, still faces British Socialists [41]—does not loom significantly. Similarly, the problem of social inequality, the existence of a caste system—in England closely linked to that of an exclusive educational system and the continued existence of a royal court—is of much smaller importance in Austria. An extensive system of general public education, coupled with the equalization of incomes, has largely met the demand for a system in which careers are open to the talented. And since, by Socialist admission, redistributive taxation has reached that optimal point at which further extension of progression conflicts with the need for incentives and meets the opposition of special interest groups *within* the ranks of the Party, the impetus given to the socialist cause by the demand for equality has largely exhausted itself.[42]

---

[39] Austrian Socialists, however, seem to limit this interest by and large to members of the "proletariat." They do not appear to play a leading role in exploring the problems of penal reform or rehabilitation and treatment of the mentally ill.

[40] *Socialism—A New Statement of Principles*, p. 32.

[41] Cf. Jenkins, "Equality," *loc. cit.*

[42] The pressures against leveling of incomes exerted by Socialist managers, members of the professional classes, and skilled workers—all of whom the SPOe wishes to comprehend within its ranks—have been mentioned in previous chapters. The impression that further equalization is not contemplated by the SPOe is corroborated by the editorial "Was hat sich geändert?" (*loc. cit.*), in which the continuing inequality of *women* was specified as the only area in which socialist egalitarianism had as yet not achieved its goal.

The third principal socialist goal, the insistence on *participation* as giving meaning to democracy—and specifically social democracy—has previously been discussed in the context of the earlier socialist demand for "economic democracy." Here, too, Austrian Socialists have reached the limit of what appears to them compatible with the efficiency of a dynamically productive economic system. They are generally unwilling to accept R. H. S. Crossman's admonition that socialism demands maximum distribution of responsibility and participation even at the price of economic efficiency.[43] On the contrary, the distance between the managerial elite and the mass of workers is increasing through the integration of the trade unions into the management stratum, the development of a group of "socialist managers," and the corresponding growth of feeling on the part of workers that they are still the subjects of manipulation at the hands of distant and irresponsible powers. Yet, apart from occasional expressions of concern, concrete proposals aiming at its reversal have not been worked out and, as far as the SPOe is concerned, are not seriously under consideration.[44]

Socialism and the Proletariat

The growing uncertainty about the fundamental principles of socialism has been accompanied, naturally enough, by the abandonment of the traditional dichotomy of capitalism and socialism and thus of the anticipation

---

[43] "In a world organized in ever larger and more inhuman units, the task of socialism is to prevent managerial responsibility degenerating into privilege. This can only be achieved by increasing, even at the cost of 'efficiency' the citizen's right to participate in the control not only of government and industry, but of the party for which he votes and of the trade union whose card he carries. *After all, it is not the pursuit of happiness but the enlargement of freedom which is Socialism's aim*" [italics added]. (*Op. cit.*, p. 29.) Socialist Union (*ibid.*, p. 56) shares this sentiment. Yet, as the basis for a political program it must be considered equally unrealistic in Britain and in Austria.

[44] British Socialists engaged in "rethinking" the principles of Socialism appear much more concerned with the urgency of this problem than are members of the SPOe. This may be a reflection of the fact that, almost without exception, the publicists of the Austrian Socialist Party are integrated into the party's leadership hierarchy, while the most vocal "independent" critic, Hindels, is too limited by his concern with the class struggle to devote his attention to problems of "fulfillment."

of a sudden transformation, peaceful or violent, of the one system into the other.

All the changes we have seen in our lifetime—full employment, planning, controls, housing programs, social security, the national health service, progressive taxation—have produced a structure to which no ready-made label can be tagged. It may be said that these changes are a part of the transition to socialism. But have any of us knowledge of a system of institutions which would mark the end of the transition? And if we had, would there be any agreement on their nature? [45]

The slowness of change is no longer resented as a source of frustration. On the contrary, it is extolled as an integral part of the goal itself, as a guarantee of its value and durability.[46] This, in turn, is only another aspect of the acceptance of the Revisionist view of state and society. The definition of "class" has become less clear-cut [47] and the state has ceased to be viewed merely as an instrument of class rule. If society is no longer divided into two irreconcilable camps but is conceived as composed of a multiplicity of partly competing, partly co-operating social groups, a case for compromise and coalition has been soundly established.[48] The atmosphere of the political struggle has been transformed; the class enemy whose elimination was once viewed as the condition of socialist triumph has become the political opponent, and coexistence with him is accepted as a prerequisite of political democracy.[49]

---

[45] *Socialism—A New Statement of Principles*, p. 41. Oscar Pollak quotes this statement with apparent approval ("Humanistischer Sozialismus," *loc. cit.*) and charges Hindels with harbouring an illusion of the past when he believes that "one day after the conquest of power . . . everything will be changed." (Oscar Pollak, "Von Geschichtsperioden, Kampfmitteln und Bündnissen," *loc. cit.*)

[46] "The more quickly and uncompromisingly the class aim is achieved, the more clearly it appears that the human aim can only be achieved in stages." (Oscar Pollak, "Linkssozialismus von heute," *loc. cit.*)

[47] Renner in the First Republic had early criticized the tendency of socialists to rely on such abstract terms as "working class" and "bourgeoisie," which, in his view, impeded rather than helped the necessary investigation of concrete social situations. (See, e.g., "Einige Erfahrungen praktischen Klassenkampfes," *Der Kampf*, XXI [April, 1928], 142–53.)

[48] *Ibid.*; Crossman has declared it to be one of the newly gained insights that "there is neither a natural identity of interests nor yet an inherent contradiction in the economic system." (*Op. cit.*, p. 8.)

[49] See, e.g., Otto Tschadek, "Unsere Gegner," *Die Zukunft*, I (October, 1946), 16–17. This attitude has always been characteristic of Renner and his followers.

One of the results of the identification of socialism with "justice" in the abstract is that the theoretical link between socialist parties and the industrial working class—a link forged in the nineteenth century by the realities of the industrial system as well as Marx's historical analysis—is severed or attenuated. Since the ethical principles inherent in socialism are underlined and socialism is linked to "underdog" in the abstract rather than to the proletariat as the historically chosen underdog, a reassessment of socialism's relation to the proletariat becomes necessary. Not only have socialist parties, for reasons of practical democratic politics, been forced to expand from "labor parties" into "national parties" but the industrial proletariat's growth of power has raised the theoretical question whether power in proletarian hands is necessarily a guarantee of a just society any more than power in the hands of any other class or group.[50]

Though these factors point toward a separation between "socialism" and the organized labor movement, there is no indication that their force is great enough to create a serious division or a split. Socialist purists who feel that their principles are being compromised by the proletariat's exercise of power are faced with a choice between adjustment to the reality of that power and the ineffectuality of political exile. A socialism preaching the ideal of justice and equity but divorced from any substantial segment

---

(See Chap. 4, *passim*.) It would be misleading to assume, however, that this change has permeated the minds of party functionaries at all levels. The considerable support which the Scharf-Hindels Left found among them in its insistence on a more vigorous prosecution of the class struggle, as well as the continued self-isolation of many party activists from "bourgeois" influences, are evidence of a "culture lag" whereby attitudes formed in the days of violent struggle persist into the present.

[50] "Socialists as such . . . cannot be guided by the immediate interest of one class alone. They identify themselves with the manual workers as the underprivileged of our society. . . . The driving-force has come from convictions, ethical convictions as to what is right and good . . . *there is no inevitability about the link between the labour movement and socialism*" [italics added]. (*Socialism— A New Statement of Principles*, pp. 45–46.) See also Andrè Philip (*op. cit.*) for a similar statement. In Austria leaders like Schärf and Waldbrunner have insisted that the SPOe is a "national party of all persons who are not themselves exploiters of the labour of others." (Schärf, *Der Wiederaufbau und die Selbständigen*, Verlag FWV, n.d., p. 5; also PTP, 1950, p. 174; Marianne Pollak, "Heraus aus der Festung," *Arbeiter Zeitung*, April 28, 1946.) In her speech, "Gibt es sozialistische Lebensformen?" Marianne Pollak stated that the Party had abandoned its *Proletenkult* and had ceased to identify virtue and progress with the industrial working class.

of the working class would not only have surrendered the last claim to the use of the term "socialism" in any meaningful sense, it would also have ceased to count as a significant political force. The principles and goals of the new non-Marxist socialism are, however, so vague and flexible that they are unlikely to withstand the impact of the demand of *Realpolitik*. Unable to divorce themselves from the organized movement which provides their political basis yet less and less convinced of the exclusive identification of the interests of the industrial working class with the national welfare, leaders of the Socialist Party will be increasingly forced into a policy of conscious manipulation, obscuring through traditional phraseology their loss of faith in the historical destiny of the proletariat.[51]

A Socialist Way of Life?

Some Austrian Socialists have attempted to evade the consequence of their own changed position by positing a spurious distinction between the socialist attitude toward the democratic state on one hand and bourgeois society on the other.[52] Being haunted by their past identification with the Party Left they are sensitive to the assertion that socialists may never assume a positive attitude toward any existing order except a truly "socialist" one. As a defensive measure they insist that a positive attitude toward the changing *state* can be and must be combined with a radically negative position toward bourgeois *society*. Their insistence on a mode of living according to specifically socialist standards, their claim that socialists are primarily distinguished by their resistance to cultural "embourgeoisement"[53] is, particularly at the present time, pathetically anachronistic. With the conscious abandonment of *Proletenkult*, the idealization of the working-class way of thought and action, and of the collectivist ideal and mode of life, the alternative modes of behavior, which in the past socialists had opposed to bourgeois standards, have disappeared.

---

[51] Bednarik ("The Central European Worker in the Ideological Vacuum," *loc. cit.*) claims to discern already "a profound scepticism" of the Socialist leadership toward the industrial workers.

[52] Prominent among them are Oscar and Marianne Pollak.

[53] "He who makes concessions [to the People's Party] in spirit, in his way of life, in morals, in the field of culture, commits a worse crime than he who concludes compromises with it at the conference table." (Oscar Pollak, "Koalition und Opposition," *loc. cit.*)

With the transformation of the Party from a class-bound, closely knit fighting community into a broad, national, moderate and conciliatory political movement, the militant virtues once distinguishing socialist *Haltung* have lost their function. Indeed, what was known as socialist *Haltung* has all but vanished from the Party. The necessity for continued political compromise, the attempt to gain new members at almost any price, the spread of the Party from Vienna into the provinces and the inclusion of strata of the population unacquainted with the Party's tradition; the elimination of the most pressing injustices and the resulting ideological uncertainty; the loss of the burning zeal and fiery intolerance among the young; and the advance of many of the rebels of the twenties and thirties to responsible and secure administrative positions: all these factors have caused and, in turn, reflect the erosion of what once was thought of as socialist *Haltung*. Today the view—advocated in the old Social Democracy only by the unpopular "practitioners"—that there exists no intrinsic or necessary relation between Socialism and a Spartan form of living,[54] is the prevalent view and is deplored only by a few remaining "purists." [55] The former hostility toward bourgeois conventions in questions of sex—the advocacy of "free love" and the campaign against the antiabortion law—has been replaced by concern for the country's population growth and conformity to bourgeois standards in sexual matters.[56] The very idea that so-

---

[54] See Renner's statement (*PTP*, 1923, p. 188): "If someone lives on the basis of his own skilled labor—even if he lives well so that he is not a pauper—he can be a socialist." Renner himself (according to Buttinger) loved to live well and had little sympathy for the more Spartan virtues that many of his fellow Socialists identified with the cause.

[55] In Salzburg I attended a folk-dance evening sponsored by the Socialist mayor of the town and a society linked to the SPOe. The contrast between the beer-quaffing Party functionaries (some had been active Revolutionary Socialists in the thirties), clad in the short leather pants of the Austrian peasantry and joyfully participating in the noisy proceedings, and a few tight-lipped "old-timers" (who had accepted the invitation out of consideration for me) regarding the goings-on with evident distaste, provided me with a most vivid insight into the changed spirit of Austrian Socialism.

[56] A comparison of the respective clauses of the Linz Program of 1926 and the Action Program of 1947 will dramatically illustrate the change. The Linz Program demanded: (1) public information centers on questions of birth control; (2) free issuance of contraceptives by health insurance doctors; and (3) "artificial interruption of the pregnancy to be declared legal when a doctor in a public hospital carries it out on request of the pregnant woman. . . ." (*PTP*, 1926, p. 184.) The relevant clause in the Action Program of 1947 reads: "The Socialist Party

cialism implied cultural as well as economic changes, that there are or should be specifically "socialist forms of living," has become alien to the mass of present-day Party members.[57] Indeed, when forced to deal concretely with the mores considered appropriate to Socialists, those in the Party who continue to insist on the distinction produce only a catalogue which any modern middle-class Polonius would pass on to his son: decency in human relations, equality for women, neighborliness, tolerance, and temperance.[58] While in the twenties Socialists took pride in identifying themselves with everything that was "radical" and "progressive" in the arts, today there reigns among leadership and members alike a philistine indifference and even hostility to artistic experimentation.[59]

Resistance to "Rethinking"

In brief, the disappearance of the utopian vision of socialism as a new society in which all ills of the present would magically vanish and of the

---

views unlimited interruption of pregnancy as the severest danger to woman's health. Public consultation offices for problems of marriage and life are to be established. Interruption of pregnancy will not be combatted by threat of punishment, but by consultation and social welfare." (*PTP*, 1947, p. 214.) See also the article by Herbert Kohlich, "Bevölkerungspolitische Inventur" (*Die Zukunft*, III [June, 1948], 185–88), in which the author argues against acceptance of the so-called "social indication" as a ground for legal interruption of pregnancy and calls for the revival of the "will to have children." (I was reliably informed that "free love" or even divorce among prominent Party functionaries is today severely frowned upon.)

[57] Marianne Pollak introduced her talk on the topic "Socialist Forms of Living" with a revealing apology for discussing such a seemingly remote question.

[58] Marianne Pollak, "Gibt es sozialistische Lebensformen?" The only specifically "proletarian" points were the admonition to resist the "bourgeois" craze for pleasure; to refuse to believe "bourgeois" propaganda; and to reject "bourgeois" (presumably risqué) jokes.

[59] The few Socialist enthusiasts for modern art are bitter about the indifference and hostility with which Party leaders and members meet their efforts at its popularization. Indications of the lack of interest exhibited by the SPOe in modern art are many: the absence of a museum housing modern art in Vienna; the failure of the SPOe to associate itself with the annual Vienna Festival of Modern Music or with Rolf Lieberman's opera, "Leonore 40/45"—stressing the theme of international brotherhood; and the fact that as its contribution to the Festival Weeks of 1953 the city administration of Vienna sponsored a traditional play whose hero was the seventeenth-century folk character "dear Augustine," renowned in song for his addiction to drink.

belief that the socialist movement was the chosen historical instrument destined to bring about this society's realization—undoubtedly a vision shared at any time only by a minority of party members—has eliminated the urge to shape the Movement itself as an advance model of that new society. In the "period of fulfillment" the unbounded enthusiasm and idealism which used to be expended, on occasion indiscriminately and intolerantly, in the service of the cause, remain today without an objective and even without encouragement. For the leaders of the SPOe are embarrassed, even frightened, by "enthusiasm." They never cease to point out that the present is not the period of prophets, teachers, dreamers, or fighters, but that of prudent and practical administrators.[60] What in Renner's time was a much-needed counterweight to the emphasis given by the Party Left to "revolutionary spirit" and deductive reasoning on the basis of abstract socialist definitions, has in the hands of his successors become indifference and even hostility to any "theorizing," to any inquiry into the nature of socialist goals and the relation between them and the political instruments designed to implement them.[61] As a result of the "permanent coalition" the leadership necessarily accepts responsibility for the existing system and defends its achievements as the justification of continued participation in government. Dissatisfaction with these achievements, comparison of reality with anticipation, inquiry into the reasons for disappointment, these are felt by the leaders to be criticism directed against themselves and their policies, criticism potentially destructive of party unity.[62]

The leaders of the SPOe, therefore, frown on rather than encourage independent efforts at "rethinking" and veil the issues behind facile slogans

---

[60] Renner, who all his life found himself opposed and criticized by the intellectual and purist wing of the Party, early developed a certain antagonism toward the socialist "enthusiasts"; he extolled, instead, the virtues of the new hero—"the hero of the computing machine, the administrator." (*Die neue Welt und der Sozialismus*, p. 10.) See also his "Ist der Marxismus Ideologie oder Wissenschaft?" (*Der Kampf*, XXI [June, 1928], 245–56) for an earlier expression of his opposition to excessive theorizing.

[61] Renner, on the contrary, always stressed the need for extensive social inquiries into the concrete problems arising out of the process of socialization; for empirical, inductive studies rather than the dogmatic deductions popular with "orthodox" Marxists.

[62] Renner long ago held that interpretations of socialist theory tended to divide and divert the masses instead of unifying them for the practical tasks at hand. ("Ist der Marxismus Ideologie oder Wissenschaft?" *loc. cit.*)

and a spirit of compulsory optimism.[63] For these leaders are fundamentally satisfied with the Party's and their own position in postwar Austria. The Party, once more a vast political organization, is integrated into the country's government and administration at all levels and has proved its widespread and growing electoral appeal.[64] These leaders take pride in the stability of the Austrian political and economic system to which the SPOe has contributed by its moderate and constructive policy; and they feel that they have obtained for the Austrian wage earner the maximum share of economic benefits which the economy was capable of providing.[65] Only demagogues, habitual malcontents, dreamers, or "subversives" can, in their view, question achievements such as these. As long as the resumption of the role of opposition does not open the floodgates of widespread re-examination of policies and beliefs, it is easier to drown doubts in rhetoric than to explore them through discussion.[66]

---

[63] This "compulsory optimism" (a feature also characteristic of the old Social Democracy much criticized by Buttinger and the Revolutionary Socialists) is illustrated by the rhetorical generalities with which the somber views of Koestler and Orwell are disposed of by Party publicists. After describing Koestler as "the spokesman of our disappointments," Oscar Pollak drowns any doubts by proclaiming: "We, however, do not resign. . . . On our fellows who remain behind we look as those who are in the wrong. . . ." ("Arthur Koestler," *Arbeiter Zeitung*, September 28, 1947); and Felix Hubalek, in answer to Orwell, insists glibly that "a democratic form of socialism can be the salvation . . . " can protect man "before the rape of the idea through the apparatus . . . if men . . . gather all their powers and concentrate them on one aim." ("Die Utopie der Gegenwart oder: der trübe Blick in die Zukunft," *Die Zukunft*, V [August, 1950], 213–15.)

[64] At a closed meeting of the SPOe, former chairman Schärf is reported (by one of the attending functionaries) as having favorably contrasted the present electoral record—a record admittedly achieved without benefit of an elaborate program or emphasis on socialist principles—with the Party's position before 1934.

[65] See, e.g., Adolf Schärf, "Rückblick auf 8 Jahre sozialistischer Politik," *loc. cit.*

[66] For this reason I have largely drawn on English sources for my discussion of the problems of principle facing contemporary Socialists. Though isolated statements by individual Austrian Socialists paralleling formulations of the English writers cited can be found, no attempts at systematic analysis have been undertaken by Austrian Socialists.

The Failure of the Left

At the beginning of this study the question why the Revolutionary Socialists failed so completely to impress their ideas on the post-1945 Party was mentioned as requiring illumination. The answer has been suggested at various points in previous chapters as well as in the discussion of the change in socialist temper brought about by "fulfilment" of many traditional socialist demands. Accidental factors, such as the presence or absence of particular personalities at decisive moments or the weakness of potential leaders of the radical Left such as Erwin Scharf, cannot be accepted as primary causes. For it is significant that the most genuine and vocal representatives of the "illegal tradition" either resigned themselves to the hopelessness of their task [67] or threw off as obsolete their past revolutionary convictions.[68] That the "historical situation" in April, 1945, was unfavorable to any social and political revolution, particularly in view of the Soviet —and therefore Communist Party—commitment to "unity of all anti-Hitlerite forces," explains in part the ascendancy which the representatives of the prewar Social Democracy could gain over the ex-R.S. spokesmen. Once the mass party, committed to the peaceful conquest of a parliamentary majority, had been re-established with the consent of the ex-R.S. element, the "illegal tradition" had lost its relevance. Its origin had been negative; it was a violent reaction to the Party's defeat in February, 1934, and to the "lack of militancy" on the part of the old Social Democratic machine and its leadership which was held responsible for the defeat. Beyond the renewed emphasis on proletarian unity and the vague notion of "rejuvenation," no positive lessons appropriate to the post-1945 democratic party could be derived from the R.S. period. But not only did the ex-R.S. group fail to influence the revived Party significantly; it even failed to become the core of a new Party Left.

The drive toward the organization of a "left opposition" within the SPOe existed and found considerable support among part of the lower-echelon functionaries, as revealed in the "Motion of 44" in 1947. But the impulse received its energy not from any assertion of positive alternatives

---

[67] E.g., Buttinger, Podlipnig.

[68] E.g., Karl Czernetz, Oscar Pollak. Pollak, today the most outspoken advocate of antidictatorial socialism, was "by an irony of history" the draftsman of the Revolutionary Socialist "Declaration of Principles," which emphasized revolutionary action and the dictatorship of the proletariat. (Otto Leichter, "Die Tradition der illegalen Bewegung," *Die Zukunft*, III [May, 1948], 140–44.)

in the realm of theory or practice, but rather from the frustration and dis-enchantment with the policies pursued by the leadership. All it could do was to oppose the demand for a "sharper struggle against the People's Party" to the official course of co-operation and conciliation.[69] The cry for revolutionary action by-passing parliament, for the use, under certain con-ditions, of violence and dictatorship as a means of achieving the socialist goal—the traditional demand associated with the Left—had become re-pulsive to socialists who had been exposed to Hitler's dictatorship.[70] Such a demand was politically unwise as well in the presence of four occupation powers proclaiming their commitment to parliamentary democracy. The demand for "unity of the proletariat" domestically and internationally was suffocated by the increasing abhorrence for the Soviet system, and potential Leftists, like Socialists elsewhere, were unable to suggest a concrete course of action involving social or economic measures which could advance the SPOe more rapidly toward a truly socialist system.[71] In a period when men were tired of ruthlessness and abstract slogans and demanded concrete pro-posals, the former Revolutionary Socialists had the choice "to adjust to the new, present methods or to move into the background." [72] With few ex-ceptions, having spent their entire lives within the orbit of the Socialist Party and afraid of loneliness and political inactivity, their choice was to make the adjustment. In some cases the price of this adjustment has been a continuing feeling of frustration and bitterness which not even the cease-less round of activities imposed on a party functionary has been able to drown. Uncertain about their role in the uncongenial environment, overly concerned with the past, they are not equipped either by temperament or training to engage in the continuing hard task of re-examining the premises of their own beliefs and of criticizing constructively policies and measures,

---

[69] See "Scharf und die linken Sozialisten," *Trotzdem,* I (December, 1948), 5.

[70] Hindels and Czernetz have reported their sense of outrage at the callousness with which Scharf commented on the repressive treatment accorded by Com-munist regimes to their opponents, including Social Democrats. (*PTP*, 1947, pp. 47–48.)

[71] Left criticism—as in the "Motion of 44" or in Hindels' and Scharf's publica-tions—contained no call for further nationalization or for specific measures in-volving planning, controls, redistribution, or workers' control. Instead, it concen-trated on the alleged failure of the Party leaders to fight more energetically for labor's share of the national product or on concessions made to the People's Party in personnel questions; as well as the one-sided attitude of hostility toward the Soviet Union.

[72] Leichter, *op. cit.*

many of them, like public ownership, long and fervently desired by them, in the light of domestic and international experience.[73]

The unwillingness or inability of active Socialists, functionaries and members alike, to take up the challenge posed by a changed environment which both fulfills and frustrates fundamental aspirations traditionally part of socialist thought [74] has resulted not only in the abandonment of the past attachment to ideology. It has also led to a refusal to study the results of measures initiated by other socialist parties and to correct methods and goals in the light of these findings.[75] Though party lines have certainly not been inflexible, responses have thus been tactical, rhetorical, opportunist, and as a result often haphazard, unintegrated, uncreative. The absence of generally accepted principles and the resulting lack of direction have already gone far toward emasculating socialist parties as parties of reform. The most practical problems of everyday political life, as Crossman has pointed out, cannot be resolved intelligently unless the Party knows where its ultimate goals lie:

Are food subsidies and price controls temporary war-time expedients, to be dispensed with as soon as we can return to the price system, or are they part of the structure of a socialist state? Does democratic socialism involve the permanence of a mixed economy and, if so, should profit-making in the private sector be encouraged or limited? Should wages be left to find their own level through collective bargaining, or is it the function of a Labour Government to modify the wages structure in the light of national interests and social justice? Is a central-

---

[73] Not even Buttinger, perhaps the most powerful personality engendered by Austrian Socialism since Otto Bauer, has been able to give substance to his vision of a future socialist society. Lacking clearly defined goals, however, his decision not to return to Austria was a wise one.

[74] One of the most flagrant examples of the Austrian Party's determination to ignore unpalatable facts and refuse to face criticism which is more than superficial has been its failure to react to the publication of Buttinger's book in a German edition in 1953. None of the SPOe publicists has officially taken notice of its existence. Another example of the tendency to gloss over rather than to examine was Oscar Pollak's facile retort to the criticism of the Marxist tradition contained in Socialism—A New Statement of Principles. Unlike the British authors of the pamphlet, he apparently sees no need for a reconciliation between ethical and Marxist socialism, explaining the changed emphasis by reference to the ever-so-handy dialectic. ("Humanistischer Sozialismus," loc. cit.)

[75] A suggestion by Marianne Pollak that a study center be set up to gather and examine the experiences of socialist parties elsewhere apparently met with no response.

ized public corporation a more socialist method of running a public utility than municipal or co-operative ownership? Does socialist principle demand that we should receive our spectacles and dentures free, but pay for travelling on nationalized railways? [76]

Each of these questions, as shown in previous chapters, is of equal relevance to Austrian Socialists. Yet, as demonstrated, not only have Austrian Socialists failed to answer them conclusively, they have even refused to face them openly and courageously. By formulating actions not on the basis of principle or even in conscious awareness of their consequences but in response to changing pressures from within and without, the SPOe has ceased to be a creative political force and a source of inspiration to its members.[77]

The positive result of the Socialist Party's transformation has been that it has not only ceased to be a threat to the system of parliamentary democracy but has become its most vigorous and effective defender. By securing the working class a home in the modern state, by raising it to a position of approximate equality with the other major segments of society, by assuring a high degree of economic security and eliminating the worst forms of pauperism, by removing the sense of grievance and opening the way to the enjoyment of a middle-class way of life by the working class, the Socialist Party appears to have fulfilled its historical mission and to have exhausted its spiritual impetus. Just as it has adjusted much of its thinking and terminology to the present age wherein a number of pressure blocs compete for a maximum share of the national wealth within the framework of a semi-public economy, it seems inevitable that eventually it will also discard or modify those structural features derived from the Party's past as a militant spiritual community—the tight organizational pattern, the hierarchy, and the elaborate inner-party machinery.

In spite of its rediscovery of the humanitarian values of socialism the Party appears too lethargic, the leadership too preoccupied with its immediate tasks and too intent on depicting its achievements as the realiza-

---

[76] Crossman, op. cit., p. 2.

[77] Several years ago Peter Maier (in "Theoretische Revision," Die Zukunft, IV [May, 1949], 147–51) and Hans Müller (in "Vom Unbehagen in der Partei," loc. cit.) warned that slogans could not, in the long run, replace hard thinking about both ultimate principles and concrete tasks. The prediction expressed by Crossman (op. cit.) and the authors of Socialism—A New Statement of Principles—that the present uncertainty in the Socialist Movement might easily lead to sterile opportunism if it is not made the basis for honest reappraisal—appears to have been largely borne out by the SPOe's development.

tion of the age-old socialist dream, to accept the intellectual challenge presented by the uncertainties and perils of the human condition at mid-century. Though the Socialist Movement is unable to fill the existing ideological and intellectual vacuum by its present mixture of "party cult, mass consumer mentality, and anti-Communism," [78] it has, by reconciling itself to the mainstream of Western tradition, become the "guarantor of an organic social development," [79] and thus an effective force realizing and conserving what has been most valuable in that tradition, the ideal of human equality and freedom.

---

[78] Bednarik, "The Central European Worker in the Ideological Vacuum," *loc. cit.*, p. 66.
[79] Seidel, *op. cit.*, p. 695.

Appendix 1. *The Electoral Position of the Socialist Party in National Elections Since 1930*

Table 1 is presented as a guide to the twenty-five large electoral districts (*Wahlkreise*) which serve as the basis for the subsequent breakdowns. By locating them in the appropriate *Land* and giving their official designation, the reader acquainted with Austrian geography will be able to obtain some indication of their location. Furthermore, the degree of industrialization in each of the *Länder* has been indicated by the percentage figures of the working population active in agriculture and industry. A breakdown of these percentage figures for the electoral districts is unfortunately not easily available.

Tables 2 and 3 present figures and percentages indicating the changes in the votes received by the Socialist Party in parliamentary elections of 1930, 1945, 1949, 1953, 1956 and 1959. Table 3 shows the position of the four parties relative to each other. Figures for 1930 have been included to allow some comparison between the postwar and prewar strength of parties. It must be pointed out, however, that in 1930 the anti-Socialist camp was split into several parties whose votes have been grouped under the two post-1945 headings of OeVP and VdU. In spite of misgivings this seems justified because of the traditional major split in the Austrian Right between the Catholic and anticlerical camps. Though the VdU is by no means merely the successor organization of the pre-1934 *Landbund* and National Socialists, the traditional split has remained and a certain continuity may be assumed.

Table 4 is frankly speculative, an attempt to gauge the degree of support or sympathy existing for the SPOe within the ranks of VdU voters. In the run-off election for President in 1951 the Communist Party gave official

275

orders to its followers to vote for the Socialist candidate while the VdU refused to adopt an official position. Thus the assumption that the increase of Socialist strength in the second round was due to the solid Communist vote plus a fraction of the Independent vote is not farfetched. As voting in Presidential elections is compulsory, the additional support could not have come from previous nonvoters galvanized into political action by the Socialist appeal.

Table 4 merely indicates that when and if former VdU supporters decide to cast their vote for one of the major parties, they are likely to split fairly evenly—though with considerable regional variations—rather than throw their weight overwhelmingly to one side or another. Any decline of the VdU and of the traditional "third (anticlerical, nationalist) bloc" may thus have less effect on the terms of the present coalition than anticipated.

TABLE 1

THE ELECTION DISTRICTS (*Wahlkreise*) *

Land *and* Population	Election District (*Wahlkreis*) Number and Name		Percentage Working in Agric.	Ind.
Wien 1,766,102			3	53
	I	Innen-Ost		
	II	Innen-West		
	III	Nord-West		
	IV	Nord-Ost		
	V	Süd-Ost		
	VI	Süd-West		
	VII	West		
Nieder Oesterreich 1,250,494			47	36
	VIII	Viertel o.d. Wienerwald		
	IX	Viertel u.d. Wienerwald		
	X	Viertel o.d. Manhartsberg		
	XI	Viertel u.d. Manhartsberg		
Ober Oesterreich 1,108,720			39	39
	XII	Linz und Umgebung		
	XIII	Innviertel		
	XIV	Hausruck		
	XV	Traunviertel		
	XVI	Mühlviertel		
Salzburg 327,232	XVII	Salzburg	31	38
Tirol 427,465	XVIII	Tirol	36	37
Vorarlberg 193,657	XIX	Vorarlberg	26	51
Steiermark 1,109,335			43	36
	XX	Graz		
	XXI	Mittel-u. Untersteiermark		
	XXII	Ost Steiermark		
	XXIII	Ober Steiermark		
Kärnten 474,764	XXIV	Kärnten	38	37
Burgenland 276,136	XXV	Burgenland	63	25

* The figures and percentages are derived from *Oesterreichs Bevölkerung in Bild und Zahl* (Oesterreichisches Statistisches Zentralamt, Wien, 1953), Tables 3 and 34.

TABLE 2

Number and Percentage of Votes Received by the Socialist Party in National Elections Since 1930 by Electoral Districts (Wahlkreise) *

	1930	%	1945	%	1949	%	1953	%	1956	%	1959	%
I	68,504	46	48,237	48	51,977	38	54,160	39	50,438	38	51,959	40
II	45,022	44	33,903	44	34,492	35	35,857	36	31,718	35	31,687	37
III	73,175	50	51,687	48	57,188	40	59,309	40	55,743	40	57,174	42
IV	137,756	67	98,586	63	112,655	56	120,874	56	116,673	55	123,947	58
V	124,517	67	86,286	64	94,844	59	101,209	59	98,784	58	104,870	61
VI	118,313	61	89,995	59	105,287	53	108,473	53	106,142	53	109,023	55
VII	136,131	66	99,520	62	108,997	55	110,650	55	103,265	54	105,826	58
VIII	66,482	33	67,852	37	81,444	35	89,905	38	93,514	39	96,013	40
IX	150,387	50	119,844	52	137,714	47	150,369	50	152,609	51	155,482	52
X	32,768	23	41,128	30	48,461	29	53,772	33	53,194	33	53,080	34
XI	41,935	24	55,606	36	63,012	32	66,745	34	67,910	35	66,168	35
XII	39,977	44	48,081	54	50,389	40	66,480	48	73,314	50	80,101	52
XIII	12,717	16	21,347	28	21,252	22	28,882	29	31,640	31	34,081	32
XIV	27,258	24	41,091	36	39,720	28	50,828	36	57,696	38	63,327	40
XV	43,256	37	48,908	43	51,215	36	65,136	44	71,833	47	74,064	48
XVI	12,780	16	20,548	27	21,466	24	25,618	28	26,455	29	26,965	29
XVII	37,005	30	49,965	39	57,752	34	65,871	35	69,147	36	75,966	39
XVIII	38,895	22	40,857	27	53,820	24	70,473	29	74,865	30	82,038	32
XIX	16,217	21	19,189	28	19,262	19	24,531	23	31,271	27	36,834	30
XX	64,217	44	61,344	48	71,974	39	78,292	42	85,083	44	89,131	45
XXI	24,054	25	35,919	36	43,930	34	48,999	38	55,795	42	57,173	43
XXII	12,520	12	22,258	21	29,016	23	31,575	25	34,576	27	36,074	28
XXIII	74,580	45	86,252	54	99,562	46	113,494	51	126,871	55	130,398	56
XXIV	68,020	39	87,572	49	101,356	41	121,775	48	128,494	48	136,967	50
XXV	50,765	38	58,917	45	66,739	40	75,240	45	76,265	46	75,587	47
TOTAL	1,517,251	41	1,434,892	45	1,623,524	39	1,818,517	42	1,873,295	43	1,953,935	45

* The figures and percentages are taken from the official reports published by the Oesterreichische Statistische Zentralamt after every national election (*Die Nationalratswahlen vom . . .*). The percentage figures refer to the Socialist share of the valid votes cast.

TABLE 3

Votes Received by the Four Major Parties in All National Elections Since 1930. Expressed in Percentages of the Valid Votes Cast, by Electoral Districts (Wahlkreise) *

	SPOe						OeVP						VdU (FPOe)						KPOe					
	30	45	49	53	56	59	30	45	49	53	56	59	30	45	49	53	56	59	30	45	49	53	56	59
I	46	48	38	39	38	40	33	47	46	42	49	47	18	—	9	13	8	10	0	6	6	5	5	3
II	44	44	35	36	35	37	36	51	49	43	51	49	18	—	11	16	10	11	0	5	5	4	4	3
III	50	48	40	40	40	42	30	47	43	39	47	45	18	—	11	15	8	10	0	5	4	5	4	3
IV	67	63	56	56	55	58	21	26	26	23	27	26	9	—	5	9	4	6	0	11	11	12	14	10
V	67	64	59	56	58	61	22	26	27	24	27	27	10	—	5	7	4	5	0	10	10	10	11	7
VI	61	59	53	53	54	55	25	33	33	29	34	33	12	—	6	9	5	7	0	8	8	8	8	5
VII	66	62	55	55	54	58	22	29	31	27	32	30	9	—	6	9	5	6	0	8	8	8	9	6
VIII	33	37	35	38	39	40	57	58	55	51	54	53	10	—	4	6	3	4	0	9	6	6	4	3
IX	50	52	47	50	51	52	36	39	40	35	39	38	12	—	4	6	3	5	0	5	6	9	7	5
X	23	30	29	33	33	34	57	67	62	59	63	61	19	—	6	5	3	4	0	3	3	3	1	1
XI	24	36	32	34	35	35	63	62	62	57	59	59	13	—	3	4	3	4	0	2	3	5	3	2
XII	44	54	40	48	50	52	37	42	30	32	38	35	15	—	26	15	9	10	0	4	4	5	3	3
XIII	16	28	22	29	31	32	61	71	53	56	59	55	7	—	23	14	9	12	0	1	2	1	1	1
XIV	24	36	28	36	38	40	56	62	46	47	52	48	9	—	23	14	8	10	0	2	3	3	2	2
XV	37	43	36	44	47	48	48	52	39	40	44	41	10	—	20	12	6	8	0	5	5	4	3	3
XVI	16	27	24	29	29	29	72	72	65	66	68	67	7	—	9	4	2	3	0	1	2	2	1	1
XVII	30	39	34	35	36	39	47	57	44	43	47	44	16	—	18	19	15	15	0	4	3	3	2	2
XVIII	22	27	24	29	30	32	64	71	56	55	63	59	14	—	17	13	6	8	0	2	2	3	1	1
XIX	21	28	19	23	27	30	57	70	56	55	61	57	22	—	22	19	10	12	0	2	2	3	2	1
XX	44	48	39	42	44	45	37	46	35	36	42	42	18	—	19	17	10	9	0	6	5	5	4	4
XXI	25	36	34	38	42	43	50	61	49	46	51	50	24	—	14	14	5	5	0	3	3	5	2	2
XXII	12	21	23	25	27	28	64	78	66	62	67	66	24	—	11	12	5	5	0	1	0	2	1	1
XXIII	45	54	46	51	55	56	37	37	32	30	33	32	17	—	14	12	6	7	0	8	8	7	6	5
XXIV	39	49	41	48	48	50	31	40	34	29	34	33	29	—	20	17	15	14	0	9	3	4	3	2
XXV	38	45	40	45	46	47	45	52	53	48	49	47	17	—	4	5	3	5	0	3	3	3	2	1
TOTAL	41	45	39	42	43	45	42	50	44	41	46	44	12	—	12	11	7	8	0	5	5	5	4	3

* These percentages are derived from the official reports published by the Oesterreichische Statistische Zentralamt after every national election (Die Nationalratswahlen vom . . .). For 1930 the OeVP column represents the combined total of the votes cast for the Christian Social Party and the Heimwehren where they ran on separate tickets; the VdU column represents the combined total of the votes cast for the Landbund and National Socialist Party. The Communist Party ran in 1930, but in no election district (Wahlkreis) polled more than a fraction of one per cent. In 1945 only three parties (the SPOe, the OeVP, and the KPOe) contested the election. In that year the electorate was exceptionally small because of the absence of many prisoners of war and former National Socialists prevented from voting.

TABLE 4

PERCENTAGE OF VOTES CAST IN THE FIRST ROUND OF THE PRESIDENTIAL
ELECTION FOR THE INDEPENDENT CANDIDATE BREITNER WHICH
IN THE RUN-OFF WERE PRESUMABLY CAST FOR THE
SOCIALIST CANDIDATE KÖRNER *

E.D.	Breitner vote % of total vote cast	Increase in Körner vote over Socialist plus Communist vote % of total vote cast	% of Breitner vote which presumably was cast for Körner in run-off
I	14.7	3.8	26
II	18.1	4.6	25
III	16.3	4.4	27
IV	7.5	2.8	37
V	6.9	1.9	27
VI	9.7	3.3	34
VII	9.1	3.8	42
VIII	6.3	3.9	62
IX	6.2	2.8	45
X	6.2	3.2	52
XI	4.9	2.9	59
XII	24.0	9.5	40
XIII	22.8	10.5	46
XIV	22.4	10.9	48
XV	17.1	8.5	50
XVI	7.4	6.6	89
XVII	36.1	13.4	37
XVIII	24.6	11.1	45
XIX	25.7	10.4	40
XX	27.5	10.4	38
XXI	20.8	8.5	40
XXII	17.4	5.9	34
XXIII	18.7	7.1	38
XXIV	24.2	10.6	43
XXV	5.1	2.6	51

* These percentages are derived from *Die Präsidentschaftswahlen vom 6. und 27. Mai 1951* (Oesterreichisches Statistisches Zentralamt, Wien, 1951).

Appendix 2. *Elections to Chambers of Labor and Work Councils*

The following tables depict the party preferences of manual and white-collar workers as expressed by their votes in elections for the Chambers of Labor (1949, 1954, and 1959) and Work Councils (concluded in 1948 and 1952).

Elections to the Chambers of Labor are held separately for manual workers, salaried employees, and transport workers. Thus they provide a unique insight into the differential appeal made by the parties to these groups. Without additional information, however, interpretation of the results listed in Tables 1 and 2 remains highly speculative. No clear and uniform pattern emerges. At least five variables—class, geographic area, nonvoting, new voters, "Independents"—affect the Socialist position in unknown interaction. Thus, the following brief observations are merely intended to draw attention to some suggestive aspects of the election results.

1. The percentage figures may obscure actual party gains or losses. Thus, while the SPOe position improved between 1954 and 1959 among Vienna manual workers by 3.6%, the Party actually obtained 12,000 votes less in 1959 than in 1954.

2. The striking decline in participation is a threatening sign for the SPOe, particularly as it is generally more pronounced among manual workers than salaried employees. The drop in Vienna appears particularly menacing.

3. The number of manual workers eligible to vote increased from 1954 to 1959 by approximately 118,000. Yet the SPOe gained less than 4,000 votes in all of Austria, while the OeVP added 16,000.

281

4. The losses of the Communist list ("Unity List") among manual workers between 1954 and 1959 were unevenly distributed. They were percentually highest in Vienna, Lower Austria, and Burgenland, lending support to the assumption that the presence of Soviet Russian occupation forces (withdrawn in 1955) had previously artificially inflated the Communist vote in those areas. The figures presented do not provide any indication whether former Communist voters turned to the SPOe or OeVP or swelled the ranks of abstainers.

5. The figures clearly indicate differential "political cultures" (related, it may be surmised, largely to religious factors) in diverse *Länder* and areas. Thus the Socialist vote *among manual workers* has ranged from close to 80% in Eastern Austria (Vienna, Lower Austria, Burgenland) to approximately 50% in Tirol and Vorarlberg in the West. Among salaried employees, where Socialist party strength is less, a similar gap—50% in the East as against around 20% in Vorarlberg—exists.

6. The figures tend to support the impression gained from Table 4 in Appendix 1 that defections from the "Independents" after 1949 affected SPOe and OeVP differently in different parts of Austria. Thus in Upper Austria and Carinthia, where the Independent lists dropped by 24.4 and 11.3 per cent respectively among manual workers, the SPOe gained roughly seven times as many votes as the OeVP. In Vorarlberg and Salzburg, on the other hand, both parties added to their strength almost equally. Among salaried employees, "Independent defectors" in Carinthia seem to have chosen the SPOe over the OeVP in a ratio of approximately 3 to 1, while in Salzburg the results were the reverse, the OeVP gaining 8.1% as against the SPOe's 2.8%.

With regard to the Work Council elections (Tables 3 and 4) two reminders may be in order. First, as indicated in Chapter 2, the election trend after 1952 indicates the growing strength of the SPOe at the expense of the Independent and Communist lists. Second, the reader's attention should be directed to the Socialist success among agricultural and forest workers. The large number of Socialist councilors elected in this sector somewhat obscures the decline suffered in some of the other industries.

TABLE 1

PARTICIPATION IN ELECTIONS TO CHAMBERS OF LABOR, 1954 AND 1959 *

Land	Manual Workers		Salaried Employees		Transport		Total	
	1954	1959	1954	1959	1954	1959	1954	1959
Wien	72.9	57.8	64.0	62.9	95.2	82.7	72.1	61.9
Burgenland	81.4	79.6	80.8	77.0	86.3	85.9	81.7	79.7
Kärnten	60.1	54.4	67.6	58.8	88.6	83.7	64.6	58.3
Nieder Oesterr.	80.6	71.7	80.9	71.5	88.0	84.8	81.4	72.8
Ober Oesterr.	77.6	71.5	76.8	72.1	88.9	85.6	78.6	73.0
Salzburg	54.2	60.0	58.2	61.2	88.6	92.6	59.1	64.0
Steiermark	73.4	67.9	74.8	68.7	85.0	82.6	74.8	69.5
Tirol	53.8	46.2	59.5	52.9	81.7	79.6	58.5	51.6
Vorarlberg	52.1	42.1	62.1	57.1	79.1	75.2	56.1	47.7
TOTAL (AUSTRIA)	71.5	62.9	67.9	64.6	89.5	83.6	72.5	65.3

* The figures represent percentage of voters to those eligible to vote. Source: *Arbeit und Wirtschaft*, XIII (December, 1959), 344–45.

TABLE 2

RESULTS OF THE ELECTION TO THE CHAMBERS OF LABOR, 1949, 1954, AND 1959 IN PERCENTAGES OF VALID VOTES CAST BY *Länder* *

Land		SPOe 1949	SPOe 1954	SPOe 1959	KPOe† 1949	KPOe† 1954	KPOe† 1959	OeVP 1949	OeVP 1954	OeVP 1959	VdU‡ 1949	VdU‡ 1954	VdU‡ 1959	Nonparty 1954	Nonparty 1959
Wien	Manual Workers	72.4	75.6	79.2	13.1	14.2	9.2	9.4	8.0	8.0	5.1	0.8	1.4	1.3	2.2
	Salaried Employees	53.7	52.9	52.0	6.5	8.1	5.2	29.8	32.3	32.7	10.0	2.2	4.3	4.6	5.8
	Transportation	76.5	73.8	77.9	11.9	14.8	9.1	11.9	11.4	10.6	—	—	—	—	2.4
	Total	68.2	68.8	70.3	11.2	12.5	7.9	15.0	15.4	16.2	5.6	1.1	2.2	2.1	3.4
Burgenland	Manual Workers	80.6	80.6	77.6	4.9	5.4	1.6	14.5	12.9	19.1	—	1.1	1.7	—	—
	Salaried Employees	50.6	46.9	44.5	3.3	7.0	—	46.1	46.1	51.4	—	—	4.1	—	—
	Transportation	77.5	79.9	82.3	3.3	4.5	1.9	19.2	15.6	15.8	—	—	—	—	—
	Total	77.2	76.8	73.4	4.6	5.5	1.4	18.2	16.8	23.3	—	0.9	1.9	—	—
Kärnten	Manual Workers	66.4	76.8	74.5	6.4	5.9	6.2	7.4	8.9	9.9	19.8	3.9	6.7	4.6	2.7
	Salaried Employees	40.4	49.5	48.6	3.0	1.7	1.6	23.2	26.4	28.6	33.4	6.2	12.2	16.1	9.0
	Transportation	69.9	73.4	73.2	9.2	8.5	10.9	11.9	15.6	13.4	9.0	—	2.5	2.5	—
	Total	63.0	71.6	69.2	6.4	5.6	6.0	10.7	13.0	14.1	19.9	3.7	7.2	6.2	3.5
Nieder Oesterreich	Manual Workers	72.1	71.7	74.5	15.9	17.2	8.7	12.0	10.4	15.2	—	0.3	1.0	0.5	0.6
	Salaried Employees	54.7	53.1	52.0	10.2	13.5	4.4	35.1	31.2	39.0	—	1.0	3.2	1.2	1.4
	Transportation	81.6	81.0	84.6	6.7	7.6	4.0	11.7	11.4	11.4	—	—	—	—	—
	Total	71.3	70.3	72.2	13.9	15.5	7.5	14.8	13.3	18.4	—	0.4	1.2	0.5	0.7
Ober Oesterreich	Manual Workers	52.3	74.1	72.8	6.3	5.7	5.0	9.9	13.1	15.8	31.5	4.6	3.8	2.5	2.6
	Salaried Employees	41.4	51.6	49.0	3.1	3.0	2.1	21.3	28.4	32.1	34.2	10.1	10.7	6.5	6.1
	Transportation	72.3	71.5	71.3	6.4	11.0	11.1	10.5	15.3	14.2	10.8	2.2	1.7	2.2	1.7
	Total	53.5	69.8	68.0	5.8	5.8	5.1	11.9	16.1	18.8	28.8	5.3	4.9	2.9	3.2

Salzburg														
Manual Workers	63.1	66.9	67.8	5.6	3.7	2.7	12.1	16.1	17.9	19.2	6.4	10.0	6.8	1.6
Salaried Employees	32.0	34.8	37.4	2.3	1.3	1.0	22.0	32.1	33.8	43.7	10.9	23.7	20.9	4.1
Transportation	76.6	76.1	74.7	8.3	5.9	6.6	7.4	11.3	14.0	7.7	1.9	4.7	4.8	—
Total	54.2	62.0	61.6	5.6	3.6	2.9	12.8	18.6	21.1	27.4	6.5	12.5	9.3	1.9
Steiermark														
Manual Workers	67.4	76.3	75.1	11.7	9.4	8.8	6.6	9.4	11.6	14.4	2.3	2.4	2.5	2.1
Salaried Employees	51.9	57.4	54.0	5.2	4.0	3.2	20.9	30.9	32.6	22.0	5.0	7.2	2.8	3.0
Transportation	70.7	71.5	71.9	11.1	10.0	9.9	10.1	15.1	16.2	8.1	1.5	2.0	1.8	—
Total	65.2	72.4	70.7	10.5	8.5	7.9	9.5	13.8	16.1	14.8	2.7	3.3	2.5	2.0
Tirol														
Manual Workers	55.2	58.6	55.9	2.7	3.5	3.5	24.8	25.0	31.2	17.3	3.5	3.7	9.3	5.7
Salaried Employees	33.4	35.6	32.9	1.6	2.0	1.7	36.8	37.8	43.8	28.2	6.5	8.2	18.1	13.4
Transportation	69.3	70.5	68.9	6.5	6.8	6.4	16.7	19.4	24.7	7.5	—	—	3.4	—
Total	54.2	55.9	52.9	3.3	3.7	3.6	25.3	26.7	33.0	17.2	3.5	4.0	10.1	6.5
Vorarlberg														
Manual Workers	47.3	52.1	50.1	4.5	4.5	3.5	27.1	31.0	36.3	21.1	7.1	7.9	5.3	2.2
Salaried Employees	22.1	25.1	20.9	1.7	—	—	46.5	49.8	54.7	29.7	13.7	18.6	11.4	5.8
Transportation	66.4	71.3	64.4	5.2	4.8	4.9	19.0	23.8	25.9	9.4	—	4.8	—	—
Total	45.3	48.8	44.2	4.1	3.6	2.7	29.6	34.0	40.0	21.0	7.6	10.3	5.9	2.8
AUSTRIA														
Manual Workers	66.5	73.2	73.9	11.0	10.8	7.3	10.6	11.3	13.9	11.9	2.2	2.9	2.4	2.0
Salaried Employees	49.1	50.8	49.0	5.7	6.4	3.7	28.5	32.1	34.6	16.7	4.4	7.4	6.2	5.3
Transportation	74.8	74.2	75.7	9.2	10.7	8.4	11.7	13.6	13.8	4.3	0.6	1.1	0.9	1.0
Total	64.4	68.6	68.4	9.7	9.9	6.6	14.2	16.0	18.6	11.7	2.5	3.7	3.0	2.7

* "Die Arbeiterkammer Wahlen," *Arbeit und Wirtschaft*, III (December, 1949), 19–22; and *ibid*., XIII (December, 1959), 344–45.
† KPOe list appeared under the title T.U. Unity in 1954 and 1959.
‡ VdU appeared under the title FPOe in 1954 and 1959.

TABLE 3

RESULT OF WORK COUNCIL ELECTIONS IN 1948 AND 1952 BY *Länder*
EXPRESSED IN PERCENTAGES OF TOTAL NUMBER OF
COUNCILORS ELECTED *

Land	Number of Councilors		SPOe		KPOe		OeVP		VdU	Nonparty	
	1948	1952	48	52	48	52	48	52	52	48	52
Wien	13,951	12,320	60	59	7	7	3	3	0	31	31
Burgenland	211	332	91	79	3	7	5	8	0	1	7
Kärnten	1,552	1,287	61	63	5	6	4	7	3	31	22
Nieder Oesterreich	3,517	1,989	63	57	11	13	4	8	0	22	21
Ober Oesterreich	2,830	2,727	73	61	4	5	4	3	2	20	30
Salzburg	1,281	1,194	55	45	6	4	1	0	2	38	49
Steiermark	3,782	4,513	69	67	6	4	2	2	1	23	26
Tirol	1,231	1,015	51	56	6	2	10	4	1	33	37
Vorarlberg	611	698	39	35	4	3	23	21	1	34	39
TOTAL	28,966	26,111	62	59	7	6	4	4	1	28	30

* The figures and percentages are based on tables published in *Solidarität* No. 51, April, 1948, and No. 166, February, 1952. (Fractions have been rounded out to the nearest full number.)

TABLE 4

RESULT OF WORK COUNCIL ELECTIONS IN 1948 AND 1952 BY TRADE
UNION EXPRESSED IN PERCENTAGES OF TOTAL NUMBER OF
COUNCILORS ELECTED *

Trade Union	Number of Councilors		SPOe		KPOe		OeVP		VdU	Nonparty	
	1948	1952	48	52	48	52	48	52	52	48	52
Employees in private enterprises	5,660	5,373	46	40	5	5	8	8	0	41	46
Building workers	9,301	6,298	73	74	5	4	2	2	1	21	19
Chemical industry	1,483	1,198	66	64	15	15	2	1	1	18	19
Paper processing industry	910	606	65	61	5	4	2	2	0	29	36
Employees in trade and transport	993	897	60	47	11	9	3	4	1	26	38
Hotel and catering trade	647	598	43	40	3	3	2	3	0	52	54
Agriculture and forestry	64	2,107	72	80	2	2	0	5	1	27	13
Food and consumer goods	1,200	1,709	63	65	8	6	8	6	0	22	24
Metal and mining	5,463	4,887	60	54	11	11	1	1	1	28	33
Textile, clothing and leather	2,857	2,334	64	61	6	6	6	5	1	24	27
Personal services and entertainment	249	104	74	63	6	6	1	0	0	19	31

* The figures and percentages are based on tables published in *Solidarität* No. 51, April, 1948, and No. 166, February, 1952. (Fractions have been rounded out to the nearest full number.)

Appendix 3. *The Ten-Point Program*

Adopted by the Party Conference of the Austrian
Socialist Party in Vienna (1952)

The Austrian Socialist Party, the party of freedom, the defender of human rights and the fighting instrument of the working population, calls upon the Austrian people to support it in the achievement of the following Ten-Point Program and to enable it to realize the program by way of democracy:

1. Struggle for Austria's freedom and independence. Integration into a united, democratic Europe and the society of free nations. Securing of human rights. Extension of democratic institutions.
2. Securing the economic future of Austria through far-sighted development of the country's productive resources, particularly the exploitation of water power and natural resources.
3. Increase of the national income through increased productivity. Liberation of the economy from the price dictatorship of the cartels. Just distribution of the national income. Increase of the living standard of the working population in town and country.
4. Full employment with the aim of assuring every person able and willing to work of a job. Elimination of unemployment among the young. Legal securing of vocational training.
5. Continuation of social welfare policy, adjustment of social welfare legislation for manual workers to that for salaried employees. Equal pay for equal work for men and women. Step-by-step increase in welfare benefits. People's pension to make the evening of life secure for all Austrians, regardless whether wage earners or self-employed.

6. Increase of public housing activity, furtherance of co-operative housing and home-ownership. Homes for young couples and single persons. Creation of a new rent law for apartments, offices, and business premises with the aim of strengthening tenants' protection.

7. Rationalization of public administration, particularly the just re-ordering and simplification of the tax system. De-bureaucratization and democratization of the economy.

8. Increase of agricultural production through improvement of the soil. Advance of mechanization. Land reform to strengthen the ownership position of the working peasant and settlement of rural laborers. Appropriate protection of tenant farmers.

9. Purity and impartiality in the judiciary and public administration. Elimination of all pull and corruption.

10. Equal educational opportunities for all children and democratic education to make of them free citizens. Protection of the family and thus reform of the obsolete family law. Appreciation of the economic and cultural importance of intellectual labor and improvement in its material position. Luxury taxes for the furtherance of art, science, popular education, and physical exercise.

Socialists struggle for a world at peace in freedom, a world which bans exploitation and domination of man by man and peoples by peoples, for a world in which the development of individual personality is the prerequisite for the enriching development of all mankind.

Bibliography

Documentary Material

1. *Governmental Publications*

Bundesamt für Statistik, *Statistisches Handbuch für den Bundesstaat Oesterreich*, Vol. XV. Vienna, 1935.

Bundesgesetzblatt der Republik Oesterreich. Oesterreichische Staatsdruckerei.

Bundesministerium für Verkehr und Verstaatlichte Industrien. *Consultation Machinery*, mimeographed, n.d.

———. *Oesterreichs Grundindustrie Verstaatlicht.* Vienna, 1951.

———. *A Social Advisory Council for the Nationalized Industries*, mimeographed, n.d.

———. *Standing Orders of the Social Advisory Council (S.A.C.)*, mimeographed, n.d.

Magistrat der Stadt Wien. *Statistisches Jahrbuch der Stadt Wien*, New Edition, Vol. III, 1930–1935, Magistratsabteilung für Statistik.

———. *Statistisches Jahrbuch der Stadt Wien*, New Edition, Vol. 6, 1939–1942, Magistratsabteilung für Statistik.

———. *Die Verwaltung der Bundeshauptstadt Wien, 1945–1947.* Vienna, 1949.

———. *Die Verwaltung der Bundeshauptstadt Wien, 1948–1949.* Vienna, 1951.

Oesterreichischer Amtskalender. Vienna: Verlag der Oesterreichischen Staatsdruckerei (annual).

Oesterreichisches Statistisches Zentralamt. *Ergebnisse der Volkszählung vom 1. Juni 1951 nach Gemeinden.* Vienna, 1952.

———. *Die Nationalratswahlen vom 9. November 1930.* Vienna, 1931.

———. *Die Nationalratswahlen vom 25. November 1945.* Vienna, 1946.

———. *Die Nationalratswahlen vom 9. Oktober 1949.* Vienna, 1950.

Oesterreichisches Statistisches Zentralamt. *Die Nationalratswahlen vom 22. Februar 1953.* Vienna, 1953.

——. *Die Nationalratswahlen vom 13. Mai 1956.* Vienna, 1956.

——. *Die Nationalratswahlen vom 10. Mai 1959.* Vienna, 1959.

——. *Oesterreichs Bevölkerung in Bild und Zahl.* Vienna, 1953.

——. *Oesterreichs Verstaatlichte Industrie.* Vienna: Verlag Carl Ueberreuter, 1953.

——. *Die Präsidentschaftswahlen vom 6. und 27. Mai 1951.* Vienna, 1951.

——. *Statistisches Handbuch für die Republik Oesterreich.* Vienna (annual).

Stadtbaudirektion der Stadt Wien. *Der soziale Wohnungsbau der Stadt Wien von 1945 bis 30.11.1952,* December 1952, mimeographed.

Statistisches Amt der Stadt Wien. *Statistisches Taschenbuch der Stadt.* Vienna (annual).

Stenographisches Protokoll. Sitzungen des Nationalrates der Republik Oesterreich, Oesterreichische Staatsdruckerei.

2. Publications of the SPOe, OeGB, Chambers of Labor

Arbeiterkammer Wien. *Jahrbuch der Arbeiterkammer Wien* (annual).

Kammer für Arbeiter und Angestellte in Wien. *Wirtschaftstatistisches Jahrbuch* (pre-1934, annual).

Oesterreichischer Gewerkschaftsbund. *Tätigkeitsbericht 1945–1947 und Stenographisches Protokoll des 1. Kongresses des OeGB.* Vienna: Verlag des Oesterreichischen Gewerkschaftsbundes, 1948.

——. *Stenographisches Protokoll des 2. Kongresses des OeGB.* Vienna: Verlag des Oesterreichischen Gewerkschaftsbundes, n.d.

——. *Tätigkeitsbericht.* Vienna: Verlag des Oesterreichischen Gewerkschaftsbundes (annual since 1948).

Sozialdemokratische Arbeiterpartei Deutschösterreichs. *Jahrbuch der österreichischen Arbeiterbewegung.* Vienna: Verlag der Wiener Volksbuchhandlung (annual, 1928–1933).

——. *Protokoll des Parteitags der SDAPDOe* (including *Bericht der Parteivertretung an den Parteitag,* annual, 1890–1933).

Sozialistische Partei Oesterreichs. *Die Aktion der Sozialistischen Partei Oesterreichs—Rede des Parteivorsitzenden Dr. Adolf Schärf auf dem Parteitag 1952, mit dem vom Parteitag beschlossenen Zehnpunkteprogramm.* Vienna: Zentralsekretariat der SPOe, n.d.

——. *Berichte der Landesparteivertretungen.*

——. *Dokumente der Sozialistischen Bewegung.* Vienna: Sozialistische Hefte, Folge 11, 1946.

——. *Lehrbriefe der SJ-Akademie.* 2 vols. Vienna: Schulungsreferat der SJOe, n.d.

——. *Merkblätter für die Schulungsarbeit,* Sozialistische Bildungszentrale.

——. *Organisationsstatut der Sozialistischen Partei Oesterreichs.* Vienna: 1946, 1947, 1949, 1950.

————. *Programm und Organisation.* Vienna: Zentralsekretariat der SPOe, 1952, 1955.

————. *Protokoll des Parteitags der SPOe* (including *Bericht der Parteivertretung an den Parteitag* and *Antragsheft*) (annual since 1945).

————. *Redeanleitungen.* Vienna: Sozialistische Bildungszentrale (SBZ).

————. *Sozialismus das Ziel.* Vienna: Verbandsvorstand der SJOe, n.d.

————. *Vorentwurf für ein neues Programm der SPOe.* Vienna, 1957.

————. *Was wird aus unserer Jugend? Wiedergabe der Enquete über Jugendprobleme in unserer Zeit, 11. und 12. Juni 1951.* Vienna: Frauenzentralkommittee der SPOe, n.d.

————. *Zum Programmentwurf,* Ausserordentlicher Parteitag, 1958.

3. Miscellaneous

Freud, Fritz. *Die Konstituierende Deutsch-Oesterreichische Nationalversammlung—Ein biographisch-statistisches Handbuch, 1919–1921.* Vienna: Verlag Karl Harbauer, 1919.

Handbuch des Oesterreichischen National-und Bundesrates 1945 nach dem Stande vom Juni 1946. Vienna: Bilderzeitung, G.m.b.H., 1946.

Handbuch des Oesterreichischen National-und Bundesrates 1949 nach dem Stande vom 1. Februar 1950. Vienna: Bilderzeitung, G.m.b.H., 1950.

Keesings Archiv der Gegenwart. Vienna: Siegler Verlag (annual).

Oesterreichisches Institut für Wirtschaftsforschung, *Monatsberichte.*

————. *Die Produktivität der österreichischen Industrie.* Sonderheft, Mai, 1949.

Books, Signed Pamphlets, and Articles

Ausch, Karl. *Austria—Conditions of Prosperity.* London: London Bureau of Austrian Socialists, 1944.

————. *Die neue Wirtschaft im neuen Oesterreich.* London: London Bureau der österreichischen Sozialisten, 1945.

Bauer, Otto. *The Austrian Revolution* (abridged version). London: Leonard Parson, 1925.

————. *Bolschewismus oder Sozialdemokratie?* Vienna: Verlag der Wiener Volksbuchhandlung, 1920.

————. *Die illegale Partei.* Paris: Editions "La Lutte Socialiste," 1939.

————. *Der Weg zum Sozialismus.* Vienna: Verlag der Wiener Volksbuchhandlung, 1919.

————. *Zwischen zwei Weltkriegen?* Bratislava (Czechoslovakia): Eugen Prager Verlag, 1936.

Bayer, Hans. *Sozialisierung und Planwirtschaft.* Vienna: Manzsche Verlagsbuchhandlung, 1947.

Bednarik, Karl. "The Central European Worker in the Ideological Vacuum," *Confluence,* II (1953), 53–69.

Bednarik, Karl. *Der junge Arbeiter von Heute—ein neuer Typ.* Stuttgart: Gustav Kilpper Verlag, 1953.

Bell, Daniel. *The End of Ideology.* Chicago (Ill.): The Free Press of Glencoe, Illinois, 1960.

Berger, Peter. "Elections and Parties in Austria," *Journal of Politics,* XII (1950), 511–29.

Bevan, Aneurin. *Der einzige Weg* (with an introduction by Josef Hindels). Innsbruck: Verlag Flöckinger G.m.b.H., 1951.

Braunthal, Julius. *Auf der Suche nach dem Millennium.* 2 vols. Nuremberg: Nest Verlag, 1948.

————. *The Tragedy of Austria* (with Appendix, "Mussolini and Dollfuss, An Episode in Fascist Diplomacy," by Professor Paul R. Sweet). London: Victor Gollancz, Ltd., 1948.

Briefs, Goetz. *Zwischen Kapitalismus und Syndikalismus.* Bern: A. Francke A.G. Verlag, 1952.

Brügel, Ludwig. *Geschichte der österreichischen Sozialdemokratie.* 5 vols. Vienna: Verlag der Wiener Volksbuchhandlung, 1922–1925.

Brunngraber, Rudolf. *Ueberwindung des Nihilismus—Betrachtungen eines Aktivisten.* Vienna: Verlag der Wiener Volksbuchhandlung, 1949.

Burnham, James. *The Managerial Revolution.* New York: The John Day Company, 1941.

Buttinger, Joseph. *Am Beispiel Oesterreichs* (consulted in manuscript), n.d.

————. *In the Twilight of Socialism.* New York: Frederick A. Praeger, Inc., 1953.

Crossman, R. H. S. (ed.). *New Fabian Essays.* London: Turnstile Press, 1952.

Czernetz, Karl. *Der Sozialismus und seine Gegner.* Vienna: Verlag der Wiener Volksbuchhandlung, n.d.

————. *Sozialisten und Kommunisten—Zwei Welten.* Zell am See: Rupert Rindler, n.d.

————. *Die Zweite Republik in Oesterreich.* London: Londoner Büro der österreichischen Sozialisten, 1944.

Deutsch, Julius. *Was wollen die Sozialisten?* Vienna: Verlag der Wiener Volksbuchhandlung, 1949.

Duverger, Maurice. *Political Parties.* London: Methuen & Co., Ltd., 1954.

Ellenbogen, Wilhelm. *Sozialisierung in Oesterreich.* Vienna: Verlag der Wiener Volksbuchhandlung, 1921.

Fischl, Hans. *Schulreform, Demokratie und Oesterreich, 1918–1950.* Vienna: Verlag Jungbrunnen, 1952.

————. *Warum allgemeine Mittelschulen?* Vienna: Verlag Jungbrunnen, n.d.

Flossmann, Ferdinanda. *Wir wollen eine gerechte Steuerpolitik.* Vienna: Sozialistischer Verlag, Schriftenreihe "Die Frau," n.d.

Forchheimer, Karl. *Keynes' neue Wirtschaftslehre.* Vienna: Verlag des Oesterreichischen Gewerkschaftsbundes, Schriftenreihe der Arbeiterkammer Wien, 1952.

Funder, Friedrich. *Vom Gestern ins Heute.* Vienna: Verlag Herold, 1952.

Gay, Peter. *The Dilemma of Democratic Socialism.* New York: Columbia University Press, 1952.

Giterman, Valentin. *Die historische Tragik der sozialistischen Idee.* Zürich: Verlag Oprecht, 1939.

Gulick, Charles A. *Austria from Habsburg to Hitler.* 2 vols. Berkeley (Calif.): University of California Press, 1948.

Hannak, Jacques. *Im Sturm eines Jahrhunderts—eine volkstümliche Geschichte der SPOe.* Vienna: Verlag der Wiener Volksbuchhandlung, 1952.

Hindels, Josef. *Von der Urgesellschaft zum Sozialismus.* Vienna: Zentraler Schulungsausschuss der SJOe, n.d.

Hiscocks, Richard. *The Rebirth of Austria.* New York: Oxford University Press, 1953.

Johnstone, Harry F. *The Restraint of Competition in the Austrian Economy.* Vienna: Economic Division, Office of the U.S. High Commissioner for Austria, 1951.

Kautsky, Benedikt. *Geistige Strömungen im österreichischen Sozialismus.* Vienna: Verlag der Wiener Volksbuchhandlung, n.d.

———. *Teufel und Verdammte.* Zürich: Büchergilde Gutenberg, 1946.

Kienzl, Heinz. *Freie Wirtschaft?* Vienna: Verlag des Oesterreichischen Gewerkschaftsbundes, 1953.

Klenner, Fritz. *Die österreichischen Gewerkschaften—Vergangenheit und Gegenwartsprobleme,* Vol. II. Vienna: Verlag des Oesterreichischen Gewerkschaftsbundes, 1953.

———. *Putschversuch-oder nicht? Ein Tatsachenbericht über das 4. Preis-und Lohnabkommen und die beiden gescheiterten kommunistischen Generalstreikversuche im September und Oktober 1950.* Vienna: Pressereferat des Oesterreichischen Gewerkschaftsbundes, n.d.

Kostroun, Ludwig. *Der neue Weg der Selbständigen.* Vienna: Verlag Freier Wirtschaftsverband, n.d.

Krywult, Josef. *Arbeiterschaft und Steuerpolitik.* Vienna: Verlag des Oesterreichischen Gewerkschaftsbundes, Schriftenreihe der Arbeiterkammer Wien, n.d.

Kummer, Karl. *Der dritte Weg—Grundsätzliche und praktische Vorschläge für eine Sozialreform.* Vienna: Verlag Typographische Anstalt, 1949.

Lauterbach, Albert. *Planung und Freiheit.* Vienna: Verlag des Oesterreichischen Gewerkschaftsbundes, 1950.

Lipset, Seymour. *Political Man.* New York: Doubleday & Company, 1960.

MacIver, Robert M. *The Web of Government.* New York: Macmillan, 1948.

Matthias, Erich. *Sozialdemokratie und Nation—Ein Beitrag zur Ideengeschichte der sozialdemokratischen Emigration in der Prager Zeit des Parteivorstandes, 1933–1938.* Stuttgart: Deutsche Verlags-Anstalt, 1952.

Merton, Robert. *Social Theory and Social Structure.* Chicago (Ill.): The Free Press of Glencoe, Illinois, 1949.

Michels, Robert. *Political Parties.* Chicago (Ill.): The Free Press of Glencoe, Illinois, 1949.

Migsch, Alfred. *Anschlag auf Oesterreich—Ein Tatsachenbericht über den kommunistischen Putschversuch im September-Oktober 1950.* Vienna: Zentralsekretariat der SPOe, 1950.

Mitrany, David. *Marx Against the Peasant.* Chapel Hill (N.C.): The University of North Carolina Press, 1951.

Moik, Wilhelmine. *Grosse Leistungen, Neue Forderungen.* Vienna: Sozialistischer Verlag, Schriftenreihe "Die Frau," n.d.

Nemschak, Franz. *Der Weg zu einem gesamtwirtschaftlichen Konzept.* Vienna: Oesterreichisches Institut für Wirtschaftsforschung, 1951.

Neu Beginnen, Auslandsbureau. "Neu Beginnen—was es will, was es ist, und wie es wurde," London, n.d.

Neugebauer, Max. *Wir wollen den inneren Frieden.* Vienna: Verlag Jungbrunnen, 1950.

Patzer, Franz. "Der Wiener Gemeinderat von 1890 bis 1952." Unpublished manuscript, Vienna, 1952.

Philip, Andrè. "Die Krise der sozialistischen Doktrin in Europa," *Rote Revue,* XXI (1951), 215–27.

Popp, Franz. *Auf dem Wege zur neuen Schule.* Vienna: Verlag der Wiener Volksbuchhandlung, n.d.

Powelson, Louise N. "The Political Parties of Austria, 1945–1951." Unpublished doctoral dissertation, Yale University, 1953.

Rauscher, Franz. *Die Verstaatlichung in Oesterreich.* Vienna: Verlag des Oesterreichischen Gewerkschaftsbundes, 1949.

Renner, Karl. *Demokratie und Bureaukratie.* Vienna: Universum Verlag, 1946.

———. *Denkschrift über die Geschichte der Unabhängigkeitserklärung Oesterreichs und die Einsetzung der provisorischen Regierung der Republik.* Vienna: Oesterreichische Staatsdruckerei, 1945.

———. *Die Menschenrechte.* Vienna: Danubia Verlag, 1948.

———. *Die neue Welt und der Sozialismus.* Salzburg: Alpenland Verlag, SPOe, 1946.

———. *Oesterreich von der Ersten zur Zweiten Republik.* Vienna: Verlag der Wiener Volksbuchhandlung, 1953.

———. *Staatswirtschaft, Weltwirtschaft und Sozialismus.* Berlin: Verlag von J. H. W. Dietz Nachfolger, 1929.

———. *Wege der Verwirklichung.* Berlin: Verlag von J. H. W. Dietz Nachfolger, 1929.

———. *Die Wirtschaft als Gesamtprozess und die Sozialisierung.* Berlin: Verlag J. H. W. Dietz Nachfolger, 1924.

Rothschild, K. W. *The Austrian Economy Since 1945.* London: Royal Institute of International Affairs, 1950.

Schärf, Adolf. *April 1945 in Wien.* Vienna: Verlag der Wiener Volksbuchhandlung, 1948.

———. *Der geistige Arbeiter in der 2. Republik.* Vienna: Verlag der Wiener Volksbuchhandlung, n.d.

————. *Der Wiederaufbau und die Selbständigen.* Vienna: Verlag Freier Wirtschaftverband, n.d.

————. *Zwischen Demokratie und Volksdemokratie.* Vienna: Verlag der Wiener Volksbuchhandlung, 1950.

Scharf, Erwin. *Ich darf nicht schweigen.* Vienna: Selbstverlag, 1948.

Schlesinger, Rudolf. *Central European Democracy and Its Background—Economic and Political Group Organization.* London: Routledge and Kegan Paul Ltd., 1953.

Schumpeter, Joseph A. *Capitalism, Socialism and Democracy.* New York: Harper & Brothers, 1947.

Seidel, Bruno. "Wesen und Wandlung des Sozialismus und seiner Sozialpolitik vom klassischen zum heutigen Sozialismus," *Zeitschrift für die gesamten Staatswissenschaften,* CIV (1951), 660–97.

Seidel, Hans. *Der Wiener Wohnungsbedarf und die Wohnbaufinanzierung.* Vienna: Oesterreichisches Institut für Wirtschaftsforschung, 3. Sonderheft, 1946.

Sering, Paul. *Jenseite des Kapitalismus—ein Beitrag zur sozialistischen Neuorientierung.* Vienna: Verlag der Wiener Volksbuchhandlung, 1948.

Socialist Union. *Socialism—A New Statement of Principles.* London: Lincoln-Prager Press Ltd., 1952.

Stupperger, Leopold. "Die Entwicklung der Arbeiterkammern in Oesterreich." Unpublished doctoral dissertation, University of Vienna, 1949.

Sturmthal, Adolf F. *The Tragedy of European Labor, 1918–1939.* New York: Columbia University Press, 1943; 2d ed., 1950.

————. *Unity and Diversity in European Labor.* Chicago (Ill.): The Free Press of Glencoe, Ill., 1953.

Sweezy, Paul M. *The Theory of Capitalist Development.* New York: Oxford University Press, 1942.

Verrosta, Stephan. *Die internationale Stellung Oesterreichs, 1938 bis 1947.* Vienna: Manzsche Verlagsbuchhandlung, 1947.

Newspapers and Periodicals

Amtsblatt der Stadt Wien
Arbeit und Wirtschaft (Arbeiterkammer Wien and OeGB)
Arbeiter Zeitung (SPOe)
Arbeiter Zeitung (illegal edition, published in Brünn, RS)
Der Aufbau—Monatsschrift für Wiederaufbau (Stadtbauamt der Stadt Wien)
Austrian Information (Austrian Information Service, New York)
Berichte und Informationen (sympathetic to VdU)
Gewerkschaftliche Rundschau (OeGB)
Gewerkschaftliche Nachrichten (OeGB)
Informationsdienst der SPOe (1945–1946)
Der Kampf (SDAPDOe)
Der Kampf (illegal edition, published in Brünn and Paris, RS)

Das Kleine Volksblatt (OeVP)
Neues Oesterreich (nonpartisan)
Der Neue Vorwärts (SAP, Scharf)
Neue Wiener Tageszeitung (OeVP)
OeGB—Bildungsfunktionär
Oesterreichische Monatshefte (OeVP)
Oesterreichische Volksstimme (KPOe)
Die Presse (conservative, nonparty)
Salzburger Nachrichten (sympathetic to VdU)
Der SJ Funktionär (1948)
Solidarität (OeGB)
Der Sozialist (oppositional inner-SPOe; mimeographed)
Der Sozialistische Akademiker (BSA)
Der Sozialistische Gewerkschafter (Socialist Fraction, OeGB)
SPOe—Betriebsvertrauensmann
SPOe—Bildungsvertrauensmann
SPOe—Vertrauensmann
Stimme der Jugend (SJOe)
strom (Verband Sozialistischer Studenten)
Trade Union News Bulletin from Austria (OeGB)
Trotzdem (SJOe)
Unsere Arbeit (SBZ, 1945)
Welt der Arbeit (SPOe, Betriebsreferat, and Socialist Fraction of OeGB)
Der Wiener Kurier (U.S. Information Service)
Wiener Zeitung (Austrian Government)
Die Zukunft (SPOe)

Index